INSIGHT

DenmarK

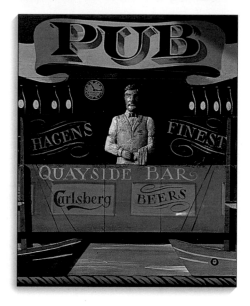

APA PUBLICATIONS

Part of the Langenscheidt Publishing Group

ABOUT THIS BOOK

Editorial
Project Editor
Jane Hutchings
Managing Editor
Emily Hatchwell
Editorial Director
Brian Bell

Distribution
UK & Ireland
GeoCenter International Ltd
The Viables Centre , Harrow Way
Basingstoke, Hants RG22 4BJ
Fax: (44) 1256-817988

United States
Langenscheidt Publishers, Inc.
46–35 54th Road, Maspeth, NY 11378
Fax: (718) 784-0640

Canada
Prologue Inc.
1650 Lionel Bertrand Blvd., Boisbriand
Québec, Canada J7H 1N7
Tel: (450) 434-0306. Fax: (450) 434-2627

Australia & New Zealand
Hema Maps Pty. Ltd.
24 Allgas Street, Slacks Creek 4127
Brisbane, Australia
Tel: (61) 7 3290 0322. Fax: (61) 7 3290 0478

Worldwide
**Apa Publications GmbH & Co.
Verlag KG (Singapore branch)**
38 Joo Koon Road, Singapore 628990
Tel: (65) 865-1600. Fax: (65) 861-6438

Printing
Insight Print Services (Pte) Ltd
38 Joo Koon Road, Singapore 628990
Tel: (65) 865-1600. Fax: (65) 861-6438

©2000 **Apa Publications GmbH & Co.
Verlag KG (Singapore branch)**
All Rights Reserved

*First Edition 1991
Third Edition 2000*

CONTACTING THE EDITORS
Although every effort is made to
provide accurate information, we
live in a fast-changing world and
would appreciate it if readers
would call our attention to any
errors or outdated information
that may occur by writing to us:
**Insight Guides, P.O. Box 7910,
London SE1 1WE, England.
Fax: (44 20) 7403-0290.
insight@apaguide.demon.co.uk**

This guidebook combines the
interests and enthusiasms of
two of the world's best known information providers: Insight Guides,
whose titles have set the standard
for visual travel guides since 1970,
and Discovery Channel, the world's
premier source of nonfiction television programming.

Insight Guides' editors provide
both practical advice and general
understanding about a destination's history, culture, institutions
and people. Discovery Channel
and its comprehensive web
site, www.discovery.com,
helps millions of viewers
to explore their world
from the comfort of
their own home and
in addition encour-
ages them to ex-
plore it first hand.

How to use this book

This fully updated edition of *Insight:
Denmark* is carefully structured to
convey an understanding of the
country and its culture as well as to
guide readers through its many
sights and activities:

◆ The **Features** section, indicated
by a yellow bar at the top of each
page, covers the history and culture
of the country in a series of infor-
mative essays.

◆ The main **Places** section,
indicated by a blue bar, is a
complete guide to all the sights
and areas worth visiting. Places
of special interest are coordinated
by number with the maps.

◆ The **Travel Tips** listings section,
with an orange bar, provides a
handy point of reference for
information on travel, hotels,
shops, restaurants and

EXPLORE YOUR WORLD
Discovery CHANNEL

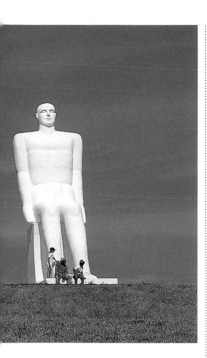

Map Legend

---‥--	International Boundary
-----	Country Boundary
⊖	Border Crossing
—•—	National Park/Reserve
-----	Ferry Route
Ⓢ	S-Tog (S-Train)
✈ ✦	Airport: International/Regional
🚐	Bus Station
🅿	Parking
❶	Tourist Information
✉	Post Office
🛉 † ⟊	Church/Ruins
†	Monastery
☾	Mosque
✡	Synagogue
◢ 🏰	Castle/Ruins
∴	Archaeological Site
∩	Cave
𝟏	Statue/Monument
★	Place of Interest

The main places of interest in the Places section are coordinated by number with a full-colour map (e.g. ❶), and a symbol at the top of every right-hand page tells you where to find the map.

more. Its index appears on the back flap, which serves as a bookmark.

The contributors

This new edition of *Insight: Denmark* was edited by **Jane Hutchings**, under the guidance of managing editor **Emily Hatchwell**. It builds on the foundations created by the writers of previous editions, most notably the late **Doreen Taylor-Wilkie**, editor of the original *Insight: Denmark*, who also wrote about Funen and its Archipelago, and North Jutland.

This edition has been extensively updated by a team of experts led by **Fradley Garner**, a writer and film narrator who lives in Copenhagen. Garner contributed the Insight On Christiansø and panels on N.F.S. Grundtvig and Millennium Transport, and, with **Bryan Wilder**, updated the chapter on Copenhagen. Wilder, an American journalist who regards Copenhagen as his home, contributed the chapter on Greenland, and updated those on Danish Churches, Architectural Heritage, North Zealand, Funen, the Archipelago, Odense, North, South and West Jutland, and Ålborg.

Jack Jackson, a freelance journalist living near Århus, contributed the features on A Modern Nation, The Danes Today and Green Power, Insights on Design and Christmas, and a panel on the Danish Resistance Movement. He updated the chapters on East Jutland and Århus.

Charles Ferro, a Copenhagen-based writer, wrote the features on Denmark's Great Outdoors and Eating Out. He updated the chapters on Beer, South and West Zealand, Bornholm and the Faroe Islands.

Glen Garner, an American-Danish writer and artist, revised the chapter on the nation's Culture and updated the panel on Denmark's Queen.

Rowlinson Carter wrote about Denmark's history from the very beginnings to 1945.

Writers whose text has been adapted from earlier editions include **Robert Spark**, **Geoffrey Dodd**, **Penny Visman**, **Michael Metcalfe**, **Vivien Andersen**, **Hugh Matthews**, **Jo Hermann**, **Stephen Rosenmeier**, **Thomas Rosenmeier**, **Ulla Plon**, **Lars Ole Sauerberg** and **Hanne Goldschmidt**.

The Travel Tips section was compiled by Copenhagen-based **Anna Lia Bright**, a research associate specialising in information about Denmark, and edited by **Anne Esden**.

Additional editorial assistance was provided by **Liz Clasen**. The book was proofread by **Eric Bailey**, and indexed by **Elizabeth Cook**.

CONTENTS

Introduction

History

Features

Natural
surroundings
but unnatural
proportions

Travel Tips

Places

A NEARLY PERFECT NATION

Small, but perfectly formed, Denmark is a country of
fun-loving, environmentally conscientious people

Hamlet can relax. There is nothing rotten in the State of Denmark. Yes, the winters can be dark and dreary. They're long, but not biting cold and there is little snow – the Danes go to Sweden and Norway to ski – and summers can be sunny, with long hours of daylight. Yes, the tax rate is among the world's highest. But taxes are ploughed back to help make this a country "where few have too much and fewer too little." The 5.1 million *danskere* enjoy the highest living standard of any nation.

The world's oldest kingdom may no longer be an empire, but the sons of those Vikings continue to pack plenty of clout. These days they're spreading their seed far and wide in canisters of frozen nitrogen: Denmark is the biggest supplier of meticulously screened and frozen human sperm on the planet – and a major purveyor of computer elements and electronic devices, windmills, agricultural products, arts and crafts and skilled professionals. Aside from some North Sea oil fields, the place has no raw materials to speak of.

Denmark is a nation of cyclists (two-wheelers outnumber bipeds) and recyclers – more than half the country's rubbish is turned into district steam heat for homes and other new things, nuclear plants excepted. Natural gas and windmills are the preferred energy sources of this windy country. It's a well-ordered land, where trains and buses, as well as people, get there when they're supposed to. The Danes revere peace and quiet, and if you jump a red light or forget your bicycle light at night, somebody will let you know.

Listen to the American writer and broadcaster Garrison Keillor in the *National Geographic*: "It is – let's be frank here – almost everyone's idea of the World's Most Nearly Perfect Nation: a clean, peaceful, well-regulated society populated by prosperous (but not greedy or rapacious), tolerant (but principled), law-abiding (but humorous), computer-literate, bi- or trilingual people who all vote in elections and are as witty as Victor Borge and have no hang-ups about sex and reside in sunny, energy-efficient homes... who can discuss (in excellent English) the infrastructure needs of developing countries or the Danishness of Woody Allen while serving perfectly poached salmon off handsome earthenware, copies of which are on display at the Museum of Modern Art in New York City."

What's left to say – except that even those doing a whirlwind tour of Europe ought to look into the attic. Especially now that it's connected by bridge and tunnel with the rest of the house. The only Hamlet you'll find stalks the ramparts of Elsinore Castle, playing to an enraptured night audience. And it's still light outside. ❑

PRECEDING PAGES: Samsø island, Stavns Fjord; serene Egeskov Castle, Funen; idle boats at dawn on Samsø island; rich agricultural land typical of Denmark.
LEFT: Carlsberg, probably the most popular beer in Copenhagen.

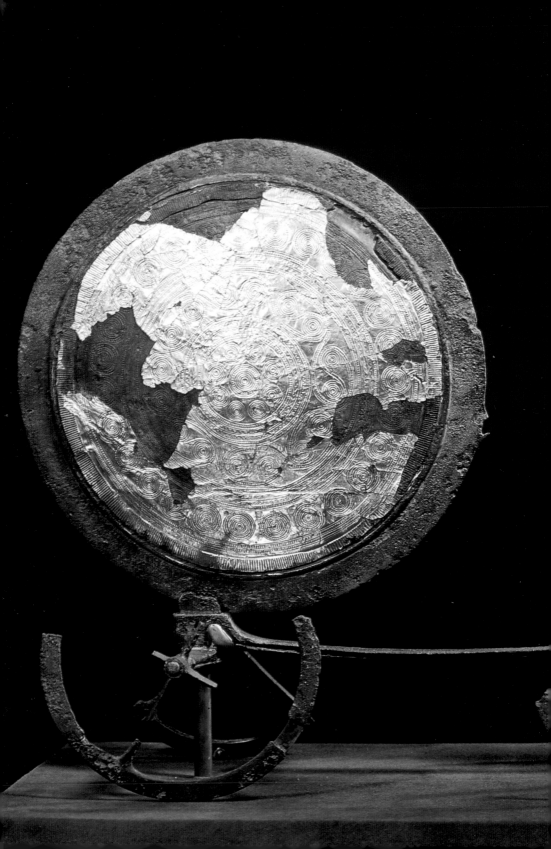

Decisive Dates

EARLY HISTORY: C.4000 BC–AD 800

c.13,000–1800 bc The Stone Age: by 4000 BC settlers are growing crops and burying their dead in dolmens.

c.1800–500 BC The Bronze Age: metalwork and weapon-making skills acquired through trade with other European countries.

c.500 BC–AD 800 The Iron Age: Grauballe Man and Tollund Man are buried in peat bogs, to be unearthed in the 1950s in a remarkable state of preservation.

500–600 AD Danes migrate from Sweden to Jutland.

THE VIKING ERA: 8TH–11TH CENTURY AD

8th–10th century Viking raids throughout Europe. Monasteries and settlements in England, France and Russia are plundered.

811 Southern border of the Danish kingdom established on the banks of the Eider River, where it will remain for about 1000 years.

940–85 Harald Bluetooth brings Christianity to Denmark; it takes 100 years or so for the country as a whole to become Christian.

1014–43 Crowns of Denmark and England united. King Knud (Canute) creates an empire including Denmark, England and Norway; it collapses soon after his death.

1066 Battle of Stamford Bridge: end of Viking era.

FROM VIKINGS TO DANISH EMPIRE

12th century Denmark re-emerges as dominant power in the Baltic.

1332–40 Denmark ruled by the counts of Holstein.

1340–75 Valdemar IV unites the country and restores the throne after a period of civil war and anarchy.

1397 Queen Margrethe I forges the Kalmar Union, a federation of the kingdoms of Denmark, Sweden and Norway, under Danish leadership.

1417 Eric VII makes Copenhagen his capital and has a palace built at Helsingør.

1449 Sweden leaves the Kalmar Union.

1460 Christian I secures the duchies of Schleswig and Holstein.

THE REFORMATION AND WARS WITH SWEDEN

1522 King Christian II is driven into exile.

1523 The Swedes elect their own king, Gustav Vasa, and the Kalmar Union is dissolved. But Norway will remain under Danish rule for another three centuries.

1530 Lutheran preachers bring the Reformation to Denmark.

1536 Christian III becomes king and declares Lutheranism to be the official state religion. After a siege of Copenhagen assets owned by the Catholic church are seized by the Crown and bishops are imprisoned.

1563–70 Unsuccessful war to recover Sweden.

1588–1648 The long reign of Christian IV brings prosperity but ends in a losing war with Sweden. The king enlarges Copenhagen, which flourishes culturally and economically, and commissions many buildings, including Rosenberg Castel and the old Stock Exchange. Castles, palaces and mansions are built throughout Denmark in Renaissance style.

1625–57 The Thirty Years War with Sweden, launched by Christian IV to check Swedish expansion, ends in crushing defeat for Denmark and Swedish occupaton fo Jutland and Funen. The war ends with the signing of the Treaty of Roskilde.

ABSOLUTE MONARCHY

1665 Frederik III deprives the nobility of power and establishes an hereditary absolute monarchy.

1711 The plague claims 20,000 lives out of Copenhagen's population of 65,000.

1729 Greenland becomes a Danish province.

1780–81 Denmark joins Russia, Prussia and Sweden in the League of Armed Neutrality to protect neutral shipping during the American War of Independence.

1784 Following far-reaching land reforms introduced during the regency of Crown Prince Frederik, about 60 percent of Danish peasants become landowners.

NAPOLEONIC WARS AND THE GOLDEN AGE

1801 First Battle of Copenhagen: during the Napoleonic Wars an English fleet under the command of Admiral Nelson destroys much of the Danish fleet in Copenhagen harbour.

1807 Second Battle of Copenhagen: to prevent Denmark siding with Napoleon, Nelson attacks and destroys the rebuilt Danish fleet, bombards Copenhagen and occupies Zealand. Defeated Denmark sides with Napoleon and suffers further defeats. By 1813 the country is bankrupt.

1814 The Treaty of Kiel. The victorious powers dissolve the Denmark-Norway double monarchy and Norway is ceded to Sweden. Denmark keeps Iceland, the Faroes and Greenland.

1810–30 The Golden Age of Danish literature, which is dominated by children's writer Hans Christian Andersen and existentialist Soren Kierkegaard.

1843 The Tivoli Gardens are opened in Copenhagen.

1847 The first railway line links Copenhagen with Roskilde.

THE AGE OF REFORMS

1848–49 Revolutions occur across Europe. Absolutism ends in Denmark. Constitutional monarchy is established under a liberal constitution, with the new King Frederik VII handing political power to the parliament. Germans of Schleswig-Holstein revolt with Prussian support.

1857 onwards Copenhagen's old ramparts are demolished to create space for dwellings. Industrialisation draws in the poor rural population, but many cannot find work. By 1900 the population of Copenhagen approaches 400,000.

1864 War with Prussia and loss of Schleswig-Holstein.

1890s Many liberal reforms in education and health – precursors of 20th-century liberal social policies.

1906 Ole Olsen founds the Nordisk Films Kompagni, still in existence today and said to be the oldest film company in the world.

EARLY 20TH CENTURY

1907 onwards with two castles destroyed by fire (1795 and 1884). Work on the third Christiansborg Palace starts, in 1918 it becomes the seat of the Folketing, the Danish parliament.

1914–18 Denmark remains neutral in World War 1.

1915 Far-reaching constitutional reform. Women are given the right to vote.

PRECEDING PAGES: Sun Chariot in the National Museum in Copenhagen. **LEFT:** King Christian II of Denmark. **RIGHT:** Queen Margrethe II.

1918 Iceland achieves full self-government.

1919 Denmark recovers northern Schleswig (but not Holstein) under the treaty of Versailles.

1924 onwards Social Democrats win power.

1929–40 Despite the economic hardships of the 1930s, a welfare state established under left-wing coalition dominated by Social Democratic Party.

1940 Nazi occupaton of Denmark. Danes trade minimal co-operation in return for limited self governemt.

1943 Germany takes complete control of Denmark. The Danish Resistance is born. Thousands of Jews are smuggled to neutral Sweden.

1944 Iceland declares independence.

1945 Denmark liberated by the British.

MODERN DENMARK

1949 Denmark becomes a founding member of NATO.

1972 Denmark joins the EEC (today's European Union). Margrethe II succeeds to the throne.

1979 Home rule for Greenland and the Faroes.

1984 Poul Schluter becomes first Conservative prime minister since 1894.

1989 Denmark becomes the first country to recognise same-sex marriages.

1993 After voting against the Maastricht Treaty on European Union in the 1992 referendum, the Danes accept a revised treaty.

1996 Copenhagen is cultural capital of Europe.

2000 Øresund bridge opens between Copenhagen and Malmo in Sweden. ❏

BEGINNINGS

Archaeology has solved the mystery of Denmark's distant past, unearthing
bones, boats, treasure – and evidence of murder most foul

Until Scandinavia introduced itself to the rest of the world in the alarming guise of the rampaging Vikings, very little was known about the remote north, and even that tended to lack the ring of truth.

The past remained cloaked in mystery until well into modern times. While the sands of Egypt offered up papyrus and clay tablets providing intimate insight into the lives of people who lived more than 1,000 years before Christ, nothing was reliably known about the Danes or about their Scandinavian cousins until they materialised as Vikings. As that news was mainly recorded by priests on the run from their depredations, the initial impression formed was not sympathetic.

When at last archaeology prised open the past, the evidence came trickling out in strange and wonderful ways. The earliest signs to date of human activity in Denmark were recognised in a pile of animal bones which, 80,000 years ago, had been tossed into a sand pit like so much litter. Amazingly, they had survived the crushing pressure of successive ice ages moving first one way and then the other over the site. That these particular bones should then have come to the attention of someone who knew what they meant completes a chain of highly improbable events.

Murder inquiry

The flukes go on. A body dug up in 1950 was thought at first to be prime evidence of a recent murder: the male victim had close-cropped hair, stubble on his cheeks and was naked but for a woollen cap. Police suspicions concentrated naturally on the rope around his neck. It transpired, however, that the luckless fellow had actually been dead for about 2,000 years, which made it a case for archaeologists rather than policemen. He joined the clues to Denmark's past, many of them objects recovered from the

---

LEFT: stone axes in Copenhagen's National Museum.
RIGHT: Grauballe Man, 2,000 years old but discovered only in the 1950s.

seabed and – more litter – from the domestic rubbish dumped by ancient Danes on the shore where they spent their summers.

Small stage, big impact

The story of Denmark unfolds against a modest backdrop. Its highest mountain, if that's the

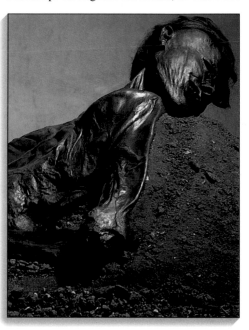

word, would struggle to be seen against the Manhattan skyline. The deepest waterfall plunges all of 122 cm (48 inches), or so it is said. The country is only 360 km (240 miles) long and not much wider; it could be swallowed 16 times by Texas alone.

Denmark's history, however, is out of all proportion to the tiny stage. The Danes wielded a powerful influence over Western and Eastern Europe. They were instrumental in the creation of the English, French and Russian empires, initially by opening eyes to the potential of seapower. The Danes like to think that it was their injection of a virile backbone into the bloodstock of the English that made the difference between the feeble warriors the Romans and then the first Danes encountered and the later empire-builders. By this tortuous logic, they therefore lay claim to moulding the English-speaking world. In France, the hell-raising Danes became paragons of piety, building cathedrals and dutifully joining the Christian crusades against Muslim infidels.

Throughout the predatory migrations criss-crossing Europe, the Danes clung with singular tenacity to the land of their ancestors. Their line of kings stretches back

THE FIRST DANES

Denmark's cultural and linguistic roots can be traced to the early Iron Age and the arrival of the Danes, a tribe from Sweden, who settled in Jutland in about 500 BC.

but they have never surrendered their independence to foreign invaders, However, they have not always been entirely their own masters. There was a nadir after the Viking glories when intruders occupied parts of every Danish province. The closest the country ever came to total capitulation, though, was the Nazi occupation during World War II, when "independence" rested on a slender semantic subtlety. The Danish flag, which according to legend descended from heaven, undoubtedly gave other European countries the idea of adopting a national flag.

Imperial pedigree

At the turn of the 15th century, the Danish-led Kalmar Union was the largest unified kingdom in Europe, covering not only Norway and Sweden but also Finland, Iceland and Greenland. The last alone, still Danish but now self-governing, is four times the size of France. Denmark once ruled Germany as far south as Hamburg, and their shared border right into modern times was a recurring trouble spot, latterly as that well-known, double-barrelled diplomatic nightmare, Schleswig-Holstein.

Contemporary Danes are usually reticent about, or even slightly embarrassed by, their imperial pedigree. It suits them better now to be thought of as beacons of responsible, decent common sense. They are not, on the whole, as stridently sanctimonious as their Swedish and Norwegian neighbours, not nearly so keen on a state forever poised to rescue its citizens from weaknesses like tobacco and alcohol.

unbroken, at least over 900 years, to one Gorm the Old, making Denmark one of the world's oldest kingdoms. But tracing the line of kings is far from straightforward. Denmark's first historian, Saxo, thought there may have been more than 50 Danish kings before the Viking Age, and an 11th-century German, Adam of Bremen, gave up trying to work out the succession: "Whether of all these kings or tyrants in Denmark some ruled the country simultaneously or one lived shortly after the other is uncertain."

Tradition of independence

The Danes lost wars, and at times bled themselves dry on improvident military adventures,

Cheerful fatalism

The modern Dane, then, is a fairly amiable soul frequently to be found with a glass of beer in one hand, a cigar in the other and a *bon mot* for most occasions. This is all a far cry from ancestors whose worst fate was to die in bed. They felt obliged to go to their graves in a happy frame of mind, no matter what. "It shall hereafter be recorded in histories," said a royal eulogy, "that King Halfer died laughing."

The cause of Halfer's death is not specified, but it was as likely as not some hideous war wound. Adam of Bremen observed of Danish criminals that they much preferred the axe to any other form of punishment – imprisonment or flogging, for example. "As for groans, complaints and other bemoanings of that kind, in which we (Germans) find relief, they are so detested by the Danes, that they think it mean to weep for their sins, or for the death of their dearest relations."

Cheerful fatalism was occasionally carried to the most extreme lengths. In one instance, a warrior who was thrown to the ground in an armed wrestling match noticed that his opponent in the process had dropped his sword. He offered to wait in the same vulnerable position while the other man retrieved his weapon to administer the *coup de grâce*. He kept his word.

going to keep it for himself. Molesworth would have scorned the idea that Denmark could ever become an artful trading nation, not least as the exporters of widely admired pork products.

Despite its northern isolation, there must have been some contact between Denmark and the Ancient World, because amber found only in the Baltic region has been discovered in Stone Age remains in Greece and even in Egyptian jewellery. The country was close to the well-worn trading routes along rivers such as the Vistula, Dneiper, Elbe, Danube and Rhine, and indeed there is reason to believe that well before the Viking Age the Danes were

Artful traders

R.M. Molesworth, sent to Denmark as "Envoy Extraordinary" by King William III of England in 1689, thought the Danes had already lost their warlike nature. Their chief characteristic, he decided, was "gross Cheating". "In their Markets they will ask the same price for stinking Meat, as for fresh; for lean, as for fat," he complained. Whenever he showed interest in some article for sale, the shopkeeper would immediately change his mind and say he was

LEFT: reconstructed dug-out canoes at the Stone Age village of Hjerl Hede, Jutland. **ABOVE:** Bronze Age burial ground at Ydby Hede, Limfjord in West Jutland.

sending furs and slaves (as well as amber) east which they exchanged for gold and bronze.

Early impressions

The first recorded voyage to Scandinavia was by the astronomer, Pytheas of Marseilles, in about 325 BC. His account no longer survives, but in its time it influenced generations of writers, including Strabo (63 BC–AD 25) who described priestesses on a peninsula, presumably Jutland, who sacrificed prisoners of war and foretold the future not in tea-leaves but in blood and intestines. This society, he said, had been discovered by a Roman expedition which had sailed around Jutland on the orders of the

Emperor Augustus in AD 5. Ptolemy produced a remarkably accurate description of the "four islands of Scania" (Denmark plus Sweden) in the second century AD, but one wonders where Pliny got his information about a purported animal whose solid legs (i.e. no knees) forced it to sleep standing upright or, at best, leaning against a tree. The creature had to walk backwards when grazing – to avoid tripping over an over-sized upper lip.

A more reliable picture begins to take shape through the observations of Christian missionaries in Charlemagne's time. Even so, flights of fancy continued to circulate well into the

Middle Ages, like one about a tribe of Amazons, larger and more impressive than some of the lesser women, who merely had beards. The Amazons produced beautiful daughters but their sons were born with the heads of dogs.

Archaeology's revelations

In the 19th century, the new science of archaeology, to which the Danes Christian Thomsen and Jens Worsaae made a substantial contribution, began to assemble a more credible picture of Denmark's prehistory. The beginnings are difficult to trace because the Arctic ice cap shifted remorselessly one way and then the other. When the ice retreated northwards, men

followed the thaw to hunt and fish. When it crept south again, they were forced to retreat to more temperate zones. Parts of Jutland escaped the ice, but elsewhere there was little chance that evidence of early human activity could survive in places which, for thousands of years at a time, were first frozen solid then awash when the ice melted.

Tell-tale bones

It was during one of these prolonged retreats of the ice that hunters who had moved in to occupy an area near the Gudenå River in North Jutland sat down to eat some deer they had killed. The marrow in the bones was a prized delicacy, and with practised hands they split open the bones to get at it. The remnants were thrown aside into a pit.

The discarded bones lay there undisturbed as apparently meaningless litter until eventually archaeologists detected that they had been split in such a manner as could only have been done by human hands. Dating techniques were employed in order to determine the age of the bones and put it at 80,000 years. It was altogether an astounding conclusion to what must have been at the time an agreeable but hardly exceptional meal.

Archaeology needs such luck in Denmark at least until it reaches the end of the last Ice Age, about 10,000 years ago. That gradual event was a mixed blessing when it happened. Although the thaw made much more inland territory habitable, seas swollen by melting ice flooded the low-lying coastal plains which, as they were warmed by the Gulf Stream, had previously been the most congenial spots for settlement.

Dug-out canoes

As the surge of tides over thousands of years would normally have obliterated all signs of an inundated coastal settlement, divers working in about 3 metres (10 ft) of water in 1976 were initially not sure what to make of unexplained humps in the seabed off Tybrind on the island of Funen.

Marine excavation confirmed more than they dared hope for: they had chanced upon a fishing village which had existed 6,000 years ago. They brought up a dug-out canoe 8 metres (26 ft) long and 80 cm (30 inches) wide which had a fire hearth built into the stern and still contained stones, which were evidently the ballast for some voyage along the Baltic coast, possibly to catch eels, in about 4100 BC.

The canoe, restored and now exhibited at the Moesgård Prehistoric Museum in Århus, was only part of the story which unfolded around Tybrind. There had once been, it transpired, a village with a road leading down to a port. The houses had perished, but there were still signs of the stone roadway and of mooring posts.

The settlement had evidently been inhabited for well over a millennium: it offered up a an

WINNING DESIGN

The 2,000-year-old Hjortespring boat which is on display in the National Museum in Copenhagen, is a prototype of Viking design hundreds of years later.

tier, which in its present state is 65 km (40 miles) long, Denmark is surrounded by sea. Furthermore, it stands like Gibraltar at the junction of two strategic seas. The need to exploit the sea, and during times of danger to defend the sea approaches, put a premium on maritime skills. Boats are therefore some of the most important items in Danish archaeology and more than 250 dug-out boats have been recovered. Many of them ended their working lives as coffins pushed out to sea.

extraordinary wealth of artefacts including pottery, stakes, bows, spears, wooden arrowheads and various implements, including fish hooks, made out of antler and bone. In addition, human remains were found: a woman and child in a grave and the scattered bones of at least four other people.

In 1987, Korshavn in North Funen produced another exciting find: a boat similar in design to the Tybrind example but 1,000 or so years older. Apart from the German frontier, which in its present state is 65 km (40

LEFT: a return to the past at Hjerl Hede Stone Age village. **ABOVE:** prehistoric gravestones near Agri (Mols) in East Jutland.

Burial chambers

A rather more benevolent and stable climate in the latter part of the Stone Age (13000 to 1800 BC) brought about rapid progress on land as well. Changing burial practices are the milestones of cultural development. The most familiar relics, of which no fewer than 23,000 examples are still to be seen, are stone cairns, or "dolmens", a number of upright stones topped by a huge capstone.

The mechanics of getting the capstone into position inspired the sort of debate surrounding the construction of the Egyptian pyramids. In any case, the dolmens imply considerable technical skill on the part of the builders. Their design became ever more ambitious until they were oblong chambers capable of holding more than 100 bodies, the approach being through stone-lined passages.

The Stone Age farmers who ended up in dolmens spent their summers at the coast. Refuse from one summer after another piled up, an unplanned treasure trove for future archaeologists. These kitchen middens, as they are called, have revealed a varied diet of birds, shellfish (especially mussels and oysters), seal and game. Food was cooked and stored in large jars which could be made to stand upright by pushing their pointed bases into the ground, a

design that probably originated in the Aegean. Nights were lit by blubber burnt in crucibles.

Trading boom

The Bronze Age (around 1800 to 500 BC) opened Denmark's frontiers. Furs, slaves and amber went out; bronze and bronze objects came in. Local craftsmen proved adept at copying the imported items and were soon producing fair imitations of bronze swords and other articles, right down to the decorative motifs.

In some respects, though, the Danes resisted change. They stuck to religious beliefs which, in common with a religious movement then

Two of the best preserved Iron Age "bog people" were discovered in the early 1950s. The Tollund Man, who was hanged and thrown into a peat bog some 2,200 years ago, can be seen at the Silkeborg Museum. His close contemporary, the Grauballe Man, now at the Forhistorisk Museum, Moesgård, had his throat comprehensively cut. Indeed, all the 160 or so bog people now recovered seem to have met violent deaths. The manner of these deaths suggests a religious ritual, probably a sacrifice to the fertility goddess for a good harvest and to ward off pestilence. Rings and necklaces found with some of the bodies were symbolic of the goddess concerned.

convulsing Egypt, was rooted in sun worship. The sun god was courted with the trombone tones of a curved horn known as the *lur*, still to be seen in the National Museum and on packets of Danish butter. The finest surviving tribute to the sun is unfortunately only a contemporary model of the original object, a huge gilded disc which, mounted on six wheels and drawn by a gilded horse, would have been carried through the fields to bless the crops.

In common with the rich classes almost everywhere, Danes who profited from the boom in commerce insisted on taking the trappings of success to their graves. They were buried with their finest weapons in oak coffins whose tannin helped to preserve not only the clothes they were buried in but also nails and hair. A young girl, interred at Egtved in eastern Jutland, was found to be wearing a short, woollen skirt wound twice around her hips, a short-sleeved jacket and a belt decorated with a large bronze disc. Her hair and nails were carefully groomed. Men generally wore kilts with shoulder straps, cloaks and tall, woollen caps.

Cold comfort

A dramatic change in the climate occurred in about 500 BC. While Athenians basked in sunshine as they built the Parthenon, temperatures a central row of wooden posts. The animals stayed at one end, radiating warmth.

Bog people

The water in Denmark's peat bogs has an acid and iron content which is responsible for vivid confirmation of people's physical appearance in the Iron Age which succeeded the Bronze. Hermetically sealed in peat, the bodies of some 160 "bog people" have been extracted in an remarkable state of preservation; most notable was the Tollund Man, who, on being removed from the turf near Silkeborg, gave police the idea they had a murder inquiry to attend to.

dropped suddenly in Denmark. For some time previously, Denmark and even Norway had enjoyed a climate rather milder than has been experienced since. Among the first casualties were the clothes worn since the Bronze Age. Kilts and short skirts were out, trousers and underwear came in. Building had to be more substantial, not only for humans but also for animals which had previously grazed outdoors all year round. The solution was the long house with thick earth walls and a roof supported on

From around the same period is one of the country's most exciting archaeological digs near Roskilde. An unusually large long-house, discovered in 1986, offered a tantalising prize of jewellery and other valuable artefacts. It was no ordinary residence, which led archaeologists to wonder whether it was Denmark's long-lost capital, the home of the early Vikings.

It is at this point that Danish history is transformed. Instead of being drawn from inanimate objects, it comes alive with people called Harald Bluetooth, Sweyn Forkbeard, Magnus the Good and Eric the Very Good. The names give a clue to their character but in any case, thanks to the scalds (bards), they are able to speak. ❏

LEFT: Nørresundby archaeological site near Ålborg in North Jutland. **ABOVE:** in the middle of a field the past can suddenly appear in the form of a grave mound.

THE IRON AGE REVISITED

*People are queuing up to forsake their modern comforts
and experience life as it was lived in the Iron Age*

A week in an Iron Age long house, wreathed in smoke, with the only light filtering hazily through a low door, may not be the most comfortable way to spend a holiday. Yet modern Danish families queue up to try out this primitive life at the Iron Age village in Lejre. The village is part of the Lejre (pronounced "Ly-ra") Historical Archaeological Research Centre, just west of Roskilde (off routes 21/23). More than just a living museum, the centre seeks new knowledge about the life and activities of ancient Danes by reconstructing their clothes, dwellings, farming, utensils and tasks.

Primitive lifestyle

A Stone Age village re-creates life here from about 5400–3900 BC. But the more popular Iron Age village spans the period from *circa* 200 BC–200 AD. The centre also features ancient graves and burial traditions, workshops and an activity area where visitors – including children – can try their hands at chopping fire- wood, paddling a dug-out canoe, and more. Finally, there is a "modern" village of farm cottages from around 1850. People who choose a holiday in the Iron Age are the raw material for the centre's research into ancient ways of life.

The centre opened in 1964 with the aim of re-creating a landscape of the past. The underlying theory was that, by imitating primitive methods of farming and living, Lejre could discover what effects different forms of cultivation had on the earth. This became a cross-check to deductions drawn by archaeologists working on sites from similar periods. It is also often faster. It may take archaeologists thousands of hours to trace patterns of life in a hut from the erosion on a clay floor. The Lejre centre needs only to leave a family to fend for itself in the Iron Age village for a couple of weeks to find that they live in a totally different pattern.

Lejre was founded by its first director, Hans-Ole Hansen. Hansen had been interested in primitive hunting weapons and household implements since his boyhood and he had already helped build a long house at Allerslev, south of Lejre.

After Danish Television took an interest in that project, the Carlsberg Foundation offered Dkr 500,000 (around £43,000/US$71,000) to expand the new "science" of recreating the past. With more volunteers, Hansen set about building the Iron Age village, using only traditional tools and building methods. It has houses, paved streets and wells, surrounded by a high wooden stake fence, as authentic as the Lejre builders could devise.

Learning lost techniques

The centre now covers many other periods of Danish history, ranging from a late Stone Age site to the reconstruction of 18th and 19th-century workshops and a "land labourer's" house of the same period. Its summer season includes training in forgotten techniques, and demonstrations of past technologies and crafts. It does this for schools and seminars as well as casual visitors. Nevertheless, in this curious mixture of academic institution, museum and visitor centre, the Iron Age village and its experimental families are the greatest attraction.

Dark and draughty

The houses, which crouch low, are copies of excavations from various parts of Denmark, with side walls around 1 metre (3 to 4 ft) high, and sloping, shaggy, thatched roofs. Inside they are dark and draughty. The reaction from modern families, used to double-glazing and central heating, is astonishment. But the

> ### OLD BOARS
>
> A cross between wild boar and domestic pig, the long-nosed pigs that snuffle through the ground are a popular attraction for visitors to the Iron Age village.

Iron Age food as well as primitive cooking utensils and instruction in how to use them.

All this is fascinating to the 100,000 or so visitors to Lejre each year. They may have no ambitions to live as our ancestors did but enjoy taking the centre's marked route back into the past. The tour lasts around three hours and is 3 km (2 miles) long. In the old workshops, ancient craftsmen make copies of prehistoric Danish pottery, fired in kilns that are sunk into the hillside. Weavers copy Iron Age garments and

houses are soon crowded with food supplies, tools, a hand spinner, tanning hides, and piles of wood for the central fire. Above hang drying plants, hunks of smoked meat and cheeses, and drying clothes, almost as smoky.

The lack of light affects the families most, and the need to bend, both to avoid the "smoke loft" and to duck under the door. It is not so much that Iron Age people were small but that they spent most of their lives doubled over. Some modern Iron Age dwellers choose contemporary garments. The centre can provide

others experiment with, and teach the skills of, natural dyeing.

The Iron Age village also includes a sacrificial bog, prehistoric dancing, and the nearest modern strains to ancient crops (from the Middle East or Pakistan), planted on ground tilled with an ard, an ancient plough. Long-nosed pigs roam the ancient village alongside Gotland sheep, old species of goats and hens, Iceland cows (Iron Age cattle's nearest modern relative) and a sturdy Shetland pony-like horse.

The Lejre Experimental Centre is at Slangealleen 2, DK-4320 Lejre (tel: 46 48 08 78; fax: 46 48 14 05; www.lejre-center.dk) and is open from 1 May to late Oct, 10am–5pm. ❏

LEFT: enjoying a working holiday at Lejre.
ABOVE: the reconstructed Iron Age village of Lejre.

VIKINGS AT LARGE

*The Vikings erupted out of Scandinavia, equipped with the finest ships
of their day, and spread terror with their lightning raids*

In 789, the Vikings descended like bolts from the blue to refute dubious theories about strange folk living in the north. The sheriff of Dorset in England was one of the first to be enlightened.

The Vikings arrived unannounced in three ships of a design very different from anything seen in English waters before. The language they spoke among themselves made no sense at all, but strangers had been turning up at English ports since Phoenician times and the sheriff assumed that the purpose of the visit was, as usual, trade. He invited them to the royal manor house to find out what they wanted and what they could offer in exchange. He was being naive. The Vikings battered him to death, bundled everything of value into their ships, including some of the startled population, and left.

Plundered monasteries

If the Vikings found the sheriff of Dorset naive, they rejoiced in the blind faith which left rich pickings for the taking in isolated, undefended monasteries. In a Christian society, monasteries were protected by their sanctity. To the robustly pagan Vikings, this was absurd, as the bodies of monks strewn around the plundered Lindisfarne monastery in Northumberland testified when the Vikings called again four years later and sailed away in ships loaded to the gunwales. A few other monasteries suffered a similar fate before the Vikings left England alone for about 40 years while they explored opportunities elsewhere. When the raids resumed, however, they were organised like annual summer outings.

The tempo of raids had every monastery in England, Ireland and France praying for deliverance from the wrath of these "Northmen" and, specifically, from their throat-cutting. The Muslims in Spain and in North Africa did more than pray. When Vikings captured Seville in 844, they fought back. The Vikings suffered a notable reverse. Those taken prisoner were too numerous to be dealt with on the city's gallows. They were hanged, and left hanging, from trees.

There may have been some method in the way the Vikings cultivated their atrocious reputation. Small raiding parties, no matter how

daring, would always have been vulnerable while moving about among a large and truculent native population. If the mere suspicion of their presence was enough to make everyone scatter, their work was made easier and they would probably have been well clear before effective counter-measures could be organised.

Vikings who fell into English hands had nothing to look forward to: scalping was routine and some wretches were flayed, their skins being nailed to church doors. As years went by, however, a growing number of raiders decided against going home for the winter and struck up a *modus vivendi* with the locals.

It meant nothing to the victims whether their

LEFT: the romanticised view – a modern "Viking" in traditional costume in the Viking play *Rolf Krake.*
RIGHT: runic stone in Jelling, East Jutland, carved by King Harald Bluetooth 1,000 years ago.

tormentors were Danes, Norwegians or Swedes, and of course Vikings did not sit down patiently to explain distinctions which, in any case, would have been far from clear in their own minds. There were then so many peripatetic chieftainships in Scandinavia, and there was so much intermarriage between the leading families, that any thought of national identities in the modern sense would be inappropriate.

Moreover, many accounts of Vikings on the warpath were by priests in no position to press questions on their pursuers. The early chronicles are therefore full of Norsemen (implicitly Norwegians) who were actually Danes, and

"Danes" who were almost certainly Norwegians. Only in the very broadest terms, then, can it be said that the Vikings who pushed eastwards by land into Russia and ultimately to Constantinople were predominantly "Swedes", while "Norwegians" sailed west to Scotland, the smaller British isles and Ireland, thence leapfrogging via Iceland and Greenland all the way to America. The "Danes" busied themselves in Germany and, in competition with "Norwegians", in England and France.

Expansionism or pagan revolt?

The impulse which caused the Vikings suddenly to abandon their isolation has been debated with the same uncertainty surrounding the tags of nationality. One of the theories put forward is that lustful pagan polygamy produced more people than the land could support. Although the tradition of dividing land equally among legitimate and illegitimate sons (in prolific numbers) would have placed a greater strain on the notoriously unyielding terrain of western Norway than on Denmark, the argument that land hunger drove the Vikings abroad is generally plausible. Less so, however, is the romantic view that the Vikings – slightly flawed, perhaps, but no more than that – were on some kind of pre-ordained mission as exemplars of egalitarianism, artistic sensitivity, good government and other qualities which mankind had been lacking since Pericles.

The Viking explosion has also been interpreted as a pagan revolt which very nearly finished off Christianity when it was on its knees in Europe, between the fall of the Roman Empire in the West and the spiritual resurgence generated by the Crusades. That threat, at least, was removed when the Vikings embraced Christianity and ploughed into their new cause the same zeal which, under pagan colours, had so recently caused universal panic. Mass conversion to Christianity was actually brought about at home less by theological dialogue than by the thrust of a sword.

Perfidious admiral

The adventures of an admiral named Hastings indicate that the Vikings were not over-awed by the mystical powers of the "White Christ", as they called Christianity. He entered the Mediterranean in about 857 with a fleet of about 100 vessels with a view to investigating and if at all possible plundering Rome. As it happens, the city he approached while it was celebrating the feast of Christmas was not Rome at all but Luna, the ancient Etruscan city.

Nevertheless, the defences looked formidable so he "had recourse to that perfidy which a Northman never scrupled to employ against an adversary". He sent word to the Bishop that he merely wished to repair and replenish his battered fleet, but he also dropped the tantalising hint that he had grown tired of seafaring and might be inclined to consider Christianity "in order to find that repose in the bosom of the church which he had had so long sighed for." The Bishop leapt at the prospect of such an unexpected baptism but regretted, having administered it, that the new convert would not be allowed to enter the city. He could, however, camp outside, and the Italians warily agreed to supply him with provisions.

The loud wailing which soon reached the Bishop's ears from the camp was explained as a lament for Hastings who had suddenly fallen ill and was not expected to live. The messenger advised the Bishop that Hastings had intimated that he would leave all his booty to the church (the

ALL IN A NAME

Now usually associated wth murder, rape and pillage, the term Viking originally referred to "men of the creek". In the 9th and 10th centuries it meant "sea robber".

bearers and reinforcements were quickly masters of the city, "which they set fire to, after committing their usual acts of ferocity". Hastings then loaded his already creaking ships with more booty and sailed for home, "not forgetting to take with him the handsomest women of Luna."

The normal authorities can only guess that Hastings was a Dane, but Denmark has undisputed title to the legendary Jomsburg Vikings, a *corps d'élite* founded by a certain Palnatoki in the reign of Harald Bluetooth (941–91) and

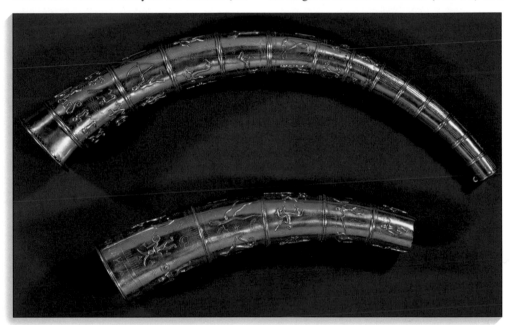

ships had profitably called at Spain, North Africa and the Balearic islands en route) provided the Bishop conceded a Christian burial within the city. Shortly afterwards, crestfallen Viking pall-bearers filed into the city with the coffin and set it down in the cathedral.

The Bishop himself was leading the service for the repose of the admiral's soul when the coffin flew open and, sword drawn, Hastings ran the Bishop through. The pall-bearers thereupon drew their weapons and Hastings, pall-

featuring such luminaries as "Bui the Thick" and Vagn, "the most unruly and turbulent youngster who ever sailed on a Viking cruise." They were based in an island camp on the Baltic coast of Germany, probably at what is now Wolin. The camp seems to have been run along the lines of a boarding school devised in Sparta. No one was admitted until proving that "he did not fear to face two men equally as strong and well armed as himself." In any case, no one under 15 or over 50 was allowed in (the turbulent Vagn, Palnatoki's grandson, excepted) and certainly not any female. No one was allowed to leave for more than one night without Palnatoki's personal permission. ❑

LEFT: one of five 11th-century Viking ships on display at Roskilde's Viking Ship Museum.
ABOVE: beautiful Viking Age golden horns.

FROM VIKINGS TO DANISH EMPIRE

The short-lived Anglo Danish kingdom gave way to the vagaries of fortune and civil war. Then the union of Denmark, Norway and Sweden was forged

When the spotlight of recorded history suddenly floods the Danish stage, it reveals what had been happening in the shadows since the days when the inhabitants were mainly occupied by spearing reindeer with flint weapons and chasing seals at the edge of the ice. The country was well on its way to becoming a recognisable nation, the scores of warring chieftainships having forged some degree of unity under the time-honoured threat of hostile neighbours.

In this case, the principal threat was Charlemagne and his Christian hordes to the south. A king named Godfred first threw up the celebrated Danevirke defensive line across the Jutland peninsula, but others like Horik pushed beyond that until in 811 Denmark had established its southern border at the Eider River.

Astonishing speed

Also in the shadows, as we have seen, the Scandinavians as a whole had been applying themselves to ship design, the development of a strong keel capable of securing a substantial mast being the key to long sea voyages.

The standard long boat was about 60 feet (20 metres) long, powered by 30 oars and a sail, but still so light that its crew could when necessary drag it across land. They could attain the astonishing speed of 10–11 knots in bursts and, as a hinged rudder on one side of the stern would fold up under impact, they could be driven on to a beach at full tilt. At this watershed in history, the emergence of the dreaded Vikings, the navy which made it possible was already a *fait accompli*.

Secrets of the sagas

Marvellous tales pour from the pages of the sagas. The rows of empty shelves in the library are suddenly crammed with information. The writers responsible for the transformation drew

LEFT: King Knud (Canute), the father of Christianity in Denmark. RIGHT: Viking burial ground at Lindholm Høje, Ålborg in North Jutland.

on the oral traditions of the so-called scalds (bards). They were expected by the kings who employed them to make the most of their victories and fine personal qualities and skip over the other stuff, but they managed by innuendo and plain cheek to present a remarkably balanced picture.

Kings and bards

The famous King Knud (Canute in English), whom we shall soon be meeting, provides a glimpse of the royal relationship with scalds. It came to his notice that a visiting Icelandic scald, one Toraren Praisetongue, had produced some unauthorised verses about him. He ordered Praisetongue to present himself the following day and recite these verses – or be hanged. Perhaps Praisetongue made some hasty revisions, but in any case the king found the verses very acceptable, especially the bit about:

Knud wards the land, as Christ,
The shepherd of Greece, doth the heaven.

Revision or not, Praisetongue not only saved

his neck with this inspired passage but was rewarded on the spot with 50 marks of silver. The verses were ever afterwards known as "The Head Ransom".

Conquest of England

The manner in which the first wave of Vikings pounced out of the north on an unsuspecting Europe is covered in the feature on pages 33–35. It recounts how these early terrorists (or cultural ambassadors, as romantics would have it) increasingly chose to remain in the lands they scourged, and that in itself gave rise to a different kind of problem. In England, the well-

CANUTE THE GREAT

King of England, Denmark and Norway, and the father of Christianity in Denmark, Canute died well before his 40th year – too young for his full potential to be realised.

He won the English throne in 1016 on the death of Edmund Ironside, whom he defeated at Assandun, Essex. The first true Dane to sit on the English throne, Canute married Emma, widow of Ethelred the Unready. He ruled the English according to their own laws and customs, but employed Scandinavian soldiers to maintain his command. Unjustly, he is chiefly remembered as a pompous idiot – commanding in vain the incoming tide to turn back – or as a poor loser at chess.

groomed Danes (they bathed on Saturdays) made a greater impression on English women than was good for them, which contributed to a war which resulted in Sweyn Forkbeard, then king of Denmark, conquering virtually the whole of England and incorporating it in a Danish empire in 1014.

War over the women of England is a lovely idea but, alas, altogether too simple. Denmark was actually suffering an economic crisis because the changing map of Europe had closed the long-used oriental trade route along the Volga, depriving Denmark, the western terminus of that route, of markets for its amber, furs and slaves in the east and cutting off its supplies of Arabic silver. At the beginning there had been plenty of substitute wealth in the unguarded monasteries of Europe, but there was a much more efficient way of extracting foreign assets. It revolved around conquest, occupation and the collection of tribute from the cowed natives. The name given to this institutionalised blackmail has a resonant historical ring: Danegeld.

King Knud – or Canute

Forkbeard the Conqueror has rather unfairly been eclipsed in history by a distant kinsman, William, who in 1066 (less than 50 years after Forkbeard's conquest) arrived in England with the descendants of Vikings who had settled in Normandy. Forkbeard was a pagan but he produced a son and heir who earned the accolade of being "the first Viking leader to be admitted into the civilised fraternity of Christian kings". The son, Knud, was said to be "of great size and strength, and very handsome except that his nose was thin, high and slightly bent. He had a light complexion and fair, thick hair, and his eyes surpassed the eyes of most men, in beauty and in keeness."

Knud was already king of England (as King Canute) when he succeeded his brother two years later and became king of Denmark as well. In England, the most familiar incident in Canute's reign is the exact opposite of what actually happened. He placed his throne on the beach but it was not to defy the incoming tide. It seems he was bored with obsequious courtiers who kept on saying that he was master of the universe. He sat on the beach and allowed the waves to engulf him precisely to demonstrate to them that he was not master of the seas, whatever they said, and to illustrate man's impotence before the might of God.

Chess games

Knud fares almost as badly in Danish folklore, which depicts him as a shocking loser at chess. It seems he was playing a game with his kinsman, Ulf the Jarl, during a lull in a campaign against Sweden and Norway when he made an ill-considered move and lost a knight. Knud put his knight back on the board and said he wanted to try a different move. This was too much for Ulf, who overturned the board and walked out. "Runnest thou off, Ulf the Coward?" the king

"whereby Ulf the Jarl met his bane". The monks in charge were appalled at the sacrilege but felt much better about it when Knud granted the church "great lands so that it became a big lordship".

Knud's conscience – the popular version of events continues – drove him to seek forgiveness for this outrage from the Pope. In reality, he had political reasons for the visit, which coincided with the coronation of Conrad IV as Holy Roman Emperor. Knud needed support for – or at least acquiescence in – his plans to expand his empire. In modern terms, then, the meeting was an informal "summit", and by

taunted. Ulf turned at the door, shouted "Thou didst not call me Ulf the Coward when I came to thy help when the Swedes were beating you like dogs," and went to bed.

In the morning, Knud told his shoe-lad to get rid of Ulf. The lad found his intended victim at prayer in St Luke's Church, the cathedral in Roskilde, and thought it was the wrong place and time for a summary execution. A Norwegian named Ivar the White had no such qualms, however, and ran his sword through him,

---

LEFT: the Middle Ages are re-enacted with gusto in Denmark. **ABOVE:** *Gaia*, a replica of a 10th-century Viking ship in the waters off Greenland.

publicly posing with these powerful personages Knud hoped to convey the impression that he was one among equals. He made a great show of it, insisting on taking a place in the coronation procession at Conrad's side.

He planned to run his empire, which included Norway, parts of Sweden and various outposts along the Baltic coast, from a capital in England. The enterprise was cut short, however, by his untimely death when he was only 37.

An imperial dream fades

Knud's various sons and heirs were not equal to keeping his imperial dream alive. One of them, Hartha-Knud, kept a united England and

Denmark going for a while but dropped dead from drink at a wedding feast in Lambeth. According to the chronicler of the period, "He never did anything royal." The English throne went to Edward the Confessor, the Danish to Magnus the Good of Norway.

On his death-bed in 1047, he passed Norway on to Sven, the Danish son of the chess casualty, Ulf. Sven "held the whole history of the barbarians in his memory, as it were in a written book" and fathered 19 children, only one of whom was legitimate and anyway died in infancy. Sven's notable qualities – "handsome, tall and strong, generous and wise, just and

brave but never victorious in war" – seem to have eluded his offspring. One of them, Harald, was known as "the Hen".

On the feeble note of royalty relegated to the level of poultry, the imperial Denmark of the Viking Age petered out. Many Danes remained in the colonial outposts and were assimilated. Those who went home retreated into a domestic madhouse, with rivals drowning one another (the preferred method was to wrap the chosen victim in heavy chains and throw him into deep water) and difficult clergymen being forced to sit in prison wearing funny hats.

Knud IV, great-nephew of his illustrious namesake, had the idea of re-conquering Eng-

land. A fleet of 1,000 ships assembled for that purpose and waited a whole summer for Knud to show up and lead them across the North Sea. He didn't, and they went home.

Knud earned the distinction of becoming Denmark's first saint, partly because at his funeral, having been murdered in church, "two days' unceasing rain stopped, the sun shone in a blue sky and all present joined in a *Te Deum*".

Wars against pagans

Never were the Danish nobility more certain of avoiding the old Viking stigma of death in bed than in the decade of civil war after 1147. Valdemar I only narrowly avoided a violent departure before rising to survey a kingdom in tatters, a third of it lost to Denmark's *bête noire*, a tribe of Baltic Slavs usually referred to as "the heathen Wends" who had based themselves on the island of Rügen. Valdemar was fortunate in being able to call on the Bishop of Roskilde to find a solution to the loathsome tribe.

Absalon, Bishop of Roskilde, is rare in history as being equally comfortable in the role of bishop, statesman, warrior, literary patron and admiral. He took to the Wends with a vengeance, storming their supposedly impregnable temple stronghold and rubbing in the humiliation by requiring the Wend priests to assemble and watch him demolish their gigantic wooden god, the four-headed Svantevit. Reduced to splinters, Svantevit was handed around to the Danish troops to be used as firewood. Absalon then marched on to the Wend capital, Garz, and did the same to the seven-headed Rugeivit. The Wends could take no more. They agreed to immediate baptism as Christians and surrendered their island, which was thereafter part of the bishopric of Roskilde.

Absalon next applied himself to the defence against pirates of a fishing village called Havn. The fortified village was first known as Kaupmanna Havn (Chapmen's or Merchants' Haven) and later as København (Copenhagen). The stronghold which Absalon built in 1168 was on the site now occupied by the Christiansborg Palace and it is fittingly his statue – on horseback, battle-axe in hand but a bishop nevertheless – which stands nearby.

Although he was somewhat overshadowed by the energetic bishop, Valdemar was always a popular king who, on his death, "was lamented by all Denmark for which he fought more than 28 battles in heathen lands and warred against the pagans to the glory of God's church so long as he lived."

Saved by the banner

With the Wends out of the way, Valdemar II pursued the Estonians with the same venom. He nearly over-reached himself at the battle of Lyndanise in 1219. His attack with an armada of 1,000 ships on the city of Reval was all but lost when a red banner with a white cross in the centre floated down from heaven. It provided

> ### THE DANISH FLAG
>
> The oldest national flag in the world is a source of pride among Danes. It must never touch the ground and only a pennant version may be flown at night.

day," a contemporary historian notes, "this Empire, and with it the hegemony of the North, crumbled to dust." Count Henry, it seems, had a grudge over confiscated property. He crept up to the tent where Valdemar and his son slept, and marched them off to the dungeon in Danneberg, his castle on the Elbe in Germany.

The unfortunate Valdemar was not released until two years later, and only then on humiliating terms. The ransom was 45,000 marks in silver, all the Queen's jewellery, arms and equipment for 100

just the tonic the Danish forces needed to turn the battle around and win. The "Danish Cloth" (*Dannebrog*) was adopted as the national flag.

Valdemar II turned Reval into a fortress, which was tantamount to annexing the Baltic as a Danish lake. Just when it looked as if Valdemar was within reach of emulating the great Knud's empire, he made a poor choice in asking Count Henry of Schwerin to join him and his son on a hunting trip to Lyø, an island south of Funen. The date was 6 May 1223. "In one

---

LEFT: an altarpiece from Skt Olai Kirke in Helsingør showing a bishop giving alms to lepers. **ABOVE:** the coming of the Dannebrog, Denmark's national flag.

knights, the whole Danish empire bar Rügen. He had to provide hostages and take an oath to keep the peace. He sought a dispensation from the Pope to be released from the vow. The Pope agreed that it had been taken under unreasonable duress. Valdemar was therefore free to seek revenge with a clear conscience but the results were disappointing. He lost an eye at the battle of Bornhoved and decided that he would rather study law. His *Liber Census Daniae*, drawn up in 1231, is the Danish Domesday book.

Tottering throne

Valdemar's four sons all became Kings of Denmark in turn, but the throne was by then hollow.

"At the death of Valdemar II," the Rye Monastery annals say, "the crown fell off the head of the Danes. From that time forth they became a laughing-stock for all their neighbours through civil wars and mutual destruction, and the lands they had honourably won with their sword were not only lost but caused great disasters to the realm and wasted it."

Murder and mayhem

For a century afterwards, most kings had only the consolation of not dying in bed. The alliance between church and state in particular broke down, the church threatening kings with

excommunication, the kings replying, for instance, by throwing the Archbishop of Lund, Jacob Erlandson, into a dungeon. He was chained and forced to wear a cap of fox tails.

The only respite from this mayhem was in the royal personage of Eric Klipping, who ascended the throne at the age of 11. In 1282 he enacted Denmark's Magna Carta at Nyborg. Parliament was to meet once a year and no one was to be imprisoned without trial. Ultimately, the high-minded Eric fared no better than his contemporaries. His misfortune was also to go hunting. Exhausted after a hard day in the field, he slumped in a barn and was found the following morning with 56 wounds to the body.

Norway was behind the assassination. The perpetrators were greeted there as heroes and made the subject of sentimental ballads. Their agent in Denmark was identified as Archbishop Jens Grand, who was accordingly thrown into a dungeon as "the lowest criminal with every circumstance of ignominy until December 1295, when he escaped". Pope Boniface VIII took a very different view of him, declaring him a martyr because "there was many a saint in heaven who had suffered less in the cause of God". Norway and Denmark embarked on a long war over the affair.

Denmark's difficulties were altogether too much for Christopher II, "the most faithless and useless ruler Denmark has ever had". He was made to step aside (he died in "extreme poverty") while the monarchy was carved up among a number of foreign princes, notably Count Gerhard III of Holstein, who also fell victim to a murderer who crept up on him in his sleep. Denmark badly needed a saviour.

Valdemar IV, only 20 or so when he ascended the throne, was determined to make himself "Restorer of Denmark" and, while being forced to sell Estonia to settle debts and to cope with the ravages of the Black Death, conceived an elaborate plot which would win back England. He offered to help France in the Hundred Years' War by invading England with 12,000 men for 600,000 florins. His son, he thought, could usefully marry a French princess.

Miraculous fishes

As the scheme came to nothing, the 600,000 florins did not materialise, but Valdemar received a windfall from a quarter which no one could have anticipated. Fantastic shoals of herring appeared in the Sound, so tightly packed that, according to a Frenchman who witnessed the phenomenon, "one may cut them in two with a sword". Everyone was obliged to eat fish during Lent but, for the poor, the ordinary kinds of fish were an unaffordable luxury.

The Frenchman interpreted the herring as divine intervention, a fish so small and numerous that Lent could be properly observed even by the most wretched peasant. Danish and German fishermen were drawn to the Sound in scenes that anticipated the Californian gold rush, 40,000 boats at a time scooping up the herring. The fish were a budget-saving godsend for the king, whose revenue from the tax imposed on catches exceeded the revenue available from all other sources put together.

Flush with money, Valdemar gave full vent to ambition. He began by capturing Visby, a rich Hansa town in Gotland, off the east coast of Sweden, and proclaimed himself "King of the Goths", a title still borne by Danish monarchs. The Hanseatic traders recognised the threat and took the 77 cities they controlled into union with Sweden, Mecklenburg and Holstein. Valdemar's campaign ground to a halt and he was forced to

OLDEST MONARCHY

The present ruler and Margrethe I, founder of the Kalmar Union, are the only two queens in a line of monarchs that stretches back to Gorm the Old (10th century).

throne, she was in the perfect position to hone her natural political abilities. Steering the baby Oluf on to the Danish throne was merely her opening shot. The addition of the Norwegian crown to Oluf's head was automatic on the death of his father in 1380. Her move on Sweden began when young Oluf reached the age of 15 and, on his mother's recommendation, started calling himself "the true heir to Sweden". The claim was based on his hereditary connection with the dispossessed Folkung dynasty and it infuriated

seek asylum abroad. In future, the victorious allies declared, they would have the last say over who ruled Denmark. They did not object when Margrethe, Queen of Håkon VI of Norway, proposed her five-year-old son, Oluf.

Grand designs

Margrethe had been married to the much older King Håkon when she was 10; she was only 17 when she gave birth to her first and only son, Oluf. As the precocious power behind Håkon's

LEFT: a 12th-century AD altar from the church at Lisbjerg near Arhus, East Jutland. **ABOVE:** an ivory crucifix in Herlufsholm Kirke, near Næstved.

King Albrecht, who occupied that throne on what he considered to be legitimate grounds.

Margrethe's designs on Sweden were set back by Oluf's death in 1387 when he was only 17. His mother (with "a dark complexion and somewhat masculine in appearance") stepped into his shoes and within a week assumed several titles, including "The Right Heir and Princess of Denmark." The Norwegian lords were impressed into recognising her as their "mighty lady and master" although this was in contravention of the Norwegian law of succession. She settled any misgivings by producing her grand-nephew, Eric of Pomerania, who met the requirements of the Norwegian Council and was proclaimed hereditary sovereign. Eric was seven. Sweden, however, still eluded her net.

Final hurdle

Oluf's contentious claim to the Swedish throne had rested on the Folkung pretender, Bo Jonsson Grip, and when Grip died Margrethe persuaded the Swedish nobles to transfer all his fortresses and most of his land to her in exchange for future guarantees of their privileges. The nobles therefore acknowledged her as Sweden's "sovereign lady and rightful master" but there was still Albrecht to contend with. He went off to recruit a mercenary army in

Germany but was routed soon afterwards by Swedish and Danish forces at Falköping.

Albrecht was dragged off the battlefield in chains and Margrethe fulfilled her long desired goal. "God," said a contemporary chronicle, "gave an unexpected victory into the hands of a woman." To which another added, "All the nobility of Denmark were seized by fear of the wisdom and strength of this lady."

Three realms united

The union of the three countries was formally enacted with Eric's triple coronation at Kalmar in 1397. He was 14. In theory, the three nations were equal; in practice, Denmark was the senior partner. Norway's participation at the coronation seems to have been through the Bishop of Orkney, and he was an Englishman.

The coronation became "the most intensely discussed single event in Nordic history" because of a contradiction in two documents drawn up at the time. One proclaimed that the three realms would forever be united under one king, the other that, after Eric, each country could choose a king from his direct descendants or, if they weren't any, from elsewhere. The immediate effect, though, was the creation of an empire which stretched from the Gulf of Finland to the Varanger Fjord on the Polar Seas and south to the Eider. It included the Orkneys, Shetlands, Faroes, Iceland and Greenland. It was twice the size of the German empire.

Young Eric turned out to be "rash, violent and obstinate", and Margrethe spent much time trying to repair the damage caused by his ill-considered and badly carried out schemes. She was on her boat in Flensborg, trying to unravel a war he had started with Holstein, when she died, thus surrendering "the greatest personal position ever achieved in Scandinavia".

In spite of her achievements, little is known about Margrethe personally. There is a glimpse of her in straitened circumstances as Håkon's bride in Norway, a letter begging him to arrange credit with a merchant in Oslo so that she could pay the servants, but little else has survived. The effigy on her tomb in Roskilde cathedral depicts her as eternally young.

Romance and piracy

Eric stumbled along, trying to undermine the power of the Hanseatic League and developing Copenhagen as a royal seat. He managed to antagonise his subjects in all three kingdoms and, in a pointed anticlimax to the optimism at Kalmar, he threw in the towel. The manner of his departure at least adds a little romance to this disappointing monarch. He went off with his favourite mistress to Visborg Castle in Gotland and there established himself as an efficient, prosperous pirate. One of the demands made of his successor, his nephew Christopher, was to suppress these piratical exploits. He declined, quipping: "Uncle must live too." ❏

LEFT: a rare depiction of Queen Margrethe in a fresco in a church at Lolland. **RIGHT:** manuscript of Valdemar II's Jutland Code, of 1241, granting legal rights.

sanabant ab oī infirmita
te. Pſeueraũt aũt Iſtan
na in ūginitate ꝓ eam
mīre ūgies nobiles ſaca
uelamina ſuſcepūt. Sã
na eps o dſ ignaoi mīr
ur qui bñ ignaoꝰ
mīis tui atꝗ ionathas
ſollēnia coluī ē apd te ī
tribulationibꝰ adiuuen IST
gnaoꝰ bñſtium iohis euu
gliſte diſaplꝰ ꝓ audio eū
eps fuit. Qn aũt diu ꝓpaue er
de oꝛaſʒ ꝓ traiani ipatoꝛ
deuictoꝛia redeunt ꝓ iāms
moꝛtē nũnati ociuʒ ꝓ libe
ſe iani ē aſſeruit. Oꝛ ea
ū ferro uincti roma dua
ꝓeꝓ tradend ibide beſthis
Cū ꝗ roliꝗ ꝓ deuoꝛand
ma ueuiſʒ ꝓ aũt ba
aꝰ duci busʒ dīc ei ꝗau.
Ignaoi mīr anyochiā re
bellare ſaas ꝓ ad dm ꝗnua
noꝛ ſiuas. Cui ignaqus
Rex dñs ius ſacſtio utuā

diguitatē affeciō. De me ꝗ
ꝗ uoluiſ ꝓtãs fac ſʒ mul
latēū me mutabis. Leuo iꝰ.
Craiaũ dicit. Cuſtodi
re eū in carcere ſiue ab
ꝗſti ut tercia die beſthis
deuoꝛandū tradar. die iꝗ
iꝰ ꝑato: leuaʒ ꝓ oīs pꝰ
ſueuerūt ut uidēt aña
ochēū eſꝓ ꝗ erat aī beſt
is pugnaticꝰ. Craiaū ꝑe
ꝗ ſeroces leones adiſꝓ mul
ti ut ſic deuoꝛarēt ꝗ ū reli
ꝗe remaneret. Tunc ignaoꝰ
dīc. ſrumentū ꝓ ſū beſthaꝛ
deuoꝛabʒ molar ut panis ꝓ
d efficiar. In ꝗuſificatōe ū ꝗ ūĝ

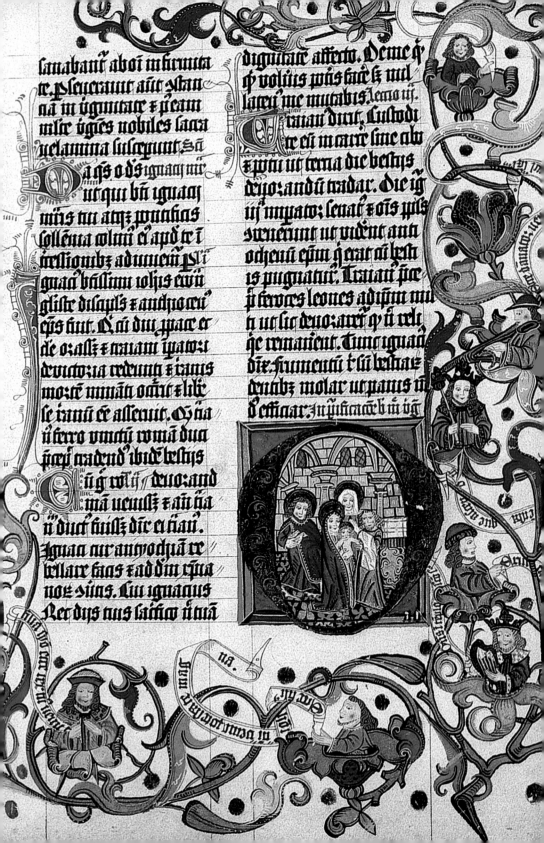

ua.

THE REFORMATION

A turbulent period of religious division, social unrest and civil war

culminated in the triumph of Lutheranism

Christian II (1513–23) brought "genius and madness" to the throne, although by then Sweden had backed out of the Kalmar union and was running its own affairs. As crown prince and his father's regent in Norway, Christian II had averted a similar move towards independence there by murdering the Swedish-Norwegian nobleman Knut Alvsson. His death, according to the playwright Henrik Ibsen, plucked the heart out of Norway, which for a long time afterwards was reduced to little more than a Danish province.

Nevertheless, Norway continued to trouble Christian, because it harboured pockets of Hansa authority in a number cities, including Bergen. It was in Bergen that the king was attracted to the daughter of a Dutch market woman and asked her for a dance. "In that dance," sighs the chronicler Arild Hvidfeldt (echoing Valdemar II's decision to take Count Henry of Schwerin along on his hunting trip), "he danced away the three kingdoms of Denmark, Norway and Sweden."

Dove tale

Christian actually married the 13-year-old Isabella of Burgundy, an arrangement which cemented links with the House of Habsburg and the Emperor Maximilian, her grandfather. But the "little dove" (Dyveke), as he called the Dutch girl, was kept at hand, a few miles outside Copenhagen. When Maximilian heard about the arrangement, he demanded the little dove's immediate expulsion from Denmark. Christian's response was to move her and her mother even closer, to a house round the corner from his palace. It seems that, living in the city centre, Dyveke may have caught the eye of the governor of Copenhagen castle, Torben Oxe.

There is some doubt as to what happened. Oxe may have made advances and been rebuffed. He may then have conspired to make her eat a bowl of poisoned cherries. In any case,

LEFT: *Dawn: Luther at Erfurt*, by Joseph Noel Paton.
RIGHT: Christian II, who ruled from 1513 to 1523.

in the fourth year of Christian's reign, the little dove died. Oxe was arrested and, over the pleading of the queen, who went on her knees before Christian, was sentenced and executed.

The affair was not merely a domestic melodrama but a symptom of Christian's attempts to tug his kingdom into the Renaissance era

taking place elsewhere in Europe. These necessitated a high degree of monarchical authority, which could only be at the expense of the nobility. Moreover, his upbringing had given him both bourgeois sympathies and a hostile suspicion of the nobility, as exemplified by Torben Oxe. Some authorities believe that Oxe was wholly innocent or, at least, that the case against him was never proven.

The real consequence of the dance in Bergen, however, was not so much the ill-fated affair but the looming figure of the mother, Sigbrit. A former student of alchemy and medicine, she came to believe that she possessed telepathic powers which gave her remote control over the king. Of common stock herself, her hatred of the nobility spurred Christian's bourgeois reservations. The idea of a king reaching over the heads of the nobility to lend a hand to the commoners is one that has inspired Danes to regard him as a prophet of the benign state.

Christian's ability to curb the power of the Danish nobility turned ultimately on events in Sweden, where "Sten Sture the Younger" (his real name was Nilsson) was hoping to claim the Swedish crown on the back of mass support for his strongly expressed nationalism. He had already seized and installed himself in a castle when Christian advanced on him with a

force of German, French and Scottish mercenaries. Sten Sture was defeated twice, the second time dying of wounds while retreating to Stockholm. His widow, Kristina Gyllenstierna, kept the resistance going from Stockholm but in the end she capitulated and on 4 November 1520 Christian was crowned king of Sweden.

The Bloodbath

Christian had been supported all along by the Holy Roman Emperor, which angered the Protestant movement brewing in Uppsala. Three days after his coronation, he secured his position with "a stroke of truly machiavellian ruthlessness". His opponents were rounded up

in the Great Square near Stockholm Castle, charged with heresy, and executed. Eighty-two lost their heads, including two bishops and the scions of many noble families.

The killings did not stop with what came to be known as the "Stockholm Bloodbath"; similar trials were held in other places on his way back to Denmark until the number of victims exceeded 600. It was a journey "marked by gallows and executions".

Visiting the Netherlands, Dyveke and Sigbrit's birthplace, Christian was hailed as a great European monarch. He met Erasmus and they discussed the impact of Luther. When Erasmus voiced criticism of the violence that had been stirred up by the reformer, Christian ventured that "mild measures avail nothing; the medicine that gives the whole body a good shaking is the best and surest".

It was a telling remark from one who was closely identified with the Holy Roman Emperor, the dispute over Dyveke notwithstanding, and a portent of the Reformation ahead. Christian had summoned a Lutheran preacher to his court in 1519, only two years after Luther nailed up his thesis at Wittenberg, and while the preacher made some converts among the Danish upper classes, the king was not yet ready to follow.

Christian continued to give a good shaking instead to the Danish nobility but he was soon in trouble both at home and in Sweden where Gustav Vasa, some of whose family had died in the Stockholm Bloodbath, led the Swedish miners in a revolt which saw him elected to the Swedish throne. Christian was helpless to do anything about it.

In Denmark he faced growing resentment over extortionate taxation and could no longer rely on his old ally, the church, not only because of the Bloodbath but also because he had confiscated the profits of a papal legate who had been doing a roaring business in indulgences. He tried to excuse the Stockholm atrocity by putting the blame on the man he had just appointed Archbishop of Lund. The bewildered archbishop was burned at the stake.

Exile and imprisonment

In December 1522 Christian's excesses drove 18 Jutland nobles, including four bishops, to offer the throne to his uncle, Frederik, Duke of Holstein. Friendless in Denmark, Christian sailed for the Netherlands with his wife, children and Sigbrit, where he hoped to rally support from the Holy Roman Emperor. "In fact," says Professor T.K. Derry, "the union of the three crowns came to a final end with the sudden eclipse of this highly gifted, but despotic and unstable ruler."

In the Netherlands Christian "became so poor that he had to pawn his jewels, his faithful queen died in 1526, and his three children were taken from his custody to be made Catholics". In the circumstances, then, he understandably

LET THEM EAT RATS

During the seige of Copenhagen people were reduced to eating dogs and cats, small birds, frogs and even rats, and they made their bread from soaked leather.

is still there for visitors to see. He outlived two of his successors, Frederick I and Christian III, and died at 77, having spent eight years of his life in exile and 27 in prison.

Civil war

Frederik, the uncle who succeeded Christian II, fudged the developing religious division by tolerating both camps. On his death, though, the issue came to a head, with part of the Council in favour of Prince Hans, who was being brought up as a Catholic, the others preferring his older

leapt at an invitation from Norwegian bishops to assume the crown of Norway independently. Aided by his brother-in-law, the Emperor Charles V, he set sail with 10,000 men and laid siege, indecisively, to Akershus in Oslo.

He was in turn encircled by Danish and Hanseatic reinforcements who, in the end, sent him into solitary confinement in Sønderborg Castle on the island of Als. With nothing else to do, he walked round and round his table wearing a path in the stone flags of the floor which

LEFT: an influx of Dutch artisans brought these characteristic breeches to Amager.
ABOVE: still hopeful of a return, Christian II in exile.

brother, the future Christian III, a Lutheran. Solving the impasse was not made easier by the arrival of Count Christopher of Oldenburg in Denmark with an army financed by the Hanseatic mayor of Lübeck, who demanded the restoration of Christian II.

Surprisingly, perhaps, the imprisoned king still enjoyed support in Copenhagen, if only among the peasants he had championed, and the so-called Count's War dragged on for two years, the last civil war in Denmark's history.

Seige of Copenhagen

Few kings have reached their throne by such a blood-stained path as Christian III, whose victorious army entered Copenhagen in 1536. By that time, the citizens (still faithful to Christian II, or more probably to their redoubtable burgomaster Ambrosius Bogbinder, a childhood friend of the king) had long waited in vain for help from Charles V. For many months Christian's ruthless German general Johan Rantzau drove back any emaciated citizen who attempted to escape, and Bogbinder equally ruthlessly suppressed talk of surrender. By July 1536, when the people of Copenhagen filed out of the city bare-headed and with white sticks to indicate surrender, there was nothing left for them to eat but "the leaves on the trees".

The Clergyman King

The new Lutheran king was now the most powerful man in Denmark. Every other citizen from noble to peasant had bled along with the scarred country, and the hold of the Hanseatic League was gone for ever.

Despite his power and unlike his relentless general who counselled vengeance, the young king decided to treat Copenhagen generously and decreed that peace was to be restored in his name. In the light of this, his nickname as "The Clergyman King" seems rather less surprising than his early activities might have indicated.

Though his German-Holstein advisers advocated an absolute monarchy, in the early days at least, Christian III knew he needed the support of the nobility and the ordinary people to bring about the reforms his Lutheranism demanded. He was wise enough also to listen to Mogens Gøye, Frederik I's chief counsellor, and the strong man of Jutland, who counter-balanced the Germans and urged moderation in the king's move against the Catholic bishops.

The revolt against the Catholic Church had begun in the reign of his father Frederik I and, as governor of the Duchies (Schleswig-Holstein), Christian had early on adopted the new faith. By 1526 Frederik declared the Danish Church independent. Lutheran preachers such as Hans Tausen, a renegade monk, were permitted to preach – although the Catholic hierarchy did not always make their mission easy. When Tausen himself was imprisoned by the Bishop of Viborg, he continued to preach to enormous crowds through the prison bars. Despite the bishops, he became Frederik's own chaplain and, later, under Christian III, Bishop of Ribe.

Purging the bishops

Apart from his zeal for religious reform, at the end of the tangle of civil war Christian III had an even more pressing need: to pay Rantzau and his German troops. The two coincided neatly and, as it did with King Henry VIII of England across the North Sea, the wealth of the Catholic Church, its monasteries and estates provided a strong second motive for dealing swiftly with the bishops.

A secret nocturnal council decided "in God's name to take these bishops by the scruff of their necks" and, during that night, Christian III rounded up the bishops, including the astute Joachim Rønnow, who had earlier appeared to support Frederik I's reforms but retained his true colours and was found hiding on a beam in his palace.

Only the Bishop of Børglum, Stygge (Ugly) Krumpen, managed to escape and he was flushed out of a baker's oven a few days later. The country's last Catholic archbishop fled the country without a finger being raised on his behalf and Danish troops marched northwards to implement the same changes in Norway. Norway, Christian then declared, would "henceforth be and remain under the Crown of Denmark… and it shall henceforth neither be, nor be called, a kingdom in itself."

Reformation sealed

The Catholic Church was dead in Denmark, Rantzau's soldiers were paid, and the people of Copenhagen, so recently humiliated, were glad to witness the downfall of their bishops. The Reformation was sealed by a council of 1,000 nobles, merchants and peasants (but no clergy) which agreed to confiscate Church lands and to the establishment of Lutheranism. Magnanimously, Christian III declared an amnesty for offences committed in the civil war, the blame for which was firmly laid at the bishops' door.

> **CHURCH COLLECTION**
>
> The monarchy emerged from the civil war stronger than ever, and buttressed by a treasury that was much enriched by the confiscation of church properties.

council and held positions of power as great as those of the nobility, the latter were less interested in holding office in the new church. Lutheran bishops and clergy were not, as their Catholic brethren had been, exclusively drawn from the ranks of the nobility. Tradesman and peasants played a significant part in church affairs. For instance, the new Bishop of Zealand, Peder, known as Palladius (1503–60), was the son of a shoemaker, yet he along with Bugenhagen was pre-eminent in shaping the new doctrines.

The bishops could be thankful that Christian felt no need to treat them as his Viking predecessors might have dealt with subjects who offended. Only Bishop Rønnow remained captive for life. In time the rest were released and given lands. Oluf Munk, last Catholic Bishop of Ribe, again became a royal councillor, after he had demonstrated his conversion by marrying and fathering six sons and six daughters.

With the diminished role of the Catholic bishops, who had been members of the royal

LEFT: Christian III, famous for his religious reforms.
ABOVE: herring market at the height of the season.

National pride

The Danish Reformation was undoubtedly German inspired, with most of Denmark's reformers looking to German universities for their religious education and the king bringing in a German, Johannes Bugenhagen, a disciple of Luther, to organise the new Reformed Church. However, this ecclesiastical reformation turned into a national and patriotic revival. Danish became the language of the church, with hymn books, services and the Bible being translated into Danish, in a surge of national feeling that looked ahead to a similar period of national pride in the 19th century. Post-Reformation Denmark was distinctly Danish. ❑

ABSOLUTE MONARCHY

Denmark enjoyed a long period of prosperity and was defeated by Sweden.
The nobles lost their power with the establishment of absolute monarchy

I n his entertaining book *The Scandinavians*, Donald Connery says: "Looking at the list of Danish monarchs for the last five hundred years is a little like watching a long volley in tennis" – his point being that one Christian is followed by the next Frederik, and vice versa.

Christian III reigned for 23 years and, with finances hugely improved by the confiscation of Church property, he presided over the recovery from civil war and instituted the centralisation of power which was to become a characteristic of the tennis volley ahead. The economic benefits were not evenly spread, however. The peasants were as badly off as ever, and many smaller land-owners, and the nascent urban middle class, were long made to suffer for taking the wrong side in the civil war.

Christian III's son, Frederik II, felt emboldened to launch his largely mercenary army against Sweden, where his counterpart, Eric, was often distracted by his ultimately futile desire to marry Queen Elizabeth of England. "There was a tremendous killing," wrote Eric of one of the battles. "The water in the river was coloured red as blood… We stuck into (the Danes) like a herd of wild boars, sparing none…" Eric went mad before the war ended. He stabbed one of his nobles to death personally, had others butchered in prison, married his mistress in private and then insisted on having her crowned in public. In the end he was put away and died nine years later of arsenic poisoning. Peace was restored at Stettin in 1570, not an inch of territory changing hands.

Full-blooded man of action

Frederik's successor, Christian IV, was "a man of action rather than reflection, brave, artistic, and interested in all kinds of practical concerns; he is the one sovereign of the long Oldenburg line who not only became a popular hero in his lifetime but has been widely and on the whole

gratefully remembered by posterity." Professor Derry's appraisal is slightly qualified by other historians: one adds that he was also "vitiated by a pleasure-loving nature, prone to excesses".

His family life has been called "full-blooded": his first marriage produced three sons, his second (a morganatic union with a

young noblewoman) another son and six daughters. When the second wife was banished for adultery, he consoled himself with her chambermaid. "The quarrels between his natural children, among themselves and with his legitimate children, caused the King much grief and misery," it is recorded.

Christian changed the face of Denmark and of Norway, not merely with many of their finest public buildings but also with new towns, whose names often boasted the royal connection. The name of the Norwegian capital, Oslo, was changed to Christiania, and a new town on the west coast became Christiansand (now Kristiansand). He trebled the size of the Danish

---

LEFT: Queen Caroline Matilde, wife of Christian VII.
RIGHT: King Christian IV, famous for his numerous children but also for his building programme.

navy with ships he helped to design, sent explorers off to find the Northwest passage, personally sailed around the North Cape into the White Sea and chartered companies to develop trade with the Far East. He liked the grand gesture. On visiting his brother-in-law, James I of England, his present was a warship.

Single combat

Like Frederik before him, Christian came round to thinking that he was ready for a war with Sweden. When the Council demurred, reminding him that the last one had been expensively fruitless, Christian threatened to declare war in

his independent capacity as Duke of Schleswig-Holstein. He had his way but, though the Danes captured two of Sweden's main fortresses and laid siege to Vaxholm, Stockholm's defensive fortress, again the war was not decisive. At one point, possibly with a view to economising, the Swedish king challenged Christian to settle the dispute in single combat, adding: "Herein if you fail we shall no longer consider you an honourable king or soldier." Christian scorned the challenge from "a paralytic dollard" and advised him to stay at a warm fireside with his nurse. In the negotiated peace of Knarød, 1613, Denmark restored some of the captured Swedish territory. But, for six years, Sweden

lost its major western stronghold, Älvsborg and its major trading station at Gothenburg until the country paid a crippling ransom to the Danes. On balance, this was a victory for Denmark over its neighbour – but one that was never to be repeated.

Christian allowed himself to be drawn into the Thirty Years' War and suffered crushing defeats first by Germany and then by a rejuvenated Sweden. He was in the thick of the fighting himself and was on the quarter-deck of his flagship when a gun exploded. Shrapnel struck him in 23 places, including an eye, but he picked himself up off the deck and ordered the fight to continue.

He felt let down by the Danish nobility and his son-in-law, Ulfeld, when ultimately forced to sue for peace on what he considered humiliating terms. He saw out the last years of his 52-year reign in the company of the loyal chambermaid, being described as "a Renaissance prince whose sense of beauty found expression in buildings which have long outlived the collapse of his political ambitions".

The practical politics behind the glitter of Christian's reign involved a steady erosion of the power of the nobility. The power did not pass to the people, however, but into the hands of the king. Although Frederik III promised a constitution that would redistribute their powers more democratically, he did nothing and the changes were "never heard of any more after that day and the Estates of Denmark did not meet again for nearly two centuries".

There was a new constitution, however, a secret one, and it is easy to imagine why Frederik kept it under wraps until his death. It did away with any pretence: power was to be invested absolutely in the monarchy.

Absolute monarchy

At the mercy of the crown, Denmark was doubly unfortunate in the untalented procession of individuals who wore it. Christian V, according to a calmly balanced view, was "weak, shallow and vain". Frederik IV was virtually illiterate when he ascended the throne at the age of 28, although he later learned to read and enjoy poetry. Christian VI's "whole appearance was unsympathetic; his voice and face were equally disagreeable". His queen was "sulky and fretful". Frederik V died of drink; Christian VII, "depraved in mind and body" as a boy, went from bad to worse. "With his drunken comrades he visited bars... where His Majesty used to break glasses, bottles, and furniture to pieces and throw them out of the windows."

A German doctor, Johann Friedrich Struensee, was retained as Court Physician to put Christian right. Christian IV's wife, Queen Caroline Matilde (a sister of George III of England), at first distrusted this "atheist, of dissolute life and elegant manners" who, furthermore, was "spoilt by women". Nor could his skills reverse

> ### LONG LIVE THE KING
>
> Christian IV's long reign saw the building of many of Denmark's most lavish palaces and mansions. There was also an awakening of the arts and sciences.

formerly been sinecures for men of influence.

His zealous reforms made enemies, not least because they were the work of a German who never learnt Danish and was "of a domineering character". A powerful group led by the dowager queen cornered the imbecilic king in his bedroom at 5 a.m. and made him sign an order for Struensee's arrest, the rest of the plan being to lock up Caroline Matilde in Kronborg Castle at Helsingør. Struensee was plucked out of bed and made to listen to a list of charges which

her husband's slide into "hopeless imbecility". She was not yet 21.

Struensee charmed the king into granting him wide powers of state, and the queen into bed. He decreed, wisely, that adultery and unchastity were no longer offences, but that was only one of 1,069 Cabinet orders through which in 16 months he tried to overhaul Danish society. He introduced freedom of the press, exercised tight budgetary controls, and laid down qualifications for holding public posts which had

---

LEFT: Christian IV's Round Tower, Copenhagen.
ABOVE: Christian IV processing through the streets on the day of his coronation.

included usurpation of royal authority, *lèse majesté* and injury to His Majesty's honour.

He was not given the benefit of his own legal reforms which, as well as legalising adultery, had abolished capital punishment for most offences and forbidden judicial torture. On 28 April 1772 the executioners first cut off his right hand, then his head. His body was drawn and quartered; the severed head mounted on a pole. As the king was in no condition to take over his duties, the Crown Prince Frederik stepped in as regent.

The queen was imprisoned in the castle until rescued by a British man-of-war despatched by George III. Although depressed by separation from her infant daughter, she became a popular figure around the old Hanoverian castle where she lived until struck down by smallpox at 23.

In 1801, the British Navy again sailed under the guns of Kronborg Castle, on this occasion 20 ships of the line among 53 under Admiral Sir Hyde Parker and Horatio Nelson. Two days later the greater part of the fleet entered Copenhagen harbour and engaged seven dismasted Danish blockships, two ships of the line and several floating batteries and gunboats. The raw recruits and students who were manning the Danish defences put up what Nelson later described as the hottest fight he had ever known.

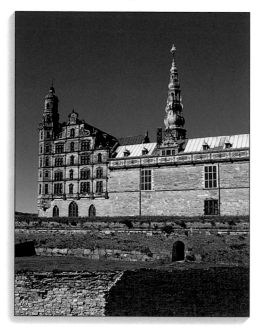

Brave crews

The cause was Denmark's ratification of an armed neutrality treaty with Russia, the latest in a series of steps to prevent Britain from searching neutral ships in case they were violating Britain's embargo on trade with Napoleon. After five hours of desperate fighting, Nelson sent a message addressed "To the Brothers of Englishmen, the Danes". In it, he offered to spare the defenders if they ceased fire. If not, he would be obliged to set on fire the batteries he had taken "with their brave crews". Crown Prince Frederik agreed to a truce and was slightly taken aback when Nelson praised an 18-year-old Dane, Peder Willemoes, who, in a tiny gunboat, had attacked his flagship for four hours. Nelson recommended that he be promoted to admiral for his pluck.

Copenhagen bombarded

Hostilities broke out again in 1807. Napoleon and Alexander I of Russia ordered Denmark (plus Sweden and Portugal) to close its ports to England and to declare war. The British reply was to send a large fleet and 30,000 troops under the command of Lord Cathcart and the future Duke of Wellington with an ultimatum: either come out formally for England or Copenhagen would be bombarded.

The sequel is a black page in the history of the British Navy. The admiral concerned later faced a court-martial for cowardice in the face of the French fleet, but there was no fleet to threaten him in Copenhagen. The Danish crown prince almost certainly desired a rapprochement with England but found it impossible to meet the deadline. Copenhagen was bombarded for three days. The university and cathedral were destroyed, as were several hundred houses. The city capitulated on 7 September.

All Danish ships and boats (more than 70 in all), with their stores and ammunition, were taken to England. The crown prince, acting as regent to the mad Christian VII, promptly concluded an alliance with Napoleon, whereupon England declared war on Denmark. Napoleon sent French and Spanish troops to shore up Danish defences, and it is said that the incomprehensible sight of these troops marching past his window was the last straw for the deranged monarch. The hard-pressed crown prince, regent for more than 20 years, succeeded him as Frederik VI.

Bankrupt and penalised

Shocked by the bombardment of Copenhagen, Denmark stayed with Napoleon while his other allies deserted him. The nation paid a terrible economic price for its stand and, by prolonging it, stood to lose even more through reparations at the Treaty of Kiel, 1814. In the event, bankrupt Denmark, having recently seen its proud navy carted off, then lost Norway to Sweden. The only faint consolation was that it retained Iceland, Greenland and the Faroes. ❑

LEFT: Kronborg Castle at Helsingør. **RIGHT:** a 19th-century courtyard typical of city life at the time.

DENMARK ALONE

Out of defeat came a cultural flowering, enlightened reforms,
and the loss of the duchies of Schleswig-Holstein

It was almost as if Denmark's intellectual community redoubled its efforts to compensate for the diplomatic and military setbacks. The generation of 1810–30 produced a Golden Age of Danish literature dominated by Hans Christian Andersen and Søren Kierkegaard.

Frederik VI, small of stature and sickly, had no real interest in literature.With his passion for military matters somewhat irrelevant in the country's reduced circumstances, he turned his hand to setting up a public school system. He coincidentally bolstered the writers' campaign to advance Danish literature and language by speaking Danish, rather than German, at court, thus breaking a centuries-old tradition.

Encouraging the use of Danish in government and in the arts was very much the spirit of the European National Romantic movement, which regarded a common language, rather than geography, as the criterion of nationhood. While the promotion of the Danish language helped to restore self-esteem when it was at a low ebb, the emphasis on language ties created for Denmark more problems than it solved.

Buffer zone

The Norwegians, too, were re-discovering their identity through language, but as far as Denmark was concerned Norway after 1814 was a lost cause. When the issue raised its head in the Danish-ruled Duchies of Schleswig and Holstein, however, the repercussions had Lord Palmerston tearing at his hair. They lingered well into the 20th century. Schleswig and Holstein represented a kind of mixed buffer zone between "pure" Denmark and "pure" Germany. The German-speakers were politically dominant in both places: in Holstein as an overwhelming majority; in Schleswig because few of the Danish-speakers, a majority in real terms, met the franchise qualifications. The Germans, on the whole, were prosperous town-dwellers,

the majority of Danes were peasant farmers.

Germany in 1830 consisted of a confederation of states and, following the overthrow of the Bourbon rulers of in France, they adopted liberal constitutions which were the envy of Danes in general and the German-speakers of Schleswig and Holstein in particular. The latter

campaigned for similar rights, implying that the two duchies would then become independent and, as such, might even abandon their Danish connection in order to join the German confederation.

Whatever reservations the Danish-speakers might have had about Copenhagen's reluctance to move with the times, they liked the prospect of German hegemony even less. Yet Copenhagen could hardly agree to liberal reforms without extending them to the two duchies, which could then vote to go their own way.

At its heart, the issue polarised into a contest between Denmark and Prussia, an inexorable route to war, but it was caught up in broad

LEFT: Denmark won the Battle of Egersund but lost the 1864 war to Germany. **RIGHT:** N.F.S. Grundtvig, founder of Denmark's famous folk high schools.

cross-currents, too. The pan-Germanic movement was counterbalanced by pan-Scandinavianism, a cause taken up by students under the influence of N.F.S. Grundtvig, who sought to develop a tolerant form of Christianity incorporating the virtues of Norse mythology, a combination which produced stirring hymns.

Grundtvig's educational ideas were the basis of Denmark's folk high schools. They were intended for rural children, the school year being concentrated in the five winter months when they could be spared from the land. Traditional book learning was replaced by emotional discussion and community singing which

sent pupils back to their farms with a lively pride in the nation's past and with a streak of idealism concerning the future.

Denmark was still without a real constitution, and reforms lay within the discretion of the ageing King Frederik. He occasionally made major advances such as the early introduction of universal elementary education. But he held back on the laws of land-ownership which might have improved the status and security of rural tenants who paid rent with their labour and a mass of workers, such as dairy maids, who put in long hours for little more than their board and lodging. Censorship laws still required newspapers to be scrutinised

by the police before they could be put on sale.

High hopes rested with the accession of Christian VIII. But he feared that too many concessions would jeopardise Schleswig-Holstein. However, Christian virtually conceded the point in his final months, and his successor, Frederik VII, sealed the matter. A witness described how, on 29 January 1848, "in a silence so profound that the stroke of the pen could be plainly heard, the king signed the order with a firm hand, thereby abolishing absolutism".

The reaction in Schleswig-Holstein was very much as predicted, with some demanding freedom (including the right to determine future relations with Germany) and others the incorporation of Schleswig with Denmark. A flicker of armed rebellion in the duchies was quickly put down by Danish forces, but their intervention attracted a huge number of German troops under a veteran Prussian commander who overran not only the duchies but also Jutland as far as Århus. King Oskar of Sweden offered a force of 15,000 Swedes and 3,000 Norwegians to repel the Germans. With Britain and later Russia taking a keen interest – the balance of power in the Baltic was at stake – hostilities were suspended, resumed and suspended again.

Humiliating blow

Denmark's southern border remained the Eider River, originally fixed in 811 and still defended by ancient earthworks little different from what they had been then. They were no match in 1864 either for the new breech-loading Prussian needle-gun, against which the Danish forces offered muzzle-loaders, nor for the Prussian now orchestrating his country's affairs, Bismarck. The Chancellor had correctly anticipated that the great powers would not intervene on Denmark's behalf and was unyielding at the negotiating table. The duchies were surrendered into his hands: Denmark thereby lost 40 per cent of what remained of its territory in Europe after the departure of Norway and Skåne.

Danes responded by making the best of what was left. The Health Society set about reclaiming the wasteland of western Jutland and settling it with rural poor. North American and Russian grain flooding the European markets

LEFT: an old etching of surveyors at work on land enclosure.
RIGHT: city street, Copenhagen *circa* 1865.

steered Danish agriculture away from cereals to dairying and cattle-breeding. The pork industry took pains to produce the kind of streaky bacon popular on British breakfast tables.

The economic revolution was painful for many country dwellers, who had to choose between joining the drift towards towns or emigrating. The growth of industry and an urban proletariat made the lingering privileges of the land-owning classes anachronistic and untenable. With every election, the Left reduced the Conservatives' position in the Folketing until, in 1884, they held only 19 out of 102 seats, although they still formed the government.

The Conservatives went on about building a ring of fortifications around Copenhagen (with the inference that the rest of the country could be sacrificed in the event of war); the socialists agitated for legislation to benefit poorer workers. They edged towards a compromise which then took on its own momentum as the genesis of the Danish welfare state. In 1901, with the Conservatives down to eight out of 114 seats, King Christian invited the majority to form a government. Celebrations greeted the *systemskiftet* (change of system), the start of a democracy that was to make 20th-century Denmark one of Europe's most liberal nations. ❑

GRUNDTVIG: FOUNTAIN OF ENLIGHTENMENT

The early 19th century was a Golden Age in which Denmark was culturally renewed. Two figures overshadow on the world scene. Hans Christian Andersen (1805–75) charmed his way into hearts, while Søren Kierkegaard (1813–55) thought his way into minds.

Less known outside Denmark is the theologian, historian, educator, statesman, scholar, activist politician and hymnist-poet N.F.S. Grundtvig. This one driven genius had greater impact on his nation than the gentle storyteller and the top-hatted existentialist philosopher.

A fountain of enlightenment for nearly 90 years, Nikolai Frederik Severin Grundtvig fathered popular movements –

particularly the folk high schools. Like circles in water, knowledge spread out from these centres. Today, over 100 state-subsidised adult boarding schools, all outside the formal educational system, teach arts, music, history, sports and many other subjects. Foreign visitors can attend; there are no entrance requirements or exams.

Grundtvig (1783–1872) helped his people grow from an ignorant peasantry who took orders from the rich and educated to an involved population who spoke up. The bishop voiced his own liberal opinions in the *Rigsdag* after a democratic constitution was adopted in 1849. Grundtvig's psalms are unequalled in Christian hymnology.

THE WAR YEARS

A movement of workers from land to town marked the early 20th century
before the onset of two world wars and Denmark's struggle to remain neutral

As Denmark moved into the 20th century, its social, political and economic structures were fluid and changing fast. The overtones of the long and often acrimonious constitutional row that had led to the *system-skiftet* (change of system) still lingered, and the great march from land to town had only just

begun. The new industrial workers and small-holders swelled the ranks of the emerging Social Democratic Party and Radical Liberal Party, making them political forces to be reckoned with.

By 1915, reforms went further and the Social Democrats and Radical Liberals combined with the farm-based Liberal Democrats to push through a monumental amendment to the Conservative constitution of 1866. This reform transferred the balance of power to the Folketing, abolished the electoral privileges of the upper chamber (the Landsting), granted the vote to women and servants, and introduced proportional representation. As a consequence,

the old Right Party, its energy sapped by the constitutional row, was transformed into the modern Conservative People's Party.

A question of neutrality

This more polarised society was tested during World War I. Denmark, like Scandinavia as a whole, was determined to remain neutral, and had an extra incentive stemming from the country's crushing defeat at the hands of the German Confederation in 1864. At first, neutrality was under acute pressure from Germany, which forced Denmark to sow mines in the Great and Little Belts through which the British navy might enter the Baltic. King Christian apologised in advance to his kinsman, King George V of Britain. As Britain was in no position to resist near-certain German invasion of Denmark if the Danes refused, his predicament gained British sympathy. Strains on both neutrality and supply lines grew as the war drew on and German submarine warfare sank a third of Denmark's merchant fleet.

The country remained neutral, however, and was thus deprived of a seat at the Versailles conference which would have been the ideal forum for re-opening the question of Schleswig on the southern border with Germany (*see Denmark Alone, page 57*). As it was, the Schleswigers themselves had to petition the peace conference for the fulfilment of an 1866 promise of a plebescite

Political drama

In the immediate wake of the war, internal tension grew. Extremist sentiments began to spread, especially among the working class, and industrial antagonism, worsening in 1919–20, led to a domestic political crisis.

After a brief but menacing period, a new government held controversial referenda separately in the northern and southern zones of Schleswig. The north returned a three-quarters majority for reunion with Denmark, but Danish euphoria was cut short by the results in the south, which showed an even bigger majority the other way. The southern border was redrawn accordingly and Danes masked their disappointment by Christian X's ceremonial return to the Duchy on a white charger.

The great levelling

From 1924, the Social Democrats displaced the Liberal Democrats as the largest political party. Despite that, an absolute majority remained constantly out of reach so that the two parties held office in turn, supported respectively by the Radical Liberals and Conservatives.

Political fragmentation and the rise of Social Democracy had forever altered Danish politics reform policies chiefly promoted by the Social Democrats and Radical Liberals, but in time adopted by most other parties. Their methods were taxation and social legislation, especially practised during the long-running coalition of Social Democrats and Radical Liberals from 1929 to 1940.

The Social Democrat leader Thorvald Stauning dominated this period. Cigar-maker and prime minister, he came to be associated with the crucial transition from middle-class rule to social democracy. With more than 30 years of political activity, Stauning became one of the 20th century's leading Danish politicians,

and, in turn, reflected an incipient levelling-out in Danish society. The former "lower" and working classes were on the rise, and the old ruling classes were in decline. Social and geographical mobility played its part in producing a more homogeneous society based on the precepts of welfare and middle-class morals, and modern Denmark was born.

All this was due in large measure to social

PRECEDING PAGES: workers at a furniture workshop in the late 1800s. **LEFT:** three Scandinavian capitals contrasted: carefree Copenhagen, snobbish Stockholm and emancipated Oslo (then Christiana). **RIGHT:** soldiers protect strike breakers in Randers.

symbolising the era between the Great Depression and the start of World War II.

World economic depression in the 1930s hit hard in Denmark, which still depended on agricultural exports. Falling prices, followed by foreign curbs on Danish exports, had a disastrous effect on farmers and seriously hit the emerging manufacturing industries. Unemployment shot up to record levels and in 1933, the Social Democrats, Radical Liberals and Liberal Democrats were forced to turn to sweeping emergency measures to avert national bankruptcy. They devalued the currency and curtailed the debt burden, banned strikes and lockouts, guaranteed farm prices and controlled production. They also continued foreign exchange and trade controls which had been introduced the previous year.

Nazi threats

Concerns over economic and social well-being were soon dwarfed by anxiety over Hitler's rise to power just over the border in Germany. Nazi rearmament again threatened Denmark's neutrality – a double blow because money saved on army and armaments had been an important factor in laying the foundations of a modern welfare state. Under this German pressure and, spurred by the Danish government's reluctant

decision in 1933 to accept the German offer of a non-aggression pact, Denmark's politicians felt obliged to close ranks. Slowly, preparations were made to upgrade its defences.

It was too late. When Germany invaded Denmark and Norway on 9 April 1940, these belated preparations proved of little avail. Organised military resistance was futile and, after a brief struggle, the Danish government yielded under protest. It did, however, secure a German agreement to respect Danish rule. The government's goal was to maintain neutrality and self-government, but it had to give in to many German demands. Sealed from

THE DANISH RESISTANCE MOVEMENT

The Resistance movement in Denmark began in 1941 when Germany demanded that the leading members of the Danish Communist Party be interned. The party went underground and, together with the Conservative Party, published the newspaper *Frit Danmark* (Free Denmark). In 1942 it launched a campaign of sabotage.

In 1943 explosives were acquired from England, labour strikes organised and riots broke out. In the same month that Germany took control of Denmark, August 1943, the Danish Freedom Council was formed to lead the fight for liberation. The council included representatives from the main Resistance groups: Communists, Free Denmark,

Danish Unity Party and The Ring, which had lost many of its pioneers in German internment and concentration camps. By the end of 1944 the Resistance had 20,000 members. Sabotage groups carried out 1,500 attacks on the railways and 2,800 attacks on industry and shipping connected to the Germans. The Resistance's greatest successes were in Jutland and Funen, where German troop transports from Norway to the Normandy front were at times cut to a quarter of their schedules.

In Copenhagen you can visit the Frihedsmuseet (Museum of Danish Resistance) in Churchill Park (open Tues–Sun 11am–3pm; entrance fee; tel: 33 13 77 14).

the outside world, farmers and manufacturers had to adapt to the German market as their sole outlet if workers were to keep their jobs.

Force of resistance

The agreement was the price the Danes paid to avoid a Nazi government and to control local Nazism; but, as the war progressed, the Germans intensified their demands. The problem became one of how far the Danish government could yield without sacrificing the essential values and interests which it had remained in office to safeguard.

The issue of how much to sacrifice spawned an organised Resistance movement against the occupation forces. The movement gained early support from Britain but was strongly opposed by the Danish authorities, who felt their position and policy could be undermined. As the Germans began to experience their first serious reversals in the war, the situation deteriorated. Supplied by air-drops from the British, the Danish Resistance resorted to widespread propaganda and sabotage.

In response to Resistance action, Germany retaliated with ever harsher methods. In August 1943, the Danish authorities reached a point where they could no longer yield to German demands without destroying their position with the Danish population. German military occupation forces took over executive power and the Danish government and monarch effectively ceased to function from 29 August 1943.

From that time, the Resistance leaders in the underground government, the Freedom Council, emerged with growing authority to direct the struggle against the Germans. Sabotage attacks and reprisals escalated in a period of lawlessness. The Germans rounded up Resistance members, policemen, military leaders and many others. Thousands were sent to concentration camps, while the luckier ones escaped to Britain and Sweden.

Lucky escape

The night before 2 October 1943, the Germans decided to "solve the Jewish question", but they failed. In a miraculous few weeks during that autumn – just before the Germans began their

round up – the Resistance and thousands of other sympathisers smuggled 7,000 Jews on to small fishing boats and other craft and across the Sound to Sweden. The 7,000 made up almost the whole Jewish population of Denmark and the Germans arrested only 202 Jews. The horrible fate of many of those unfortunate 200 in the concentration camps is proof of what the rest would have faced but for their astonishing escape.

Peacetime rule

In the war's closing stages, the old political leaders were obliged to seek contact with the

Freedom Council. Military personnel, released from internment, were placed under the Council's direct command to bring an infusion of new and trained men. By the time British troops entered Denmark on 5 May 1945, Denmark was a recognised ally of the victorious Allied Powers.

The relationship between the Resistance movement and the politicians was another matter; but, despite residual friction, a coalition government of political parties and Resistance leaders made the transition to peacetime. It restored lawful authorities, and enacted comprehensive (if controversial) powers to punish collaborators. ❑

LEFT: German tanks roll into Denmark, 1940.
RIGHT: Danish troops guard the German battleship *Prinz Eugen* at the end of World War II.

A MODERN NATION

In the second half of the 20th century Denmark took its place on
the international stage and built on its reputation for quality and innovation

World War II marked a key turning point for Denmark. It steered free from its isolated neutrality and jumped into global politics and business, settling into a role that it continues to shape to this day.

In 1945, after five years of German occupation, Denmark joined the United Nations in the hope that the organisation would bring security and peace. The Cold War changed that idea immediately. The threat of the powerful Soviet Union, close to Danish borders, encouraged Denmark to join NATO, the Western defence alliance. For the first time in 150 years Denmark was assured of help in the event of attack.

In 1948, Denmark became part of the Organisation for European Economic Co-operation, an offshoot of the Marshall Plan, now the OECD. The country also joined the European Free Trade Association, which nudged the country's economy into an international arena and dismantled trade and currency restrictions. Denmark, Sweden and Norway also formed the Nordic Council in 1952, largely thanks to Denmark's Social Democrat prime minister, Hans Hedtoft. Since then, the council has co-operated in economic, social, environmental and cultural affairs, as well as communications.

In January 1973, Denmark joined the European Community. To this day, the Danish Parliament has backed continuous membership and integration into the European Union, but the public has been divided on the issue. A referendum on the single European market in 1986 barely passed, and the Maastricht Treaty on Europe's economic and political union was rejected in 1992 with 50.7 percent "no" votes. After a compromise between political parties, the treaty was put before the public again a year later and passed with 56.7 percent of the votes. The debate was passionate. After the second referendum, police opened fire on demonstra-tors in Copenhagen – for the first time in Denmark's post-war history – as protesters lit fires in the streets and threatened police.

Benefits for all

Politics since 1945 has centred around Denmark's welfare state, which gives all

citizens – not just the poor and the needy – benefits in all areas. The Social Democrats, who make the welfare state their main focus, have been the largest single political party since the war. Through the years, whether or not they were in power, they have influenced policy-making, helping to shape the basic tenets of Denmark's welfare society. Key leaders have included Hans Hedtoft in the early 1950s followed by the successful H.C. Hansen, J.O. Krag and, in the early 1970s, Anker Jørgensen.

Population growth and a zeal for improved living standards in the 1950s and 1960s helped vigorous expansion in every sphere. Welfare policies brought retirement pensions and free

LEFT: wind farms across Denmark generate more than 10 percent of the country's power.
RIGHT: high standards are adhered to in construction.

medical and social services, along with a host of developments and improvements in other social areas. At the same time, the Social Democrats initiated educational reforms, which led to the expansion of higher and adult education as well as increased public support for the arts.

Royal emancipation

The right wing Liberal Democrat and Conservative parties, vying for second place in party size, have also led the country through key developments. In 1953, the Liberal Erik Eriksen led a major constitutional reform,

abolishing the *Landsting* (upper chamber) to leave the *Folketing* as the sole legislative body.

At the same time, the revision introduced a much-applauded change in the rights of succession in what is the world's oldest monarchy, making it possible for a woman to succeed to the throne. In January 1972, Margrethe, the popular daughter of King Frederik IX, became Queen and has continued a down-to-earth monarchy in true Scandinavian style since then (*see page 82*).

The right wing parties have also taken control during years when the economy struggled. The comforts of the "cradle-to-grave" welfare

WHO'S WHO IN DANISH POLITICS

Since 1945, the Danish political situation has been complex. No one party has gained an absolute majority since the beginning of the 20th century. It has been known for up to 10 parties at once to sit in the *Folketing*, the one-chamber parliament, forming complicated coalition governments. In protest in 1994 the comedian Jacob Haugaard ran for the *Folketing* – and won.

The parties (with percentage of votes cast in the 1998 election and their areas of interest):

Social Democratic Party: old workers' party, in favour of maintaining the welfare state (36%).

Liberal Party: privatisation, agriculture (24%).

Conservative Party: traditional right-wing views (9%).

Socialist People's Party: further left than the Social Democrats (7%).

Danish People's Party: on the far right, nationalistic and anti-foreigners (7%).

Centre Party: slightly right-wing, pro-European Union (5%).

Social Liberal Party: exact centre, swing votes (4%).

Unity Party: the "Red-Green" party, anti-European Union, pro-environment (3%).

Christian People's Party: Christian foundation, slightly right-wing in its views (2%).

Others: (3%).

system – free medical care, education, child allowances, rent subsidies, pensions and almost full pay for those out of work – worked well in the boom years of the 1960s. But they proved too much in the harsher 1970s and 1980s, and by the 1990s were swallowing up half of Denmark's gross domestic product.

In addition, the country's necessary dependence on international trading has made its balance of payments vulnerable to world economic trends and, again and again, the

PUMPING OIL

Denmark discovered oil and natural gas in the North Sea in 1972, just before the global oil crisis pummelled the country's economy. By the 1990s Denmark was self-sufficient in energy.

led by Conservative Poul Schlüter, seized the power from Social Democrats. Over the next decade, inflation was brought under control and Danish foreign debt was reduced, partly because the country had become nearly self-sufficient with respect to energy as a result of North Sea oil and natural gas discoveries (*see left*).

In 1993, prime minister Schlüter resigned after a judicial inquiry ruled that he had lied about measures to prevent Tamil refugees entering the country from Sri Lanka. A new

government in power has been forced to cut back welfare programmes severely.

New times

In the 1970s, a number of social movements steered politics – from the women's movement to youth to "green" policy and nuclear energy protests. The international economic crisis hit Denmark in 1974 and the country struggled under a stagnant economy, unemployment and high inflation. By 1982, a right-wing coalition,

LEFT: agriculture and food processing make an important contribution to Denmark's export economy.
ABOVE: new technology in the printing industry.

coalition, led by the Social Democrats under prime minister Poul Nyrup Rasmussen, came to power. Nyrup, as he is called, has focused on maintaining and reforming the welfare state, and helping to move Denmark to a strategic advantage in an era of increased international competition and European integration.

Bringing home the bacon

Until the end of the 1950s, agriculture was the primary driver behind the Danish *kroner* and politics. While the focus has shifted, the farming sector continues to leave its mark today. Danish pork, poultry and dairy products have solid export markets in Britain, the United

States, Japan and the Middle East. Denmark has shipped bacon to Britain for well over a century – in the process building a strong shipping sector and skill in handling perishable foods. Food exports to the United Kingdom, more than any other single factor, motivated Denmark's decision to join the European Community in 1973. If Britain did not join, Denmark was not interested.

The foundation of Denmark's agricultural success was built partly on the co-operative movement, begun in the 1860s, which introduced quality standards and effective modern marketing methods, developed export markets

one of the world's leading fishing nations and a major exporter of fish and fish products. Models of wooden ships hang in every Danish church, as if to remind congregations to be thankful for the fruits of the sea.

Danish fishing vessels land nearly 2 million tonnes of fish a year, mostly cod, plaice, mackerel and herring caught in the North Sea, Baltic Sea and Kattegat regions. The vessels are generally smaller than those used in other countries, and they operate mainly in the near to medium-distance waters, returning to port frequently to land catches while they are fresh.

In a maritime echo of agriculture's co-oper-

and new products. Co-operatives dominate production and processing today, though farming's contribution to the economy fell after the 1960s. As industrialisation took over, farm structures changed. In 1960 there were 200,000 farms; four decades later there were only 60,000. Most are worked by the owner alone, and many farmers are forced to run the tractors and combines in the early mornings and late evenings – while having second jobs in the day.

Fruits of the sea

Like farming, fishing dominates Denmark's character, even though its importance has diminished in the last decades. Denmark is still

ative system, crew members are paid by results. Half the income from a voyage goes towards maintaining the ship itself, while the rest is distributed on a fixed scale. The skipper may get the biggest share, but even the cabin boy can find himself rich after a successful voyage.

Quotas, periodic algae and industrial pollution, particularly in the Kattegat and Baltic, have seriously affected total catches in recent years and made fishing less profitable for many trawler operators and crews.

At the end of the 1950s, industry overtook agriculture as the main contributor to the Danish economy in terms of exports, employment, and share of gross national product. It has continued to grow steadily since. Then, as now, industry has meant manufacturing. Denmark lacks the raw materials that have helped to build major industrial companies in neighbouring Sweden. Most raw materials must come from abroad, while companies must export to be able to turn a good profit.

Danish industry began mainly as a supplier to agriculture, making tilling equipment, parts for pig sheds and dairies and food processing factories. Agriculture also provided the basis for other

OVERSEAS AID

Denmark generously donates 1 percent of its gross national income to international aid. Much support goes to the Baltic states, Eastern Europe and Africa.

seemed to stimulate the inventiveness of many more young Danes. Lego, the toy company, was founded in 1932, while Bang & Olufsen, internationally famous for home electronics of exquisite design, started in 1925, and paint and lacquer manufacturers Dyrup began in 1928.

In the depths of the 1930s Depression, a farmer's son, Mads Clausen, built refrigerator controls from parts that he had made at the family farm. Clausen's resulting company, Danfoss, is today one of Denmark's biggest

forms of production. Animal glands were used for insulin production by Nordisk Gentofte and Novo – since merged to form Novo-Nordisk, the world's largest insulin producer. Today, Novo-Nordisk uses biotechnology to make a product that is identical to human insulin.

Industrial roots

Many of today's most successful Danish companies had their start in the years between the two world wars. The Depression years

---

LEFT: a waterside car boot sale, Denmark style.
ABOVE: fishing is not as important to the economy as it once was, but it remains a major source of income.

industrial employers. It is the world leader in the production of heating and refrigeration controls, with production plant in seven countries.

Finding niches

The lack of raw materials, heavy taxation and high wage levels make production in Denmark relatively expensive, and high volume production is not competitive. Danish industries have thus been forced to rely upon quality, spiced with a flexible approach and a willingness to take smaller orders not considered worthwhile by bigger producers. To survive, the Danish manufacturer has to be a skilful niche player and spot gaps that are of no particular interest to competitors in other countries. A prime example of this is electronics. If you want a gadget to measure noise level, or blood gas, or something to monitor the condition of a patient in intensive care, you'll find it in Denmark, where companies like Radiometer, Coloplast, and Brüel Kjær have found their niche.

Equipment for people with a hearing disability is another speciality that Danish companies Widex, Oticon and Danavox have exploited so successfully that they hold more than 30 percent of the world market for hearing aids. All of these companies have found success by their focus on the quality of their products,

and they have become another chapter in Denmark's post-war success in industrial design – using the principle of form and function to shape their products (*see Insight On Danish Design, pages 102–103*).

Denmark also leads the world in production of wind turbines, which began in the early 1980s and then grew exponentially in the late 1990s as the world became aware of the benefits of renewable energy. Vestas Wind Systems, the world's largest wind turbine manufacturer, along with NEG Micon, Bonus, Nordex and others are a few Danish companies which have helped to change wind from a grassroots industry to a serious player on the

global power market. The sales value of the Danish wind industry is more than 7 billion *kroner* a year, double the size of the Danish fishing sector.

The way ahead

As Denmark moves into the next century, it faces a number of challenges if it is to continue as one of the world's most affluent, comfortable and peaceful countries. The 5.2 million Danes enjoy a standard of living almost unparalleled in the rest of the world, with excellent systems for social welfare, health and education. But the welfare system is in crisis for future generations as the national debt continues to grow, and living standards have begun to decline. Welfare, health and education buckle under the strain of government austerity and local cutbacks.

The nationalist Danish People's Party has taken advantage of the situation and gained seats in the *Folketing*, rallying against immigrants and refugees who, the party claims, are only a burden to the Danish economy. The popularity of the party's message has brought a dark cloud over Denmark's previous history of strong international aid.

Meanwhile, the Danes have found their traditional, slower paced way of life speeded up in recent years. Transmission towers have cropped up like weeds across the landscape to help to control the huge use of mobile cell phones. The Internet, e-mail and the World Wide Web have taken the country by storm.

A system of bridges has replaced ferries, making transport fast and efficient (*see opposite*). The Øresund Fixed Link over the sound between Copenhagen and Malmö, Sweden, is affecting business, society and culture to a degree that business leaders, politicians and experts have only begun to grasp; the new urban region has become the eighth largest in Europe, attracting several international companies to the area.

The Denmark of today has, in general, discovered more and more its true talents. Small, maybe. But the country's knack in scurrying between the cracks of potential in global business and politics has given it strength and a promising future. ❏

LEFT: Denmark is renowned worldwide for the skill and vision of its designers.

Millennium Transport

Getting about in Denmark with its more than 400 islands used to be slow going. All road and rail links between Jutland in the west and Copenhagen in the east relied on ferries. This is a civilised way to travel, but it took almost five hours to get from Århus to the capital. You could fly the distance in 25 minutes.

Ferries still ply the Danish straits but the country is now bridged from east to west. Copenhagen to Århus now takes just three hours, and Odense is an easy day trip. Denmark finally joined hands in 1998 with the opening of the Store Bælt Link, spanning the 20 km (12 miles) of water between Funen and Zealand with a four-lane motorway and two tracks of rails. The Lille Bælt Bridge between Jutland with Funen had existed for years. The Great Belt project involved the construction of Europe's biggest suspension bridge and an equally impressive railway tunnel. More than 6½ million cars passed the toll booths in the first year alone.

Nevertheless, July 2000 marks the opening of the most symbolic link: the new bridge-tunnel connecting Europe with Scandinavia; Copenhagen, Denmark, with Malmö, Sweden. The two countries have been separated for the last 8,500 years by the Øresund strait, 20 km (12 miles) wide.

This enterprising project is an integral part of the new Øresund region, encompassing eight cities and more than 3 million people, and it's rapidly growing into northern Europe's biggest commercial, technical and population centre. It's already one of the world's major transport hubs.

Land at Kastrup International Airport, and you're greeted by award-winning design and function. From here, new road and rail links whisk you to central Copenhagen in less than 15 minutes and to southern Sweden in less than 30 minutes.

The Øresund region's cities are well-preserved in history and architecture, and have resisted the temptations of urban sprawl. A rich mixture of culture and entertainment complement a clean, varied natural environment. Depending on the season, you can enjoy a beach, play golf, sail, surf, fish, cycle, skate or ski, all within a 100-km (60-mile) radius of Copenhagen.

Meanwhile, major transportation projects continue in greater Copenhagen. An automated, light-rail network called Metro is scheduled to begin service in 2002. This has required the construction of underground stations at several key points in the city as giant machines bored through the limestone deep beneath the streets.

When completed, the Metro will link with the existing "S-Tog" (S-Train) network and various parts of Copenhagen in a new way, round the clock, and during rush hour, every 90 seconds.

One stop on the Metro line is Ørestad, a "new town" project located between central Copenhagen and the airport. Ørestad is being constructed around the concept of a high-quality environment for business, living, culture and shopping. The

master plan calls for six neighbourhoods linked by parks, canals, boulevards and the Metro. These will evolve over a number of years but several new "tenants" have already staked their claims. Among them are Copenhagen University and the Danish National Broadcasting Company (DR).

All regions of Denmark are now easily accessible by car or train, or by bicycle. It takes less than three hours to drive from Esbjerg, where North Sea ferries arrive from Germany, the Netherlands and UK, to Copenhagen. From the German border in south Jutland to Skagen, the trip is four hours.

Many of Denmark's smaller islands are still accessible only by sea, allowing you to take the ferry, and enjoy a time-honoured mode of travel. ❑

RIGHT: Ørestad – the new "model" town that is a symbol of Denmark's developing infrastructure.

THE DANES TODAY

They're warm, fun-loving and friendly. But they can also be cool and reserved. It all depends where you meet them

Danes have two reputations in the world, one at home and another abroad. Outside Denmark, Danes are known as warm, curious, friendly, funny, charming. Whether met on a mountain track in New Zealand, a small town in Midwest US or a savanna in East Africa, Danish travellers – in their modest way – bring on laughs and a sense of pure enjoyment for life. They try not to act too offended when, outside Europe, one too many people ask: "Is Denmark the capital of Sweden?" or "What language do you speak – Dutch?" The Dane gives a short, firm geography lesson on the spot, reminding with a smile that Denmark is, in fact, the oldest monarchy in the world, from AD 935.

At home, Danes have a different reputation to foreign visitors as distant, sombre, even cold. They keep to themselves. Danes are quite aware of this image, and blame it on the wet, cool climate. "Not much of our social life happens on the pavements or out in front of the home," says Frans Kjær Nielsen, a Danish language teacher in Århus. "We spend much of our time indoors with our families and friends."

Inside this thin barrier of social contact, Denmark is one of the warmest countries in the world. People are genuine. They speak their minds. They thrive on making life cosy, relaxing and enjoyable – from the most festive occasion to the most mundane coffee break at the office. To experience this, one has to go where the Danes are.

On the dockside

In the early mornings on the docks of Skudehavnen, a harbour on the northern edge of Copenhagen, crews of fishermen empty their morning's haul of herring from nets into crates. Most harbours like this around Denmark have a fish market of some sort. Here, things are

PRECEDING PAGES: Danish football supporters in high spirits; girls in national costume, Greenland.
LEFT: "Roligans" ready to cheer on their team.
RIGHT: enjoying a quiet, Sunday stroll.

more "tax free". At the *Sorina København* boat one autumn morning, fisherman Erik Sørensen says it's time for a break and hands out bottles of beer. That seems to attract others, who compliment the *Sørensen's* crew on a good catch. They get beers, too.

"We Danes, we love beer," Sørensen says,

his orange rubber overalls covered with scales. A man rides a squeaky bicycle onto the dock, pulling a little trailer. One of the fishermen fills it with herring, and a blue bank note is quickly exchanged. "We sell only to my uncle," Sørensen says with a little smile.

A few minutes later, two more men buy a load of fish, followed by a woman who fills an empty baby buggy. Sørensen looks uncomfortable. "They are my uncles, too."

Culture of food

In this sea-faring land, where model ships hang below the ceiling murals in every village church, fish – particularly herring, mackerel, eel and cod – belongs to one of the basic food groups in Denmark, joined by an elaborate variety of dairy products, rye bread, cakes and pastries and coffee and wine.

In Denmark, when people meet, they eat. When they go for a drive or a walk, they make sure they've got a supply of food, coffee and cake. At work, they break at mid-morning for buns and coffee and in the afternoons someone might bring back slices of layer cake from a nearby bakery.

Danish rye bread is the foundation of society. Extremely dense and usually packed with undigestible seeds and grains, it could be used to build walls if one ran out of bricks. Sliced and spread with goose lard or butter, Danish rye is topped with arty combinations of foods for *smørrebrød*, Danish open sandwiches.

"It's a very Danish tradition," explains Camilla Jørgensen, a tall worker wearing white clogs who fills bags with orders in a local *smørrebrød* deli in Copenhagen. The smell of pickled herring permeates the air. "Children eat like this when they go to school. The parents put together a food box for the kids, then they split it. People normally have one egg, one meat and one fish. You eat it everywhere."

At a festive lunch, *smørrebrød* is at its zenith.

TAXING FOR EQUALITY

Denmark is a society of non-extremes where, as Danes themselves say, "few have too much and fewer have too little". The welfare system gives everyone the same opportunities: free health service, education, support for the elderly and handicapped, unemployment benefits, pensions, and more. The system carries a price: goods and services are taxed at 25 percent, and 50-70 percent of income is taxed. This equality carries through to social norms. Everyone is on first-name terms, the formal address, *De*, being reserved mainly for the Queen. Dress is casual, and a tie in the workplace is rare, except for insurance salesmen, bankers and undertakers.

"You must have two or three kinds of herring," explains Hanne Christensen of Svendborg, Funen. While her husband, Carl, adds that fiery shots of cold aquavit must "go down like hail stones".

"And then you need a little warm dish, like fried fish with lemon and remoulade," Hanne says. "Some sliced meats," adds Carl. "Small tenderloin steaks. Danish meatballs with red cabbage." "And then cheese and fruit salad at the end," says Hanne.

That cosy feeling

Such a lunch is what Danish *hygge* is all about. *Hygge* (pronounced "HEU-guh") stands for any and every sense of cosiness, and it is found everywhere in Denmark. A good meal has *hygge*, a casually stylish room or house can have *hygge*, a story, a walk in the woods, a meeting at a café, even a person can have *hygge*.

Cakes, coffee and candlelight are usually key ingredients. Parties for weddings, birthdays, anniversaries and the like have *hygge* at their core. Long tables are decorated with flowers and candles and creatively folded napkins. A three-course meal is usually interspersed with songs

GIVE A LIGHT

To encourage that very Danish sense of well-being known as *hygge*, candles and candle holders, rather than toasters and appliances, are the most popular items for wedding gifts.

food", and guests gradually take the hint. *Hygge* was born, no doubt, indoors during the grey winter months. From November to February, Danes go to work in darkness and return home again in darkness. But warm candle-light fills flats, homes and offices in natural defence. During *Jul* (Christmas), live candles decorate Christmas trees indoors, around which families join hands and sing carols. Small, local ferries light up the black water with strings of white Christmas lights. On New

and speeches, which end in a collective "Hurrah!" Wine flows freely.

As the Danish poet and troubadour Benny Andersen writes in a song well known among Danes, "One must keep the mood wet. I'm drunk and I'm feeling great."

Six hours into such a celebration and filled with spirits, a party-goer has a chance to get up from the table – usually to fetch some coffee and cookies and sit down again. Later yet, the hosts serve the final course, called "get out

LEFT: camping out and eating – two very popular pastimes for most Danes.
ABOVE: farmhouse holidays involve young and old.

Year's Eve, the Queen gives her annual talk to the nation on television, and fireworks spark and pop, lighting up the cold sky at midnight.

Spring in the air

By February, winter seems to drag on forever. In his essay, *Oh! To be Danish*, the author Klaus Rifbjerg writes of this time: "Sure, it can be grim, and now and then we might want to turn our collar up and jump in the river. But then the light suddenly changes and there's a melody in the air, a whiff of spring to come, the smell of the sea and a blackbird singing on a rooftop." Fields of fluorescent yellow winter rape blossom in May, and the days turn long. In

The Queen

People quip that if Denmark's few republicans were ever to end the monarchy their first choice for president would be Margrethe Alexandrine Thorhildur Ingrid. Even in circles where it is fashionable to put down royalty, the Queen's abilities and skills are recognised. Plainly, the Danes love their queen.

Born on 16 April 1940, a week after the Nazis occupied Denmark, Margrethe was hailed as a welcome ray of light breaking through the darkness of occupation. No one then imagined she would

ever rule the country: the Danish constitution specified male inheritance of the throne, and not until 1953 was it amended so that a woman could ascend – if there were no male heirs. The constitutional change was ratified by referendum, so that Margrethe became the first Danish Queen to be elected by the population. She has two younger sisters, Benedikte and Anne-Marie.

Renowned for her outrageous hats, Margrethe in fact wears many hats, including monarch, mother and grandmother, and artist. She keeps herself politically informed, meets her government weekly and has a full round of social and diplomatic functions. But Margrethe doesn't hide the fact that she has a life outside the job. First comes

her family: her husband Prince Henrik (French-born as Count de Laborde de Monpezat), and their two sons, Crown Prince Frederik (born 1968) and Prince Joachim (1969).

In August 1999 Margrethe assumed a new role, as grandmother, when a son was born to Prince Joachim and Princess Alexandra. The attractive and charming businessman's daughter from Hong Kong entered the royal family with a splash in 1996 and soon became wildly popular, not just with her mother-in-law, as she quickly picked up the rudiments of the Danish language (a must for anyone who wants to win over the Danes).

Margrethe was 13 when she became heir-apparent, and from that moment her education was meticulously planned. After graduation from the Danish gymnasium (upper secondary school) she studied national and international law at Danish and foreign universities. She also found time to attend lectures in archaeology, a favourite subject, and take part in digs. Even military service was included. She served in the Women's Flying Corps, and the WAAF in Britain. Certainly, Margrethe could claim to be Europe's best-educated monarch.

Some say Margrethe inherited her artistic talent from her mother's family, the Swedish Bernadottes. An accomplished painter with several exhibitions, Margrethe commands the highest prices of any Danish contemporary artist. All profits go to charity. In 1999, a painting of hers became a Red Cross poster to benefit the refugees of the war in Kosovo.

Margrethe has twice translated books into Danish. The first in partnership with Prince Henrik when, under a pseudonym, they published the Danish translation of Simone de Beauvoir's novel *Tous Les Hommes sont Mortelles*. In 1988, she translated a Swedish novel, Stig Stramholm's *Dalen*. She was fascinated by J.R.R. Tolkien's *Lord of the Rings* and illustrated it, again using a pseudonym. Her most ambitious work was in 1987, when she designed the costumes and scenery for a TV production of Hans Christian Andersen's *The Shepherdess and the Chimney Sweep*.

The family lives at Amalienborg in Copenhagen, where the Queen Mother, Queen Ingrid, also resides, and at Fredensborg in Northern Zealand.

Thankfully, the Danish media still show a modicum of propriety when covering the royal family. Anything else, to be sure, would not be the Danish thing to do. ❏

LEFT: Margrethe II, Queen of Denmark, being greeted with flowers at an event in Århus.

spring and summer, city Danes bike out to their garden houses on the edge of town and country Danes collect dead branches and greenery into huge piles on the beaches and in the countryside.

On the evening of 23 June, Midsummer's Eve, those piles of wood are topped with an effigy of a witch and set on fire to drive bad spirits from the land as Danes gather around the bonfires and sing. In July, nearly the whole country goes on vacation for three weeks. Barbecues are lit, bathing-suits donned, clothes abandoned.

Harvest time

By late summer, farmers' tractors haul grain and hay, holding up traffic. Towns hold harvest parties, children start school and families hunt for mushrooms and berries in the beech and oak forests. People start to complain about the diminishing light and increasing rain, and soon the frost hits and temperatures can drop so low the sea freezes solid. So, the Danes light a candle, make some *hygge* with homemade hot cocoa and buns, and look forward to *Jul* again.

The story is the same all over Denmark – from all the regions of "mainland" Jutland to the islands of Funen and Zealand, to Bornholm in the Baltic Sea, and on any of the other 80 or so inhabitable islands. Each region has its own special traditions, songs, foods and even its own dialects, and these must be experienced in person.

Spirit of co-operation

A sense of togetherness and looking out for each other can be felt not only in family *hygge*, but in society as well, starting with the generous welfare system. Workers unions are strong, and the co-operative spirit prevails. Only four out of 100 Danes do not belong to an association, and 76 belong to at least two.

"We have a joke that if two Danes sit together for five minutes, they will start an association," says Frans Kjær Nielsen in Århus. The tradition started after 1864, when Denmark lost a chunk of southern Jutland to Germany in a war. Farm and factory workers formed gym-

---

RIGHT: Danes enjoy the fresh air, even in the city, where open air concerts are popular.

> ## THE EYES HAVE IT
>
> During a *skål* (pronounced "skoal"), or toast, lift your glass and, in as casual a way as possible, make eye contact with everyone present before drinking.

nastic sports associations in order to build a stronger defence in future wars. Meanwhile, farmers started the world's first dairy co-operatives, finding that as a team, they could gain a more prominent position in agricultural production.

The sense of togetherness has not always come through in tough times, however. In 1998, a general strike that included truck drivers sent the country into a panic. Many Danes emptied market shelves, fearing they would die of starvation or disease before

the strike was over. Items like toilet paper and milk were gone within hours. Black markets for fresh yeast – the most sought-after item – sprouted up in railway stations and parks, its price 20 to 30 times its real value. After a couple of weeks, radio talk shows had topics like, "What to do with old yeast and milk."

When the strike ended after five weeks, the Danes laughed at themselves for the way they acted. This was Denmark, a country that had been proud of helping society and keeping level headed in the worst situations. But on this occasion Denmark had, simply, lost its cool.

In the 1960s and 1970s, Denmark experienced the first recent wave of immigrants –

Turkish "guest workers". It was not until the early 1980s, however, that the effects of immigration on the Danish culture were felt.

Tolerating newcomers

The revolution in Iran brought a stream of refugees, and other global conflicts brought refugees from the Far East, Middle East, the Balkans, Somalia, and elsewhere. At first, the Danes welcomed the newcomers, who brought with them new religious beliefs, traditions and cuisines.

"Denmark today is so different from

MANY VOICES

More than 100 dialects are spoken in Denmark. Some vary greatly. People in South Jutland are hardly understood by the residents of Copenhagen.

Denmark just 20 years ago," says Karen Fyhn, who lives in East Jutland. Her husband, Henrik, comments, "When I was a child, it was really something special to see a foreigner, to come home and say, 'I saw a black person today.'"

In the next decades, however, the Danish social democracy, traditions, norms and welfare system were thrown into question by newcomers and Danes alike. Denmark found itself unprepared in how to deal with cultural misunderstandings, how to teach Danish effectively to thousands of immigrants every year, and how to help integrate them into the job market and society.

Immigrant education

When Frans Kjær Nielsen began to teach Danish in Århus in 1985, the only option for foreigners was a local night school, which also offered hobby classes like painting and gardening. Only a couple of Danish text books were available.

Fortunately, Nielsen says, things got better. The country passed immigrant education laws and established special schools, as well as improving teacher-training. Today, teaching materials fill entire school libraries. Immigrants also take courses in Danish society and culture shortly after they first arrive.

The effort has been slow to show results; unemployment is high among immigrants, who have tended to congregate into their own neighbourhoods, making it more and more difficult to interact with Danes. By the late 1990s, small ultra-nationalistic political parties and a tabloid press attempted to turn public opinion against foreigners.

While politicians and public officials have tried to work things out on paper, the greater part of Danish society seems to be tolerant and in favour of change – it takes personal effort from both sides, many have pointed out.

One letter in a national newspaper, addressed to the immigrants of the nation, said: "If you see a Dane on the street, smile. Many of us will smile back." ❏

SOUL FOOD

To the Danes, a life without education is like a sailing boat without wind. All children must attend school until 9th grade, after which about half go on to high schools and half into vocational training. Many young people, especially after they've turned 18, head off around the world – something that colleges of higher education and work places prioritise among applicants. Employers send their staff on additional courses for skill development. Danish folk high schools, the invention of N.F.S. Grundtvig (*see page 59*), are popular among all ages, but especially teenagers. Here there are no exams, just art, song, dance, languages, sport – anything that is good for the soul.

LEFT: Denmark has its fair share of immigrants, the number of which increased in the late 20th century. **RIGHT:** people gather around the bonfire to celebrate Midsummer at Valdemar castle.

GREEN POWER

*Enlightened environmental policies, organic food, wind farms and bicycles
are all part of Denmark's quest for a sustainable future*

On Kultorvet square in Copenhagen one autumn morning, a huge side of beef hangs by the door of a butcher shop, dripping blood near a customer's baby buggy. No worry – it's organic blood. "What I sell here is medicine – and chemical-free," says the owner Jens Slagter, whose family has been in the

business so long his last name means "butcher" in Danish. His shop went organic in 1989 when he found that Danes wanted organic foods. Today he can hardly keep up with demand.

"Green" thinking pervades Denmark – starting with agriculture, energy, transportation, waste, construction and even taxes. At the consumer level, organic foods are so popular that their prices have fallen to nearly equal non-organic foods. Farmers can go to schools to learn organic methods, and green farm co-operatives have created popular networks where customers subscribe to a big bag of fruits and veggies every week. A federal "green fund" is doled out to projects that help Denmark work to a goal of sustainable development. One of these projects is a nationwide system of Green Guides, who offer advice and tips to consumers on how to choose environmentally friendly products and how to save energy in the home.

Visitors to Denmark will notice within minutes of their arrival two signs of the country's greenness: windmills and bicycles. Windmills dot the landscape – including the area around Copenhagen's airport – churning out clean energy. Bicycles, meanwhile, outnumber cars in some city areas, and the streets are built for them with special lanes and even traffic lights.

Renewable sources

Denmark likes to prove to itself and the world that it is one of the most progressive countries in the ecology sector. In one bold goal, for instance, 35 percent of the nation's energy is to be generated from renewable sources by 2030. At the rate things are going, the country will probably surpass the goal sooner than planned. The government has even chosen the island of Samsø, between Jutland and Zealand, to produce all of its energy by renewable sources in years to come.

Most Danes believe the environment to be the single most important political issue, and since the oil crisis of the 1970s, saving energy has been a top priority in Danish politics. Successive governments have kept fuel prices artificially high and have funded the research and implementation of alternative forms of energy. The energy crisis created an interesting situation in Denmark. On the one hand, the government tried to balance a tottering budget with high energy taxes. On the other hand a large group of people responded with enthusiasm and persistent interest in energy matters, and blamed the government for taking too little action. What evolved was a new perspective, not so much out of worry about the economy as out of concern for the environment.

Through a mix of laws, taxes and voluntary commitment, a whole new set of initiatives to reduce pollution and "energy gluttony" arose.

Can ban

Some of the ideas have gained both recognition and controversy worldwide. The best known is probably the re-use of glass and plastic drinks bottles, along with a "can ban" on drinks. A costly deposit persuades people to return empty bottles to shops; a beer bottle, for example, is re-used 30 to 35 times before it is remelted. The system, which Denmark hails as the most successful in the world because of the waste it avoids and the raw materials it saves, has in fact brought Denmark before the European Court of Justice over its trade restrictions on canned drinks.

products to be sold until they are first proven safe for nature.

Environmental impact is always assessed before anything is built and before any new laws are passed. Today, the huge amount of waste from the country's building sector is nearly all recycled. Housing is built not only to be energy efficient, but a movement towards organic, natural building materials is gaining force in Denmark. Near Århus in Jutland, a collective has created its own "sustainable" town. Houses are built with organic materials, plots of organic farmland are worked, rainwater is collected and waste turned to compost. ❑

In the international sphere, Denmark makes its mark in climate protection policies, chemicals and taxes for vehicles, emissions and energy consumption. The government has cracked down on pesticides since 1994 and removed hundreds of products from shelves that have been found too harmful for the environment, and passed laws to restrict farmers' spraying. Denmark is also one of the few countries of Europe that will not allow new

PRECEDING PAGES: a path through the forest, just one part of the environment that Denmark cherishes.
LEFT: the Danes recycle many different materials.
RIGHT: electric cars have had mixed success.

WIND POWER

Denmark isn't the windiest place on earth, but it makes good use of the gusts it gets. In the early 1980s Danish-produced windmills began to sprout up across the country and around the world. By the early 1990s parts of the Denmark were generating much of their energy from wind. The government's goal for wind to produce 10 percent of the country's power consumption by 2005 was surpassed in 1999 and now, as a result of two successful offshore test wind farms, plans are in place to take to the seas for future development. Today, wind turbines built in Denmark produce up to 2 megawatts of power at a cost that competes with coal power.

THE CULTURAL SCENE

Denmark is a small country that thinks big culturally: many of its artists, writers, film-makers and musicians have achieved international acclaim

For a small country, Denmark has a lot to show for itself. Denmark and the Danes pop up all over the world, once you start looking. The Danes have always been an outgoing people. Many great artists and writers have found that the development of their talent, and often also public recognition, have been possible only on the world stage. (Correspondingly, the Danes generally are most impressed with those of their fellow countrymen who make it big abroad.)

For that reason, the great neo-classical sculptor Thorvaldsen went to Rome to study and stayed for 40 years. The most famous painter of the post-war era, Asger Jorn, spent the pre-war years in Paris. Denmark's two most famous names in literature, Hans Christian Andersen and Karen Blixen, both made their names overseas, and Blixen even wrote in English (as Isak Dinesen).

The Danish silent movie actress, Asta Nielsen, worked in Germany. Victor Borge has lived the American dream, twinkling his piano keys and humour, and Jacob Riis, emigrating to New York in the late 19th century, became a famous reformer photographing the ghetto poor to show how the other half lives. Lars von Trier's *Breaking the Waves* (1996), which film critics voted the best Danish movie ever, is entirely in English, without even a single Danish actor.

Then there were those who stayed home. Søren Kierkegaard (1813–55), the father of existentialism prowling the cobbled streets in the inner city on his daily walks, Kierkegaard's top-hatted crow-like figure was the popular butt of caricature. Today he is studied at universities the world over, and people learn Danish to read the original version of existentialism.

Historically, the narrow confines of Danish society, with its predominantly agricultural base

---

PRECEDING PAGES: modern Danish fabric design. **LEFT:** ballerina from the Royal Danish Ballerina in a painting by Hans Voigt Steffensen. **RIGHT:** Hans Christian Andersen immortalised in Copenhagen.

and petit bourgeois mentality, presented too many limitations and too few opportunities. Yet they were products of a society which allowed a baker's son (Christian Købke) to become an artist and a poor cobbler's son (Hans Christian Andersen) to become one of the world's greatest storytellers (*see page 227*).

Support for the arts

A sizeable chunk of the Danish national budget is allocated to the support of the arts. Funds are channelled into public productions, making art, both with a small and a capital A, generally available and accessible throughout the country. The current policies are based on the underlying egalitarian philosophy of N.F.S. Grundtvig (*see page 59*), which has pervaded Danish society since the end of the 19th century. A theologian and philosopher, Grundtvig (1783–1872) pointed to the spoken, live word as the road to a humane and Christian community in the name of enlightenment (the equivalent of the Danish word *oplysning*, which also means information). Grundtvig penned most of the nationalistic anthems and religious hymns Danish school children still sing today.

Even more, official policy encourages a positive interaction between arts institutions and grassroots culture. Official funds are given not only to theatres, film, individual artists and fine-art museums but also to libraries, folk high schools, open universities and evening classes, music and film clubs and schools, youth clubs and even sports clubs.

Of course, this system has a built-in elitism, as there will always be those who are "government approved" and those who are not.

PETER HØEG

Denmark's most famous contemporary author, Peter Høeg (born 1957) achieved international success in 1991 with *Miss Smilla's Feeling for Snow*, which made it to the top of the best-seller lists in London and New York. In the hands of the Danish director Bille August, the novel was turned into a Hollywood film. The murder mystery and voyage of self-discovery examines the touchy relationship between Denmark and the Inuit people of its former colony, Greenland. Høeg's characters, Smilla included, are often misfits, inhabiting the grey zone on the fringes of normality. Other titles include *A History of Danish Dreams* (1988) and *The Borderliners* (1994).

Literary heritage

Denmark's strongest art tradition is literary. Though it may have been a while since it last happened, Danish authors have still won more Nobel Prizes per capita than any other country. Henrik Pontoppidan (1857–1943) and Karl Gjellerup (1857–1919) shared one in 1917, and Johannes V. Jensen (1873–1950) repeated the feat for literature in 1944.

The tradition reaches back to the sagas and medieval folk songs, to Ludvig Holberg in the Age of Enlightenment, the Romantic poet Adam Oehlenschläger (1779–1850), to Hans Christian Andersen and Søren Kierkegaard in the 19th century. Georg Brandes (1842–1927), the most influential personality in Danish letters from 1871 to World War I, wrote Denmark into the modern century. In the 1920s and 1930s there was a strong realistic movement in Danish literature, with writers such as Martin A. Hansen, Hans Kirk and H.C. Branner leading the way.

Today, more than 20 percent of public funds for culture go to the public libraries. Sixty-five percent of adults and nearly 80 percent of young people use the libraries. Authors receive remuneration not for their lending rates but according to the number of volumes on the shelves. In most cases, the "library money" is what keeps them afloat.

No doubt a fair share goes to Klaus Rifbjerg (born 1931) who has more than 100 titles to his name, starting with his then scandalous novel *Chronic Innocence* in 1958. Having survived the radical movement of the 1960s and early 1970s, Rifbjerg is now literary editor of Denmark's largest publishing house, Gyldendal. He still turns out a novel or two a year.

A highly prolific and beloved author from the 1970s until his death in 1993 was Dan Turèll, beat poet and "Karma Cowboy", known for his musical recitals and rapid-fire delivery. A Copenhagen landmark – a café is named after him – "Uncle Danny" also found time to write more than 40 mystery novels.

On the stage

More than one-third of the state funds allocated to the theatre go towards financing the National Theatre, Det Kongelige Teater. This includes

LEFT: Peter Høeg, now a household name.
RIGHT: Meryl Streep and Robert Redford in a scene from *Out of Africa*, a film based on Karen Blixen's life.

Gamle Scene, which stages opera, ballet and large-scale productions, and Nye Scene. A state institution, it is also home to the Royal Opera, the Royal Ballet and the Royal Danish Orchestra. A quarter of the public funds go to 20 smaller Copenhagen theatres – such as Dr Dante and Fiolteatret, where much good innovative work is shown – as well as stages in the three largest provincial towns, Århus, Odense and Ålborg.

The most popular Danish playwright remains Ludvig Holberg (1684–1754). A child of the Enlightenment, Holberg wrote in the comedic tradition of Molière. Holberg is always playing somewhere in Denmark. Grønnegårdens Teater, which performs outdoors in the tree-lined courtyard of Kunstindustrimuseet, stages a Holberg play at least every other summer, often using over-the-top costumes and milking the plays for laughs.

Sophisticated dramas

A bright young playwright today is Nikoline Werdelin, who has taken her witty, risqué style from the pages of her popular comic strips to the stage. Her sophisticated dramas, such as *The Blind Painter*, play to packed houses.

Moreover, some 100 touring children's theatre companies, as well as a handful of per-

KAREN BLIXEN: THE AFRICA CONNECTION

Take a look at your 50-*krone* note. The lady in the hat is Karen Blixen, Denmark's female national poet and novelist, otherwise known by her pen name, Isak Dinesen. Her life was as exotic and eventful as her tales. Born on 17 April 1885 she was raised at Rungstedlund, a large estate overlooking the Sound between Denmark and Sweden. Her beloved father committed suicide when she was 10. Her marriage of convenience to a Swedish relative, Baron Bror von Blixen-Finecke was in many respects a rejection of her strict upbringing. So was her subsequent escape to Africa. She wanted his title, and he wanted her money to start a farm in Kenya. He not only lost her fortune but also gave her syphilis, and the marriage was dissolved in 1925. Her love affair with Denys Finch-Hatton, an English aristocrat, is the backdrop for *Out of Africa* (1937), later a successful film starring Meryl Streep as Blixen. In 1931 her world in Kenya collapsed with the failure of the coffee farm and the death of Finch-Hatton. After returning to Denmark, she wrote *Seven Gothic Tales* (1934), which brought her international acclaim. This was followed by *Winter's Tales* (1942), *The Angelic Avengers* (1946), *Last Tales* (1957) and *Anecdotes of Destiny* (1958). She died in 1962 at Rungstedlund where she is buried. The Karen Blixen Museum opened here in 1991.

manent theatres, such as Det Lille Teater (The Little Theatre) in Copenhagen, cater for the youngest audiences. Only a select few receive state support. Others make do on their own, like the popular Batida musical theatre company, which since the mid-1980s has delighted children all over Denmark and throughout much of the world.

Denmark's excellent children's culture overall is another reason why the smallest Scandinavian land is considered such a good place to raise children.

TOPICAL STORYLINES

Urban crime dramas, like *Pusher* (1996) and *Bleeder* (1999), by filmmaker Nicolas Winding Refn, feed off the tensions between Danes and immigrants.

The silver screen

Denmark's Nordisk Film Kompagni, founded in 1906, is the oldest film company on the planet still in operation. Its polar bear logo is familiar to all Danes. This is where Carl Th. Dreyer (1889–1968) began his career. The films of Dreyer, a master of psychological realism, are still shown at film festivals and schools the world over. His works include *The Passion of Joan of Arc* (1928) and *The Word (1955)*.

Today, Danish cinema revolves around the Danish Film Institute. Founded in 1972 to distribute public funds to feature films, the institute may be the prime example of a successful government-sponsored art industry.

The organisation reads scripts and puts up half the funds for the movies. A quarter of its budget is allocated to productions for children and young people.

In 1982 the state increased its funding and this, coupled with the establishment of the Danish Film School, jump-started the industry, which now reels out 15 or so productions a year.

The programme started paying off with prizes a few years later when Danish films took Academy Awards for the best non-English language movies two years running. *Babette's Feast*, directed by Gabriel Axel and based on a story by Isak Dinesen (Karen Blixen), won in 1986, and *Pelle the Conqueror* triumphed the following year. Directed by Bille August and based on a story by Martin Andersen Nexø, it starred Max von Sydow as Pelle's father.

The 1990s heralded a new, edgier Danish cinema, and the prime mover was Lars von Trier. A darling of the international film festival circuit and master of publicity, Lars von Trier manages to get the kind of funding that his Danish colleagues can only dream of. As the director-producer puts it, the Danish film legislation "has made it possible for me to direct films I would not have been able to make anywhere else in the world."

Von Trier is part of the circle of Danish film-makers who formulated the Dogma 95 manifesto, a set of rules designed to turn movies away from the Hollywood bent. Featuring shaky hand-held cameras and all-on-location shooting, the Dogma movies tell chilling, true-to-life stories.

Von Trier has helped to pave the way for all sorts of movies, including those of his "Dogma" brothers, Thomas Vinterberg (*The Celebration*) and Søren Kragh-Jacobsen (*Mifune's Last Song*) who have both won awards for their personal, off-beat dramas at major international festivals.

Making music

The Music Council, which was founded in 1976, distributes state funds for musical activities of all kinds. The classical tradition still attracts the most money, to symphony orchestras and opera companies in Copenhagen, Odense and in the big provincial cities,

Odense, Århus and Ålborg. Northern and Southern Jutland also have their own professional orchestras, and there are many small chamber music ensembles.

Live performances are well attended, thanks to a heavily subsidised subscription system, which has brought ticket prices down to a level acceptable to the Danish public.

Historically, the Romantic period produced writers of *Lieder*, operettas in the German tradition (Friedrich Kuhlau 1786–1832, famous for the score of *Elverhøj*) and ballet music – by J.P.E. Hartmann (1805–1900), Niels W. Gade (1817–90), and H. C. Lumbye (1810–74), also

1925, this Dane was borne along by a powerful and dramatic internal drive, rapidly abandoning inherited traditions of form.

In addition to his popular symphonies, which were on the repertoire of orchestras from Stuttgart to San Francisco, Nielson wrote three instrumental concertos, choral music, piano pieces and two operas. What put Nielsen on the map was Leonard Bernstein's recordings – with the New York Philharmonic – of all six of his symphonies.

The classical music season traditionally focuses on the winter months, but in Denmark there are concerts throughout the summer in

famous for the Viennese-style *Champagne Gallop*) – mostly commissioned by August Bournonville, master of the Royal Danish Ballet School.

Turning from Romanticism, the Funen composer Carl Nielsen (1865–1931) placed Denmark firmly on the international music map (*see page 216*). Although influenced by Mozart and Brahms, Nielsen ignored contemporary developments to follow his own path. From his first symphony in 1892 to his sixth and last in

LEFT: Danny Kaye, playing the writer in the film *Hans Christian Andersen*. **RIGHT:** a stark scene from a stark film – *Breaking the Waves* by Lars von Trier.

LARS VON TRIER, FILM DIRECTOR

Avant-garde bad boy or pretentious self-promoter? Whatever the Danes may think of him, Lars von Trier (born 1956) is certainly never boring. A prime mover in wresting Danish cinema out of the staid folk comedy and coming-of-age genres, von Trier has brought European art cinema to a large Danish audience. A product of the Danish film school, von Trier broke through with the dystopian *Element of Crime* (1984), followed by *Zentropa* (1991), *Breaking the Waves* (1996) and *The Idiots* (1998). Von Trier's real popular breakthrough came with *The Kingdom I* and *II* (1994 and 1997), two television mini series about oddballs at Copenhagen's main hospital.

Copenhagen's Tivoli Concert Hall, as well as at music festivals across the country, culminating in the Århus Festival in early September.

Summer is also the time for all popular forms of music to "come out in the open". For 10 days in July, the annual Copenhagen Jazz Festival fills the streets, cafés and concert halls of the city for more than 300 performances by cream-of-the-crop jazzmen and women, many of them from overseas.

What Paris once was to American writers, Copenhagen still is to American musicians. Here they find an informality and intimacy, combined with enthusiasm and talent, helping

genres which are attracting computer-savvy music-makers with funky names like Dog Tractor and Doubled Muffled Dolphin. A unique Nordic brand of soul music seems to be the radio standard.

Raw-larynxed singer Thomas Helmig is "world-famous in Denmark". So is Lars H.U.G., a former 1980s avant-garde figure who later spent three years on a government grant writing and recording a best-selling English-language album of jazzy songs.

Most young bands like to sing in English for the proper international sound, but sadly it often costs them a certain innate poetry. A few bands

to make Copenhagen the jazz capital of Northern Europe.

When the Danish Radio Big Band was established in 1964, it attracted Thad Jones and other legendary players, who set up residence in Denmark. Trumpeter Thad wrote for, inspired, and conducted the band. Saxophonist Jesper Thilo, bass player Niels-Henning Ørsted Pedersen, the trumpeters Palle Mikkelborg and Jens Winther, all international names, had a common nursery – the Big Band.

Like most other Western countries, Denmark has spawned its own variants of contemporary music genres, from rock to rap and beyond. Electronica and techno are important new sub-

have had smash international hits, such as Aqua and Michael Learns to Rock.

Summertime music festivals all over the country lure the young, and slightly older, by the tens of thousands to lap up top international and Danish bands. Roskilde Festival is the biggest (*see opposite*), followed by the festivals in Ringe and Skanderborg. Other festivals cater to more specific musical tastes, such as the Tønder Festival for folk music.

Visual arts

In Denmark, historically rich in literature, the oils did not really start flowing until the 19th century with the arrival of C. W. Eckersberg

(1783–1853), who is generally regarded as the father of Danish painting.

Eckersberg made the obligatory study tour to Rome via Paris where he worked under David, who taught his pupils to study nature and see with their own eyes. Eckersberg returned with this philosophy of *voir beau et juste* which he passed on to his own pupils Marinus Rørbye, Christen Købke, Wilhelm Marstrand and Constantin Hansen, painters who formed the nucleus of what became known as The Golden Age, from about 1815 to 1848.

The next group of importance were the "Skagen painters". This group coalesced

known for his quiet interiors, this "Danish Vermeer" also did landscapes and portraits of serene beauty in a subdued colour scheme – a standard against which many Danish painters still define themselves. In 1998, Hammershøi was the subject of a travelling exhibition organised by the Guggenheim Museum.

Germinating in the isolation of the German occupation, the most important Danish modern art movement, Cobra (including artists from Copenhagen, Brussels and Amsterdam), came to full bloom in the post-war years. The group was founded by Asger Jorn (1914–73) and drew inspiration from sources ranging from

around the artist couple Michael and Anna Ancher (1859–1935) and P. S. Krøyer (1851–1909) who, distancing themselves from stiff academic tradition and the stuffiness of the capital, settled in the northernmost tip of Jutland. Attracted by the light and motifs of the seascapes and local Skagen fishing population, they painted vibrant, naturalistic works in the last decades of the century.

Perhaps the most famous Danish painter of all is Vilhelm Hammershøi (1864–1916). Best

LEFT: a painting by Martinus Rorbye (1803–48), one of the early Skagen painters.
ABOVE: fun and high spirits at the Roskilde Festival.

ROSKILDE FESTIVAL

Originating in 1971 as Denmark's answer to America's Woodstock, the annual Roskilde Festival attracts 90,000 young people from all over Scandinavia and Germany for four days of music. A list of the bands that have played Roskilde over the years reads like a pantheon of international pop and rock music stars, including David Bowie, Bob Marley, U2, Bob Dylan and R.E.M. Naturally, any Danish band worth its salt plays Roskilde. Striving to stay relevant, the organisers add new styles like electronica and techno to the play list. Festival profits go towards supporting local Roskilde charities and youth organisations.

German Expressionism and French Surrealism, to primitive art and children's art. In a more narrative vein, painter and sculptor Henry Heerup reached back to old-style Nordic visual imagery and Viking curlicues.

The highest-profile contemporary artist is Per Kirkeby (born 1938). Grounded in the 1960s school of experimental art and dipping into Pop Art, Kirkeby is a painter of monumental abstractions and a part-time designer of massive brick sculptures for the public space.

OPEN HOUSE

Don't miss Copenhagen's annual Kulturnat (Culture Night) in October, a popular "Copenhagener affair," when museums, galleries and performance spaces throw open their doors to special events.

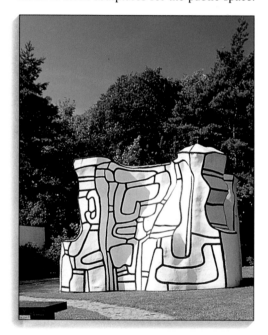

Bjørn Nørgård (born 1947) gained notoriety in 1970 when he led a horse into a field and butchered it, preserving the event on film and pieces of the horse in jars. Today the academy professor makes draperies for the Queen that hang on castle walls.

Galleries and museums

For today's art, look to the galleries. Copenhagen's gallery scene is concentrated in the streets around Kongens Nytorv, where the Royal Academy of Fine Arts and Charlottenborg are located. Galleri Nikolai Wallner in Store Kongensgade and Galleri Susanne Ottesen in Gothersgade are two of the most prominent. Nikolaj Church, now a public gallery, is also worth a visit. Nikolaj will advertise current art events and openings that lie off the beaten track.

Denmark has a wealth of art museums. In the 1990s, museums such as Arken, in Ishøj south of Copenhagen, and Trapholt, in Kolding, have arisen in buildings that make architectural art statements in their own right.

The mecca of all museums, the Louisiana Museum of Modern Art in North Zealand with its sculpture garden sweeping down to the Øresund sound, is a must-see. Jutland has the Ålborg and Århus Art Museums, as well as museums for several individual Cobra artists – Asger Jorn in Silkeborg, and husband-and-wife painters Carl Henning Pedersen and Else Alfeldt in Herning.

In Copenhagen, the State Museum of Art houses a comprehensive international collection dating from the 13th century, and entire rooms each for Emil Nolde, the Danish-German expressionist, Edward Munch and Hammershøi. In 1999, a new wing was added, in the open glass-and-steel style that defines Danish architecture now, with space for large-scale Minimalist works.

The Hirschsprung Gallery features 19th-century artists of the Golden Age and turn of the 20th-century Skagen painters, though the Skagen Museum is really the place to go to see them. The neo-classical sculptor Thorvaldsen has a museum of his own, built to his specifications when he returned from Rome in 1838 after having spent 40 years abroad. Sponsored by the capital's merchant class, the museum also served as a direct statement to the king by the powers that would soon beget the young democracy.

Ny Carlsberg Glyptoteket is a 19th-century gem with extensive collections of Roman and Egyptian art. In 1998, a new wing was added to house its 19th-century French and Impressionist art collections. Look for the Degas bronze ballerina with the cloth skirt, one of just three casts made. And be sure to descend the long staircase to the mummy room. ❏

LEFT: exhibit in the sculpture garden of the renowned Louisiana Museum of Modern Art, North Zealand.

Danish Royal Ballet

For more than a century and a half, the Danish Royal Ballet and its male dancers have been major movers of world ballet. Leaping onto the world stage, Peter Schaufuss went on to lead the London Festival Ballet and the Berlin Ballet, and Peter Martins became artistic director at the New York City Ballet.

Both are products of the Royal Danish Ballet School with its great masters Harald Lander (1905–71) and August Bournonville (1805–79). It was Bournonville who created what we know as "classical ballet," and whose methods still form the core of the teaching today.

Despite his French name, Bournonville was born in Denmark, son of the ballet master Antoine Bournonville, who had danced under Galeotti, the first ballet master of the school. August studied in France but returned to Denmark and went on to lead Danish ballet for 50 years.

Over the years he choreographed some 50 full-length productions. Of the 10 that have survived, *Napoli*, *The Dancing School* and, *La Sylphide* are still performed regularly the world over.

Bournonville trained his dancers according to a strict series of weekly programmes or "schools" – one for each day of the week. His Friday school is still in use and is shown on the stage in *The Dancing School*. The schools consist of long sequences of step compositions.These exercises promoted the qualities he needed for his graceful and dramatic style, as well as the strength to perform the "new" techniques of pointwork for women and leaps for men. The exuberance and beauty that define his ballet also give it its "Danishness".

The next big change came with Harald Lander (1905–71), who was ballet master from 1932 to 1951. His success lay in how he played off the contrast between contemporary choreography and loyalty to the Bournonville tradition. With a repertoire built around his wife and prima ballerina, Margot Lander, the Ballet soared to new heights. His most successful works included *Etude* (1948) and *Quarrtsiluni* (1942), both with music by Knudåge Riisager.

During the German occupation the Ballet became a focal point of national pride, and after the war Lander forged a company of dancers that

RIGHT: Denmark has produced fine ballerinas, but it is the men that have achieved the greatest success.

delighted audiences throughout the world, cementing the success of Danish ballet.

Lander's most successful student, Flemming Flindt, served as balletmaster from 1966 to 1978. Flindt restaged traditional ballets such as *The Nutcracker* and *Swan Lake*, and created memorable modern pieces such as The Lesson, based on a story by Ionesco, and *The Miraculous Mandarin*, to music by Bartok. He also worked with Ionesco on *The Triumph of Death* (1971), featuring his wife Vivi Flindt, all-around nudity and music by Thomas Koppel.

Frank Andersen, artistic director from 1985 to 1994, continued the Bournonville tradition. Most

memorably, he persuaded Queen Margrethe, an accomplished artist, to design the sets and costumes for *A Folk Tale*. In 1999, Aage Thorndal-Chistensen became ballet master, assisted by his wife, Colleen Neary, as first director. The Royal Ballet's repertoire today presents the best of the classical and the modern, spanning the range from Bournonville to Balanchine.

The home of the Royal Danish Ballet is Det Kongelige Teater (The Royal Theatre) in Copenhagen, and the season runs from 15 August to 1 June. The summer is devoted to the overseas tours that continue to demonstrate to audiences how a nation of only 5 million people can produce some of the world's best dance. ❏

A FLAIR FOR DESIGN: FUNCTION WITH FORM

*When a nation of craftsmen mixed with a late
move towards industrialisation in the 1900s,
a new school of design was born*

A chair may be something to sit in, and a lamp may help to light up a room, but Danish designers have made these objects more than ordinary in the last 50 years. Behind glass in museums and in use in a wide range of places from conference rooms to homes, Danish design has brought a sense of elegance to everyday life.

"It always starts with a task," says designer Hans J. Wegner. "I never say to myself I'm going to make a piece of art. I tell myself I want to make a good chair" (Wegner's Round Chair, above). Danish designers "subtract and subtract" unnecessary elements from products and tools to find true function and form, says Jens Bernsen of the Danish Design Centre. "Sometimes these designs even turn out to be beautiful."

In Copenhagen, you should visit the Danish Museum of Decorative Art, Bredgade (open Tue–Fri 10am–4pm, Sat–Sun 12–4pm, closed Mon; entrance fee; tel: 33 14 94 52), and the Danish Design Centre, H.C. Andersens Boulevard (open Mon–Sat 10am–5pm, Sun 11am–4pm; entrance fee; tel: 33 69 33 69). A good place for furniture is Illum's Bolighus.

△ **URSULA**
Ursula Munch-Petersen designed this well-loved table service for Royal Copenhagen.

▽ **PH LAMP**
Poul Henningsen saw light fixture as more t just light, but someth to create a sense of s

▽ **CYLINDA LINE**
The architect Arne Jacobsen designed this stainless steel line of household objects for the company Stelton, and it is now one of the most recognised in Denmark.

DESIGN IN THE HOME

For all its elegance, Danish design is not something limited to galleries and museums. In Denmark, it is found everywhere – hotels, restaurants, cafés, offices, and most importantly, homes. Nearly every Dane, it seems, has some sort of sleek designer lamp hanging over the dinner or coffee table.

For special occasions, such as weddings, birthdays and office receptions, Danes give arty salad sets, candle holders, salt and pepper grinders, pot holders – even mixing bowls (*pictured above*).

"The kitchen drawer is good design's enemy number one," says Erik Bagger, whose wine serving tools are well known in Denmark. Danish-designed products are meant to be used, however, meaning that Denmark probably has the most stylish contents of kitchen drawers anywhere in the world.

The visually striking sound systems designed by Bang & Olufsen are praised worldwide, and are found in many a Danish home. Even cupboard handles and other household fittings are part of the Danish design world.

◁ **EGG CHAIR**
Many of Arne Jacobsen's designs were intended for specific buildings or, in this case, hotel lobbies.

▽ **IC3 TRAIN**
Gone are the days of lumpish locomotives. Even Danish trains have a high quality of design.

CHURCHES

Few people may go there to worship these days, but Danes still take pride
in the rich diversity and abundance of their churches

There is perhaps no better way to get a sense of Denmark's history than by visiting some of its churches. Danes are not, on the whole, faithful churchgoers, but the fabric of the Evangelical Lutheran church and the nation's cultural inheritance are fiercely guarded everywhere. Interesting old traditions remain. Many Danish churches have a model ship hanging in the sanctuary as a reminder of the Danish maritime tradition and the sailors who work so far from home.

Early Christian churches

Christianity was introduced in Denmark in 826 by the French Benedictine monk Ansgar, and the small town of Jelling in eastern Jutland is presumed to be the site of the first officially-protected Christian church.

The first historical statement of Denmark's conversion to Christianity appears in runic on the Jelling Stones: "King Harald raised this monument to the memory of Gorm his father and Thyra his mother, (the same) Harald who won all of Denmark and Norway, and made the Danes Christian."

The stones, from about 985, stand today beside a small 11th-century church. Below it lie the remains of two older, wooden structures. The uppermost of these may have been built by King Harald Bluetooth after his conversion. According to legend, this occurred after he witnessed an astonishing act of faith by a missionary monk named Poppo, who carried red-hot iron in his hands without any apparent pain or injury.

By 1200, some 2,000 churches had been built around the country, and those standing today tell the story of Denmark. Little architecture survives from the Middle Ages apart from the churches, and their upkeep is evidence of social bonds and coherence through the centuries.

PRECEDING PAGES: Føvling Kirke in Jutland.
LEFT: a beautiful altar in Vor Frelsers Kirke in Copenhagen. **RIGHT:** detail inside the Domkirke in Maribo, South Zealand.

They are often found on hills, and their towers afford sweeping views of the rolling landscape.

Middle-Age Danish churches have characteristic shapes. Built of brick and stone, many of them whitewashed, there is usually a tower built much later, especially in the 16th century. Their naves and apses are Romanesque in their

foundations, built from the 10th to 12th centuries. In many cases the Gothic period, roughly 1250–1500, saw the churches enlarged and Gothic vaults erected on the earlier structures. To see purely Romanesque churches, visit west and north Jutland; the Gothic churches are abundant elsewhere in the country.

Modest solidity

Like the Danes who worshipped there, the churches are not grandiose. Denmark has no ecclesiastical marvels on the scale and magnitude found elsewhere in Europe. The churches in Denmark bear witness to the modest solidity of Danish culture and piety, and were built and decorated largely by peasant craftsmen. Even city churches speak not of the nobility, but of wealthy tradesmen whose touchingly crude, carved and painted epitaphs mark the passing of daily life.

Fortress-churches

One uniquely Danish kind of church architecture is found in the round fortress-churches of Bornholm, Zealand, Funen and northern Germany. They were built in certain villages as refuges in times of war, and had wells and thick walls resembling the curtain walls of medieval Europe. Extremely narrow battlements and

windows helped them withstand the sieges which occurred, particularly in the Baltic. Østerlars Kirke on Bornholm is a fine example, while the church at Horne on Funen shows how some were altered by Gothic additions.

In Copenhagen's Christianshavn district, visitors should see Vor Frelsers Kirke (the Church of Our Saviour), which has a splendid spire with an external winding staircase to the top. Unless you have a good head for heights, forgo the climb, magnificent though the view is, and visit the interior of the 17th-century sanctuary, with its large windows and cheerful light.

Christianskirke, also in Christianshavn, is amusing because the 17th-century burghers used their own boxes instead of pews. It was like being in a private theatre but perhaps it served a practical purpose, as Danish sermons in the 16th and 17th centuries could last for several hours. It could be restful to put the pulpit oratory at a peaceful distance by closing the doors for a while. Marmorkirken (the Marble Church) in the capital was finished in the 19th century. It speaks of Copenhagen's ambition to rival Rome and the Pantheon. Although it's a sombre affair inside, the extension is splendid.

Ribe Domkirke (cathedral), in Denmark's and Scandinavia's oldest town, is the largest and perhaps the best-preserved Romanesque church in the country. Its current shape is from 1176, the year a fire destroyed its predecessor.

It is a beautiful place. Climb the stairs to visit the flat-topped bell tower for a wonderful view of the marsh and farmlands of southern Jutland. In common with other churches built around the same time, Ribe Domkirke originally lay outside the centre of the city – probably because its missionary activity wasn't completely accepted by the still-pagan Vikings of the nearby town.

While in the area, it is worth taking the time to visit Christ Church in nearby Tønder. It was built in 1591 and retains a tower from the late Middle Ages, but otherwise is notable for its use of space and light.

Denmark's most beautiful Gothic churches are at the former Cistercian monasteries of Løgumkloster, just north of Tønder, and Sorø on Zealand. Both were built during the second half of the 12th century, and are examples of the most important development in Danish architecture during the 12th century: the introduction of red brick.

Royal resting place

From Viking times through the Middle Ages, Roskilde, just west of Copenhagen, was a great religious, cultural and political centre. There are 14 parish churches and five convents in the area, as well as the magnificent cathedral, Roskilde Domkirke, the burial place for almost all Danish Kings and Queens.

Excavations have shown that building began around the year 1000, and chapels are still being added. The two most impressive are those of King Christian IV, in Dutch Renaissance style from 1641, which has beautiful murals; and the chapel of King Frederik V from

1770, masterwork of the architect Harsdorff. The cathedral has an enormous variety of architectural styles, both medieval and Renaissance, and has grown like a living organism over a millennium.

Haderslev Domkirke and Sct. Olai Kirke in Helsingør, both rebuilt in the 1400s to fit more closely the ideal basilica type found in northern Germany, are other noteworthy churches.

A trip to the university town of Lund in southern Sweden, once part of Denmark, and the cathedral there is also a memorable after-

CHURCH-SHY

Although nine out of ten Danes officially belong to the state-supported Evangelical Lutheran Folkskirchen, regular churchgoers number fewer than one in twenty.

doorways to the nave, which evoke the spiritual change required by the Catholic church as demons and ogres were replaced by Christian symbolism. Notice the frescoes, from the Middle Ages, which also help one distinguish Romanesque from Gothic style.

Lively frescoes

One notable example is Fanefjord Kirke on the island of Møn, where the vaults of the double nave display medieval man's lively experience of important events in the Old and New Testa-

noon's excursion from Copenhagen. The Archbishop of Lund was the primate of Denmark at the time of its construction and, although it has suffered a major fire and reconstruction, it remains an outstanding example of Romanesque architecture in southern Scandinavia.

A great majority of early Danish churches, it is believed, were built on pagan sites. Quite often, a well is found in the crypt below the altar, and this is also true in Lund. Note also the granite-carved figures, especially above the

LEFT: Roskilde, the Bishop's residence and Cathedral.
ABOVE: the round church at Østerlars, designed as a fortress for times of war.

ments. Unlike those of the Sistine Chapel, the paintings still show the artist's sense and use of space. They were all obliterated during and after the Reformation in 1536, but careful restoration continues as layers of whitewash are removed to reveal these beautiful scenes.

Modern tributes

Denmark has also built remarkable churches in modern times. To honour the 19th century educational reformer N.F.S. Grundtvig (*see page 59*), an impressive church bearing his name was built in northern Copenhagen. And Jørn Utzon, architect of the Sydney Opera House, is responsible for a church in the suburb of Bagsværd. ❏

THE ARCHITECTURAL HERITAGE

The Danish islands and countryside are bejewelled with
some 800 fortresses, castles and manor houses

The evolution of Denmark's fortresses, castles and manors can be traced to the early Middle Ages, when a wealthy property owner might surround his home and a cluster of smaller outbuildings within a palisade or moat.

Stone buildings first appeared in Denmark around 1075, but the only remains of a tower, of Zealand, where Gåsetårnet (the Goose Tower) from the early 1300s overlooks the remains of the fortress and the harbour below, and at Hammershus (from 1255) on Bornholm.

The Romanesque style, with its rounded arches and window openings, was gradually replaced in the 13th and 14th centuries by the

from around 1100, can be found near Bastrup Sø (lake) on Zealand, just west of Farum.

The most interesting ruins in Copenhagen are those below Christiansborg Palace, the Danish parliament in the city centre. Here you can see the foundations of the original castle from the late 1160s built on top of the remains of the village of Havn by Copenhagen's founder, Bishop Absalon.

Other good choices are the ruins of Korsør (about 1280), Kalø Slot near Århus, (the foundations were laid in 1313) and Gurre Slot just southwest of Helsingør (late 1100s). The best preserved ruins in the country are either in the town of Vordingborg, on the southwestern coast

Gothic, with its more intricate, pointed archways and subtle detail. The best examples of Gothic architecture include Gjørslev (circa 1400), about 10 kilometres (6 miles) south of Køge on Zealand, and Rygård (from 1525), between Nyborg and Svendborg on Funen.

Hamlet's castle

Renaissance influence on Danish architecture began around 1550 as appearance surpassed defence as a design consideration. Examples of the transition from Gothic to Renaissance style include Gisselfeld and Borreby on Zealand, as well as Nakkebølle, Årbæklunde, Hesselagergård and Egeskov, all on Funen and from the

1500s. The first public monument in Renaissance style is Kronborg castle in Helsingør, built by King Frederik II. Shakespeare called it Elsinore Castle, and made it the setting for *Hamlet*.

The most obvious examples of Renaissance construction appeared during the reign of that voracious builder, King Christian IV. He adopted Dutch Renaissance style and the architect Hans van Steenwinckel – and nearly bankrupted the nation in doing so.

There are no castles in Denmark on the grand

> **ROYAL TREASURES**
>
> The museum at Rosenborg Slot houses the private property of Denmark's royalty and the beautiful crown jewels. I t is an intimate and lovely building.

and complete whole. Built as the royal summer house outside the city walls, the castle is now at the heart of the city near Nørreport Station.

The styles of the many manor houses vary, but they generally emphasise balanced proportion and scale. Mostly open and friendly, they speak of the comfortable rural life of the aristocracy. Early examples are Hesselagergård on Funen, or Holmegaard near Næstved, southwest Zealand. Hvidkilde on Funen is from around 1550, but with later additions. Gavnø, south of Næstved,

scale of Versailles, but quite a number of accessible and historically important ones are open to the public. These include Kronborg, Frederiksborg, Dragsholm, Gavnø Slot (castle) and Egeskov Slot. Amalienborg Palace, an outstanding rococo complex in Copenhagen, is the official residence of the Royal Family, and some of its rooms are open for guided tours.

When in Copenhagen, visit Rosenborg Slot, dating from 1617, and the surrounding Kongens Have (Royal Gardens) which form a rare

is from around 1400. Closer to Copenhagen is Søllerødgård, dating from the late 17th century.

Where to stay in style

Castles and manor houses require upkeep, and today many of them have opened their doors as hotels. Gammel Vraa castle in north Jutland is one of Denmark's loveliest, and its restaurant is all candlelight. Sophiendal Manor House from the 1870s in east Jutland features four-poster beds. It has roaming herds of Angus cattle, and their beef is on the menu. Hvedholm Slot in south Funen, built in 1570 and rebuilt in "Rosenborg" style in 1880, offers a view over to Fåborg and the Funen Archipelago. ❑

LEFT: Hesselagergård manor house, Funen.
ABOVE: the grand interior of Rosenholm manor house in Jutland.

THE GREAT OUTDOORS

The Danes are enthusiastic about active pursuits, whether cycling to work, hiking the coastal paths, casting a rod or skippering a yacht

Denmark offers a well-manicured countryside and breathtaking seascapes ideal for outdoor activities. The Danes themselves will take advantage of any opportunity to do something outdoors, regardless of the time of year. In the warmer months they'll seemingly use any excuse to be in the sunshine, whether eating breakfast on a sunny terrace or enjoying an all-day excursion. In the cooler part of the year, all it takes is the proper clothing.

Mild climate

Meteorology is not an exact science, especially in Denmark, where the weather is fickle due to the many factors influencing it. Carrying a raincoat, and often a jumper, is advisable even in the summer months. The Danish weather is mild; the winters are not bitter, the summers not too hot and for the bulk of the year the temperatures are between 1–10°C (35–50°F). Winter temperatures generally fluctuate around freezing point and summers usually are a breezy 13–24°C (55–75°F).

At the water's edge

With more than 7,400 km (4,600 miles) of coastline, the waters surrounding Denmark are a playground for outdoor activities. No point in the country is more than a 45-minute drive from the sea and many inland waterways or fjords are even closer.

Kayaks, canoes, rowing boats, smaller sail or motor craft may be hired at resort centres along the coasts or beside the larger lakes. The Gudenå river system in Jutland is a favourite for excursions on the water. For the more experienced sailor, yachts can be chartered from marinas around the country, complete with crew if need be.

The air is hardly still in Denmark, and the windsurfing is excellent. Seasoned surfers may prefer the exhilaration of the North Sea, while beginners can try their hand in the lee of a fjord, bay or on an inland lake.

Danish beaches tend to be very child friendly, although the waters along the west coast of Jutland have some strong currents and undertows. The beaches of the islands that dot the

coast are normally a sugary sand, and in some areas there are so few people you might think you were on a deserted island. Beach volleyball has grown into a major sport on larger beaches, with organised tournaments and informal pick-up games now a common sight.

Out for a hike

Hiking or just strolling along the coast is a favourite of Danes and visitors alike. Amber hunting can be a fruitful venture along the shores of Bornholm or western Jutland. Bornholm is also known for its sheer cliff walls that separate the beaches. A fine outing in southeast Zealand is a hike along Møns Klint, 100-metre

(330-ft) high chalk cliffs forged by calcareous shells hundreds of millions of years ago.

A good catch

Denmark is an El Dorado for the angler, with great opportunities for salt and freshwater fishing. To begin with, visitors and Danes alike need a national fishing permit, which can be obtained at local tourist offices and post offices. The reasonably priced permits apply for a day, week or year. Generally, anglers may fish freely in salt water, but rights for streams, lakes and ponds are mainly privately owned. Check with tourist offices or at an angling shop for details of local permits, daily limits, minimum sizes and other restrictions.

Coarse fishing is a big sport in Denmark and the landscape is dotted with water courses full of bream, carp, rudd, roach, perch and other species. Many of the same waters hold pike or zander that will test a rod and the ability of its holder. Salmon are on the comeback in the Gudenå river system, and can be caught along some coastal areas, especially on Bornholm.

The streams of Jutland and Funen hold some real trophy brown trout, ideal for fly and spin fishermen. Grayling can be found in a few streams in central-north Jutland, while rainbow

AN ANCIENT LANDSCAPE

The Danish countryside has been blessed with a notable variety of plants and fungi. When agriculture began to take form in Denmark around 6,000 years ago, man began to influence the landscape. Species that once only inhabited coastal areas migrated inland and new habitats emerged. The oldest moorlands appeared around 4,000 years ago and some stretches of this habitat in central Jutland are only around six to seven centuries old. The oldest beech forests, now common in eastern Denmark, date from around 1500 BC. Wooded areas in the eastern part of the country tend to be mainly hardwood, while in western Denmark there are more conifers.

trout that have escaped from fish farms have begun to thrive in Danish waters.

A favourite of Danish fishermen is fly or spin casting for sea trout from the coast. Cod, gar, herring, mackerel and flatfish are also a sought after by surf casters. Charter boats take individuals out in search of deep-water species.

Rural pursuits

The Danish countryside is a breathtaking patchwork of forests, dunes, marshes, moors and

LEFT: windsurfing is a particularly popular water sport. **RIGHT:** swans and coot gather in a quiet fjord in North Jutland.

meticulously manicured farmland. In every type of landscape walkers will find paths or trails that stretch for miles, and a labyrinth of winding country roads.

Hærvejen is a bicycle and walking trail that stretches from the German border to Viborg in north-central Jutland. Traders and travellers beat this path a few thousand years ago, and much of it still looks as it did during Viking times. All along the route there are inns, hotels or hostels, as well as shops for provisions.

The bicycle is an important mode of transport and source of fun for Danes and visitors alike (*see page 119*). Denmark has thousands of miles of foot/bike paths and bikes may be taken on most trains and ferries. Tourist offices can provide detailed maps of routes.

Another wheeled activity is roller/in-line skating, which has become an immensely popular pastime. It would seem logical that skaters should use bicycle paths – and many do – but this is actually prohibited. Traffic laws state that skaters must share the pavements with pedestrians, using common sense as a guideline.

The view from the saddle

For those who would like to view Denmark on horseback, riding stables (mostly in Jutland)

LIFE IN THE WILD

The National Forest and Nature Agency estimated in 1995 that the number of breeding, naturally occurring species in Denmark include 49 mammals, 209 birds, five reptiles, 14 amphibians, 37 freshwater and 110 saltwater fish. A person need only travel a few minutes from the centre of any city to find wildlife habitat.

In forested areas, the most commonly spotted animals are fox, deer, hedgehogs, martens, badgers, hare and rodents. It would not be unusual to find these species in suburban districts, and most cities have modest fox populations. Rural waterways host otters and mink, while seals can be seen frolicking along the coastline. Some smaller whales and porpoises venture into Danish waters, although sightings are rare.

Birds of prey include hawks, buzzards, falcons, owls, osprey, and some larger eagles. Both the inland and coastal waters provide an excellent habitat for water fowl. Denmark provides a resting or wintering grounds for 17 species of migratory sea birds, and around 20 percent of their total population makes its winter home in or pays a visit to Danish waters. The mute swan was chosen as Denmark's national bird. With only three or four pairs left in the country in 1926, the swan was declared a protected species. Now there are around 4,000 breeding pairs.

offer special holiday trips with half or full board. A horse can also be hired by the hour or day, complete with lessons or a guide if requested.

For spectators of equestrian disciplines, the main annual event is the Hubertus Hunt held in the Royal Deer Park in Klampenborg just outside Copenhagen on a November Sunday. The meet draws thousands of people who normally combine a Sunday afternoon stroll with the excitement of the race. A favourite gathering place for many is near water obstacles to cheer good-natured riders who have to wade out of the water after a spill.

Hole in one

Golf is the fastest growing sport in Scandinavia, and its popularity has exploded in Denmark in the past few years. Nearly all clubs and courses welcome visitors, and in most cases you needn't be accompanied by a member. The number of pay-and-play courses is relatively small, considering the growing size of the sport, and these tend to show signs of wear from the many novice players who frequent them. It would be wiser, and more of a challenge, to find a private club.

The better clubs impose maximum handicap restrictions, usually around 25–30. Green fees are reasonable, and excellent courses are no more than a few minutes' ride from the centres of urban areas. All of them will challenge a handicap, with the natural beauty of the Danish landscape providing the hazards.

Copenhagen Golf Club, the oldest in the country, is set in the Royal Deer Park, a 15-minute drive north of the city centre. Golfers must share the course with herds of wild deer as the park once was a royal hunting ground. A high number of courses remain open year round and set up winter greens at lower prices.

Huntsman's prey

Hunting is a classic sport that has seen a slight revival in the past few years, but for the visitor it demands both a hunting licence and normally the rights to use a tract of land. It's not simple to get started, but not impossible either. Many farmers will allow the use of fields for wing shooting, or wooded areas for deer. Another possibility is hunting for water fowl along coastal areas, but this demands some investigation to find a suitable area. A central place for gathering information is the Jagt-og Skovbrugsmuseum, a museum dedicated to hunting (Folehavevej 15–17, 2970 Hørsholm; tel: 42 86 05 72).

Winter sports

Winter temperatures normally fluctuate around freezing point and accumulations of snow are infrequent. In fact, there were only eight white Christmasses in Denmark in the 20th century.

Jutland normally gets more snow than eastern Denmark and has a few modest ski slopes. All around the country, however, there are lovely spots for cross-country skiing – when there is snow.

The same holds true for ice skating; when the lakes and ponds freeze, people quickly get out their blades. Lakes in central Copenhagen and other cities are smoothed to create wonderful outdoor rinks.

Football

For spectator sports, the dominant attraction is football. With the exception of national team matches and championship games, it is fairly easy to get a good seat in the home stadium of a top-division team. ❏

LEFT: you can even join a roller-blading class if you are so inclined.

On Your Bike

The bicycle is the single most common mode of transportation in Denmark and it's not unusual to see the rich and famous peddling along rural byways or urban thoroughfares. It is estimated that every other Dane owns a bicycle and uses it regularly. For city commuting it is often the fastest mode of transport, and many people use a bike as a link to mass transit.

There are thousands of miles of bike paths all around the country. In cities they normally run parallel to motor traffic, while in rural areas they may often be separate. With very, very few exceptions, you can go anywhere on a bike. At any time of day or night, in all seasons, you will see cyclists – a grumpy stream on a Monday morning, a cheerful flow on weekends.

With the Great Belt Bridge now open and the Øresund Bridge to Sweden opening in 2000, it is possible to bike from Skagen at the northernmost tip of Jutland, south and then eastwards across the country and into Sweden. Ferries accommodate cyclists and trains will shuttle you across the major bridges. Bicycles may also be taken on certain commuter trains for a small charge.

The City of Copenhagen came up with a brilliant idea a few years ago, the City Bike. The bicycles are placed strategically at stands around the inner city. Cyclists put a 20-kroner coin into a slot to unlock a bike, and it's theirs for as long as they like. When the bike is returned to a stand, the 20 kroner is refunded. The bikes may only be used within the old ramparts of the city, but this is where the sights are. It would be wise to carry a lock, to prevent someone else from getting the 20-kroner deposit and leaving you stranded.

Danish families also find cycling a good way of communing with nature, a preoccupation of all Scandinavians. As the schools close in June, it is common to see a family setting off with three or four bikes, toddler on the baby seat, heavily laden saddle bags and perhaps a small box-trailer.

For visitors, the passion for cycling brings benefits. Many tourist offices offer all-in holidays which cover hire of cycles, routes, accommodation and meals. It is also possible to hire bikes at most railway stations and in modest-sized towns, with the added advantage of easy spares for a machine

RIGHT: cycling is a pleasure in Denmark, whether you cycle on the road or on one of the many cycle paths.

that goes wrong. The view from the bike is the ideal way to see the country. Denmark in spring and summer is sweet with the small pink saucers of wild roses which bloom in hedges and bushes and right down to the edge of the beaches. You can jump off a bike to examine an interesting plant, stop at one of the white churches, or to view an idyllic thatched farm with cross-timbered walls and painted beams. On a Danish island it is simple just to lay down a bike in the grass and dip into the sea which, in the Great or Little Belts, Kattegat or Baltic, is calm and warmer than the North Sea.

One of the best areas for cycling is Funen and its islands of Ære, Langeland and Tasinge, where

manor houses, castles and pretty villages proliferate. The island of Bornholm has a number of cycle routes and is another favourite with cyclists. Also worth exploring are the isolated beach roads linking the fishing villages and dunes of Jutland.

Be aware that the police will write out tickets for traffic violations on two wheels. Pedalling creates a thirst, but bicycling while intoxicated is a serious offence. Lights are required 20 minutes after sunset until 20 minutes before it rises again. Traffic lights and signage must be observed and signalling a turn or stop is part of the safety regime. Most petrol stations, department stores and, of course, bicycle shops carry an assortment of mandatory, or handy equipment. ❏

EATING OUT

The open sandwich, or smørrebrød, epitomises Danish food.
It ranges from the most basic fare to elaborate, sculpture-like creations

The principal contribution that Denmark has made to world cuisine is the open sandwich. Called *smørrebrød* (literally, "buttered bread"), it can be enjoyed in countless variations.

As is the case in most nations, popular foods stem directly from the farmers' fields. Danish farmers had the butter and the grains, mainly rye, so this is the basis of the open sandwich. The concept is the centrepiece of any luncheon, but the Danes may eat *smørrebrød* at all three main meals, or as between-meal snack.

The sandwiches originally appeared in rural districts. According to some sources, cattle breeders from the former Danish, now German, areas of Schlesvig and Holstein took the idea northwards with them through Jutland.

It was in the mid-19th century that the sandwiches began to assume their present form when they were served as the evening meal – usually composed of leftovers from the hot meal consumed in the afternoon. The afternoon repast also included a coarse-grained bread, usually rye or a mix of grains, and nothing went to waste. The combination of bread topped with meat, fish or vegetables became a substantial offering before retiring for the night.

How the sandwich spread

The idea spread from the country to towns and cities by word of mouth, and with the help of the newly-completed railway grid. Travellers would grab a bite at a provincial station and carry the idea home with them.

During the industrial revolution, workers began carrying the sandwiches to the job, and at around the same period butchers were opening shops instead of selling at market. They began offering various cold and smoked cuts of meat, so the selection of toppings expanded. By the start of the 20th century, the open sandwich had

largely replaced the hot afternoon meal, and was also the Danes' preferred choice for lunch.

Limitless potential

As long as you start with the buttered bread – or pork dripping if preferred – anything can be put on top of it. Probably the simplest form is a

slice of rye with a layer of pork dripping topped with sugar, a rural favourite that is still eaten by many traditionalists. Even the lowly potato, sliced and garnished with a seasoned dressing, raw onions or chives and sea salt can be a feast. At the other end of the spectrum the finest caviar or truffles adorn the bread.

Some restaurants, most notably Ida Davidsen in Copenhagen, feature sandwich menus that are scrolls several feet long and they haven't nearly exhausted the possibilities.

To be sure, the sandwiches vary in size, so when ordering *à la carte* it would be wise to inquire how many "pieces" constitute a meal. Sometimes one can be enough, but if you have

PRECEDING PAGES: herring hung out like washing on the island of Bornholm. **LEFT:** the famous open sandwiches feature in most Danish buffets. **RIGHT:** herring turns up in many different guises.

more of an appetite you might start with fish, followed by meat and then cheese toppings.

While each chef usually has a speciality, a couple of sandwiches have gained national popularity. "Sun over Gudhjem" is named after the town on Bornholm, which is Denmark's sunshine island and the place best-known for its smoked fish. The sandwich consists of smoked herring, radishes and raw egg yolk. It's not to be missed when visiting the island.

Oskar Davidsen, Ida's grandfather, came up with a sandwich that was a favourite of a circus veterinarian who frequented his restaurant. It consists of rye bread spread with dripping, liver pâté, salt-cured cold pork and aspic, and has come to be known as, "The veterinarian's late evening snack".

Ordeal by meal

The prime season for the full-blown Danish lunch is during the Christmas holidays, although visitors will find eateries offering sumptuous buffet tables all year round.

For the novice, the art of constructing a proper open sandwich can be difficult to master. Ask for help; there are fixed rules about what topping to put on which bread, and the correct garnishes to complement the main fea-

THE SCHOOL OF SKÅL

Standard table manners apply in Denmark, but toasting with beverages, or *skål*-ing, is a near-sacred ritual. The correct way to *skål* is to lift the glass, look at the person you want to *skål*, say the word and lift the glass slightly, drink, look at the person again, and put the glass back on the table. Not only is it good etiquette to *skål*, it's also a great way to flirt.

There are also rules about when to *skål*. A gentlemen must ensure that the lady on his right has something on her plate and in her glass. She must be the first he *skåls*, followed by the lady on his left a few minutes later. Never drink until the host has given a welcome toast to the gathering, or, if this isn't done, until he *skåls* the woman on his right. It is also the host's duty to *skål* each guest individually, if the size of the party allows this. The hostess may also *skål* her guests, who in turn, may *skål* her. It is not good form to *skål* a person who is older or of higher rank:, let the "senior" take the initiative, and returrn the gesture within three minutes. A gentleman should also *skål* the man sitting to the left of his wife/partner, as well as her.

The gesture may be made with non-alcoholic drinks, though not with a water glass. It can also be done with an empty glass, but you should go through the motions of taking a sip and conceal the empty glass.

ture of a sandwich. Rye bread is used with most toppings, except for more delicate seafood and cheeses. "Aged cheese", however, is an exception to the rule: it is served on rye bread spread with dripping. The cheese is then topped with raw onion, aspic, raw egg yolk and a splash of dark rum.

Pace yourself

When confronted by the buffet table, start with the herring, which is generally marinated, curried or smoked. At this point it must be said that nothing goes better with the fish (and most of the selections to follow) than beer and snaps, the Danish *akvavit.* As the Danes say, "The fish need something in which to swim." Other types of fish – mackerel, cod, gar, salmon, shellfish – feature in this part of the meal, too. A word of advice; pace yourself, there will be a lot more to come, and these ordeals can extend for several hours.

After the fish, move on to the cold cuts or cured meat and sausages, and the various meat-based toppings. Once again, the table will probably be laden with a host of temptations, but save room: there's more to come. Between each phase in the ordeal the Danes usually take a break, often called a "smoking pause", and it's worth bearing in mind that one in every three people over the age of 13 smokes.

The next course consists of hot dishes, sausages, Danish meatballs called *frikedeller,* fried pork tenderloin, fillet of sole, and possibly more. By this time, many people skip the bread and eat their *smørrebrød* without the *brød.* Another breather, and then it's time for the cheese – generally a selection of Danish and imported cheeses served with fruit, sweet peppers and radishes.

While the Danish lunch may seem to eclipse other meals, remember that the feast described above would mainly be for festive occasions, and would be the main meal of the day.

Danish breakfasts may seem somewhat spartan compared with a classic English breakfast. A roll or bread with a slice of cheese is a popular choice, but cold cuts of meat, yoghurt, and cereals also have broad appeal. What stands out

> ### BARGAIN BUFFET
>
> If you happen to see a restaurant sign stating "*sildebord*" – usually on Sundays – do give it a try. It means a herring buffet, normally at a ridiculously low price. The profit comes from the beer.

at the breakfast table is the coffee; Danish coffee is a richly textured brew, and it's strong. The Danes drink a lot of coffee, throughout the day, but there is also "afternoon coffee" to tide people over until the evening meal. This is a cup of coffee with cake, biscuits, pastry or a small cheese open sandwich.

Traditions upheld

The Danes eat their evening meals relatively early, and many restaurants close their kitchens at around 10pm. Traditional

Danish cuisine has always centred on the bounty of the fields and the seas. It is hearty fare, usually featuring pork or fish, potatoes and another vegetable. A gravy or sauce almost always accompanies the main *entrée*, and the main vegetables are peas, carrots, beets, cucumbers, and members of the cabbage family. New Danish potatoes are pure joy, and a good chef will take pride in serving them.

While Danish cooking has been strongly influence by French cuisine, there has been a revival of traditional Danish dishes in the past decade and many restaurants now feature them, especially some of the out-of-the-way places not mentioned in tourist guides. ❑

LEFT: sticky cakes for tea or dessert are a favourite.
RIGHT: humble-looking street stalls like this are a common sight in Denmark.

BEER, GLORIOUS BEER

The Danes are among the world's most enthusiastic beer drinkers – and they know a thing or two about producing it, too

Two Danish words that can prove invaluable to the visitor are *øl* and *skål*. The former has a linguistic link to ale, while the latter means bowl and stems from the Viking habit of shouting for more drink from the common bowl. Use the word *øl* to order a beer, and say *skål* as a social ice-breaker, because drinking beer in Denmark is almost as prevalent as breathing air. Despite some recent slight drops in sales figures, the Danes are the third largest per capita beer drinkers in the world, just behind Germany and the Czech Republic.

From pilsner to porter

The 15 breweries in the country produce around 150 varieties of beer. Most of them are of the pilsner type – the lighter brew first developed in Pilsen, Czechoslovakia – but there is the entire spectrum up to the stouts and porters. The basic ingredients for nearly all of them are barley, water, yeast and hops. One brewer, Thisted Bryghus maintains the tradition of using bog myrtle (also known as sweet gale) as the seasoning in place of hops, which did not appear in Denmark until around the year 1000. Before that, bog myrtle was the predominant "spice" for beer – and probably what whet the Viking palate in mead.

The brews range in strength from the brand NAB, with less than 1 percent alcohol, to concoctions of double-digit alcohol strength that can liven up a party fast. A decade or so ago, a few breweries began producing "annual brews", with the alcohol content based on the year: in 1991 the strength was 9.1 percent, in 1996 it was 9.6 percent, and so on. Each year, one-tenth of a percentage point was added. As the millennium approached, many feared that in 2000 the alcohol content would be 00 percent.

While beer drinking remains nearly as popular as ever, the art of matching the correct beer to traditional dishes is all but lost, although a small group of purists has launched a crusade to

LEFT: Tuborg comes to town in Copenhagen.
RIGHT: there's never a wrong moment for a beer.

enlighten the population. Few epicureans would dream of washing down raw oysters with a cold porter or stout, but in fact they are wonderful together. Hearty meat-and-potato dishes balance perfectly with stronger beers, while the slightly darker, "Bavarian-style" Danish beers complement game, smoked fish and pork

roasts. The basic pilsners go well with seafood dishes – and almost anything served at the table. An anonymous Dane once quipped: "Beer goes well with almost any dish, and the exceptions should be avoided at all costs."

The amber-coloured beverage fits naturally into any social situation. In fact, the bottle opener has earned the pet name, "society's helper" and a person carrying one – and almost everybody does – is said to be "fully dressed". By the way, we refer only to bottles here, because environmental concerns prohibit the sale of canned beer and sodas in Denmark. Some within the EU protest the ban, but most Danes would consider it unnatural to drink the national beverage from a can. And people like the design of the bottle which fits the human hand perfectly. That's why a bottle of beer nested in a loose grip is called a "hand beer".

The Danes can use the most unlikely instruments to open a bottle of beer: a screwdriver, a disposable lighter, a coin, a pen, a shoe heel, a key – even a folded newspaper. Some Danes maintain that anyone who is extremely thirsty can open a bottle with a soggy hot dog bun; first freeze the bun and then prise off the cap.

The test of a true beer drinker – and a real mate – is to hand the person two unopened bottles of beer. If he or she can open one bottle

with the other, replace the cap and open the second without creating a gush of foam, that's a true beer drinker. If you are handed an unopened bottle, or one spewing foam, then the person is not a real mate.

Strict drink-drive rules

Beer drinking is acceptable behaviour anywhere, with the exception of the workplace. It is not unusual to see a respectable man or woman sit on a city bench and drink a bottle of beer. The Danes have an exceptionally casual attitude towards drinking, unless a person mixes drinking and driving, which will cost a lost licence, a stiff fine, or time in jail.

Cafe and pub culture

In the past 20 years, the café has largely replaced the pub as the preferred spot to drink. "Let's go to a café" roughly means, "Let's go to a pub", and many establishments are open all day and through most of the night.

The popularity of the café ushered in a renewed taste for draught beer, but the brew connoisseur should beware; inexperienced service staff seem to consider the chore of pouring a glass of draught to be about the same as filling a glass with soda or a cup with coffee. Drawing a proper draught beer is an art. Conventional wisdom around Copenhagen has it that the best draught in town is served at Gammel Kongevej Number 90, a pub that is referred to by the number of the address. Should you order a draught and happen to be thirsty, be sure to order a bottle of beer to nurse while the bartender painstakingly draws your draught.

The inroads cut by the café, however, did not mean the extinction of the pub. There's still one on every street corner, unless it happens to be in the middle of the block. In downtown Copenhagen there is an area by Nikolai Church called the "minefield". Early in the 20th century, bohemians of the city began to congregate at a couple of pubs in the area. They drew artists, poets and other creative types who filled the watering holes. Over the years, numerous other pubs opened to accommodate the thirsty bohos and their followers. The bohos would step into one house for some quick refreshment, but afterwards it was nearly impossible to walk down the pub-dotted street in any direction without meeting an acquaintance and having another drink. So, the bohemians began calling the area a minefield, and before long, the practice of marching from pub to pub became know as walking the "death route".

The imagery may sound dangerous, but it was all foamy fun, and many an artist paid off his bar bill by trading a painting or doing a mural on the spot. The walls of several pubs remain decorated with this artwork to this day, and some lucky publicans have allegedly sold some of the works for small fortunes. Walking the Copenhagen minefield is still a very popular form of entertainment.

Past rituals

Beer is deeply rooted in the history of Denmark. For centuries it was served morning, midday and evening and it was always at hand should thirst strike in the middle of the night. One reason the drink gained immense popularity in urban areas a few centuries ago was because the water was unfit to drink. No feast or burial was complete without beer. In centuries past, newcomers to a village often bore gifts of beer. The drink was also used as legal tender to pay off public fines or debt. When a farmer died, his widow had to supply a whole barrel in his honour. If she died first, he only had to provide half

> ### THANK GOD FOR BEER
>
> The first official prayer book issued by the Danish church in 1569 contains reference to the practice of giving thanks for beer at a mealtime before expressing gratitude for the food.

tioned as early as 1454. Copenhagen brewers set up a Brewers' Guild in 1622, probably with the aim of regulating quality, and in 1687 the Guild began a system of rotation so that each member brewed an equal amount.

Special yeast

The yeast used in brewing is very important to the flavour and a 19th-century discovery led to the formation of the industry as it is today. Carl Jacobsen, the founder of Carlsberg Breweries, is usually

a barrel "and not a drop more". Ironically, even into the 20th century a wife's value was rated according to her abilities to bake and brew.

Before the introduction of more scientific methods, brewing was a seasonal activity, timed to coincide with harvests, holidays and the cycle of the moon. People drank what was brewed, but since it was a rather hit-or-miss discipline, additives such as sugar were used to make it palatable.

The first brewery, Kongens Bryghus, is men-

given the credit for developing an ideal yeast culture. In fact, Emil Christian Hansen was the revolutionary brewer who cultivated this special yeast, *saccaromuces carlbergensis*, for Carlsberg, to ensure a uniform, first-class brew. This has formed the basis of every Carlsberg brew since the mid-19th century.

Instead of keeping Hansen's discovery a secret, Jacobsen, as head of the brewery, declared that anyone who wanted to use this special yeast could buy it, a concession that continues to this day. The introduction of Carlsberg's yeast so vastly improved standards that fewer farms brewed their own, and Danish brewing became an industry. ❏

LEFT: Carlsberg's famous dray horses leave the brewery in Copenhagen. **RIGHT:** beer is not just a young person's drink in Denmark.

YULETIDE GOOD CHEER: A DANISH CHRISTMAS

Christmas is a warm light on the calendar of the dark Danish winter. Candles glow and families gather – that's after the infamous office party

The Danish word for Christmas is Jul, meaning "wheel". It comes from the old Viking celebration of mid-winter in which the wheel of time turns once again.

In the 10th century a Norwegian king ruled that Jul should coincide with the Christian celebration of Jesus's birth, 25 December. Most Danes set up a Christmas tree inside their homes on the evening of 23 December, decorating it with homemade ornaments, a star for the top and real candles on the branches.

On Christmas Eve, many Danes go to a late afternoon church service, followed by a huge feast at home. Some families have roast turkey stuffed with prunes and apples, some have roast pork with sour red cabbage, others have roast goose or duck. Dessert is always rice porridge.

After dinner, the candles are lit on the tree and everyone gathers around it to sing carols. Then they open gifts from each other. Families spend the following days until New Year's Eve together.

▽ **DECORATIVE TRADITIONS**
Danes have always made their own Christmas decorations. Straw figures are also sold from stands outside homes in the countryside.

▷ Every year the popular Carlsberg horses lead a Christmas procession along Strøget, through the heart of Copenhagen's main shopping district.

△ **MARZIPAN PIGS**
Christmas *konfekt*, shaped like mice and pigs, is made from marzipan, chocolate, nougat and other goodies.

▽ **CHRISTMAS EVE**
It is traditional to join hands to dance and sing carols around the tree. Dressing up is optional.

FUN AND GAMES AT THE OFFICE PARTY

The one most notorious tradition of *Jul* is *Julefrokost*, the office Christmas lunch. This is where the stresses, strains and inhibitions of daily working life are cast aside.

Employees plan an afternoon in December to hold their party. The *Julefrokost* begins with *sild og snapps* – marinated herring on rye bread – washed down with *aqvavit* and strong Christmas beer. Most people need only a couple of shots of *snapps* before they feel its inebriating effects, and the afternoon usually goes downhill from there, depending on how one wants to remember it.

More food and drink follows, and any flirting that might have been going on during the year tends to get more serious.

Then the revellers hit the town to embarrass themselves further at local haunts. Thankfully for some, *Jul* happens only once a year.

△ **DOUBLE CLAUS**
Denmark hosts an annual Santa convention, which attracts "Kris Kringles" from around the globe – in the off season, of course.

▷ **HOME TERRITORY**
Where is the North Pole? Danes claim *Julmanden* (Santa Claus) lives in their Greenland, but the Finns argue otherwise.

PLACES

*A detailed guide to the entire country, with principal sites
clearly cross-referenced by number to the maps*

White beaches, well-groomed farmland, gentle hills, islands large and small: this is Denmark. Nowhere is very far away, especially now that a network of motorways, railway lines and spectacular bridges link west to east from Germany, through Denmark to Copenhagen and across the Øresund to Sweden. Ferries still play their part, linking islands and crossing "fjords", as the Danes call their larger lakes, for this is a nation with a strong seafaring past.

Denmark is neatly beautiful rather than grand. Encouraged by the mild climate, the fields are early spiked with green; a month or two later, the countryside glows with fruit blossom and sharp yellow rape seed followed by the golden tinges of the harvest fields. Alongside every road, wildflowers push pink, blue and yellow through the verges, best seen from a bicycle – a popular way to travel. Brightly painted half-timbered buildings echo nature's colours; medieval churches and Renaissance castles dot the landscape.

Zealand, in the east, holds the capital, Copenhagen, Scandinavia's liveliest city, and Hamlet's castle, Kronborg at Helsingør (Elsinore), high above the narrow sleeve of water which leads to Sweden. Jutland, in the west, has Denmark's only land border with mainland Europe. The North Jutland seascapes and quality of light have captivated artists over the centuries; west-coast sands stretching as far as the eye can see draw summer holidaymakers. East Jutland has an intricate lake system, fine for canoeing and watersports, and also Århus, Denmark's second city, with an international arts festival in the autumn. Funen, sandwiched between Jutland and Zealand, is called the Garden of Denmark, with Odense, the birthplace of Denmark's most famous writer, Hans Christian Andersen. Far-flung in the Baltic is the island of Bornholm, home to craftspeople and a popular holiday destination.

Copenhagen is the cultural capital, but every town has its museum and every castle its collection, covering subjects as diverse as Viking boats at Roskilde, shipwrecks, sand dunes and Iron-Age bog men in Jutland and a wealth of art. The Scandinavian tradition of open-air museums such as Den Gamle By (Old Town) in Århus bring the past to life. Accommodation can be found in friendly Danish inns, palatial manor houses, and a wide range of hotels. Holiday cottages and camping sites abound.

Across the seas lie the Faroe Islands ("Sheep Islands"), a bird-watcher's paradise, while further to the northwest, Greenland is attracting the adventure traveller with its hiking routes, dog-sledding expeditions and coastal cruises. ❑

PRECEDING PAGES: the old architecture of Odense on Funen; Copenhagen's legendary Tivoli Gardens; Legoland's Mount Rushmore Memorial, East Jutland.
LEFT: Tønder in southwest Jutland, once famous as a lace-making centre.

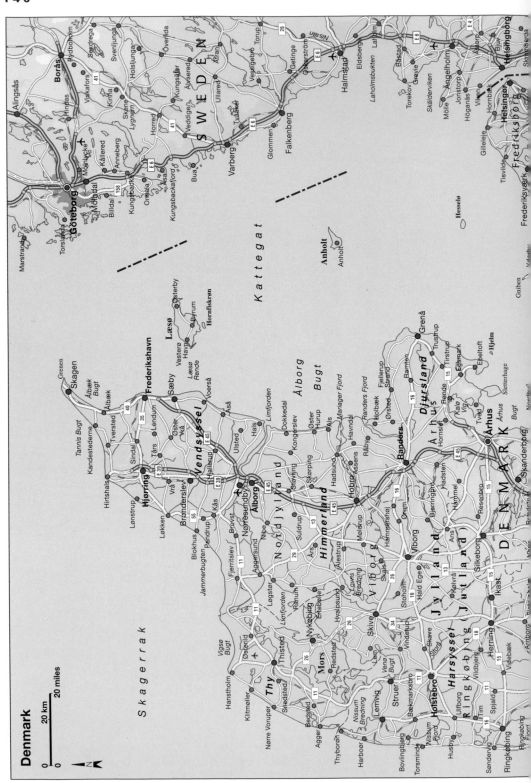

Denmark

0
20 km
0
20 miles

N

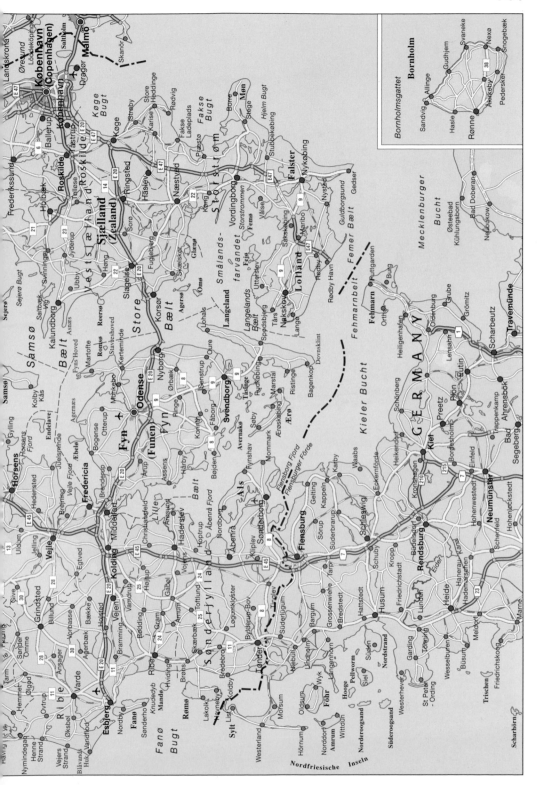

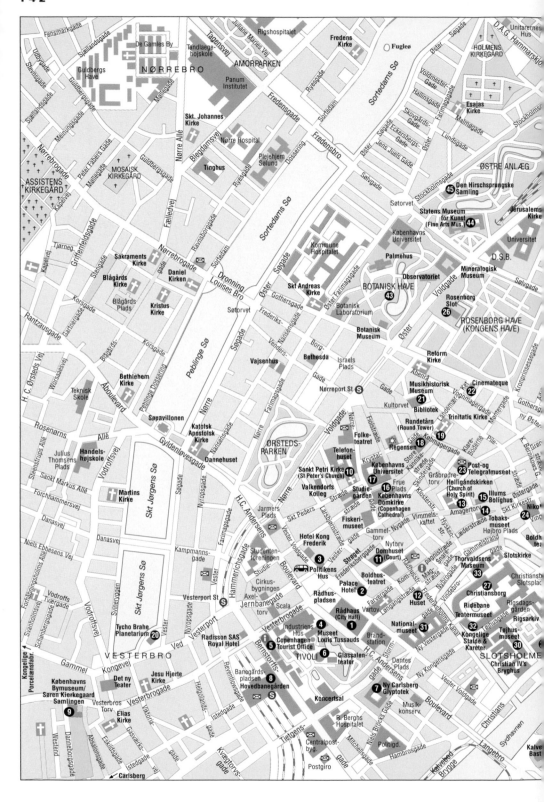

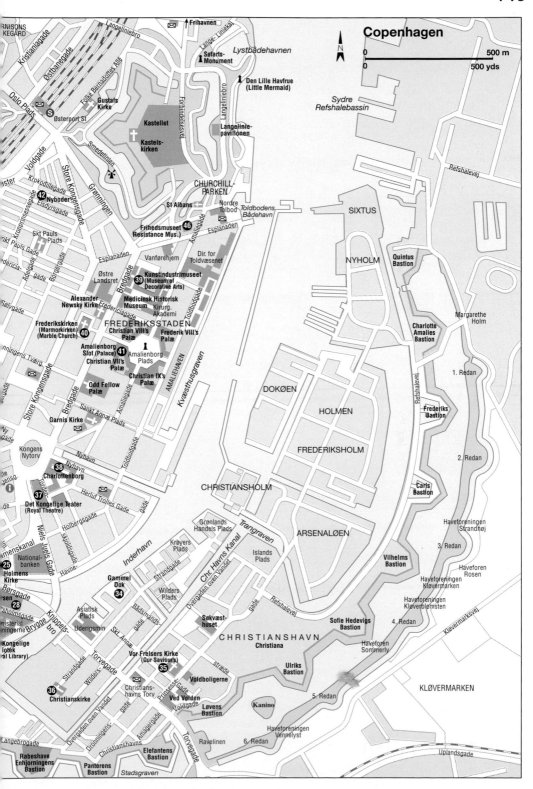

Copenhagen

0 ——— 500 m
0 ——— 500 yds

GARNISONS KEGÅRD

Frihavnen

Langelinie

Lystbådehavnen

Søfarts-Monument

Den Lille Havfrue
(Little Mermaid)

Sydre Refshalebassin

Østbanegade

Oslo Plads

Østerport St

Gustafs Kirke

Folke Bernadottes Allé

Voldgade

Krokodillegade

Store Kongensgade

Grønningen

Kastellet

Kastels-kirken

Langelinie-pavillonen

Refshalevej

42 Nyboder

Elsdyrsgade

CHURCHILL-PARKEN

St Albans

Nordre Toldbod

Toldbodens Bådehavn

SIXTUS

Skt Pauls Plads

Skt Pauls Gade

Adelgade

Borgergade

Frihedsmuseet 46
(Resistance Mus.)

Esplanaden

NYHOLM

Quintus Bastion

Sølvgade

Esplanaden

Vanførehjem

Dir. for Toldvæsenet

Østre Landsret

Kunstindustrimuseet 39
(Museum of Decorative Arts)

Margarethe Holm

Alexander Newsky Kirke

Medicinsk Historisk Museum

Kirurg. Akademi

Charlotte Amalies Bastion

Frederikskirken
(Marmorkirken)
(Marble Church) 40

FREDERIKSSTADEN

Christian VIII's Palæ

Frederik VIII's Palæ

1. Redan

Amalienborg Slot (Palace) 41

Amalienborg Plads

Frederiks Bastion

Christian VII's Palæ

Christian IX's Palæ

Odd Fellow Palæ

Garnis Kirke

Sankt Annæ Plads

2. Redan

Kongens Nytorv

Nyhavn

38

Charlottenborg

Carls Bastion

37

Det Kongelige Teater
(Royal Theatre)

Herluf Trolles Gade

CHRISTIANSHOLM

Haveforeningen Strandhøj

Holbergsgade

Grønlands Handels Plads

Trangraven

ARSENALØEN

3. Redan

Inderhavn

Kroyers Plads

Islands Plads

Vilhelms Bastion

Haveforen Rosen

National-banken 25

Holmens Kirke

Gammel Dok 34

Wilders Plads

Chr. Havns Kanal

Haveforeningen Kløvermarken

Børsgade

28

Asiatisk Plads

Bådsmands-gade

Overgaden oven Vandet

Refshalevej

Haveforeningen Kløverblomsten

Kongelige jotek (al Library)

Uderigsmin

Skt Annæ

Søkvæst-huset

Sofie Hedevigs Bastion

4. Redan

CHRISTIANSHAVN

Christiana

Haveforen Sommerly

Vor Frelsers Kirke
(Our Saviour's) 35

Ulriks Bastion

36

Christianskirke

Christians-havns Torv

Voldboligerne

Ved Volden

Løvens Bastion

Kanino

5. Redan

KLØVERMARKEN

Rabeshave Enhjorningens Bastion

Panterens Bastion

Elefantens Bastion

Ravelinen

6. Redan

Haveforeningen Vennelyst

Uplandsgade

Langebrogade

Stadsgraven

COPENHAGEN

Denmark's capital city is the liveliest and most informal in Scandinavia. Enjoy the cultural sights and chic shops of the old streets by day and the buzz of the city by night

Map on pages 142–43

Copenhagen (København) is the liveliest – and many claim the most fetching – of the Scandinavian capitals, with things to see and do all the time. When Denmark briefly ruled all Scandinavia, the city was the capital of three countries. Now with a bridge and tunnel link across the sound to Sweden, this is the Øresund region's cosmopolitan hub.

With Europe's longest pedestrian mall, she is also a "walking city," the first capital to offer the pleasures of ambling down a link of streets free of motor vehicles and exhaust fumes. And the casual pace of crowds strolling on Strøget suggests a carefree and relaxed lifestyle. Toddlers in pushchairs, young people, old people, students gathering to enjoy a beer or watch a street musician – all seem happy in their surroundings.

"Their exuberance is evident in the striking new architecture of the city's museums," reported the *New York Times*, "and the surprises begin as soon as you arrive: at Copenhagen Airport, the dramatic new steel-and-glass Terminal 3 is covered by... a delta-shaped glass roof. Trains whisk passengers into the city, a six-mile trip, in 12 minutes... and from July 2000, they'll run to Malmö, Sweden, in 35 minutes."

PRECEDING PAGES: Christiansborg, a Copenhagen landmark. **LEFT:** streamers flutter over Rådhus. **BELOW:** the Little Mermaid.

Explore by canal boat

A good way to get a first feel of Copenhagen is from the water. Take one of the 50-minute canal boat trips that leave from Gammel Strand every 30 minutes after 10am (Apr 1–late Oct; tel: 33 13 31 05). Or, if you're the adventuresome type, explore the waterways in a kayak for two hours, starting at the same place. A guide paddles ahead of you (Copenhagen Adventure Tours, tel: 40 50 40 06). You'll be surrounded by the city: wharfs and warehouses, some now converted to exposed-beam hotels; the new waterfront "Black Diamond" annexe of the Kongelige Bibliotek (Royal Library); the Royal Palace, Amalienborg, set in a cobblestone square where the noon-time Changing of the Guard is as it always was; Gammel Dok architecture centre; quays with the ferries to Malmö in Sweden and the overnight ship to Oslo; Holmen, the Royal Danish Navy base; Vor Frelsers Kirke (Our Saviour's Church) with its curious outside spiral staircase. And that modest little rock-top waterfront icon with a tendency to lose her head: the Little Mermaid, north of Churchillparken.

Copenhagen is always the "city of green spires". Copper plates, etched green by salt air, clad the spires of castles and churches like Vor Frelsers in the old city, and tower over the medieval street network and newer houses. The Old Town you visit today would have looked different but for two devastating fires

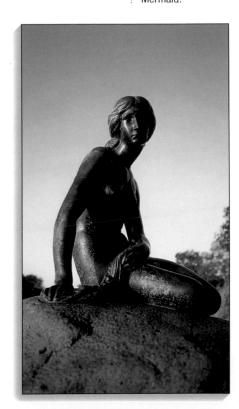

and a terrible bombardment. Blazes, in 1728 and 1795, licked and leaped along the straw-roofed houses and turned most of the half-timbered medieval town to ashes. Only a few solidly-built structures survived. Helligånds Kirken (Church of the Holy Ghost), Skt Petri Kirke, the Rundetårn (Round Tower) and Nikolai Kirke (now a centre for exhibitions of Danish and international contemporary art) still stand proudly. When Admiral Lord Nelson and the British fleet bombarded Copenhagen in 1807 the toll was also heavy. The old Copenhagen Cathedral fell victim.

After these catastrophes, laws were passed ensuring that houses built on the burnt-out spaces be made of brick or stone and have hard roofing. No more half-timbered dwellings with thatched roofs to trap sparks. So most city centre buildings today are baroque or neoclassical.

Historic trading post

Before 1167, Copenhagen was just a trading post called Havn (Harbour), which gave fairly easy access to Skåne (Scania) across the Øresund. Skåne is now part of Sweden. But in those days southern Sweden was part of Denmark, and the village of Havn enjoyed a position in the middle of the kingdom. As wars and unrest changed the geography of Denmark over the centuries, København (Merchant's Harbour) gradually moved to its point on the eastern shore of Zealand (Sjælland) , the country's main island.

In 1167, King Valdemar I commanded the local bishop, Absalon of Roskilde, to fortify Havn in order to protect it against Wendic pirates. Absalon built a fortress on the spot where the Parliament building now looms across the canal from Højbro Plads (Square), where his statue now presides. Copenhagen was on

"And I hiked around Copenhagen, along earthworks and remains of moats and along the pier where cruise ships tie up, to the statue of the Little Mermaid... looking small and forlorn, and beyond to the magnificent fountain of Gefion..."

— GARRISON KEILLOR

NATIONAL GEOGRAPHIC

BELOW: the castle of Frederiksborg, which now houses the National History Museum.

the way to becoming Denmark's biggest and most important town. The fortress became Christiansborg, *borg* meaning castle. Centuries later, it remains the seat of Danish politics, housing the single-chamber Folketing (Parliament).

During the long and fruitful reign of Denmark's most famous king, Christian IV (1588–1648), Copenhagen solidified its role as the country's seat of power. This many-talented monarch and visionary town planner built Børsen, said to be the oldest Stock Exchange in Europe, a stunning Renaissance red brick structure with a spire of four entwined dragons (Christian loved dragons), steep copper roofs, tiny windows and gables galore.

The most imposing of all Christian's works, Rundetårn (Round Tower), was planned by the king as an observatory, where you hike up a wide spiral ramp to the roof, stopping at exhibitions en-route, and finally enjoying a panorama of Old Copenhagen. Imagine what Good King Christian would have thought of the Tycho Brahe Planetarium and Space Theatre, with its permanent exhibition and hourly Omnimax films. Christian's palaces include Rosenborg, which houses the crown jewels.

At various times the Swedes, British and Germans all tried to conquer Copenhagen. The Germans occupied the country during World War II, but they never subdued it. The Swedes came close, in 1658. The Swedish army had taken almost all of Denmark. Arriving in Copenhagen, the enemy was confronted by King Frederik III and his townsfolk on the ramparts. Men, women and children used every means at their disposal, including boiling pitch, to scare off the Swedes. The king's advisers suggested he flee with the royal family. But seeing those Copenhageners on the battlements, His Majesty allegedly retorted: "I will die in my nest!" No need for that; the Swedes recognised greater will, if not superior force, and they backed off.

Copenhagen has many times outgrown the cramped space within its abandoned medieval fortifications. The capital now houses more than a quarter of the Danish population. This is the main reason for Copenhagen's sovereign dominance of the country. No other Danish city carries the same political, economic, social or cultural clout.

City Hall Square

Rådhuspladsen (**City Hall Square**) is the nexus of Copenhagen. Rådhuset (City Hall), on the southeastern side, is the administrative and political heart of the city, and the streets around the square form a central traffic hub. Here are connections to the airport, and prime arteries to the suburbs. Many bus routes converge on the square, and it's only a short walk to Hovedbanegården (Central Railway Station). Rådhuspladsen is also the spot from which any signpost or milestone in the country measures its distance to the capital, and most streets in the city have their lowest house numbers at the end closest to the square.

The square was not always at the centre of things. A little over a century ago, this site was actually outside the town gates, one of which was at the top of Strøget, the main chain of pedestrian streets. Until the 1850s the square was Halmtorvet, the haymarket, which had to be kept away from the narrow town

Map on pages 142–43

Discount punch cards for travel on buses and trains are available for 10 journeys.

BELOW: guarding Amalienborg Palace, the Queen's residence.

TIP

The Copenhagen Card offers unlimited travel on buses and trains, and admission to 60-plus top museums and sights. Cards valid for 24, 48 and 72 hours, with a brochure, can be bought from the Tourist Office, railway stations, hotels and travel bureaus.

BELOW: Bishop Absalon's statue, Rådhuspladsen.
RIGHT: out and about in the city.

streets because of the space it took, as well as the mess and fire hazard it posed. Rådhuspladsen was established as the site of the City Hall in 1900, and designed with the shell-shaped *piazza* of the Italian town of Siena as its model. Shortly after it was finished, however, the shell shape was sacrificed on the altar of burgeoning traffic; the trams in particular needed space for their platforms and rails. Now it's buses, and a bus terminal has been opened at the northern perimeter, restoring some of the original charm of this showcase square.

Rådhus ❶, the City Hall itself, may look old, but it's one of the city's newer architectural wonders (open 9.30am–3pm, free; tours in English, 3pm, for a fee; tel: 33 66 25 82). The building was designed by architect Martin Nyrop, built in traditional red brick and finished in 1905. Constructed in the national romantic style, its inspiration was drawn from medieval Danish and Norwegian architecture with a touch of the *palazzo* style of northern Italy. The façade and interior are trimmed with historic details from Nordic mythology. Above the main entrance you'll notice a relief depicting Bishop Absalon. Can you spot the polar bears above, to his left and right? A tip of the icecap to Greenland, once "Arctic Denmark", today a self-governing protectorate.

Inside the foyer, look for the entrance to **Jens Olsen's World Clock** (open 10am–4pm; entrance fee). The clock's more than 14,000 parts function in some 570,000 different ways. Its star dial mechanism shows the path of the pole star in resettable periods, making it the world's slowest moving designed mechanism, and the "most accurate and complicated clock in the world", according to the *Guinness Book of World Records*. Driven by hanging weights and crank motors, this marvel of astromechanics should lose just four-tenths of one second in 300 years. The clock shows time around the world, positions of

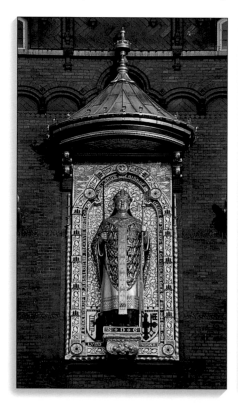

the planets, and the Gregorian calendar. The foyer also features a limestone relief of important townsmen, and a fresco portrays the first town council.

Looking for a bird's eye view? The 105-metre (346-ft) tower is for you (open daily; entrance fee). An elevator lifts you high above the city and into its tallest tower. On a clear day you can see some 50 km (30 miles) in all directions, across the sound to Sweden to the east and all the way north to Elsinore.

Endearing statues

Outside City Hall find the seated statue of Denmark's best-loved fairy-tale writer and poet, Hans Christian Andersen. Children love to crawl up in his lap and touch his top hat. The nearby dragon fountain was designed by Danish artist Joakim Skovgård and turned on in 1934. On the opposite (northwest) side of the square is a modest statue of a Danish soldier, commemorating the 1864 war against Germany in which the Danes suffered many casualties and lost the southern part of the Jutland peninsula, adjoining Germany. On the main street, **Vester Voldgade** (Western Wall Street), at the northeast corner of the square, look up to a pillar supporting a bronze statue of two Bronze Age lur players, whom the artist confused with the Vikings.

Also on Vester Voldgade are two of Copenhagen's fine traditional hotels. Closest to City Hall is the **Palace Hotel** ❷, one of the few buildings in the Jugendstil, and further north, past the square, **Hotel Kong Frederik** with the stylish and pricey Queen's Pub restaurant.

Three of Denmark's major newspapers are housed on Rådhuspladsen: *Politiken* and its tabloid sister, *Ekstra Bladet*, in **Politikens Hus** ❸, and next door, *Aktuelt*. You'll find Copenhagen's largest English-language bookstore,

Map on pages 142–43

When a virgin passes beneath the statue of the lur *players on Rådhuspladsen, it is said that the men blow their horns.*

BELOW: cafés in the square offer the chance for a break.

TIP

Plan ahead: ask the Copenhagen Tourist Office for websites for museums' and galleries' forthcoming attractions (tel:+45 33 11 13 25; fax: +45 33 93 49 69; e-mail: touristinfo@woco.dk; www.woco.dk).

BELOW: the bright lights of Tivoli.

Boghallen, on the street level of Politikens Hus; the kiosks around here sell magazines and newspapers in many languages.

On the western perimeter, on **H.C. Andersens Boulevard**, it's hard to miss a castle-like red brick building nicknamed "Little Rosenborg". There's an entrance to Tivoli Gardens (*see below*) and **Museet Louis Tussaud's** ❹ (open late Apr–mid-Sept 10am–10pm; mid-Sept–late Apr 10am–6pm; entrance fee; tel: 33 11 89 00). Although much smaller than Madame Tussaud's in London, the waxworks museum offers a line up including all the kings and two reigning queens of Denmark (Margrethe I and II) and many other notables, historic and contemporary. There's a Chamber of Horrors in the basement.

The **Copenhagen Tourist Office** ❺ lies across the street from Central Station, at Bernstorffsgade 1, near the corner of Vesterbrogade. This traveller's ganglion has it all: information on sights, cultural activities, transport, eating places, events. A prime source is the free magazine *Copenhagen This Week* (website www.ctw.dk; e-mail ctw@online.pol.dk). You'll find lots more local news and listings in the weekly English-language tabloid newspaper, *The Copenhagen Post*, distributed free by some hotels and sold at Danish State Railway kiosks and Seven-Eleven stores.

Magical Tivoli

Other Scandinavian cities have their pleasure gardens and parks, but Copenhagen has **Tivoli** ❻, which outshines them all. Tivoli's main entrance is on Vesterbrogade (open late Apr–late Sept: Mon–Fri 11 am–midnight; Sat–Sun 11am–1am; also at Christmas; entrance fee; tel: 33 15 10 01; www.tivoli.dk). Tivoli (try spelling it backwards) is a Scandinavian rainbow of gardens, open-air amusements, restaurants, cafés, theatres, an open-air stage and a major concert hall, home of Sjællands Symphony Orchestra. International artists perform here in all seasons (box office, tel: 33 15 10 12).

With 5 million visitors each year, the park is more popular than any other Danish attraction. The site was once part of the fortification and demarcation area surrounding the city, but in 1841 an enterprising journalist, Georg Carstensen, convinced King Christian VIII that if people were well entertained they were less likely to talk politics and sedition.

The king gave him permission to establish a park "to provide the masses with suitable entertainment and fun", with the proviso that he also "remove anything ignoble and degrading". A quick glance at the happy faces watching the fireworks as they whiz across the lake on a summer midnight would seem to prove Carstensen correct in his political theories. That same lake and several of the walks are reminders of the old moats and fortifications. Tivoli is famed for its shady walks under proud old trees, coloured nightlights and the abundance and diversity of the bedding plants, 140,000 of which are replanted every summer.

The youngsters who march and play in the Tivoli Guard (a Royal Guard in miniature) have been favourites with both children and adults ever since the park opened in 1843. For children, the greatest thrills come from the rides, the roller-coasters and

Map on pages 142–43

merry-go-rounds. The outdoor Peacock Theatre presents pantomimes and ballets every day. In recent years the lake has been machine-frozen for winter ice-skating, and the pleasure mecca's portals are thrown open at Christmas time, when there are tempting stalls and gentler rides for wide-eyed *julebørn*.

Tivoli is also the place to enjoy a good meal, coffee and cake, or a drink. The park has more than 20 restaurants, and some of them are among the most stylish and expensive in the city. The tall tubes in front of the "Moorish" palace, close to the Vesterbrogade entrance, contain bubbling water. This is an unusual sculpture designed by the Danish nuclear physicist Niels Bohr. Bohr was inspired by gazing at his aquarium.

Tivoli is highly recommended, but it's wise to take plenty of cash along: the place is not inexpensive.

Dining out

For relaxed refreshment or a stylish dinner, the **Copenhagen Corner Restaurant** on the corner of H. C. Andersen's Boulevard and Vesterbrogade is a good up-market choice. From your table, you get a broad vista of Rådhus-pladsen. Check out a masterpiece of Danish painting – P. S. Krøyer's two women in white strolling on the beach at Skagen, a fishing village on the northern tip of Jutland. Is it a copy? Ask your waiter.

On the same side of the boulevard, past Tivoli, set aside some time for **Ny Carlsberg Glyptotek** ❼ (open Tue–Sun 10am–4pm, closed Mon; entrance fee; Sun and Wed free). This three-building museum offers a fine art collection begun by the brewer Carl Jacobsen and maintained by the New Carlsberg Foundation. There are exquisite collections of ancient Egyptian, Greek, Roman

The Copenhagen Post, *Denmark's English-language weekly newspaper, has features and lists of what's on. Order a free copy to be sent to your home before you leave (tel: +45 33 36 33 00; e-mail info@cphpost. dk; www.cphpost.dk).*

BELOW: Harlequin on stage at Tivoli's Peacock Theatre.

and Etruscan art, as well as some French masterpieces. The conservatory houses displays of modern sculpture, and there are frequent concerts, some in the lush, palm-lined indoor Winter Garden (stop for coffee and pastry). A glazed arcade connects the garden with the new building. Opened in 1996, a century after the original museum, "the chest" now houses the fine collection of French paintings, including Monet, Sisley and Pissarro, and 72 Degas bronze sculptures. When your appetite for art is satisfied, climb the stairs to the 300-sq metre (3,230-sq ft) roof terrace paved with pale granite. Treat your eyes to this roof landscape and the spires and towers of Copenhagen.

The New Danish Design Centre, 27–29 H.C. Andersens Boulevard, is a showcase for arts and crafts. After dark, interior lighting turns it into a glowing diamond.

Doing business

The street leading out of the western side of Rådhuspladsen is **Vesterbrogade**, and adjoining the square is Copenhagen's central business and entertainment district. Walk down the street, away from City Hall, and past the entrance to Tivoli, towards one of the city's few high-rise buildings, the 22-storey **Radisson SAS Royal Hotel**, designed by the Danish architect Arne Jacobsen.

Across the street from the hotel is **Hovedbanegården (Central Railway Station) ❽**, which is also the terminal for the shuttle bus service to the airport. Dating from 1912, the now renovated station offers one of the few service centres for young inter-railers in Europe. Here they can rest, take a shower, and stow their backpacks safely. There are many shops, banks, fair-to-good restaurants, a post office and information service. When people agree to meet "under the clock", they mean the big one inside the main hall of the station.

Out in the middle of Vesterbrogade, in front of the station, stands an obelisk called **Frihedsstøtten (Pillar of Freedom)**, commemorating the liberation of

BELOW: taking a rest during Copenhagen's riotous carnival.

Denmark's peasants. The feudal system was abolished more than 200 years ago in favour of free, smallhold farmers. The obelisk was conceived by the artist Nikolaj Abildgård in 1792.

The major international airlines and travel agencies are situated in this area, as are several cinemas. At **Axeltorv (Axel Square)** you can hardly miss the pink, orange, blue and violet **Palads Theatre**, with nine cinemas and a disco popular among teenagers. Copenhagen cinemas show foreign features in their original-language versions, with Danish subtitles – not with foreign voices dubbed in. Close to the Palads look for the domed **Cirkusbygningen (Circus)**. One of the few permanent circus buildings anywhere, for well over a century it's been home to the venerable Benneweis clan, and books leading European clowns and acts (tel: BilletNet 70 15 65 65).

The iron and brick sculpture on Axeltorv is the work (1987) of native son Robert Jacobsen, and marks the square's transition to a cobbled pedestrian area. Across the street lies **Scala**, a newer multi-storey shopping centre and entertainment complex, with more restaurants of varying quality.

Cultural mix

Behind Central Station lies **Vesterbro (Westbridge)**, one of Copenhagen's old residential districts, today a blue-collar community. The dominant street, **Istedgade**, used to be a red-light district and is still a bit shabby (but that, too, is changing). With its cheaper tourist hotels, the street still has some porn shops and prostitutes. Copenhagen as a whole may be safe to walk in at any time of night, but this is a sleazier part of town. Istedgade and its side streets are a drug hub, and junkies do hang out here. Be careful, especially after dark. That said,

Map on pages 142–43

TIP

Borrow a bike: there are two-wheelers tethered at 120 outdoor "corrals" around town. Put a coin in the slot and take a bike. Return it to any rack, lock it and get your coin back.

BELOW: a plethora of badges.

TIP

Have tea or coffee overlooking Strøget, the main pedestrian street, at Fogtdals Fotocafé, Østergade 22, and see a striking photography exhibition. Ask for a window table.

Vesterbro is a vibrant area, with thousands of southern European, Middle Eastern and Asian immigrants mixed with a Danish working-class population.

Many students have also discovered the charms of this lower-rent neighbourhood. It's a fetching blend of old-fashioned food and clothing stores and shops filled with the exotic scents of unusual fruits, vegetables and spices, run by immigrants. The area offers a number of good ethnic restaurants, such as **Shezan**, Victoriagade 22 (tel: 31 24 78 88), Copenhagen's first Pakistani restaurant where, over the years, prices have stayed reasonable.

Københavns Bymuseum & Søren Kierkegaard Samlingen ❾ – the Copenhagen City Museum – offers an historical and ethnological showcase for the works of Denmark's pioneer existential philosopher, Søren Kierkegaard (Vesterbrogade 59; tel: 33 21 07 72; open May–Sept: 10am–4pm, closed Tue; Oct–Apr: 1–4pm, closed Tue; entrance fee, free Fri). Also, there's a slide show picturing 1000 years of the city's history. Take a long look at the ceramic scale model of old Copenhagen, out front. Just south of the museum, **Absalonsgade** has been turned into a museum street, with original cobblestone pavements and old street lamps. Keep exploring before you walk back to the city centre – there's always something going on in Vesterbro.

The medieval city

If Rådhuspladsen is the heart of Copenhagen, then **Strøget**, the 1.6-km (1-mile) pedestrian shopping street, is the spine. It has endless shops, small and large, street vendors and buskers galore, workshops, cellar galleries and Illums Bolighus, the department store that showcases superb Danish and international design, and usually has a special exhibition on the ground floor. Strøget is where

BELOW: see the sights by bike.

Copenhageners and visitors alike go to shop or just to promenade and look at window displays. All year round, street musicians play classical, rock, jazz and exotic folk tunes, attracting crowds of listeners.

Starting at Rådhuspladsen, Strøget meanders through five streets and four squares before it runs into Kongens Nytorv, the largest square in the old town. At the southwestern end, closest to Rådhuspladsen, are **Frederiksberggade** and **Nygade**, the more lively part of Strøget, with many small clothing and record shops, and snack and burger bars. Nygade leads to a large open area made up of two squares, Gammeltorv and Nytorv (the Old and the New Square). Before the great fires of the 18th century, a block of houses separated the two, but new fire regulations required more space between buildings and the houses were never rebuilt.

Gammeltorv, Copenhagen's oldest marketplace, dates back to the Middle Ages, when it was the scene of jousting tournaments. Peep inside the gate of No. 14 to see a relief depicting the history of the square. The old village pond once lay where No. 10 stands today, and a plaque commemorates Havn, the original town. The **Caritas Fountain** in the centre dates from 1608; it was donated to the town by King Christian IV, who thought it would make a proper contribution to the water supply, as well as the beauty of Copenhagen. On festive occasions golden apples placed on the jets dance on the water, much to the delight of the watching children. Two of old Copenhagen's main streets lead from Gammeltorv: Nørregade goes north and, as its name suggests, Vestergade leads west.

Vestergade was the village street in the Middle Ages, before Copenhagen began to grow. The rows of neo-classical houses in Vestergade are the best example of the rebuilt city that followed the fire in 1795, and old merchants' houses stand behind several of the gates. Hans Christian Andersen lived in No. 19 when, as a young man, he first arrived in Copenhagen from Odense.

The area behind Vestergade is one of the few remaining residential areas in the inner city. Living in the picturesque old houses is a mixture of old-time Copenhageners, artists and students, and here you find some of the more exotic clothing shops. There are squares and side streets with quiet old courtyards made beautiful by plants and garden furniture. People love to sit outside when the evenings are long. Under the trees, Copenhageners at pavement cafés talk, laugh and munch Danish pastries – called *wienerbrød* (Viennese bread) in Denmark – with coffee, beer and sometimes *akvavit*.

Sankt Petri Kirke (St Peter's Church) ⓾, on the corner of Nørregade and Skt Pederstræde, dates back to the time of the Hanseatic League and is the oldest church in Copenhagen. The Chancelry towards Nørregade was built in 1450 in Gothic style. Though first used as a Catholic Church, it was converted into a cannon foundry when the Reformation came to Denmark in 1536. The church was reconsecrated in 1585, and today serves a German Lutheran congregation.

Walk back to **Nytorv**, where Copenhagen's first town hall, Domhuset, was situated. In 1805 the present large, rose-coloured building with columns replaced the old town hall, which was destroyed in the fire 10 years earlier. Like most

Map
on pages
142–43

Buskers are a familiar sight on Strøget, the city's main shopping street.

BELOW: Kultorvet on a summer's day.

Most public phones don't take coins. Buy a "Telekort" card at kiosks, hotels and TeleDanmark stores.

buildings on Nytorv, it was built in the neo-classical style prevalent during the rebuilding, and designed by one of Denmark's leading architects, C. F. Hansen. The buildings behind and to its left were formerly used as a debtors' prison. When the present City Hall at Rådhuspladsen opened, the old structure became the seat of the **Domhuset (Copenhagen City Court)** ⓫.

A mob of 10,000 citizens demonstrated against absolute monarchy in front of the Domhuset on Nytorv in 1848. King Frederik VII wisely saw the necessity for change, and his acceptance of a constitutional monarchy in the same year allowed Denmark to avoid the revolutionary bloodshed which most other European nations suffered.

Søren Kierkegaard, the 19th-century philosopher, lived in the house on the corner of Nytorv and Frederiksberggade. Walk along Rådhusstræde (leading to the southeast from Nytorv) to the little square, Vandkunsten, on the right-hand side, and Magstræde with the youth centre **Huset** ⓬, a reminder of the 1960s, on the left. At the end of that decade, hippies and squatters occupied Huset and demanded a place of their own for various activities. The city, which owned the run-down building, agreed to establish a cultural centre, and Huset is still frequented by young people of all ages. It contains several bars with different kinds of music, from rock to jazz, a good and relatively inexpensive restaurant, a video art centre, a gallery and a cinema.

In the same building, but around the corner from Magstræde, is **Use-It**, a publicly-run information centre for young travellers.

Farvergade, **Kompagnistræde** and **Læderstræde** are, in fact, one uninterrupted pedestrian street with the three names in sequence. They run just southwest of, and parallel to, Strøget, and are lined with shops dealing in oriental

BELOW: musicians greet visitors to the Royal Danish Porcelain building.

rugs, antique furniture, silverware, china and curios. The prices aren't exactly low, but on a good day it's still possible to find a fair deal.

Apart from these three streets, the whole of this immediate neighbourhood is the place to find interesting gifts – whether art prints and posters or silver, pewter and china. Danish-made products are almost always good value, and you can find inexpensive presents such as hand-made glass spheres which hang inside a window to reflect the light and catch a breeze, lovely table decorations and long-lasting candles, which Scandinavians light to welcome guests.

Cobblestone streets

With their cobblestones and old houses, **Magstræde** and its extension, **Snaregade**, are among the most enchanting in Copenhagen. Although most of the white-painted houses date back to the second fire at the end of the 18th century, Magstræde contains two original 16th-century Renaissance houses (No. 17 and 19) which survived the flames. The Italian composer Giuseppe Sarti lived in No. 10 until he had to leave Denmark in 1775 because of overwhelming debts.

From Nytorv, continue along Strøget on **Vimmelskaftet** toward Amagertorv. On the left side of Vimmelskaftet is a narrow alleyway, Jorcks Passage, which leads to Skindergade, and Fiolstræde, another pedestrian street. **Amagertorv**, the widest part of Strøget, has lots of street musicians.

Helligåndskirken (Church of the Holy Spirit) ⓭, which stands on the north side, dates from the 14th century and was originally a monastery and hospital. The church and tower which still remain are from the late Renaissance and show a strong baroque influence. While the nave is almost unadorned – as

Map on pages 142–43

At the famous Carlsberg Brewery, Ny Carlsbergvej, visitors can witness the whole process of brewing, ending with a glass of the best (tours Mon–Fri 11am and 2pm).

BELOW: the founder of Carlsberg, and also his wife, are immortalised on the brewery building.

THE WALK OF THE TOWN

On your feet is the best way to discover this old town of narrow streets and cobbled courtyards. The "Crosstown Copenhagen Tour" starts outside the Tourist Information Office on Bernstorffsgade, across from Central Station (May–Sept: Tue and Fri 10.30am).

Led by the indefatigable Richard, the first stop is Rådhuspladsen, where the western wall came down in the 1850s to let the city expand. "Also," says Richard, "it was dirty and terribly crowded inside." He sets off along streets following the curve of the canal which once extended to Strøget – now Europe's longest pedestrian mall – pausing at the City Court House, profiled like a Greek temple. By the canal a buxom woman serves fishcakes. Over Amagertorv looms a Dutch Renaissance building from 1616, the mayor's residence taken over in 1911 by Royal Copenhagen Porcelain works. Today, side by side, are Royal Copenhagen, Georg Jensen silver, Holmegaard glass, and Illum's Bolighus with Danish gifts and furnishings. Then there's the Royal Theatre and the elegant Hotel D'Angleterre, where Victor Borge stays. And Nyhavn, where you can take a canal tour. What's this – Amalienborg Palace? Just in time for the noon-time changing of the guard. Have two hours really passed?

Ottilia Jacobsen

Visit the Royal
Copenhagen Porcelain
factory at Smallegade
37, Frederiksberg, just
a 10-minute walk
from the city-centre
store. It's a fascinating
half-day, and a chance
to buy good pieces
and seconds (tours:
Mon–Fri 9, 10, 11am,
1, 2pm; entrance fee;
tel: 31 86 48 59).

BELOW: taking
advantage of a
sunny spot.

required by the Reformation – the portal is sumptuously baroque. The oldest part, the wing towards Valkendorfsgade, which was the old hospital, is medieval. It is now used for book fairs, exhibitions and charity functions. A monument to the Danes who died in concentration camps during World War II stands at the churchyard gate nearest Strøget. It was designed by Kaare Klint, the furniture designer.

For tobacco aficionados, Amagertorv 9 is one of those rare places you find where you least expect it. W.Ø. Larsen is a smokers' emporium and houses the **Tobaksmuseet (Tobacco Museum)** ⓮, with its display of ancient pipes, tobaccos and smoking history (open Mon–Thu 10am–6pm, Fri 10am–7pm, Sat 10am–5pm; free; tel: 33 12 20 50). The opposite side of Amagertorv is occupied by the shops most often visited by tourists: **Illums Bolighus** ⓯ (modern design), and the flagship stores of **Royal Copenhagen Porcelain** and **Georg Jensen** silver.

Back on Strøget, the Stork Fountain in Amagertorv is the most popular in Copenhagen and the place where hippies gathered in the early 1970s. Before 1850, Amagertorv was the main traffic junction where streets from the city's four gates met. To the north is **Købmagergade** – yet another pedestrian shopping street – and to the south, **Højbro Plads**, with the equestrian statue of Bishop Absalon, Copenhagen's founder standing proud. Look past Absalon and see the canal which surrounds Christiansborg, the seat of the Danish Parliament.

Latin Quarter

The area north of Vimmelskaftet and Amagertorv is the old **Latin Quarter**, where the University of Copenhagen has its main building. The Latin Quarter is bordered on its other sides by Nørregade, Nørre Voldgade and Købmagergade,

and is a great place to go for a cosy dinner and a drink on a night out. The university has long since outgrown its space in the city centre, and moved the Faculties of Medicine, Science and Humanities to the other side of town. The Law School and a few other departments are still scattered around the area.

Centrally placed in the Quarter is **Gråbrødretorv (Greyfriar's Square)**, which can be reached from Strøget by walking past the west side of Helligåndskirken and through the picturesque narrow passage at the corner where Valkendorfsgade turns to the right. The cobblestone square is one of the most beautiful in town and a popular place to enjoy a summer evening meal or drink. The buildings surrounding it are baroque houses in bright colours, built after the first fire of 1728. Some 40 percent of the town was destroyed in the flames, with 74 streets and more than 1,670 houses ruined.

Leave Gråbrødretorv by way of Lille Kannikestræde and turn left at Store Kannikestræde (Little and Big Canon Streets) to **Københavns Domkirke (Copenhagen Cathedral)** ⑯ on the left. The original cathedral was destroyed in the 1728 fire and its replacement was hit by an English incendiary bomb during the siege and bombardment of 1807. The current structure is from 1829, designed by C. F. Hansen in neo-classical style and inspired by the Basilica in Rome. Inside the church are statues by the sculptor Bertel Thorvaldsen.

Many of the city's museums admit children for free.

Immediately north of the cathedral is the main building of the **Københavns Universitet (University of Copenhagen)** ⑰, founded in 1479. The seat of the University Board, beside Nørregade, dates from 1420 and is the oldest building in Copenhagen, while the Commons building (Kommunitetet), also on Nørregade, was at one time used as a dormitory for students and professors and dates from 1731. On the right side of the University, alongside Fiolstræde, is the

BELOW: the historic Round Tower and Observatory.

University Library. In an exhibition on the first floor, you can see the book *Defensor Pacis* (Defence for Peace), pierced by a cannon ball in 1807.

Fiolstræde is known for its antiquarian bookshops, and **Krystalgade** is the site of Copenhagen's **synagogue**. On the corner of Krystalgade and Købmagergade is **Regensen ⑱**, the oldest of the student dormitories. Regensen was founded in 1623 by King Christian IV, but only the wing facing Store Kannikestræde is original. The rest dates from 1731, having been rebuilt after the fire of 1728. The arcade in Købmagergade was established in 1909.

From antiquity to modern hardcore, the love-life of Homo sapiens is told in a tasteful setting at the Museum Erotica, Købmagergade 24 (open May–Sep 10am–11pm; Oct–Apr 10am–8pm; entrance fee).

City landmark

Across from Regensen is one of Copenhagen's most fascinating buildings. The **Rundetårn (Round Tower) ⑲** was built in 1642 as an observatory for Denmark's world-renowned astronomer, Tycho Brahe. It still has a viewing platform on the top which offers a breathtaking panorama on clear days and nights (open Sept–May: 10am–5pm; Jun–Aug: 10am–8pm; observatory mid-Oct–mid-Mar: Tue, Wed, 7–10pm; entrance fee; tel: 33 73 03 73).

The tower stands 36 metres (111 ft) high, and to reach the roof one walks up a 200-metre (620-ft) spiral ramp. The ramp won international fame in 1716 when Tsar Peter the Great rode a horse to the top; the Tsarina Catherine was driven up in a carriage. While Rundetårnet is mainly an observatory, it also serves as a tower for the attached **Trinitatis Kirke**. Built in Nordic Gothic style in 1656 for students, the church has an exquisite baroque altarpiece, made in 1731 by Friedrich Ehbisch, and a fine 1757 Rococo clock above the pulpit.

BELOW: Tycho Brahe Planetarium, for a journey through space.

One of the city's novelties, the **Tycho Brahe Planetarium ⑳**, at Gammel Kongevej 10 in the southwest of the city, near Sankt Jørgen's Lake, also

commemorates the astronomer (open Tue–Thu 9.45am–9pm, Fri–Mon 10.30am–9pm; entrance fee; tel: 33 12 12 24). Its space theatre has Omnimax film performances which fill the huge dome with pictures so that the audience, in reclining seats, travels through the stars or moves deep under water.

Another 70 metres (230 ft) up Købmagergade away from Strøget is **Kultorvet** (Coal Square), with Copenhagen's main municipal library. The small street **Åbenrå**, with its restored 18th-century houses, is just behind the library. No. 30 houses the **Musikhistorisk Museum (Museum of Music History)** ㉑ and its collection of European musical instruments from as early as the 11th century (open 1–3.50pm; May–Sept: closed Thu; Oct–Apr: closed Tue, Thu, Fri; entrance fee; tel: 33 11 27 26).

From Åbenrå, turn north to Gothersgade. No. 55 is the Danish Film Institute, home of **Cinemateque** ㉒, which celebrates Denmark's trailblazing successes in cinematography, and every month has a new programme of international and Danish films (performances: Tue–Sun 9.30am–10pm, closed Mon; tel: 33 74 34 12). Return to the Rundetårn, and opposite, in Store Kannikestræde, is one of Copenhagen's finest old houses: **Admiral Gjeddes Gård** at No. 10 has retained its half-timbered oak walls, for which trees were felled on the site in 1567. No. 12 is another old students' dormitory, **Borchs Kollegium**, and No. 11, with a picturesque yard and garden, was a professor's residence from 1750.

On the corner of Købmagergade and Valkendorffsgade is one of the city's main post offices, housed in a fine baroque palace. The **Post-og Telegrafmuseet (Post and Telecommunications Museum)** ㉓ is at Købmagergade 37.

The last section of Strøget, from Købmagergade to Kongens Nytorv, is the home of the exclusive and expensive: fashion shops, furriers, jewellers and

Map on pages 142–43

Copenhagen's bus network is extensive and one of the easiest ways to get around.

BELOW: Kongens Have, a peaceful spot in a busy city.

TIP

Catch the latest in Danish cinema at Filmhuset, a smart complex at Gothersgade 55, run by the Danish Film Institute. You can call up a list of titles and release dates at www.dfi.dk.

Copenhagen's two main department stores, **Illum** at the corner of Købmagergade and Strøget, and **Magasin du Nord**, across the small square on Bremerholm. **Østergade**'s reputation as the street with the best shops for women's fashions dates back several centuries, and the street was also the first in the country to feature "panorama" shop windows, around 1828.

Behind Østergade, on the right-hand side, is **Nikolaj** 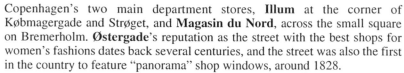, named after the patron saint of sailors. The tower from 1591 is in Dutch Renaissance style while the church itself was built in 1917. It is no longer consecrated as a church, but is owned by the City of Copenhagen and used as an art gallery for Danish and international exhibitions.

The area behind Nikolaj, bordering the canal, has quiet cobblestone streets and well-preserved houses from the end of the 18th century. **Holmens Kirke** 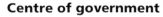, beside the Danish National Bank on Holmens Kanal, was built in 1619 and is the Royal Chapel and Naval Church. The modern **Nationalbanken** (National Bank), covered with marble from Greenland, was designed by Arne Jacobsen and erected in the 1970s.

The area on the other side of Østergade has been restored over the past 30 years and is now a small, exclusive shopping area and the place to find many of the city's popular cafés. Passing through picturesque **Pistolstræde**, with its restored houses, one comes out at **Grønnegade**, which has several pre-18th-century houses. It was once the slum of Copenhagen, but has been refurbished. **Gothersgade**, at the end of Grønnegade, marks the boundary of Copenhagen's medieval area. The area beyond Gothersgade was developed in 1647 when the town was extended north with land still known as New Copenhagen.

Heading northwest, the **Reform Kirke (Reformed Church)** at No. 111 is a fine baroque building, built in 1688 with red brick from Holland. It was consecrated to serve a Calvinist congregation from Germany, France and Holland and, even today, has services in French and German.

Across from the Church, **Kongens Have** (King's Garden) has been a favourite with Copenhageners for centuries. With its tall old trees, statues, shadowy walks and grassy lawns, the park constitutes an important "breathing space" in the densely packed city. It's a fine place to go for a picnic, or to relax away from the noise of town.

Rosenborg Slot , in the eastern corner of Kongens Have at Øster Voldgade 4A, is also one of Copenhagen's most attractive sights. King Christian IV's exquisite palace in Dutch Renaissance style is now a museum, and contains three centuries-worth of royal treasures, as well as the crown jewels (open May–Sept: 10am–4pm; Oct: 11am–3pm; Nov–Apr: 11am–2pm, closed Mon; entrance fee; 33 15 32 86).

BELOW: Rosenborg Slot, a Dutch Renaissance masterpiece.

Centre of government

Slotsholmen (Castle Island), surrounded by canals, is the seat of the Danish Parliament and government ministries. The imposing **Christiansborg** ㉗ (Palace), built on the same spot as the original old castle of Copenhagen, contains Parliament, the Prime Minister's office, the Supreme Court and the Royal Reception Chambers. The public may join free conducted tours of the **Folketinget (House of Parliament)**, and the Royal Reception Chambers (tel: 33 37 55 00).

Bishop Absalon built a fortress on this little islet in 1167, and from 1416 it was the home of the Danish king. Absalon's fortress was replaced by a new castle in 1367 and in the 1730s King Christian VI, Denmark's first absolute monarch, ordered a new, more suitable palace. This one, a magnificent baroque building, burned in 1794 and was replaced yet again with a new palace which, ill-fated as it was, also burned down in 1884. The present version of Christiansborg is less than 100 years old, built between 1907 and 1928. The granite façade was made from stones gathered in every parish in the country. The equestrian statue, erected on the Palace Square in 1876, depicts King Frederik VII (1843–63).

When the foundations for the present Christiansborg were dug in 1906, Denmark's National Museum excavated the remnants of the oldest buildings on the site, and the ruins of Absalon's old fortress and the medieval castle are now accessible to visitors (open 9.30am–3.30pm, closed Mon; entrance fee).

Map on pages 142–43

The crown jewels are among the many royal treasures held at Rosenborg Slot.

Architectural sights

Southeast of Christiansborg is another of Copenhagen's best-known buildings, **Børsen (Stock Exchange)** ㉘, built in 1619 in Dutch Renaissance style by King Christian IV. Its prominent spire is formed by the entwined tails of dragons representing Denmark, Sweden and Norway. Continue towards the harbour with Børsen on the left, and a right turn on to the harbour front leads to the entrance to the garden of **Det Kongelige Bibliotek (Royal Library)** ㉙. Kongelige Bibliotek dates back to 1482 and is the largest library in Scandinavia, with more than 2.5 million volumes, 4 million charts and pictures, and more than

BELOW: the palace of Christiansborg, Denmark's seat of government.

55,000 manuscripts, including some by famous Danes such as Hans Christian Andersen, Søren Kierkegaard and Karen Blixen (Isak Dinesen). Of special international interest is the library's Judaic Department.

The newest addition to the library, completed in 1999, is the "Black Diamond", a modern extension in black polished granite perched on the water's edge. It was designed by Århus architects Schmidt, Hammer & Lassen. The area where the Library Garden now stands was once a naval harbour, and you can still see mooring rings on the walls of the old buildings along the side. With its statue of Kierkegaard and a goldfish pond in the centre, the beautiful garden has a peaceful atmosphere.

Natural yarns and finished handiwork can be found off the beaten track in a little cellar shop, Sommerfuglen (Ditte Larsen), Vandkunsten 3, behind the National Museum.

The building to the right contains government offices, while the long building on the left, built in 1598, houses **Tøjhusmuseet (Arsenal Museum)** ❸⓿ and its unequaled collection of old weapons (open 12 noon–4pm, closed Mon; entrance fee; tel: 33 11 60 37).

The arcade of the building opposite the library, which houses the National Archives, leads back to Christiansborg. Turn left and continue across the canal. To the right on Frederiksholms Kanal is Denmark's **Nationalmuseet (National Museum)** ❸❶, commendable for its collections of ancient "bog" finds from the Stone, Bronze and Iron Ages. The museum also has fine historical and ethnographical collections (open 10am–5pm, Wed 10am–9pm, closed Mon; entrance fee, Wed free; tel: 33 13 44 11).

BELOW: sailors on the harbourfront.

Cross back over the canal to Slotsholmen on the old Marble Bridge to see the well-preserved riding grounds from the 1740s. They are bordered by the only surviving buildings from the first Christiansborg, destroyed by fire in 1794. In the wing on the right-hand side is the **Kongelige Stalde & Kareter (Museum**

of **Royal Stables and Coaches**) ❸❷ (open May–Sept: Fri–Sun 2–4pm; Oct–Apr: Sat–Sun 2–4pm; entrance fee; tel: 33 40 10 10), and adjacent to that, the old court theatre and **Teatermuseet** (open Wed 2–4pm, Sat–Sun 12 noon–4pm; entrance fee; tel: 33 11 51 76). It is one of the oldest court theatres in the world, designed in 1766 by the French architect Nicolas-Henri Jardin. French acting troupes and Italian opera singers performed here for royalty and the court in the early years of its existence, and there were often masquerades. The equestrian statue on the riding grounds depicts King Christian IX, who died in 1906.

Continue through the main entrance to Christiansborg, go back to the palace square and turn left to arrive at the Palace Chapel, erected in 1826. With the Pantheon of Rome as its ideal, the church is formed as a small temple and has a row of classical columns in front.

Behind the chapel is **Thorvaldsens Museum** ❸❸ which contains the works of Denmark's great sculptor, Bertel Thorvaldsen (1770-1844), who lived and worked in Rome for 40 years (open 10am–5pm, closed Mon; entrance fee; tel: 33 32 15 32). Thorvaldsen lies buried at the centre of the museum, which opened in 1848. On the outside walls a coloured frieze with life-size figures depicts Thorvaldsen's triumphant homecoming from Italy in 1838.

Colourful Christianshavn

Cross the harbour via the Knippelsbro bridge to reach **Christianshavn**, one of Copenhagen's oldest and most colourful residential areas. Christianshavn was built on an island in 1617 by King Christian IV and is surrounded by the original – and still nearly intact – star-shaped ramparts. It is worth a visit for its special atmosphere, marked by its proximity to the water. Apart from the harbour, the

Map on pages 142–43

Throughout the year the Danes sieze the chance to don traditional costume and dance.

BELOW: exploring Christianshavn by canal boat.

Christiania

I n 1971, a group of hippies founded Christiania, to launch what they claimed would be an alternative society. The hippie playground in the heart of the city has survived as one of the more exotic features of Copenhagen.

You will find the area in Christianshavn in what in 1971 was an abandoned 19th-century military barracks. Since then, the Christianites (as they call themselves) have converted barrack blocks, workshops and powder magazines into dwelling houses, workshops, restaurants and shops, where they can live and work. The 41-hectare (84-acre) site is surrounded by the original, 300-year-old star-shaped fortified walls.

Since the beginning, Christiania has been at the centre of worldwide public and media interest but, despite political disputes and police raids, the 1,000 inhabitants continue to live their unconventional lives. Many Danes are fiercely opposed to the existence of this unusual "suburb"; however, neither politicians nor police have taken any steps to close the area. On the contrary, in 1981 Christiania was given official status as a social experiment.

The main problem for the core of true Christianites, who have faithfully continued the idealistic fight, has been Christiania's magnetic attraction for criminals and drug dealers. Many Danes maintain that the "Free State" has become a hard-edged haven of thugs and drugs. Among Christiania's harshest critics have been the governments of Sweden, Norway and Finland, who look on the area as a regional centre of the drug trade and claim that Christiania has become a haven for countless runaway teenagers.

As part of their belief in their way of life, the Christianites refuse to condemn the open sale of hashish and marijuana, but in recent years they have successfully campaigned against hard drugs. The area's suggestively named "Pusher Street" was once thickly lined with drug dealers of all kinds but now the trade in hard drugs has moved to other parts of Copenhagen, and hashish and alcohol are still Christiania's favoured stimulants.

The dark side of the "Free State" has also created another problem: Christiania's disastrous relationship with the Copenhagen police. The only police to enter the area are riot squads. For their part, the police claim that, when they do patrol Christiania in the normal way, they are threatened by the inhabitants and risk having bottles, stones, and firebombs hurled at them by angry residents.

Despite all the stains that have come to tarnish the original bright ideals, Christiania survives. The real reason may be practical: political anxiety on the part of politicians in general and the Copenhagen authorities in particular. As it is, the Christianites, unwilling to move and opposed to the idea of their lives being directed by the establishment outside, are conveniently gathered in one place. To scatter them around Copenhagen, where there is already a critical housing shortage, could simply create a new set of problems. Visitors who want to see for themselves can take the number 8 bus to Prinsessegade. ❑

LEFT: colourful murals decorate old barracks buildings in the "free state" of Christiania.

island is surrounded by tree-lined moats and has a central canal. To the left, on the Christianshavn side of Knippelsbro, is the Danish Foreign Ministry, housed in big grey buildings which were completed in 1980. Further along the harbour wall are two old warehouses placed at right angles to it. Both have been meticulously restored. The first one, **Eigtveds Pakhus**, is closed to the public; the second one, **Gammel Dok** ❹, houses the Dansk Arkitektur Center (Danish Architecture Centre), which features various exhibitions, a bookshop and café (open 10am–5pm; entrance fee; tel: 32 57 19 30).

Until recently a run-down, working-class neighbourhood and the site of Denmark's largest shipyard, Christianshavn has changed its appearance greatly in recent years. Thanks to its central location, it has become fashionable and now features a quaint mixture of smartly renovated 18th-century city houses, big apartment blocks, old and new industry and commerce, and a good deal of the state's administration. On a summer day, the canal attracts all kinds of people, who enjoy a beer and the leisurely pace at the wharf.

Take a stroll down the streets of Christianshavn and glance into the courtyards of some of the old houses. **Strandgade 12**, an old merchant's house, has a beautifully restored courtyard, as well as a fine baroque wrought-iron gate. Other interesting courtyards can be found at Strandgade 6 and 44, which housed the old Strandgade barracks. **Amagergade 11**, at the other end of Christianshavn, is said to have the finest courtyard in town, and is surrounded by old galleries. Christianshavn is also the home of Christiania, the hippie-style "free city" whose colourful inhabitants have set their mark on the whole area (see opposite).

Two of Copenhagen's more notable churches are also on Christianshavn. **Vor Frelsers Kirke (Church of Our Saviour)** ❺ in Prinsessegade attracts the most attention. Built in red brick in 1694, its tall copper-clad tower from 1750 is a Copenhagen landmark. For a magnificent view over Copenhagen, the tower is open to visitors who dare to climb the 150 gilded steps on the outside of the spire – not a trip for windy weather.

Christianskirke ❻ in Strandgade is a Rococo building from 1754 with an unusual interior. It was built as a theatre, with three of the walls covered with boxes, including one for the royal family.

"New Copenhagen"

Returning to the city, one leaves the narrow eastern end of Strøget and enters the spaciousness of **Kongens Nytorv (King's New Square)**, another of Copenhagen's most cherished spots. Here, the **Hotel D'Angleterre**, on the corner of Østergade and Kongens Nytorv, is the grand old hotel of the city, offering first-class suites to the rich and famous, and a very good restaurant.

The square, one of the largest in the city, was laid out in 1660 to follow the French model of a *place royale* with an equestrian statue in the middle. The original statue of King Frederik V contained too much lead, however, and collapsed quietly; in 1946 it had to be re-cast. The small garden with the statue and surrounding garden is called **Krinsen**. In late June every

The Danish Foreign Ministry offers its encyclopaedic book, *Denmark* (1996), on the net in English, German and French: www.um.dk/danmark/denmark.

BELOW: Vor Frelsers Kirke, landmark of Christianshavn.

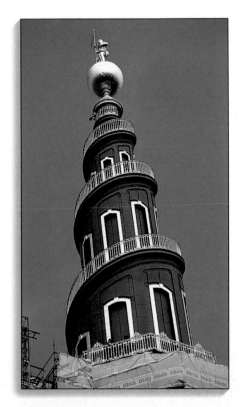

year, the new high school graduates dance around it to celebrate the end of their final examinations.

Although the quiet charm of Kongens Nytorv is disturbed by traffic, it is still one of the most stately places in Copenhagen. Dominating it is **Det Kongelige Teater (Royal Theatre)** ❸❼ which borders the square to the south. The theatre is the national stage for ballet and opera, as well as drama. August Bournonville, the influential choreographer, created a number of repertory pieces for Denmark's world famous Royal Ballet in the first half of the 19th century (*see page 101*). Company members are still the world's leading performers of the Bournonville School, and companies everywhere are eager to recruit Danish ballet dancers. The present theatre was designed in the 1870s, taking the Parisian Opera as its ideal.

Amber is sometimes referred to as "Nordic gold". You can see some fine examples in the museum and gift shop at Kongens Nytorv 2.

Another prominent building on the square is **Charlottenborg** ❸❽, on the corner of Nyhavn. Since 1754 it has been the home of the **Royal Academy of Fine Arts**, where painters, sculptors and architects receive their formal training. Go through the front gate at Charlottenborg, and into the back courtyard to find the Charlottenborg Udstillingsbygning (Charlottenborg Exhibition) and varying exhibitions of contemporary Danish and international art (open 10am–5pm; entrance fee; tel : 33 13 40 22).

Charlottenborg's neighbour, **Kongens Nytorv 1-3**, is also a part of the Academy of Fine Arts, and was built in 1740 by C. F. Harsdorff, Denmark's great classical architect. The building also served, in the mid- and late 18th century, as a model for new construction in Copenhagen.

BELOW: sculptures embellish the Marble Church.

Thotts Palace, at Kongens Nytorv No. 4, was built in 1680 and today houses the French Embassy.

Nyhavn quaysides

The narrow waterway of **Nyhavn** was dug by soldiers in 1673 and is another famous Copenhagen landmark. Old wooden schooners line the quay, and the north side is a charming combination of sailors' bars and new restaurants. The south side was always "the nice side" but the north side used to be "the naughty side" where sailors on shore leave would spend their liberty drinking, whoring, and being tattooed. While there are still a few of the old bars left, Nyhavn is now a perfectly safe place for a lively evening.

Hans Christian Andersen also fell for the charms of Nyhavn, and lived in no less than three places here: a plaque commemorates his residence during the 1860s at No. 67, and for shorter periods he lived in numbers 18 and 20.

Kongens Nytorv and Nyhavn are the southern borders of **Frederiksstaden**, an area built in the 18th century by the well-to-do who wanted stately homes close to the centre. In contrast to the winding streets of medieval Copenhagen, Frederiksstaden is marked by wide, straight streets laid out in a regular pattern.

Walk up one of the streets leading north from Nyhavn, to reach **Sankt Annæ Plads**, a long tree-lined square with an equestrian statue of King Christian X, the grandfather of Margrethe II, the present queen.

Christian X reigned during the German occupation between 1940 and 1945, and his daily rides around the city on horseback became an important symbol of liberty for the population during those years. Legend has it that, in proud contempt of German regulations that Danish Jews wear a yellow Star of David to identify themselves, the King rode the streets wearing a star on his own sleeve. **Bredgade**, at the northwest end of the square, and **Amaliegade**, which leads north, were the main residential streets of the area. Both are lined with

Map on pages 142–43

Copenhagen's harbour and canal tours sail past many of the city's sights. Board at Nyhavn, at Holmens Kirke, or on Gammel Strand at Christiansborg.

BELOW: Nyhavn, a bustling corner of Copenhagen.

large houses which today are offices. **Odd Fellow Palæ** at Bredgade 28, one of Copenhagen's finest rococo palaces and the home of a leading concert hall, burned down in 1991 but has since been restored. Bredgade and its parallel twin, Store Kongensgade, are the main shopping streets of Frederiksstaden.

At Bredgade 68 is **Kunstindustrimuseet (Museum of Decorative and Applied Arts)** with historic European and Oriental works, as well as a library (open Tue–Fri 10am–4pm; Sat–Sun 12 noon–4pm; entrance fee; tel: 33 14 94 52). The building dates from 1757 and was originally a hospital.

In Bredgade 62 is the **Medicinsk-Historisk Museum (Museum of Medical History)**, which is still reminiscent of the old hospital (guided tours Wed–Fri and Sun 11am, 1pm; free; tel: 35 32 38 00). Opposite the museum, three domes tower over Alexander Nevski Russian Orthodox Church, which was built in 1881 by the Russian government and contains a number of fine icons.

Frederikskirken , popularly known as Marmorkirken (Marble Church), lies at the western end of Frederiksgade. Marmorkirken was meant to be a grand monument, but the king ran out of money during its construction and the church was not completed until the 1870s. When the project was resumed it was built not in marble, but in limestone. From the dome, which is accessible to visitors, there is a splendid view across the sound to Sweden. The statues outside the church represent important Danish churchmen and theologians.

Royal residence

Amalienborg Palace , directly across Bredgade toward the harbour, is the residence of the Royal Family, one of Europe's less assuming royal domiciles. Nevertheless, the Royal Guard are always on duty, and the changing of the

Science-minded? Medicinsk-Historisk Museum, Bredgade 62, in the old surgical academy, features antique instruments, medieval diseases such as leprosy, and "cures"— some of which were worse than the disease.

BELOW: a statue of Frederik V surrounded by the four palaces of Amelienborg.

guard at noon every day is a sure attraction for both children and adults. Amalienborg's four separate palaces were originally planned as the centrepiece of the grand plan for Frederikstaden, but King Frederik V did not want to assume the expense of building the palaces himself. Instead, he offered a 40-year tax holiday for those who would foot the bill. Nikolaj Eigtved designed the four rococo palaces which were completed in a masterly manner in the middle of the 18th century. Only in 1794, when Christiansborg was destroyed by fire, did the Royal Family finally move in.

The exquisite equestrian statue in the middle of the square represents Frederik V and was made by the French sculptor Jacques Saly. Det Østasiatiske Kompagni (East Asiatic Company), one of Denmark's most prosperous trading companies of the day, promised to finance the statue, but there was disagreement between the artist and his backers and it took 20 years to complete the work. In 1771 Saly returned to France a sick man, bitter about the miserly fees he had received, while the stockholders of the East Asiatic Company complained equally bitterly about the enormous amounts they had had to spend.

Polar bears steal the show at the Zoo in Frederiksberg Have.

The other end of the east-west axis through the plaza ends in **Amaliehaven**, a modern park donated to the city by the A. P. Møller shipping company in 1983. The park was given a somewhat mixed reception by Copenhagen residents. Although the location is popular among strollers, the park is often referred to by locals as the "Deep-Freeze Mausoleum". Behind the park are three 18th-century warehouses – the Blue (which is actually red), the Yellow and the West Indian.

Walk west, past Marmorkirken, and turn right on to Store Kongensgade to visit Denmark's oldest housing development, **Nyboder** ㊷. The long rows of

BELOW: Tato Bob, one of Nyhavn's tattoo shops.

ochre houses were built in 1638 by Christian IV as quarters for the Danish Royal Navy, and the 616 apartments are still used for staff and retired officers.

Harbour, parks and lakes

In contrast to the busy streets, the natural areas around Copenhagen add a welcome openness to the city. The harbour which cuts through the city on the eastern side, a string of parks on the western side and the outer belt of artificial lakes mean that there is never any great distance to greenery and water. They provide residents and visitors with much-needed breathing space, and the trees help to clean polluted air.

The five parks, including Tivoli, lie in a semicircle around the inner city like a string of pearls. They were established in the middle of the 19th century when the fortifications were abandoned, a far-sighted piece of city planning.

Ørstedsparken, named after Denmark's famous 19th-century physicist Hans Christian Ørsted, known for his discovery of the principles of electromagnetism, is marked by its winding lake and large, shadowy trees. Adjoining it on the north side is **Israels Plads**, a large square which houses one of the city's fruit and vegetable markets and, in the summer months, an antique and flea market on Saturdays. Israels Plads is five minutes' walk from **Nørreport**, the city's busiest subway station.

Just north of Israels Plads and Nørreport Station is **Botanisk Have (Botanical Gardens) ⑬**, at the corner of Gothersgade and Øster Voldgade (open summer: 8.30am–6pm; winter: 8.30am–4pm; free; tel: 35 32 22 40). Visit the rosarium, the perennials and a huge conservatory with tropical and subtropical plants. Adjacent to the Botanical Garden lies **Østre Anlæg (Eastern Park)**, with lovely

The characteristic sign of the Danish Royal Mail.

BELOW: taking a break in the Botanical Gardens.

shadowy lawns, a large playground which is popular with children, and two important museums.

At the southeast corner of the park, near Sølvgade and Øster Voldgade, is **Statens Museum for Kunst (National Fine Arts Museum)** ④, which exhibits Danish and European works, including a large Matisse collection (open 10am–5pm, Wed 10am–8pm, closed Mon; entrance fee; tel: 33 74 84 94).

On the west side of the park (with an entrance from Øster Farimagsgade) is **Den Hirschsprungske Samling (Hirschsprung Collection)** ④, a commendable private collection of 19th-century Danish art (open 11am–4pm, Wed 11am–9pm, closed Tue; entrance fee, Wed free; tel: 35 42 03 36).

Kastellet (Citadel), the most northeasterly of the parks, is the only one to have kept its old ramparts intact. Part of the area is still military property. The headquarters of Copenhagen's Defence Forces and the Danish NATO headquarters are here, too.

Churchillparken, a tiny park just south of Kastellet, provides a home for **Frihedsmuseet (Danish Resistance Museum)** ④, which commemorates the Danish underground fighters of World War II (open May–mid-Sept 10am–4pm, Sun 10am–5pm, closed Mon; mid-Sept–Apr 11am–3pm, Sun 11am–4pm, closed Mon; free; tel: 33 13 77 14). The museum exhibits objects, pictures, books and publications to recognise and explain the attitudes and reactions of the Danes to German Occupation. From passive resistance and civil disobedience to active sabotage and fighting, the achievements of the Resistance movement and its co-operation with the Allies are described.

Nearby is **Skt Albans Kirke**, Copenhagen's Anglican church. Services are in English, and the congregation includes residents and visitors. Immediately

Map on pages 142–43

For treasure and trash visit the city's antique and flea markets. Try Israels Plads on Saturday, 8am–2pm, and Gammel Strand, Friday and Saturday 9am–4 pm.

BELOW: Nyboder, built in 1638 as quarters for naval officers, and still used today.

Map
on pages
142–43

TIP

Wonderful
Copenhagen on the
internet? Yes, with
events updated every
week: www.ctw.dk.

BELOW: postcard
selection.
RIGHT: work and
leisure at Nyhavn.

beside the church is the city's largest monument, the magnificent **Gefion Fountain**, dedicated to the Nordic goddess Gefion.

Gefion had four great sons fathered by a giant from the Jotunheim massif (the home of the giants) in Norway. When Odin, king of the Gods, decided that the heavenly kingdom needed more land, he sent Gefion and her four sons to try her skills of persuasion on King Gylfe of Sweden. The king was sufficiently charmed to tell the goddess she could take as much land as she could plough in one day. Quickly transforming her sons into oxen, Gefion set to the task and by nightfall she had ploughed a huge area of central Sweden. That is how, so the story goes, Denmark got the island of Zealand, while Sweden gained its largest lake as the beautiful waters filled the empty space to form Lake Vänern.

North of Langelinie, Europe's busiest cruise ship pier, at **Frihavnen (Free Harbour)**, renovations have been taking place along the lines established in London and several other European cities whose harbours have been rejuvenated since they fell idle in the late 1960s. The most architecturally interesting of the new buildings is **Paustians Hus (Paustian's House)**, designed by Jørn Utzon, who also designed the Sydney Opera House. Paustian is one of Copenhagen's finest furniture stores, and the building also houses a good restaurant.

On the west side of the inner city is another distinctive body of water. Three artificial lakes stretch about 2.5 km (1½ miles) from Østerbrogade in the north to Gammel Kongevej in the south. With their regular shapes the three linked lakes, **Sortedams Sø**, **Peblinge Sø** and **Skt Jørgens Sø**, resemble a river and provide the city with a peaceful place to go for a walk, as well as a home for flocks of birds. The lakes were dug to add to the city's western defensive perimeter and also served as a fresh water supply. On display at Christiansborg are the remains of the wooden pipes used to provide water underneath the palace.

Food and fun

Danes are confident that they provide the best food in Scandinavia, and few who have stood at a lavish *store kolde bord* (cold table) in a Copenhagen restaurant will disagree. This magnificent spread of herring, fish, meats, pâtés, salads and desserts usually also includes warm dishes, and there is an earlier, more modest cold table in most hotels for breakfast.

At night, Copenhagen is lively with scores of restaurants serving all kinds of excellent cuisine. Traditional night spots lean towards jazz but the city offers the whole spectrum of music, dance and rave. Almost all of them stay open late, and some all night. Luckily, there's always a restaurant or two open when you've had enough.

At weekends from Tivoli Gardens comes the sound of military music, played by the Tivoli Guard, dressed up as a youthful replica of the Royal Copenhagen Guard, as they parade along the paths. In summer, the evening ends with the crackle and whoosh of fireworks.

On summer evenings like this, when darkness is short, the gardens, squares and pavement cafés are full until well into the night. Copenhagen feels like a city that enjoys itself around the clock. ❑

NORTH ZEALAND

Art, literature and the high-life rub shoulders on the "Danish Riviera", which leads north from Copenhagen along the Øresund coast to Helsingør and Hamlet's castle

Map on page 182

Unless they prefer city life, people who work in Copenhagen look to the north as the most desirable and impressive place to live. It also makes a classic tour for visitors, with its green and undulating countryside, beech forests, lakes and good beaches (particularly on the extreme north coast) as well as numerous castles, manor houses, royal hunting lodges, art galleries and museums, all within an easy drive of the capital.

The coast road from Copenhagen to Helsingør is officially called Strandvejen, but is also known as the "Danish Riviera" for its stylish houses and fine views across the Øresund to Sweden. The drive along here is delightful at any time of year, but is particularly spectacular in summer with the infinite varieties of blue that make up the clear Scandinavian sea and sky scapes, and hauntingly dramatic in the occasional hard winter when the Sound is frozen into Arctic scenes that glisten in the winter sun.

Small protected harbours punctuate the road. They shelter working fishing boats and millionaires' yachts alike, and several converted marine buildings now house fresh fish restaurants, which range from those offering plain and simple fare to true gourmet food.

The annual "Round Zealand" yacht race in mid-June is one of the world's largest sailing events. It often attracts up to 2,000 entries, and offers some exciting spectator sport from Strandvejen.

Midsummer festivities

If you are in this area on Midsummer's eve you will have an unforgettable and enchanting experience. Revellers crowd around the bonfires on the beaches, fireworks displays light the skies and a procession of ships passes through the Øresund, blasting their horns to celebrate the peak of the short, intense Danish summer and positively the best-loved Scandinavian night of the year.

While it's true that the essence of North Zealand can be glimpsed in a day, it really warrants more time, either by an overnight stop at a charming Danish *kro* (inn) or by taking several day tours from Copenhagen. A car gives flexibility for touring, but there are good bus and train services from Copenhagen to Helsingør and other towns in this area. Many of these are covered by the excellent value Copenhagen Card (*see Travel Tips, Getting Around*).

Starting from Copenhagen, drive north through Hellerup, past the former Tuborg breweries. Continue through the fashionable suburb of Charlottenlund to **Klampenborg ❶** where just 15 minutes' drive from the city centre you come to an ancient 1,000-hectare (2,500-acre) royal deer park known as **Klampenborg**

PRECEDING PAGES: harbourside picnic. **LEFT:** the chapel at Frederiksborg. **BELOW:** deer park at Klampenborg.

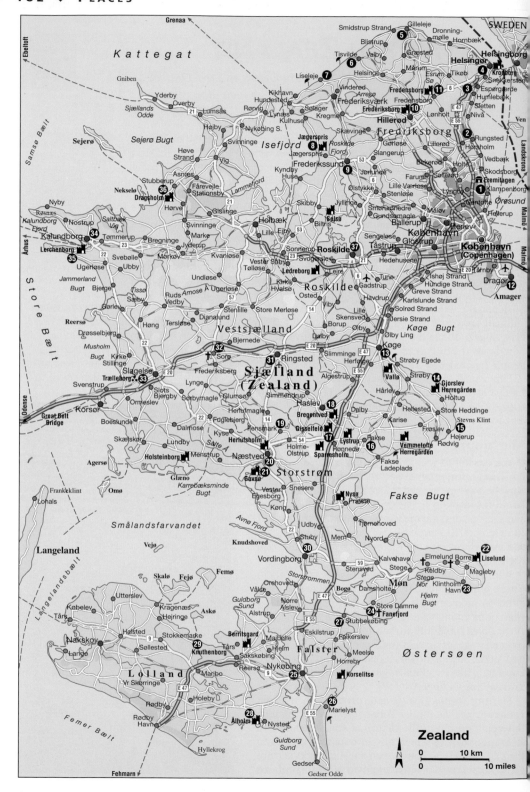

Zealand

Dyrhaven, first mentioned in official documents in 1231 (open daily). You can leave your car here and take a horse and carriage drive through the woods and parkland. Too often this form of transport is just a catch-penny tourist attraction but here, although it can be expensive (it is essential to agree a price before you set off), it is the ideal way to see the park. Forest walks are indicated by yellow spots painted on trees.

In another part of the deer park lies what is claimed to be the world's oldest fun fair, **Bakken**, a forerunner of the far more sophisticated Tivoli. Bakken heralds the start of the Danish spring every year when it opens its famous red gates on 1 April. **Peter Lieps'** rustic restaurant in the forest is the place where the locals go to drink hot chocolate or beer after winter walks, or as a romantic summer rendezvous.

Art lovers will enjoy the quiet elegance of the nearby **Ordrupgaard** (Art Gallery) at Vilvordevej 110, in a charming house so little changed since it was built in 1918 that it gives an insight into the lifestyle of wealthy Copenhagen citizens of that time (open 1–5pm daily, closed Mon; entrance fee; tel: 39 64 11 83). It has a permanent collection of Danish and French paintings, which include major works by Matisse, Corot, Manet, Renoir, Sisley and Gauguin.

Gourmets should also be aware that one of Denmark's best restaurants is to be found in the conservatory of the **Skovshoved Hotel**, situated just a few minutes' walk from the small harbour on the old Strandvejen, which runs one block inland from the sea in Klampenborg.

Out of Africa

Continue north from Klampenborg past **Eremitagen**, the stately, royal hunting lodge and through **Skodsborg**, with its alabaster-white sanatorium and health spa. Then descend into **Vedbæk**, where a popular beach and yacht harbour lie opposite Hotel Marina.

Less than half an hour's leisurely drive from Copenhagen brings you to **Rungsted ❷**, famous now for Rungstedlund, the family home of Karen Blixen, the Danish writer known as Isak Dinesen whose bestselling book, *Out of Africa*, became a film starring Meryl Streep and Robert Redford. Karen Blixen died and was buried here in 1962, and her home is now open to visitors as a museum devoted to her life, the **Karen Blixen Museet** (open May–Sept: 10am–5pm; Oct–April: Wed–Fri 1–4pm, Sat–Sun 11am–4pm, closed Mon–Tue; entrance fee; tel: 45 57 10 57).

Modern art centre

At **Humlebæk ❸**, art-lovers could easily spend an entire day at the **Louisiana Museum for Moderne Kunst (Louisiana Museum of Modern Art)**, at Gl. Strandvej 13 (open 10am–5pm, Wed 10am–10pm; entrance fee; tel: 49 19 07 91). It was opened in 1958 with a collection of Danish art aiming "to show the interplay between art, architecture and landscape". New galleries have since been added and frequent international exhibitions are held in a breathtaking setting overlooking the Øresund to Sweden. The rich permanent collection includes sculptures set in the

Rungstedlund, home of the writer Karen Blixen in Rungsted.

BELOW: the Great Hall at Kronborg, Hamlet's castle.

surrounding gardens. There is a children's wing, and a varied programme of films and concerts.

Hamlet's Helsingør

Helsingør ❹ is perhaps best known as the main ferry crossing to Sweden which takes just 20 minutes. But it's also famous for its massive Renaissance-style **Kronborg**, Hamlet's "Castle of Elsinore" (open May–Sept: 10.30am–5pm, Apr–Oct: 11am–4pm, Nov–March: 11am–3pm; closed Mon; entrance fee; tel: 49 21 30 78).

Originally built by King Eric of Pomerania when he introduced the "Sound Dues" – fees to be paid to the Danish crown by all ships passing through to the Baltic – Kronborg has been rebuilt several times. It has provided a fabulous backdrop for many international productions of Shakespeare's play, *Hamlet*. Even today, its atmosphere is eerie and smells of intrigue and royal plots.

Inside, the richly decorated King's and Queen's chambers and the 62-metre (203-ft) long Great Hall are worth seeing. Down in the dungeons, Kronborg holds the statue of Holger Danske, a slumbering Danish Viking chief who, according to legend, will awake and fill Danes with his fighting spirit when the country is in danger. His name was used as a codeword by the Danish Resistance during World War II.

Helsingør is one of Denmark's most historic towns, with entire streets of well-preserved, colour-washed buildings. The 15th-century **Skt Mariæ Kirke** and the **Carmelite Kloster** (Convent) are among the best preserved Gothic buildings in the world. Hans Christian Andersen, who lived in Helsingør for a time, described it as "one of the most beautiful spots in Denmark, close to the

Frederiksværk in north Zealand was Denmark's first water-powered industrial town. It grew in the 17th century around a powderworks and cannonball factory, which are now museums.

BELOW: enjoying an afternoon beer in Gilleleje.

Map
on page
182

Sound, which is one mile wide and looks like a blue stream swelling between Denmark and Sweden".

The coast road leads on to **Gilleleje ❺**, the most northern town of Zealand, a fascinating, small working fishing port, which has a fish auction each morning. Gilleleje played a heroic role in World War II. From here many Jews escaped to neutral Sweden through the efforts of the Danish underground and local fishermen. **Hos Karen og Marie**, housed in an unpretentious green-painted wooden building, is one of the best fish restaurants anywhere. Ask to sit upstairs facing the harbour.

If the weather is good, you could return via the sun-worshippers' beaches of **Tisvilde ❻** or **Liseleje ❼**, or carry on to **Sølager**, taking the short ferry to Kulhuse and drive through a forest of ancient oak trees to **Jægerspris Slot ❽** (open May–Sept 10am–noon and 1–5pm, closed Mon, guided tour every hour; Apr–Oct: Sun and holidays 10am–noon and 1–5pm; entrance fee; tel: 47 53 10 04). The rooms occupied by King Frederik VII are left unchanged. At the end of June, Viking plays are staged at **Frederikssund ❾**, 6 km (4 miles) away, with audience participation and traditional feasts.

As one turns inland for the return to Copenhagen, **Frederiksborg ❿**, built between 1605 and 1621, is on the outskirts of **Hillerød**, 36 km (22 miles) from the capital on the E47 (open Apr–Oct: 10am–5pm; Nov–Mar: 11am–3pm; entrance fee; tel: 48 26 04 39)). Apart from the chapel, most of the castle was burnt down in 1859, but rebuilt to the original plan within six years. The interiors were finished with large grants from the brewery king, J.C. Jacobson.

Under the Carlsberg Foundation, Frederiksborg has been Denmark's National History Museum ever since. The most notable rooms are the Council Hall, Knights' Hall, where the walls are hung with shields presented by many famous visitors, and the chapel with its original Compenius organ, built in 1610. It makes a fine setting for concerts held in July and August. North of the lake is one of the best baroque gardens in Northern Europe, and to the west is a large English garden with a small 1581 Renaissance château which King Frederik II used as a bath house. In summer, the lake offers boat trips.

Just 9 km (5 miles) from Hillerød is the royal palace of **Fredensborg ⓫**. The palace was built in Italian style in 1722, and is now used as a residence for the Danish Royal Family in spring and autumn (open for guided tours when the Royals are not in residence; tel: 33 40 31 87 for details).). There is a formal French marble garden west of the palace. The park that leads to a delightful lake called Esrum Sø, has a distinctive collection of sculptures.

The ancient, thatched **Sollerød Kro**, next to the even more ancient **Søllerød Kirke** lies in an idyllic village near Holte on the northern outskirts of Copenhagen. It's is one of the best restaurants in Denmark.

The last stop before returning to Copenhagen is **Frilandsmuseet (Open Air Museum)** at **Lyngby**, a re-created village of Scandinavian farm buildings from the 1700s and 1800s (open late-March–Sept: 10am–5pm, closed Mon; Oct: 10am–4pm, closed Mon; entrance fee; tel: 33 13 44 11. ❑

Marienlyst Slot in Helsingør was remodelled by the French architect, Jardin, in the 1760s. It features Louis XVI interiors, paintings and silver (open daily noon–5pm).

BELOW: waterside Frederiksborg.

SOUTH AND WEST ZEALAND

*A detour from the main east-west highway reveals colourful
Zealand, rich in culture and tradition, the white cliffs
of Møn, and the islands of Falster and Lolland*

Map
on page
182

The southern and western areas of Zealand have traditionally been the port
of entry for new people and ideas coming from the Continent. Many of
today's routes – whether rail, motor or by sea – are founded upon the ways
travellers and traders took many centuries ago. This section of the island has
been the scene of strife in years gone by, but now it is an enchanting expanse of
rolling hills, lush woodland and some wonderful seaside geography. On an
early summer's day the fields radiate an almost surreal green alternating with the
cartoon-yellow of rape fields in bloom, and each season yields a new palette of
colour. Zealand is rich in history, tradition and culture, and despite the main
traffic arteries that cross the region, many people simply pass through without
stopping to enjoy some of the secret jewels of Denmark.

Over the centuries, this part of Zealand played an important political role in
the development of Denmark and the Viking influence was also strong. There
are remains of a 1,000-year-old Viking fortress at Trelleborg in the south.
Roskilde to the west was an important trading centre in Viking times and today
its museum holds five magnificent Viking ships. It was also once the seat of the
reigning monarch and, after the Danes were converted to Christianity, the town
became one of the most important religious centres in Northern Europe.

PRECEDING PAGES:
the white chalk
face of Møns Klint.
LEFT: Roskilde
cathedral, burial
place of monarchs.
BELOW: corn field at
Maribo, Lolland.

Roaming geese

In the 19th century, more peaceful "invasions" of
artisans came to south Zealand to teach their skills
and some of their rituals now form part of local
festivals. In spite of the presence of the international
airport on Amager island, the old fishing village of
Dragør ⓬ has streets of half-timbered houses where
geese still roam, and the descendants of the Dutch
immigrants who brought their knowledge of horti-
culture to Denmark celebrate their traditional Shrove-
tide customs. With a barrel suspended over the course,
men dress in fancy costumes ride their horses at full
tilt, lances outstretched to spear and splinter the barrel
in half. It certainly enlivens a bleak Danish winter.

The international motorway to Germany runs from
Copenhagen past **Køge** ⓭, with its popular bathing
beaches crowded with sun-loving Danes, and summer
camp sites. Inhabitants claim that Køge has more half-
timbered houses than any other town in Denmark. The
oldest, dated 1527, stands at 20 Kirkestræde. Visit **Skt
Nikolai Kirke**, which has one of Denmark's most
beautiful town church interiors. Not far from the market place is **Hugo's Vinkælder** (wine shop) which
has one of the oldest inns in Denmark serving good
old-fashioned draught porter.

About 7 km (4 miles) south of Køge is **Vallø**, a
beautiful Renaissance castle surrounded by a moat

TIP

After a shaky start, the Arken Museum of Moderne Kunst (Art) at Ishøj, on the coast road to Køge, just south of Copenhagen, has earned a reputation for presenting excellent art by world masters (open Tues–Sun 10am–5pm; entrance fee; tel: 43 54 02 22).

BELOW: Gisselfeld Slot, a Renaissance castle near Haslev.

and park land (gardens open daily; exibition open May 14–Aug: 11am–4pm; entrance fee; tel: 56 26 74 62). Its two massive towers are unmistakable. Since 1737, the castle has been owned by a charitable trust, set up to provide a dignified setting for the unmarried daughters of noblemen in their later years. A few of these women still live here but are unlikely to patronise the **Vallø Slotskro**, an old inn opposite the castle specialising in traditional Danish food.

Bay of battles

Køge Bugt was the scene of two great naval battles between Denmark and Sweden, and the Danish National Anthem celebrates the first of these with the words: "King Christian stood by the lofty mast." Some claim that the king actually watched from Skt Nikolai Kirke.

On the way to the Stevns Klint chalk cliffs is **Gjorslev Herregården** ⓮, situated between Magleby and Holtug. The manor has a crucifix-shaped ground plan and was built in 1400 for the then Bishop of Roskilde (not open to the public). **Stevns Klint** ⓯ on the south headland of the bay may not be quite as dramatic as the chalk cliffs on the island of Møn further south, but they are very impressive when the sun illuminates them in brilliant hues of white. How long this will last remains a question; the waves pound ceaselessly against the structures, undermining the lower layers of chalk, and every once in a while whole sections crumble into the sea. The 13th-century **Højerup Kirke** at the top is only precariously intact in its fight with the sea. In 1928, the sea won a partial victory when some of the building crashed down the 40-metre (130-ft) cliffs.

Fakse ⓰, 20 km (12 miles southwest) has a nice beach near **Vemmetofte Herregården** (Manor), and is also the home of a very successful brewery. Fakse

Breweries claims that all its beers are brewed with "coral water" because the town lies on what was once a prehistoric coral reef.

Map on page 182

Northwest from Fakse, 5 km (3 miles) south of the ancient town of **Haslev**, Hans Christian Andersen is said to have found inspiration for what is perhaps his most famous story, *The Ugly Duckling*, in **Gisselfeld Slot** ⓱, a castle built in 1554 (grounds and stables open daily; castle closed to the public). On the southern outskirts of Haslev is **Bregentved Slot** ⓲, with its copper spire, which is Zealand's largest private estate (open Wed, Sun and public holidays; tel: 56 31 20 19). In springtime near the town of **Dalby**, 6 km (4 miles) east, don't miss the intoxicating sight of the vast cherry orchards which supply the **Cherry Heering Distillery** there.

The **Holmegård Glassvæk** (**Glassworks**) at **Fensmark** ⓳, 20 km (12 miles) west of Dalby, was founded in 1825, when glassmakers were brought from Norway and Bohemia. This is a popular target for tours from Copenhagen (taours Mon–Fri 9am, 10am, 11am, 1 and 2pm; entrance fee; shop open Mon–Sat, May–Sept also Sun noon–5pm; tel: 55 54 50 00). Visitors can watch the fine pieces being formed, as highly-skilled glass blowers show what is required for the special artistic objects created by the company designers. The **Glass Museum** has a notable collection which reflects the history of this famous company. At the shop "seconds", often with almost indiscernible flaws, are superb bargains. If you are in luck, you may be able to hear music played by the company's famous glass band. The band uses instruments made of glass.

Herlufsholms Kostskole (School) in **Næstved** ⓴, 5 km (3 miles) southwest of Fensmark, is one of Denmark's most prestigious private boarding schools. It was founded in 1565 by the nobleman Herluf Trolle and his wife, who were

LEFT: cycling in South Zealand.
BELOW: glass-blowing at Holmegård.

childless. The public are admitted to the courtyard, park, and chapel at limited times (chapel open May–Sept: 11am–4pm; free; tel: 55 72 17 70). The tombs of Herluf Trolle and his wife lie together behind the altar, below a crucifix that is one of the art treasures of Europe. It was carved from a single elephant tusk, and is believed to have originated in southern France in the middle of the 13th century. How it arrived at Herlufsholm remains a mystery.

Næstved has been an important trading town for most of its history and has an attractive city centre. The Gothic **Skt Peder Kirke** has a richly carved pulpit from 1671 and **Skt Mortens Kirke**, built around 1300, has a lavishly decorated altarpiece. An interesting museum of local history is housed in **Helligåndshuset** (House of the Holy Spirit), Ringstedgade 4. Built in 1492, it is well worth a visit (open daily 10am–4pm; entrance fee; tel: 55 777 08 11).

Gavnø Slot ㉑ is situated on a tiny island linked by road, 6 km (4 miles) southwest of Næstved (open May–Aug: 10am–4pm; entrance fee; tel: 55 70 02 00). In the 13th century it was used as a pirates' castle, but in 1398 Queen Margrethe bought Gavnø and turned it into a convent. It became a private manor house in 1584 and today has Scandinavia's largest privately owned picture collection. An annual flower fair is staged in its magnificent gardens.

Cliffs of Møn

The island of **Møn** ("The Maid") to the east is linked to Zealand by road bridges. According to legend, its spectacular stretches of luminous white chalk cliffs, topped with beech woods and studded with fossils, became a refuge for the most powerful of Nordic gods, Odin, when Christianity left him homeless. This now-peaceful place has been invaded by "every Northern tribe". Møn has

BonBon-Land at Holme-Olstrup, 5 km (3 miles) northeast of Næstved, is a family amusement park based upon a selection of zany sweets that hit the market a decade ago (open daily May–Sept).

BELOW: strange formations on the cliffs of Møn.

Bronze-Age tombs, 13th-century churches with medieval frescoes, and primeval forests with more varieties of wild orchids than anywhere else in Denmark. Over the past 200 years, most of the "invaders" of Møn have been writers and painters, lured there by the inspiration of its beauty and drama.

Liselund Slot ㉒ is a thatched mini-château, built in 1796 (open May–Oct, guided tours bookable in advance, 10.30 and 11am, 1.30 and 2pm; entrance fee; tel: 55 81 21 78). Hans Christian Andersen wrote his tales *The Tinder Box* and *The Little Match Girl* in a summer house known as Swiss Cottage on the estate. At one time Liselund had several other buildings but they were swallowed by the sea when part of the cliff collapsed. South of the cliffs, the fishing port of **Klintholm Havn** ㉓ has a good hotel and seafood restaurant, Ålekroen, which specialises in smoked, fried, or stewed eel.

Møn's churches are famous for their frescoes, particularly those at Keldby, Elmelund and **Fanefjord** ㉔, the last standing in a beautiful setting on an isolated hill which overlooks the narrows of Grønsund. Beside the church is the longest barrow grave in Denmark, **Grønjægers Høj**. The island's main town of **Stege** has a town gate and medieval ramparts.

Beach holidays on Falster

The Farø bridges, completed in 1985, connect Zealand to the island of **Falster**, and the ferry routes to Germany. The main town on the island is **Nykøbing** ㉕, famous for **Czarens Hus (Tsar's House)**, Langgade 2, where Peter the Great stayed in 1716, the year of his famous horse-riding exploit up the steep 200-metre (620-ft) winding ramp in Rundetårnet, Copenhagen. It is now a museum (open 11am–10pm, closed Sun; entrance fee; tel: 54 85 28 29). The area around

Map on page 182

Dressed for the part: the Middle Ages Centre, Nykøbing.

BELOW: Liselund, the miniature palace on Møn.

SMALL TREASURES

Zealand consists of vast expanses of farmland, and the many landowners of days past accumulated their own art collections. The castles and manors were often tiny museums in themselves, but today many of the works have found their way into local museums.

Odsherred in northwest Zealand juts into the waters of the Kattegat. The long stretches of powdery-sand beaches and rolling dunes attracted artists and in the 1930s an Odsherred school of painters was formed, led by Bovin, Swane and Hartz. The **Odsherred Kunstmuseum** displays their work, alongside contemporary artists (open Apr–Dec: 11am–4pm; closed Mon; tel: 59 65 24 23). At Nykobing, the **Anneberg Samlingerne** is the largest, privately-owned collection of antique glass in northern Europe (open May–Sept: 10am–5pm, closed Mon; tel: 59 91 38 00).

Further south, the **Vestsjællands Kunstmuseum** in Sorø includes a fine collection of 18th and 19th century art from the Funen and Skagen schools, as well as works by Abildgaard, Juel, Eckersberg, Lundbye, Dalsgaard and Marstrand (open mid-May–mid-Aug: 10am–4pm; mid-Aug–mid-May: 1–4pm; closed Mon; tel: 57 83 22 29).

In addition, numerous galleries and craft workshops can be found carrying on the artistic traditions of the region.

Marielyst , 10 km (6 miles) to the southeast has some 20 km (12 miles) of fine white sand dunes where local families take traditional beach holidays, and neighbouring Bøtø has a well-known nudist beach.

On the north coast, **Stubbekøbing** ㉗ is a market town with ferry connections to Bogø and Møn. It has the largest veteran motorcycle museum in northern Europe, Stubbekøbing Motorcykle og Radiomuseum, Nykøbingvej 54, with old radios also on display (open Apr–May: Sat, Sun and holidays 10am–5pm; June–Sept: daily 10am–5pm; entrance fee; tel: 54 44 22 22).

On safari in Lolland

There is a choice of road bridges from Falster to Lolland, to reach one of the island's main attractions, **Ålholm Slot** ㉘, near the old seaport of **Nysted**. The castle dates from the 12th century (open July–Aug: daily 11am–5pm; Sept–June: Sat, Sun 11am–5pm; entrance fee; tel: 54 87 10 17). It was once known as the robber's castle, and has one of the world's finest collections of rare cars with all sorts of oddities and also the special train carriage which the Ålholm Baron's father, then foreign secretary, used on his travels.

From Ålholm, the road north and west runs past the beautiful lakes to **Maribo** and on to **Knuthenborg** ㉙, a safari park at Brandholm (open May–Oct: times vary; tel: 54 78 80 88 for opening hours; entrance fee). In the far west, the **Tårs-Spodsbjerg** crossing connects the island with Langeland and Funen.

Around West Zealand

To continue the tour, drive north across the bridge from **Orehoved** in Falster to **Vordingborg** ㉚, Zealand's southernmost town. Vordingborg features the

The Historical Botanical Gardens in Vordingborg, south Zealand, feature an impressive collection of plants "that have been of service to art, beauty and medicine for generations", as it was stated during the opening ceremony in 1921.

BELOW: the dining room at Ålholm Slot on Lolland.

Gåsetårnet (**Goose Tower**), which dates from 1370, and the ruins of a fortress that was once the second largest in Scandinavia. These are now Denmark's best-preserved medieval buildings (open Sept–May: 10am–4pm, closed Mon; entrance fee; tel: 55 37 25 54). About 50 km (30 miles) north is **Ringsted ㉛** in the heart of Zealand, with **Skt Bendts Kirke**, dedicated to all Danish kings who bear the name of Valdemar. Inside the church, the tombs and coats-of-arms are a tribute to the time when this modest country town was one of the most important in Denmark.

Heading west 17km (10 miles), the next stop is **Sorø ㉜** and **Sorø Kirke**, part of the oldest abbey in Denmark. Behind the altar is the tomb of Bishop Absalon of Roskilde, founder of Copenhagen. The former abbey building is now a boarding school, **Sorø Academy**, set beside a lake which makes a beautiful setting for a peaceful walk.

Traditional timber-framed farmhouse near Maribo.

The road continues west to **Slagelse** where, 5 km (3 miles) from the centre, is **Vikingeborgen Trælleborg ㉝**, an abandoned Viking fortress some 1,000 years old (open late-Mar–late-Sept: 10am–5pm; late-Sept–mid-Apr: 1pm–3pm; entrance fee; tel: 58 54 95 06). It was once a huge fortified camp that housed 1,000 Vikings. One of the houses has been reconstructed outside the circular walls and on a cold spring day it is easy to understand how tough the life here must have been, despite the Vikings' reputations as hardy souls.

Continuing north, **Kalundborg ㉞** is a ferry port for Jutland via the island of Samsø. Despite a turbulent history, Kalundborg is now a quiet place known chiefly for its magnificent five-towered church, built in 1170 by Esbern Snare, brother to Bishop Absalon. It is surrounded by ancient buildings in Linde-gaarden, one of which holds the town museum, **Kalundborg Bymuseum**,

BELOW: Skt Bendts Kirke, Ringsted.

Map on page 182

The annual Roskilde Festival (late June, early July) is the oldest outdoor popular music festival in the world. The event is orderly, well equipped and caters for a wide range of tastes.

BELOW: Viking ship hall in Roskilde's museum.
RIGHT: selling bread at the re-created Viking fortress of Trælleborg.

Adelgade 23 (open May–Aug: 11am–4pm, closed Mon; Sept–Apr. weekends and holidays 11am–4pm; entrance fee; tel: 59 51 21 41).

Lerchenborg ㉟, around the fjord to the south, has a Music Week in August (castle open for guided tours of 25 persons or more; tel: 59 51 05 00 for details), and a road leads from its courtyard to the **Røsnæs peninsula** where there is a windmill and lighthouse.

Dragsholm Slot ㊱ 25 km (15 miles) northeast of Kalundborg at **Fårevejle** was the prison of the Earl of Bothwell, the ill-fated husband of Mary Queen of Scots, who in 1567 fled to Denmark in a vain hope of sanctuary after her downfall. Chained to the dismal walls, the earl waited long for death. His cell is open to the public, and Dragsholm itself has become a hotel and restaurant.

Viking town

Perhaps the main highlight of Zealand is the town of **Roskilde ㊲**, Zealand's second largest town, 20 minutes by train west of Copenhagen. Its Domkirke (cathedral), built in 1170, is the burial place of generations of Danish monarchs. Their elaborate tombs lie inside chapels to the main cathedral. The most impressive chapels are those of King Christian IV, built in 1641 in Dutch Renaissance style with magnificent murals, and the chapel of King Frederik V from 1770, the masterwork of the architect Harsdorff.

Modern excavations at the Domkirke have revealed that building began around AD 1000 and was probably completed in 1410. Even today, chapels are still being added and the cathedral has a sense of being alive. There are many treasures, not least the gold triptych altarpiece built in Antwerp in 1560 and the much loved St George and the Dragon clock, which chimes on the hour.

Roskilde's **Vikingeskibshallen** (**Viking Ship Museum**), beside the water on Strandengen, is one of the great delights of Denmark (open May–Sept: 9am–5pm; Oct–Apr:10am–4pm; entrance fee; tel: 46 30 02 00). Its five ships were found in 1962 at the mouth of the Roskildefjord. The vessels had lain there since the 11th-century defenders of Roskilde had sunk them to block the entrance of the fjord against enemy attack. The restored ships include a warship of the type portrayed in the Bayeux Tapestry and an awe-inspiring longship, the dreaded Viking man o'war, immensely seaworthy and used for long-range raiding. It was easily large enough for a crew of 40 or 50 men.

The vessels are superbly displayed in a way which makes them seem to sail on the fjord once more, and they illustrate the outstanding shipbuilding skills of the Vikings. A film tells the story of the complicated excavations to recover the Viking ships.

The museum has been expanded in recent years to include more outdoor activities. The builders, however, faced serious problems because it seemed that with every spade of earth that was dug up, a new Viking or medieval artefact was uncovered. Visitors will still see the experts rinsing silt to uncover even more ships and Viking and medieval lore.

To end the day with a truly Viking flavour, turn into the museum restaurant for a draught of the favourite brew of these hardy sailors, *mjød* (mead). ❑

BORNHOLM

*The Baltic island of Bornholm is a favourite haunt
of both artists and holidaymakers, who are attracted by its
peaceful lifestyle and natural beauty*

Bornholmers, and for that matter most Danes, will be happy to relate the tale of creation of Bornholm: when God had finished creating Scandinavia, he had a few leftovers from the very best features of the regions, so he gathered them all up and tossed them into the Baltic Sea. The tale perfectly illustrates the island's nickname, "Scandinavian in a nutshell", since Bornholm features such a variety of landscapes typical to different areas of Scandinavia.

The enchanting island stands in the middle of the Baltic Sea between Sweden and Poland. Although the island seems remote, Copenhagen is only seven hours away by ferry, and 30 minutes by plane. The ferry trip to southern Sweden takes about two and a half hours. It is a peaceful place; an area of 588 sq km (227 sq miles) is home to about 48,000 Bornholmers and the island has a wealth of natural history. There are no large towns and almost no industry; visitors have a perfect opportunity to relax.

It is an island of contrasts. Rugged, rocky shores, and miles of long, sandy beaches alternate along the coast. There are small picturesque fishing villages and pleasant market towns; peaceful forests and working farm fields lie side by side. All of Denmark's natural variety is packed into Bornholm.

PRECEDING PAGES: anywhere is a good spot for a picnic. **LEFT:** Bornholm's seven-stemmed tree on fertile soil. **BELOW:** an inland waterfall.

Living history

The past is everywhere on the island. Passage graves from the Bronze Age and monoliths from both the Bronze and Iron Ages are numerous. Stone carvings, most likely built in praise of the gods and maybe to induce them to provide good weather, are found in many fertile agricultural areas.

Bornholm was a maritime centre in the Baltic Sea during the Iron Age. Jewellery, coins, and relics from as far away as Rome and the Near East have been discovered and two forts, both known as **Gamleborg**, found in Paradisbakkerne (The Hills of Paradise) and at Almindingen Skov, date from the Viking period. It is generally believed that Bornholm became a part of the Kingdom of Denmark at around that time. On stormy days 1,000 years later, one is reminded of the strategic importance of the island, as fishing boats, freighters, and yachts take shelter from heavy seas.

Hammershus ❶ was built in the Middle Ages to defend the island against attack, and is today Scandinavia's largest fortified castle (open Apr–May: 10am–4pm; June–Aug: 10am–5pm; Sept–Oct: 10am–5pm; free; tel: 56 48 24 31). It stands on a huge, rocky knoll on the northwest corner of the island, and the ruins are impressive. At the time the castle was built (around 1250), Bornholm was owned by the Archbishop of Lund (in what is now southern Sweden, though then part of Denmark); he was openly

Nykirke, north of Rønne, one of Bornholm's historic round churches.

at war with the Kings of Denmark. In a brief period of its history, Hammershus was occupied by soldiers from Lübeck (1520), and the Swedes (1645 and 1658), and it was regularly plundered until 1822, when it was placed under the protection of the National Museum. Restoration continues on what is today the most magnificent relic of the history of Bornholm.

There are amazing examples of medieval architecture in the four round churches: Østerlars, Nylars, Nyker, and Olsker. When the Slavic Wends ravaged the island, they were occasionally used as places of refuge, and stand as further reminders of the historic importance of the island. During the 14th, 15th and 16th centuries Hanseatic merchants from northern Germany would move in during the herring season (May to September).

In the middle of the 17th century the island was occupied by the Swedes during one of the many wars with Denmark. The Swedish commandant, Colonel Printzenskjöld, was murdered in a conspiracy in 1658, and the islanders drove the Swedish forces from the island two years later. By popular consent, the islanders then gave themselves and the island to the Danish King Frederik III (1648–70). Their allegiance to the kingdom has had a notable effect ever since.

Almost 300 years of peace followed, until the last occupation of Bornholm during World War II. When Germany capitulated to Allied forces on 4 May 1945, the German commandant on the island refused to surrender. After warning the local population to evacuate, the Russians then bombed the two largest towns (Rønne and Nexø), and brought about the German surrender.

Strong separatist feelings still exist among Bornholmers, some of whom wish for independence from outside rule for the island. Their banner is a Danish flag with a green cross instead of the familiar white one.

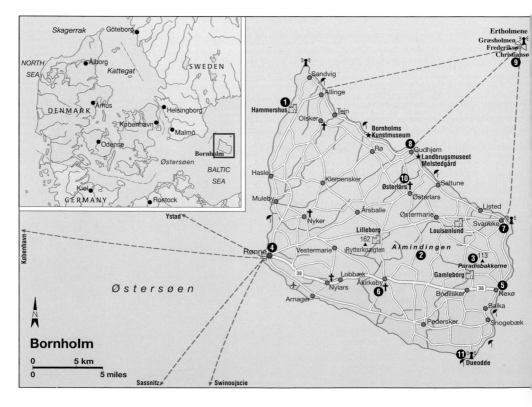

Abundant flora

The variety of plant life on Bornholm is almost overwhelming. No other part of Denmark has more hours of sunshine. The long summer and mild autumn weather encourages plants which are otherwise only found in France and Italy. The northern part of the island is extremely rocky and, by radiating heat picked up from the sun, the rocks keep the surface warm enough for figs, grapes, mulberry trees and other plants from southern Europe to grow well.

About 20 percent of Bornholm is woodland, making it Denmark's most densely wooded county. **Almindingen ❷**, in the centre of the island, is Denmark's third largest forest. **Paradisbakkerne ❸** has more and wilder vegetation than Almindingen; it is best enjoyed on foot.

Sweet cherry trees blossom in June and give a colourful show. Their berries ripen in late July and August. Red orchids are common on the banks in the river valleys and thousands of woodland flowers, especially blue, yellow, and white anemones, cover large areas.

Numerous geological faults make the island's surface a mosaic of rocks of varying age and type. Impressive formations remain from the Mesozoic, Paleozoic, and Pre-Cambrian periods, and geologists return frequently to study them. The sea has battered the steep coasts during the 12,000 years since the last Ice Age, creating especially beautiful cliffs in the north and west.

Island life

There is little industry, but Rønne and Nexø are important fishing ports, and the harbours are full of life. Small farms are scattered all over the island: the average farm is 20 hectares (50 acres) or less. Unlike their counterparts elsewhere

Map on page 202

TIP

A Baltic storm tends to churn up amber, which washes ashore. Go beachcombing early and remember that amber doesn't sink as quickly as stone. Another test is to tap it on a tooth - amber won't clink like stone.

BELOW: summer visitors prefer camping.

in Denmark, farmers on Bornholm were never indentured to wealthy landowners – the most important result of the islanders' loyalty to the Danish throne – and the result today is that really big estates do not exist.

Climate, natural history and the sea all influence the mentality of Bornholmers. One may get the impression that they are reserved; but history has taught the islanders to be restrained in making new friendships. Most visitors are attracted by their quiet and friendly ways.

From early July until the end of August is holiday time. During this period the population of Bornholm is four times greater than during the rest of the year. Though most of the residents are unmoved by tourists, a tiny minority still dreams of profits from casinos and tower-block hotels to rival the Costa Brava, but such dreams are unlikely to come true. Some years ago local politicians, concerned about potential damage to their island's environment, initiated what is known as the "Green Island Project". This effort to preserve the natural beauty of Bornholm and to raise the environmental conciousness of its inhabitants, as well as the rest of Denmark, has borne considerable fruit. The project has received financial support from the European Fund for Regional Development.

The confined area and isolated position of Bornholm provide an ideal laboratory in which to study changes in the environment. Recycling and alternative energy projects have been developed with the hope that the example of Bornholm will lead to a greater responsibility towards the natural world.

Åkirkeby's Automobil Museum contains an intriguing collection of cars, motorcycles and the equipment to repair them (open May–Oct: Tue–Sat 10am–5pm; entrance fee; tel: 56 97 45 95).

Around Bornholm

Rønne ❹, with 15,000 inhabitants, is the largest town on Bornholm, and its harbour is one of the largest provincial ports in Denmark. Ferries depart daily for Copenhagen and Ystad, in southern Sweden, and in high season one can also catch a boat to Germany or Poland. Buses from the harbour provide connections to all parts of the island nearly every hour. The area around the main square is the centre of town.

Some parts of the town have been well preserved, especially in the area just east of Skt Nikolai Kirke. The beautiful **Kastellet (Citadel)** is on the east side of town; today it is a military museum, **Forsvarsmuseet** (open May–Oct: Tue–Sat 10am–4pm; entrance fee; tel: 56 95 65 83).

Bornholm has inspired many Danish painters, as well as having produced a few of its own: Oluf Høst is probably the best known. **Bornholms Museum**, at Skt Mortensgade 29, has a collection of paintings by Høst and other artists, as well as ceramics and historical exhibits, and is well worth visiting (open Tue–Sat 10am–5pm; entrance fee; tel: 56 95 07 35).

Rønne Theatre, Østergade 7, is the oldest private theatre still operating in Denmark.

Nexø ❺ (population of 3,000), is an old fishing town on the east coast. The population still depends on the fishing industry for survival, but increasing pollution in the Baltic Sea forces some local fishermen to sail as far as the Indian Ocean and the coasts of Africa in order to maintain their standard of living.

Åkirkeby ❻ (around 1,400 residents) is the main town in the southern part of Bornholm, and the only

BELOW: enjoying the summer sun in Svaneke.

one of the larger towns situated inland. The name of the town can be roughly translated as "the town of the church-by-the-stream".

The town was an ecclisiastical centre and its church, **Åkirke**, was built around 1150 as a chapter house in the Archbishopric of Lund. The large tower was extended around 1200, and at the same time it was fortified with walls even heavier than those of either Hammershus or the round churches. It is especially well known for its sandstone baptismal font, imported from Gotland (southern Sweden) in around 1200. The font depicts the life of Christ in 11 relief carvings; the figures are explained in runic script, and end with the signature of the stone-cutter, "Sighraf, master".

The easternmost town in Denmark, **Svaneke ❼**, has a population of about 1100. For centuries, the success of shipping captains has fuelled its prosperity. The largest buildings were originally merchants' houses; north of the town is an old Dutch mill, and nearby an untraditional water tower, built by the architect Jørn Utzon in 1951. In 1975 Svaneke it was awarded the European Gold Medal for Town Preservation.

Bicycling downhill is forbidden in **Gudhjem ❽** ("good home"), a very pretty place, built on steep rocky slopes down to the water. The huge windmills around the town once provided electricity. The former railway station has been converted into a model train museum, **Bornholms Model Jernbane Museum**, and provides an excellent way of exploring local history (open mid-May–early Oct: 1pm–5pm, closed Sat; free; tel: 56 47 04 85).

For an insight into the island's history, visit Bornholms Museum, Rønne.

There is an agricultural museum, Landbrugsmuseet Melstedgård, just south-east of Gudhjem at **Melsted**, a settlement which first gained prominence as an important trading centre during the Middle Ages. The 17th-century farm features

BELOW: swimming off the coast of Christiansø island.

HAVEN FOR ARTISTS

Bornholm has the largest concentration of craftspeople in Europe. Around 150 years ago artists began to come to the island, attracted by the Baltic light. Many came as visitors and stayed and by the beginning of the 20th century a small colony of Swedish and Danish artists had established itself. Over the years their works gained a reputation which drew other artists and prospective customers. Nowadays Bornholm is a centre for Danish handicrafts and applied art.

Most potteries, ceramics and glass-blowing workshops are open to the public. Visitors are welcome to look over the artist's shoulders, and in some places actually play a hand in making something. In addition, each hamlet and village has a number of jewellers, silversmiths, wood turners and cabinet-makers, textile artists and more.

In summer a handicrafts tour bus takes visitors around selected workshops to sample the wide range of craftwork being produced. Bornholms Kunstmuseum (Art Museum of Bornholm), perched on Helligdomsklipperne (Sanctuary Rocks) between Gudhjem and Tejn, contains an extensive collection of works by painters from the Bornholm School (open May–Oct: 10am–5pm; July–Aug: also Wed until 9.30pm; Nov–Apr: 1pm–5pm, closed Mon; entrance fee).

exhibitions depicting life on the land and agricultural implements (open mid-May–late Oct: 10am–5pm, closed Mon; entrance fee; tel: 56 48 55 98).

From Gudhjem Harbour one can sail to the group of islands collectively known as **Ertholmene**. The largest of these are **Christiansø 9** (*see Insight On Christiansø, pages 208–209*), and **Frederiksø**, about 20 km (13 miles) to the northeast. With a total population of about 130 between them, they are interesting places to visit. A naval base was constructed here in about 1864, but today only fishermen and their families live on this "fortress in the sea". The islands are rocky, with castle towers, batteries, and cannon serving as reminders of the past. To the northwest is the uninhabited island of **Græsholmen**, protected as a sanctuary for seabirds. The top of the lighthouse, which once housed political prisoners, provides a good view of the islands and is worth a visit.

Østerlars Kirke 10 (consecrated to St Laurentius), just over 4 km (2½ miles) southwest from Gudhjem, is the largest of the four famous "round churches" of Bornholm. The enormous support pillars create the impression of a fortress, which was the second purpose of the structure. Inside the church (built around 1150), the vault is painted with fine frescoes of biblical scenes. On the north wall of the oval-shaped choir, stone steps lead to the second storey, where the hollow central pillar has two entrances. The outer wall has a watchman's gallery. The double altar piece was painted by the local artist Poul Høm. The dual-purpose of church and fortification is rare except in Denmark.

Festivals and food

Scandinavia offers numerous classical music festivals, and one of the most important is held on Bornholm. From the middle of July until the beginning of September, many visitors come only to hear the music. In the winter season professional Danish theatre companies visit. Rønne Theatre provides an excellent and intimate stage for their work; local amateur theatre groups also perform.

The contrast between the busy summer season and the quiet life of the rest of the year is obvious. Some like it, some do not. Almost all the residents are members of one club or another: pigeons, stamps, mushroom-picking – every conceivable hobby has a club of its own – and the various sports all have their own fans, too.

During the summer months, freshly landed herrings are delivered to the smokehouses. Here they are turned from their original silver colour into the "golden Bornholmers" dearly loved by Danes, which can often be seen drying on stands outside. Elderwood gives them their special taste. One can eat them warm from the oven or put them on black bread, sprinkle them with salt, and add chopped chives, radishes and an egg yolk on top.

Baltic salmon is said to be the finest edible fish in the world, and is normally available here. Pickled herrings were once served for breakfast, but now they're a lunchtime speciality. The best spiced herrings are produced on Christiansø. Farm products are of high quality, and one can often find a good bargain at roadside stalls.

Bornholm by bike

Of course, one can rent a car or take a bus, but still the best way to travel around Bornholm, like the rest of Denmark, is by bicycle. You hire a bike for a couple of days to escape the noise, smells and hassle of traffic. An extensive network of bicycle paths has been established on former railway rights-of-way. It is easy to find houses, hotels, and campsites en route, but remember to book lodgings in advance in the summer season. Use the tourist offices to solve problems or answer questions.

Residents often rent rooms or houses to visitors – at various prices. Bear in mind that there are many tourists on the island during the summer season, and that most are drawn to the southeast part of the island and to its wonderful beaches, **Dueodde ⓫** and **Balka**.

Future dilemmas

During the late 19th and early 20th centuries the island attracted immigrants from the impoverished districts of southern Sweden who came to look for prosperity on Bornholm. For a closer look at that phase of the island's history, read the novel *Pelle Erobreren* (*Pelle the Conqueror*), by the Danish writer Martin Anderson Nexø. In those days the immigrant Swedes earned their living on the farms and in the granite quarries; today the situation is reversed, as young Bornholmers seek work in the high-technology factories of heavy industry in southern Sweden. Will Bornholm survive because of, or in spite of, the tourist industry? Its status as a "Green Island" necessarily competes with the practical need to develop industry and keep its younger people. Yet the importance of tourism to the local economy cannot be ignored. ❑

Map on page 202

Aboard the ferry to Christiansø, a popular summer excursion from Bornholm.

BELOW: one of the many herring smokehouses.

CHRISTIAN'S ISLANDS: THE "PEA-POD ROCKS"

*Denmark's easterly possession, Christiansø is
just twice as big as the deck of an aircraft carrier,
but it offers the best natural harbour in the Baltic*

Only the Post Office
recognises the island of
Christiansø as part of
Bornholm, lying just 20
km (12 miles) east
from Denmark's Baltic
outpost. Denmark has
more than 400 islands,
79 of which are
inhabited. The sea was
the prime source of
income for the smaller
communities, but today tourism plays a key role.

Christiansø, its two tiny neighbours and all
that's on them still belong to the Danish Navy,
which fortified the outposts in 1658 to control
shipping in the Baltic Sea. Fortifications
surrounding the two inhabited islands are the
prime attractions for the many visitors who dock
in the old harbour for day-long visits. Ferries
depart from Svaneke on Bornholm throughout the
year, and from Allinge and Gudhjem in summer.

BRING A BOAT OR TENT

Accommodation is sparse. If you want to stay
longer and don't know anyone with a *hytte*
(cottage), it's advisable to bring your own boat or
a tent. The *kro* (inn) serves good meals, and you
can buy groceries and
drinks at the shop.

A century ago, the
air and light attracted
painters, and the
island authorities
still give artists
special attention. The
shades of the sea and
sky are a perennial
challenge to painters and
photographers. Each sees
the islands through special
eyes, and all find
something to
remember
them by.

▷ **THE ISLANDS**
Frederik's and Christian's
islands are all rocks and
red roofs. Behind lies
Grassholm, inhabited only
by birds, and tiny Tat with
an automatic light.

△ **STUCK-UP GLOVES**
Fishermen's gloves dry on
poles in front of the
wheelhouse insignia of
Toni Ann, the first modern
fishing vessel to be based
on Christiansø.

◁ **HOURS OF SUN**
A glass ball atop the
lighthouse focuses
sunlight on a card,
charring a line
across it to provide
a daily record.

△ **OLD BARRACKS**
Christiansø harbour is
fronted with old buildings,
modernised for the year-
round residents – there
are some 125 people
living on the island.

PARTY-TIME ON FREDERIKSØ

Across the footbridge from Christiansø, fishermen's houses border the narrow street on Frederiksø, the second pea in the pod, leading to the "Moon". That's the name of the newer of two dance halls. The older one was in the round stone Little Tower (*above*), which lent its name though not its shape to the nearby new "Moon".

After the tourists have departed on the last ferry at 4pm, the local bar comes to life.

"The lighthouse keeper is the king and keeper of the keys," says Erik Hoffmann, a mainland marine biologist who used to tie up his little research vessel on the island overnight. "He finds some kids to run up and down the street yelling, 'Big ball on the Moon tonight!'"

Refreshments appear and musicians materalise. "There's always someone who can play," says Hoffmann. "I remember Søren, an accordian player. And Henning on his squeeze box. There was always a Swede on banjo, and a flute player, too."

△TIME FOR A BEER
After the visitors have sailed away, native islanders gather for their "five o'clock meeting" and a beer on the Green.

◁ TOURIST FERRY
Big boat in a little harbour, this ferry from Bornholm calls on the island three times a day. Frederiksø's smaller tower peeks over her wheelhouse.

FUNEN

Bridging the water between Zealand and Jutland is the island of Funen, "Garden of Denmark" and home to some of the most beautiful castles and manor houses in the country

Map on page 214

Denmark's central island of **Funen** (*Fyn* in Danish) is known for its natural beauty, flowered gardens, castles and manor houses. Danes call it "the Garden of Denmark". Cycling tours take you along hundreds of kilometres of marked routes. Here, too, lies historic Odense, the birthplace of author Hans Christian Andersen (*see page 227*). South Funen and the island archipelago are a paradise for anglers and yachtsmen.

Funen's title is particularly apt for an island that is a mixture of winding roads, neatly groomed fields and trimmed hedges. Old village farmhouses often have thatched roofs, with lilac trees and spikes of pink hollyhock swaying against their white walls.

Funen's 3,458 sq km (1,335 sq miles) snuggle neatly into a rolling landscape with no hill higher than 137 metres (450 ft). Everything is tucked into a convenient circle. It might have been designed to provide a couple of days, or even a week, of comfortable touring by car or, even better, by bike.

Shelter and soil

There are two main cities. Odense in the centre is the birthplace of Hans Christian Andersen and is devoted to his memory. Svendborg to the south is the gateway to the islands of the Funen Archipelago (*see page 231*). Some are no more than a rocky speck but, where nature has been kind in providing shelter and soil, everything grows.

Funen is also an island of manors and country houses. Until 1788, the peasants were tied to a particular landowner and worked as feudal tenants. Danes regard the abolition of villeinage as one of the major events in Danish history. It was the start of Denmark's system of social rights, which now makes the country one of the most liberal in the world. Today, the manor houses seem benevolent, even protective, and many are hotels and restaurants where you can enjoy a drink or eat outdoors in the long Scandinavian twilight.

Funen provides much of the country's horticultural produce and corn. Tomatoes and cucumbers sprout in the greenhouses. The island also provides the house plants which grace windowsills all over Europe.

The Funen circle

When coming from Copenhagen, the usual way to reach Funen is by train or car, across the mighty Great Belt bridge to Nyborg on Funen's east coast. A Little Belt bridge links it to east central Jutland on the opposite side. Your choice then is circling the islands from Nyborg or Middelfart, and basing yourself either in Odense or Svendborg to make excursions. Distances in Funen and its islands are short, as they are in most

PRECEDING PAGES: murals at the house of Hans Christian Andersen, Odense. **LEFT:** drystone wall, typical of Funen. **BELOW:** sailing at Svendborg.

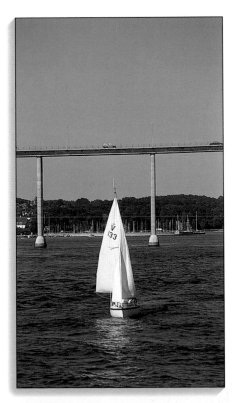

TIP

The Great Belt Link at Nyborg, completed in 1998, is Europe's biggest suspension bridge. The view is spectacular from a car or bus, but if you take a train, all you see is the inside of a tunnel.

of Denmark. Driving is easy but the most satisfying way to see Funen is on bicycle. You can stop at a gate to look at a prize sheep or lean your bike beside one of the little white-washed churches to take a look inside. Above all, you can inhale the scent of clusters of wild flowers that lie on either side of the roads below wild rose hedges. Soon it may feel as though Denmark is not so flat after all, but the effect of the fresh air and exercise is marvellous.

Most older towns on Funen started as fishing ports and trading centres. There is a tradition of seamanship, particularly in south Funen and the islands. Since the days when Funen ships plied the seas of the world, the shipping trade has shrunk in size. Today, these calm waters and their quaint seaports have become havens for leisure sailors who set their course from all over northern Europe.

Grand defences

Before heading north out of **Nyborg ❶** for Kerteminde and the Hindsholm Peninsula, take a look at **Nyborg Slot**, one of the oldest of Denmark's royal

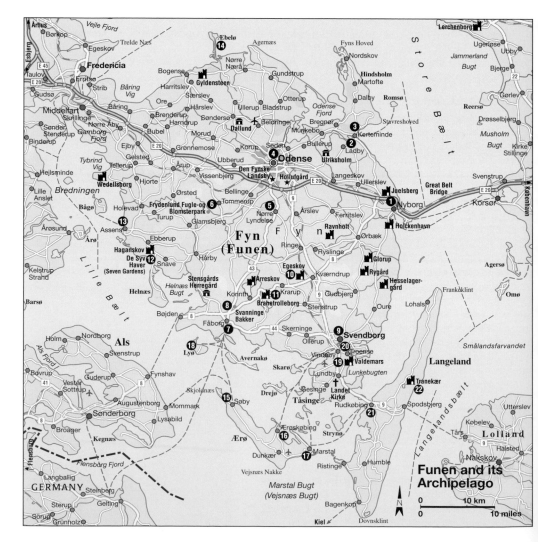

castles, which dates from 1170 (open March–May: 10am–3pm, closed Mon; June-Aug: 10am–4pm; Sept–late Oct: 10am–3pm, closed Mon; entrance fee; tel: 65 31 02 07). It was built to defend the country from the Wends of North Germany and, during the Middle Ages, was the meeting place for the three ruling powers of monarchy, nobility, and clergy. But fashions change. Copenhagen became the seat of power and, in 1722, much of Nyborg Slot was demolished to provide building materials for Odense Castle. Today, part of the original ramparts and moat remain to give a magnificent view, and the castle has a fine interior of great echoing, empty rooms, with a 30-metre (100-ft) banqueting hall.

About 15 km (9 miles) north from Nyborg, a short detour just southwest of Kerteminde takes you to the underground remains of a Viking chieftain's burial ship at **Ladby ❷** (open Mar–May and Sept–Oct: 10am–4pm, closed Mon; June–Aug: 10am–5pm; Nov–late Feb: 11am–3pm, closed Mon, Tue; entrance fee). With him in his 22-metre (72-ft) Viking ship, the chief took what he prized most: his weapons, hunting dogs and 11 horses (*see box, page 218*).

Kerteminde ❸ is the island's foremost fishing village, with old half-timbered houses in Langegade, and a couple of museums. Most towns in Funen have little workshops and craftspeople of many different skills, and Kerteminde offers stoneware and pottery at local shops.

Many of the island's traditional manor houses are today put to new uses. Not far from Kerteminde is one of the most beautiful, **Ulriksholm**, which has become a hotel. At Ulriksholm, visitors share a more gracious past, with an obligatory ghost and four-poster beds in many of the rooms.

Kerteminde leads north to the peninsula of **Hindsholm**, which pushes out into the Kattegat. It has a more dramatic landscape than the rest of Funen, and

Map on page 214

The first Danish constitution was drawn up in 1282 at Nyborg Slot, above.

BELOW: typical thatched-roofed houses on Funen.

Carl Nielsen

At the height of his fame at the banquet for his 60th birthday, the composer Carl Nielsen told the audience that his mother had always said to him: "Don't forget that Hans Christian Andersen was poor like you." There may have been something about the 19th-century air of the island of Funen which inspired poor boys to rise to fame but it is more likely that Nielsen was inspired by this most famous of Danes, 60 years Nielsen's senior. Their circumstances were similar. Both came from humble homes. Both left Odense to seek fortune in Copenhagen. Both were successful.

Carl Nielsen was born in 1865 in Nørre Lyndelse, 10 km (7 miles) south of Odense. His father, Niels, was a tradesman and also a folk musician who was in great demand for his traditional dance tunes. Playing the violin was a source of additional income for Niels, but his principal instrument was the cornet which he played with the local music society.

From musical society and peasant gatherings, young Carl gained an education in, and love of, the music of Haydn and Mozart as well as the traditional airs of Funen. The latter's flavour, along with the island's light-hearted humour, he incorporated in his *Springtime in Funen*, written in his fifties.

At the age of 14 Carl became a trombonist in the Regimental Band of Odense. He was also an accomplished violinist and had begun to play the piano and compose. His earliest compositions, at the age of eight, were two dance tunes – and all this while working as a grocer's apprentice.

Like Andersen, Nielsen wrote a memoir, *My Childhood*, and like Andersen, Nielsen took himself to Copenhagen when he was 18. There he introduced himself to the composer Niels W. Gade, and to J.P.E. Hartmann, director of the Copenhagen Conservatoire and the greatest name in Danish Romantic music. At this stage Neilsen's main instrument was the violin; his aim was to compose.

At the Royal Theatre Orchestra, where he became second violinist, he found another patron in the Norwegian conductor and composer, Johan Svendsen. In 1908 Nielsen had graduated to first conductor when Svendsen retired and, in the meantime, Svendsen had encouraged Nielsen to compose. Nielsen worked right across the range of composition from symphonies and other orchestral and chamber music, concertos, organ and piano works, to opera, choral music and songs.

At 25, he won a prestigious fellowship which allowed him to travel, and went straight to Dresden to steep himself in Wagner's ideas and to Berlin.

Nielsen composed two operas: the dark drama of *Saul og David* and *Maskarade* (Masquerade), a comic opera with much in common with Mozart's *The Marriage of Figaro*. Both operas are popular in Denmark, along with many of his great choral works, such as *Hymnus Amoris*, written in his thirties.

On Nielsen's 60th birthday in 1925, the king dubbed the composer Knight Commander of the Order of the Dannebrog, and the day culminated in a gala concert in Tivoli Gardens and a great banquet. ❏

LEFT: Carl Nielsen, the acclaimed composer, set out from Odense in search of fame and fortune.

some excavated barrows to indicate long habitation. Southwest of Kerteminde in the centre of Funen lies **Odense ❹**, Denmark's third-largest city and home of fairytale author Hans Christian Andersen (*see page 223*).

Just south of Odense is **Den Fynske Landsby** (Funen Village, Sejerskovvej 20), which gives a feeling of the whole island (open Apr– mid-June: 10am–5pm; mid-June–mid-Aug: 9am–7pm; mid-Aug–Oct: 10am–5pm; Nov–March, 11am–3pm; always closed Mon; entrance fee; tel: 66 13 13 72). It contains around 20 old farm buildings from different areas, with a vicarage, workshops, a windmill and water mill. Many of the buildings are still in working order. Funen Village is a delightful spot where the blackbirds whistle in competing chorus on a summer afternoon.

At **Nørre Lyndelse ❺**, 13 km (8 miles) south, stands the childhood home of Denmark's foremost composer, Carl Nielsen (*see box, left*). A few rooms have been converted into the **Carl Nielsen Museet**, a memorial to the man who wrote about this area in his book, *My Childhood in Funen* (open May–Sept: 11am-3pm; Oct–Apr: 11am–3pm, closed Mon; entrance fee; tel: 66 13 13 72).

Before taking the direct route south to Fåborg, detour 20 km (12 miles) west to the Tommerup and Vissenbjerg area, home of **Frydenlund Fugle-og Blomsterpark ❻**, literally a bird and flower park, with 2,000 species in idyllic surroundings (open April–Sept: 10am–4pm; June–Aug: 10am–6pm; entrance fee; tel: 64 76 13 22).

The Kerteminde landscape has attracted some of Denmark's most renowned artists. Their work can be seen at the town's Johannes Larsen Museum in Møllebakken (tel: 65 32 37 27).

Tuneful Fåborg

Fåborg ❼ on south Funen is a lovely little town where **Klokketårnet**, a carillon, chimes out a hymn four times a day. It's the largest carillon in Europe and the town's main landmark. Places to visit include **Den Gamle Gård** (**Old Manor**), at Holkegade 1–3, built in 1725 and established as a museum in 1932 (open mid-May–early Sept: 10:30am–4:30pm; entrance fee; tel: 62 61 33 38).

BELOW: shopping on two wheels.

If you could chose only one place to visit in Fåborg, it must be **Fåborg Museum for Fynsk Kunst**, at Grønnegade 75, an art gallery with a wonderful collection by the "Funen artists", mainly from the period 1880–1920 (open Nov–Mar: 11am–3pm, closed Mon; Apr–May: 10am–4pm; June–Aug: 10am–5pm; Sept: 10am–4pm; entrance fee; tel: 62 61 06 45). This 1915 gallery, now restored, shows the typical style of the Funen painters, renowned for their use of light, and includes work by Peter Hansen, Fritz Syberg and Johannes Larsen, and sculptures by Kai Nielsen.

From Fåborg, the next major town to the east is Svendborg. The area between these two places can well claim to be the most beautiful in Funen. Its hilly terrain is the result of the last Ice Age, 12,000 years ago. The heather-covered **Svanninge Bakker ❽**, about 10 km (6 miles) north of Fåborg, is a national park. **Svendborg ❾** is a beautiful market town and a good centre for touring. Along with Fåborg, it is the gateway to the southern islands.

Egeskov Slot ❿, situated 14 km (9 miles) north of Svendborg, is one of Denmark's most famous historic sights (open May: 10am–5pm; June: 10am–6pm;

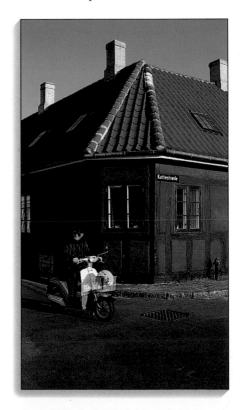

July: 10am–8pm; Aug: 10am–6pm; Sept: 10 am–5pm; entrance fee; tel: 62 27 10 16). Egeskov means oak forest, and the oaks were felled around 1540 to form the piles the castle stands on . This well-preserved castle has gardens that range from Renaissance and baroque to English and French designs, elegant enough to gain admiration even from professional gardeners.

Egeskov houses a **Veteranmuseum (Veteran Motor Museum)**, with a fine collection of old cars, aircraft, motor cycles, and horse-drawn carriages (open 10am–4pm). Egeskov's restored banqueting hall, used as a concert hall, is open to the public. The castle grounds also feature a re-creation of its 200-year-old **maze**. The "labyrinth", as it is now called, has 1.6 km (1 mile) of paths screened by 2,200 tall bamboo shoots. Egeskov's owner in 1985 asked a remarkable Dane to redesign it – Piet Hein. The late architect, writer and scientist first saw the old maze in 1938, and his restored labyrinth is claimed to be the biggest island maze in the world. The terminally "lost" can use one of the strategically-placed emergency exits.

From Egeskov, drive southwest towards Fåborg, and after 13 km (8 miles) you will pass **Brahetrolleborg** ⓫, once a Cistercian abbey, and later a baronial castle. Here, at the end of villeinage, Johan Ludvig Reventlow allowed his peasants to burn a wooden horse to symbolise his granting of their freedom.

Along the west coast

From Fåborg, turn northwest to explore Funen's west coast. Almost immediately you see the impressive gates of **Stensgårds Herregård**, a three-winged manor house hotel. Steensgårds is a lovely place to stay with period-style bedrooms, modern bathrooms, and the ideal spot for a meal in the garden (tel: 62 61 94 90).

Bogense in north Funen has been a seaport and official market town since 1288. Many of its old, half-timbered houses stand intact around the ancient market square.

BELOW:
Hunting Room
at Egeskov Slot.

BURIAL SHIPS OF OLD

One of Denmark's most remarkable archaeological discoveries is the Ladby Ship in northeast Funen. About 1,000 years ago, a Viking ship with a magnificent dragon's head and tail was hauled up on land near Ladby. The body of a high-ranking man, possibly a prince or a warrior, was placed at one end and at the other the bodies of several horses and dogs. It was then roofed over with planks and buried. The body and some artefacts were removed years later and the man was possibly reburied elsewhere in Christian fashion, as was the body of King Gorm in Jutland. The burial ship was rediscovered in 1935 and is now visible in all its Viking splendour through a domed covering (*see page 215*).

In nearby Glavendrup to the west lies Denmark's best preserved Bronze Age stone ship, including a stone bearing Denmark's longest runic inscription. Part of it reads: "Ragnhild raised this stone in honour of Alle the Pale, priest of temples, high-esteemed lord of hosts. Ö Sote cut these runes in memory of his master. May Thor hallow these runes. May he who damages this stone or removes it to serve the memory of another become a wraith."

These ship burials are thought to symbolise a voyage across the sea to the land of the dead.

Just south of Assens at Ebberup are **De Syv Haver (The Seven Gardens)** ⓬, outstanding gardens created by Tove and Gunner Sylvest (open mid-Mar–Oct: 10am–5pm; entrance fee; tel: 64 74 12 85).

In the town of **Assens** ⓭ you can visit the Willemoes Mindestuer (Memorial Rooms), Østergade 36, the birthplace of Danish war hero Peter Willemoes (open June–Aug: 10:30am–noon, 2pm–5pm, closed Mon; also open Easter and autumn holidays; entrance fee; tel: 64 71 11 90). In the Napoleonic Wars, he commanded a defence battery with such bravery during the British bombardment of Copenhagen that Nelson himself is said to have complimented him. It is a museum of cultural history, largely devoted to marine subjects.

Fifteen kilometres (9 miles) north from Assens on the road to Middelfart, a broad west-facing bay at **Tybrind Vig** is a site for underwater archaeology. This northwest area gradually becomes flatter as you approach the coast. The exception lies just north of Middelfart, where the landscape ends in steep dramatic cliffs down to the sea. Off the little town of **Bogense**, 25 km (15 miles) northeast of Middelfart, at low tide you can walk to the island of Æbelø ⓮, an unspoilt landscape rich in undisturbed wildlife.

The town pump at Bogense on Funen's north coast.

About 3 km (2 miles) east of Bogense is the castle of **Gyldensteen**, a late-Renaissance building with an impressive gatehouse (closed to the public). Here, Karen Blixen (pen name Isak Dinesen), author of *Out of Africa*, wrote some of her books during the German Occupation of Denmark in World War II. The early seat of the Blixen-Finecke family, **Dallund Manor House**, lies 13 km (8 miles) to the southeast.

From Bogense, you can complete the Funen circle by touring along the wild, sparsely populated north coast to the Hindsholm Peninsula and Kerteminde. ❑

BELOW: a Danish landmark, the 16th-century Egeskov Slot.

ODENSE

Map on page 224

The university town of Odense lies at the heart of Funen. A buzzing cultural centre, Odense is also renowned as the birthplace of the writer, Hans Christian Andersen

O dense is the quaint but lively capital of Funen and, with some 200,000 people, is Denmark's third-largest city. Odense is rich in history and famous as the home of 19th-century storyteller Hans Christian Andersen, the deity of Danish literature.

The first official reference to Odense is found in a document from 988 by the German Emperor, Otto III, in which he grants certain tax privileges to its church community. But Odense had certainly been in existence a long time before that. Its name stems from Old Norse and means "the sanctuary of Odin," the wise and mighty chief god. So the place was important enough to be worthy of Odin's protection before the Christian conversion of Denmark.

Barely 100 years after Emperor Otto's charter, King Knud II was murdered by some of his rebellious subjects in the wooden Skt Albani Kirke (church). They were dissatisfied with the exorbitant taxes he imposed to support raids against England. The Pope responded by canonising the martyred king as Skt Knud, and his grave was transferred to the stone church he built just a year before his death.

In 1139 this church was reconsecrated as **Skt Knuds Domkirke** Ⓐ (Cathedral) and, with a few modifications, is one of the most beautiful landmarks of Odense today. It's adorned with a finely detailed, gilded altarpiece made by Claus Berg in Germany in 1521. In the crypt lie the remains of King Knud and his brother, Benedict, both murdered in Odense in 1086.

PRECEDING PAGES: an old windmill at Skovsgårde. **LEFT:** Odense, ancient and modern. **BELOW:** a local resident.

Garden city

The most striking feature of today's Odense is its gentle beauty. It's largely a garden city, with green foliage as characteristic as red brick and roof tiles.

From the slightly elevated vantage point of the highway just west of Odense, the city's skyline is broken only by the cathedral tower in the very centre, the high-rise hospital of Odense University, the Thrige-Titan engine factory, and the harbour cranes.

In few other cities will one find a river in the centre of town that is clean enough to offer amateur fishermen both sea trout and eel. Urban anglers are a familiar sight. This is an accomplishment considering that Odense was once a polluted industrial city as so many others in Europe. Today, the quarter around the old factory buildings at Kongensgade and Vestergade has been revitalised and is a popular magnet for young people and the university crowd.

In the summertime the place is teeming with life, especially during performances of live music. Every Saturday from June to August, river boats depart from Munkemose at Filosofgangen and shuttle people

TIP

The Odense Adventure Pass is sold by the Odense Tourist Bureau and offers major savings on public transport, guided tours, museums and attractions. It's valid for 24 or 48 hours.

about 3 km (2 miles) south to Fruens Bøge (Madame's Beech Tree), where jazz ensembles play. Perhaps the most spectacular conversion has been the transformation of the old city slaughterhouse, Kægtorvet on Ruggårdsvej into the headquarters of Denmark's second state-owned television channel.

The former textile mill, **Brandt's Klædefabrik ⓑ**, at Brandts Passage 37-43 off Vestergade, is now a spacious multi-purpose building for permanent and travelling exhibitions, concerts and shows, complete with café-restaurant and cinema. It houses Denmark's only Museet for Fotokunst (Museum of Photographic Art, tel: 66 13 78 16); the Kunsthallen art gallery, featuring a varied programme of exhibitions (tel: 66 13 78 97); Dannmarks Grafiske Museum (The Danish Museum for Printing, tel: 66 12 10 20); and Tidens Samling (The Time Collection, tel: 65 91 19 42) which follows 20th-century daily life and fashion from 1900 to the 1970s (all open 2 Jan–30 Dec: 10am–5pm, closed Mon; July–Aug: 10am–5pm daily; entrance fee).

For modern design and architecture, visit the **Blangstedgård ⓒ** area to the southeast of the city, where architects and construction firms have presented the latest ideas on different kinds of housing and town planning. The post-modern wave in architecture has combined with traditional Danish craftsmanship in many of the buildings here, a combination at which the Danes excel.

Odense University was designed with daring architectural vision in concrete and rusted iron. It was built here in the southeastern outskirts in the prosperous 1960s, and is a relatively recent addition to the city. But its four faculties (medicine, natural sciences, humanities, and political science with business studies) have already gained considerable recognition in the international scientific community.

BELOW: open-air concert at Brandt's Klædefabrik.

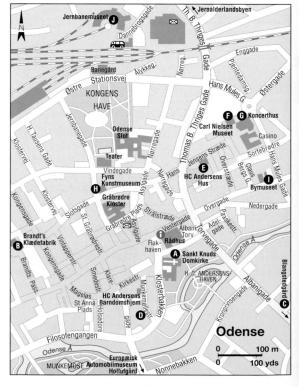

Famous personalities

Odense is best known as the original home of storyteller Hans Christian Andersen. The composer Carl Nielsen also spent his early years in the city.

Map on page 224

Munkemøllestræde ⓓ west of the cathedral is the tiny cobblestone street with the tiny house where Andersen grew up in the early 1800s (open Apr–Sept: 10am–5pm; Oct–Mar: noon–3pm; entrance fee). This is a simple shoemaker's cottage where his family lived in one room. It holds many childhood mementos and also letters from the novelist Charles Dickens and the "Swedish Nightingale", the singer Jenny Lind, long admired by Andersen. The street has been lovingly restored and the houses are inhabited, so the neighbourhood still lives on.

Hans eventually left Odense to find fame and acclaim in Copenhagen. He did, first in Denmark, then in Europe and the rest of the world. His tales have been translated into every written language on earth (*see page 227*).

Northeast of the cathedral, not far from the humble house, is the outstanding **Hans Christian Andersen Hus ⓔ** on Hans Jensens Stræde (open Sept–mid-June: 10am–4pm; mid-June–end Aug: 9am–7pm; closed Mon; entrance fee; tel: 66 13 13 72). The museum houses a large collection devoted to the writer's life, with pictures, letters, manuscripts, and personal belongings. One room is a re-creation of his later study in Copenhagen, evocative enough to give the feeling that he could have sat there the night before.

Carl Nielsen, although not as well known as Andersen, is nonetheless associated with modern composers such as Schönberg and Stravinsky (*see page 216*). Not only did Nielsen compose music which is now on the international concert repertoire, he enriched the Danish song tradition with a number of new tunes

BELOW: re-creating the stories of Hans Christian Andersen.

Map on page 224

Every Wednesday and Saturday markets fill the plazas and squares around Odense Koncerthus, selling everything from fresh produce to antiques.

inspired by the local folk traditions, the best known being his *Springtime in Funen*. Nielsen's childhood home lies outside Odense in Nørre Lyndelse. The formal **Carl Nielsen Museet G** is in Odense at Claus Bergs Garde 11 and is also devoted to his wife, Anne Marie Nielsen, who was a sculptor of no mean talent (open 10am–4pm; entrance fee).

Odense supports a variety of theatres and a major concert hall, **Odense Koncerthus G**, on Hans Mules Gade. It houses the city's symphony orchestra as well as visiting orchestras, and ensures that the tradition of stagecraft and music flourishes. In 1982, the score of an unknown symphony by Mozart was found in the city archives. It is now officially known as the *Odense Symphony*.

Artistic heritage

Head west from the Town Hall along the main shopping street of Vestergade and turn right along Jernbanegade to reach the **Fyns Kunstmuseum (Funen Art Gallery) H**. The museum (open 10am–4pm, closed Mon; entrance fee; tel: 66 13 13 72) focuses on Danish art from 1750 onwards. It also features international artists, works by young sculptors and has a special exhibit of concrete art.

The progress from drab provincial town to lively city is relatively recent, which helps to explain Odense's restless energy. The **Bymuseet (City of Odense Museum) I**, at Overgade 48–50, illustrates this urban history with displays from the Viking Age, medieval times and reconstructed houses from the 16th century to the present (open 10am-4pm, closed Mon; entrance fee; tel: 66 13 13 72). You can also relive Odense's history and prehistory at **Hollufgård**, Hestehaven 201, a manor house in the south of the city which houses an archaeological centre (open 10am–4pm, closed Mon; entrance fee; tel: 66 13 13 72).

The **Jernalderlandsbyen (Iron-Age Village)** in northern Odense at Stor Klaus 40 is a reconstructed ancient environment built according to discoveries from archaeological excavations. The prehistoric dwellings have been converted into active workshops where craftspeople practise forgotten skills (open Jan–late June: Mon–Thu 8:30am–3.30pm, Fri 8:30am–2pm, closed Sat, Sun; late June–early July: Mon–Fri 8:30am–4pm, closed Sat, Sun; July: Mon–Fri 8:30am–4pm, Sun 10am–4pm, closed Sat; entrance fee; tel:66 18 09 87).

Vintage road and rail

Rail enthusiasts will be pleased to know that Odense is also home to one of Scandinavia's most popular railway museums, **Jernbanemuseet J**, behind the station at Dannebrogsgade 24 (open 10am–4pm; entrance fee; tel: 66 13 66 30). Here are working locomotives, carriages and wagons in a real station setting from the age of steam. The museum also includes an exhibit of model ferries.

Just southeast of Odense is the **Europæisk Automobilmuseum (European Automobile Museum)**, Fraugde Kærbyvej 203, with some 100 cars and vehicles from around the 1950s (open Apr–Sept: 10am–5pm; entrance fee; tel: 65 95 18 80).

Odense is at once young and old, cultural and technical. The lucky visitor can spend days exploring it. ❑

BELOW: catching up on local events.

The magic of Hans Christian Andersen

Although his fairy tales had been read by generations, Hans Christian Andersen himself was not widely known internationally until Hollywood made a film of his life in 1952. Portraying him, Danny Kaye immortalised the song *Wonderful, Wonderful Copenhagen*; and, arguably, the film, the song, and the Little Mermaid (a character from one of Andersen's stories) have done more for tourism in Denmark than all its natural delights put together. An Andersen maxim was: "To travel is to live," which forever endears him to the travel industry.

His own life story, *The Fairy Tale of My Life*, written in 1855, is as fascinating as any of his well-loved tales. The son of a poor shoemaker's son, he achieved national acclaim in his lifetime, travelled the world, and was a guest of the rich and famous.

He was born in 1805 in Odense, on the island of Funen. The H.C. Andersen Barndomshjem (Childhood Home) is a small half-timbered house in Munkemøllestræde where, from 1807 to 1817, he lived with his parents. This house became a museum in 1930 and is today a part of the main Hans Christian Andersen Museum in Hans Jensens Stræde, where the writer was born (*see page 225*).

Founded in 1905, the museum contains many of his pictures, letters, manuscripts and books. In the reconstruction of his Copenhagen study Andersen's day boots are thrown carelessly aside and it is easy to see from their length how tall he must have been.

Quite apart from his skill as a writer, Andersen had a good singing voice and gifts as an artist. At the age of 14, he set off to Copenhagen to attend the Royal Theatre School and "become famous". Though his only success there was a walk-on part as a troll, the Theatre Board was perceptive enough to realise his gifts and found him a place at a state grammar school in Helsingør. His travels began early with a visit to Germany, and ranged widely. Later, he stayed in the castles and manor houses of his patrons but Copenhagen remained his permanent home.

Though he is now best known for children's fairy tales, Andersen wrote other books. His first, in 1831, *Shadow Picture of a Journey to the Harz Mountains and Saxony*, was the result of his early travels. Through his life, he continued to write poems, novels and plays and, in fact, his earliest taste of fame came from an obviously autobiographical novel, *The Improvisatore*, which described the rise to fortune of a poor Italian boy.

His early fairy tales, including *The Tinder Box* and *The Princess and the Pea*, were published in 1835 and brought him immortality. But his diaries record unrequited love and loneliness. In 1840, he met the Swedish singer Jenny Lind, "The Swedish Nightingale," and fell deeply in love with her, though she always called him "brother". His fairy tale, *The Nightingale*, was inspired by her.

When told he was to be made an honorary citizen of Odense in 1867, Andersen replied that it was "an honour greater than I had ever dreamt of." He died in 1875. ❑

RIGHT: the story-teller Hans Christian Andersen, whose childhood home can be seen in Odense.

FUNEN ARCHIPELAGO

Map on page 214

A short ferry crossing from southern Funen lie the islands of the archipelago, a haven for cyclists, anglers, sailors, ornithologists and those in search of tranquillity

You could spend a lifetime trying to visit all the islands of the Funen Archipelago and still miss a few. Only 19 are inhabited permanently and you would need not just time, but also a boat. On some of the islands, only birds make up the solitary population. Even the largest islands hold no more than a few thousand people, and others just a couple of families. But whatever the difficulties of getting there, these islands, with their untouched landscape and contented yellow beaches, make a marvellous holiday.

All summer long, the harbours of the main islands are full of boats from Denmark, the rest of Scandinavia, Germany and as far away as Britain. You can take day trips aboard wooden sailing ships or longer cruises through the archipelago. As you might have guessed, this is also an angler's paradise.

The **Funen islands** are a cradle of Denmark, dotted with prehistoric monuments proving that primitive people lived here thousands of years ago. As the Viking era ebbed, pirates saw the value of the islands for plunder, and they devastated the communities. In turn, many of the islanders became wary and savage, and took wicked revenge on shipwrecked mariners. But prosperity eventually returned and by the middle of the 19th century, the south Funen Archipelago was the second largest naval base in Denmark.

Today, past glories of the sea are a memory. Some of the more distant islands are depopulating, at least the natives, as young people often leave to make a living in the cities. Holiday residents usually replace them, but their presence is seasonal. The traditional industries of fishing and farming have declined and, though many of the larger islands have been able to turn to tourism and to providing yacht havens, distance is still a problem.

The irony is that only in the depth of a cold winter can some of the islanders forget their isolation, when the ice is thick enough to carry a car – just as it once carried an invading Swedish army.

PRECEDING PAGES: re-creating life as it once was. **LEFT:** hoeing in the beetroot fields. **BELOW:** attractive Ærøskøbing.

To the islands

Fåborg and Svendborg, with regular ferry services, provide the best jumping-off points from Funen. From Fåborg, it is just a short trip to the most beautiful island of all, Ærø.

Take the car ferry to **Søby ⑮** at the north of the island and, before you set off, visit its 12th-century church, Store Rise. At **Tingstedet** nearby, there is a 4,000-year-old barrow. Even if you have chosen to drive around Funen, to get the full flavour of the lovely island of Ærø, leave the car behind at Fåborg and hire a bike for the short cycle run from Søby to **Ærøskøbing ⑯**, the main town, and the old naval port of Marstal to the southeast. Cycling is easy and

Built in the 17th century, Valdemars Slot on Tasinge is worth visiting for its fine museum, Tea Pavilion and attractive location.

the roads wend past fertile fields and thatched farmhouses, medieval churches and windmills. The American author, Temple Fielding, said that Ærøskøbing was one of the five places that one should see in the world. Certainly the cobbled streets, with their brightly coloured houses, almost seem like a film set.

The oldest house, rosy-coloured and half-timbered, dates from 1645, and the citizens of this perfect small town pay for their privileges by accepting rigid controls on what they may do and not do to their homes. Look particularly at the doors of the little houses, all painted differently.

Ærøskøbing also has the **Flaske Peter Museum**, a "ship-in-a-bottle" collection of around 750 models, which is well worth seeing, and a similar collection of more than 520 **sailors' pipes** from all over the world (open May–Sept: 10am–5pm; Oct–Dec: 1–3pm; entrance fee; tel: 62 52 29 51). Det Gamle Posthus (The Old Post Office) is Denmark's oldest.

Marstal ⑰ was once one of Denmark's greatest ports, which might have held up to 300 wooden sailing ships in its harbour. The tradition of wooden ships continues today because the town has one of the few Danish shipyards which still builds in wood. Marstal is also famous for its collection of model ships at the **Marstal Søfartsmuseum** (Maritime Museum, open Oct–May: 10am–4pm, Sat 11am–3pm, closed Sun, Mon; May–Sept: 10am–4pm; June–Aug: 9am–5pm; July 9am–9pm; entrance fee; tel: 62 53 23 31).

Lyø and Avernakø

From Fåborg, ferries also run to the nearer but smaller islands of **Avernakø** and **Lyø** ⑱, both of which have good, inexpensive inns. Lyø's main village is beautiful, with 11 ponds lining the main street, and no trace of the strife of 1223, when King Valdemar and his son were captured by German warriors.

These and other islands are paradise for ornithologists but, though nature is the main attraction, in May you can see the ceremony of raising the 30-metre (100-ft) *Majstang* (Maypole). As late as the early 20th century, the islanders believed that crops would not grow without this ancient fertility rite.

The Southern Islands

Svendborg is the best gateway to the southern islands. The first island, reached by a narrow bridge, is **Tåsinge**, with some 5,000 inhabitants. This idyllic island was the setting for the tragic love affair between the Swedish Count Sixten Sparre and a Danish tightrope artiste, Elvira Madigan. Their sad story, which ended in suicide in 1899, was immortalised by the Swedish film director Bo Widerberg in a 1967 film; the couple lie in the graveyard of Landet Kirke.

On Tåsinge, you soon come to **Valdemars Slot** ⑲, one of Denmark's oldest privately owned castles, with a wonderful view over Svendborgsund (open May–Sept: 10am–5pm; entrance fee). It was built in 1640 by King Christian IV (responsible for much Danish architecture) for one of his sons, Prince Valdemar Christian. Most interesting is the castle church, with an excellent restaurant underneath. The church itself is lit only by candles. The Tea Pavilion,

mirrored in its own lake like the Taj Mahal, is now a café and looks over **Lunkebugten Bay**. The loveliest village on Tåsinge is **Troense** , which the Danes pronounce with dove-like sounds that match its gentle charm. Troense was once the home port for many sailing ships. Sitting on the veranda of the Troense Inn is one of the pleasures of a Funen summer. The slim masts of the sailing boats gather in the harbour against a darkening sea, and their wind-burnt owners carry their gear up to the inn.

Langeland

The next island is **Langeland**, literally "long land", connected to Tåsinge by a causeway-bridge. One of its famous sons was H.C. Ørsted, the discoverer of electromagnetism, who was born in the main town of **Rudkøbing** ㉑. Another famous resident was N.F.S. Grundtvig, a clergyman and founder of modern Danish education. Grundtvig in the 19th century preached "popular enlightenment," and the value of folk high schools, which are now an important part of the Danish education system (*see page 59*).

On the same road to the north of Langeland is the dramatic 13th-century **Tranekær Slot** ㉒ (not open to the public). To the south, Ristinge and Bagenkop both have excellent bathing beaches. In fact, nowhere along the coast of Funen and its islands are you far from good places to swim and sail.

All this tranquillity and beauty means peace and recreation to visitors, so it's sad to think that the real islanders are too often persuaded to move elsewhere to find work. Tourism can help to bring some prosperity, but the families that live on the small farms are hoping that new means of agriculture and the movement towards natural organic food may restore a stable prosperity to these islands. ❑

Map on page 214

TIP

Whether driving, cycling or walking, follow the "Daisy Routes" marked by a flower sign. These guide you past some of the most beautiful scenery in south Funen and the rest of Denmark.

BELOW: summer on the waters of the archipelago.

EAST JUTLAND

From the high point of Sky Mountain to the shimmering Lake District, from ancient rune stones to modern Lego bricks, East Jutland is a land of contrasts

The magic of East Jutland is not just in the air but in the water, the trees, and the ground as well. This area, which faces east to the Kattegat Sea, includes the Lake District around Silkeborg, and Himmelbjerget (Sky Mountain), at 147 metres (482 ft), one of Denmark's highest "mountains" and a place of pilgrimage for many Danes. The Gudenå, Denmark's longest river, runs north through East Jutland towards Randers on the Randers Fjord, and the Djursland peninsula – one of the most beautiful spots in the country – juts out into the Kattegat. To the south, East Jutland stretches as far as the towns of Vejle and Fredericia. The largest town is Århus ❶ (*see page 247*), Denmark's second largest city, situated on the east coast and famous for its autumn arts festival.

Tour by boat

By far the strongest motivation for a holiday in Eastern Jutland is a love of nature, outdoor life and active pursuits. The rivers that criss-cross the countryside make it the perfect place for botanists and bird watchers, mushroom and berry hunters, walkers and cyclists, anglers and sailors. It is possible to canoe all the way from the spring of Gudenåen in Tørring, through lakes Mossø and Julsø to Silkeborg, and farther on through Tange Sø to Randers. The trip takes at least four days, six to seven with children in the boat, and local tourist offices can reserve canoes.

The view from the top of **Himmelbjerget** ❷ over the Lake District is magnificent – a fact not missed by the hundreds of motorists who stop here daily in summer months. One flank of the mini-mountain runs down into Julsø lake, the starting point for the paddle-steamer MS *Hjejlen*, which has carried passengers to Silkeborg since 1861. The world's oldest paddle-steamer still in use, the *Hjejlen* is a relaxing way to see the Lake District. People with houses and cabins along the shores compete with each other to keep their gardens tidy for passers-by.

Skanderborg ❸ lies at the southeast end of the lake chain, the area's oldest community, with a charter granted more than 400 years ago and a 12th-century royal palace, built on a lake promontory. The chapel, **Slotskirken**, and a round tower are all that remain of this once strategic fortress, which fell into ruin in the 1700s. A model of the castle is on display at the **Skanderborg Museum** (open Jun–Aug: Tue–Sun 10am–4pm; Sept–May: Tue–Fri 2–4pm, Sat–Sun 1–4pm; free; tel: 86 52 24 99).

Skanderborg also hosts "Denmark's Prettiest Music Festival" in August every year, held in a beech tree forest on the edge of Lake Skanderborg. Music festivals are a culture in themselves in Denmark, where hundreds or even thousands of people camp for several

PRECEDING PAGES: rolling landscape of East Jutland. **LEFT:** heading up Himmelbjerget. **BELOW:** in pensive mood.

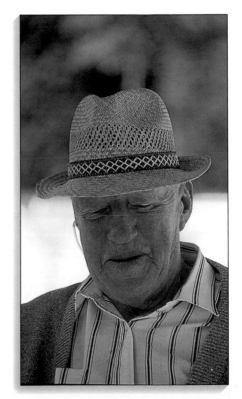

days to enjoy music from almost every genre, from classical to techno. **Ry ❹** is the town closest to Himmelbjerget, small and full of life, particularly during the summer when campers, canoeists, walkers and cyclists use the town as a base for sightseeing or excursions into nature.

The **Them ❺** district, west of Ry, is in the heart of woodland that forms some of Denmark's most untouched nature. Lakes snuggle between the trees, some with their waters protected against pollution, such as **Tingdalsøerne**, where the waters are the only habitat for a few rare plants. This is the "divide" of Jutland; to the east are gentle vistas of water and trees, while towards the west, wide stretches of moor lead to West Jutland. One fun summer excursion is to take the old **steam railway** from Bryrup to Vrads, which runs past lakes, over dams and heather moors and through the forest.

Gammel Rye, just south of Ry and Himmelbjerget, is the Lake District's smallest and oldest town. It was a cultural centre in the Middle Ages and as a result has several churches and **Skt Søren**, a notable holy spring. Opposite the

"Kroer" (inns) offer Danish meals in beautiful settings. Svostrupkro and Kongensbrokro, along the Gudenå River, were once frequented by bargemen.

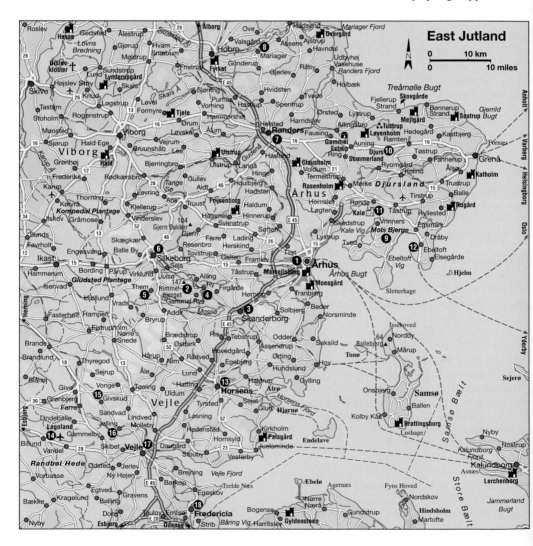

spring is a system of deep, sunken roads, formed in the Middle Ages as the sandy soil gave way under heavy traffic of the time.

Map on page 238

Prehistoric man

Silkeborg ❻ at the northwest end of the Lake District, was founded in the 1840s by paper manufacturer Michael Drewsen, who is now commemorated in a statue in **Torvet**, the main square. But if the town is young, the **Silkeborg Museum** (open May–Oct: 10am–5pm; Oct–May: Wed, Sat–Sun noon–4pm; entrance fee; tel: 86 82 14 99) has some of the oldest relics in the country. The remarkable centrepiece is the **Tollund Man**, who was hanged and thrown into a bog 2,200 years ago. His surprisingly well-preserved body was discovered by two local farmers in 1950 who rushed to report their discovery to the police. At first, most believed he was the victim of a modern crime. The museum displays the corpse as it lay when discovered but only the head is genuine; the rest of the body was unable to be preserved.

The **Silkeborg Kunstmuseum (Museum of Art)** is built around the glorious, colourful and playful work of the painter Asger Jorn, who was born in Silkeborg. His paintings and sculptures are complemented by those of 20th-century artists such as Dubuffet, Arp, Alechinsky, and others from the COBRA (Copenhagen, Brussels, Amsterdam) group (open Apr–Oct: 10am–5pm, closed Mon; Nov–Apr: Tues–Fri noon–4pm, Sat–Sun 10am–5pm; entrance fee; tel: 86 82 53 88). The privately-owned Galerie Moderne supplements this collection with changing exhibitions of painters and sculptors from the same period.

Northwest of Silkeborg, the Gudenå winds through the hills of **Gjern Bakker**. Along the river banks are an old road from Viborg to Skanderborg, once

BELOW: gathering mushrooms in early autumn.

Baroque Town Hall in Randers, on the Gudenå River.

reserved for kings and nobility, and the towpath used by bargees to pull their barges back to Skanderborg from the fjord port of Randers. Nowadays, the towpath has a less arduous role as one of Denmark's foremost nature trails. There are several protected areas around the railway town of **Gjern**, also the ruins of abbeys at **Tvilum** (where the church still stands). Other ruins by Alling lake were built by monks some 700 years ago.

The river meanders northeast to **Randers ❼**, an industrial centre where several buildings from the Middle Ages to the 17th century have been preserved. Vintage trains run throughout July from Randers north to Mariager or east to Allingåbro. **Mariager ❽** is the northernmost town of the area, known as the "town of roses", with its cobbled streets and half-timbered houses.

Vikings and castles

The **Djursland peninsula** has white beaches in the north, forests with deer and other animals, and the **Mols Bjerge ❾** (hills) on their own smaller peninsula in the south, part of a beautiful nature reserve. Tall, modern wind turbines churn clean electricity gracefully from several places along the rolling landscape. Potters and painters have made Djursland into a large art colony, their home galleries marked by hand-painted road signs that say *kunst* (art) or *keramik* (pottery). About 12 km (7 miles) east of Randers, **Hegedahl** in Fausing is just one of many galleries with regular customers who stop every year on their way to summer vacation spots on the peninsula. Along with the natural beauty, historical monuments from prehistoric to Viking times abound in Djursland.

Castles and manor houses flourish in this part of Jutland, one of the best being **Gammel Estrup** (open Apr–Oct: 10am–5pm; Nov–Mar: 11am–3pm;

BELOW: a great form of transport for all ages.

MOLS BJERGE

Ancient history meets beautiful nature at Mols Bjerge with cairns and grave mounds from prehistoric times scattered over the hills. The most impressive relic, the **Posekjær Stenhus** barrow (Denmark's Stonehenge), lies along the road from Agri to Grønfeld. From here one can follow the trail to **Tinghulen** (The Court Hole), a 25-metre (80-ft) ravine. This great crevasse was caused by a huge lump of ice trapped below the ground's surface as the Ice Age came to an end. With its sharp acoustics, Tinghulen was used as a "court room" until the late 17th century. A trail from here passes through heather-clad hills and forest to the Bronze Age burial mounds of **Trehøje**.

Only 200 years ago this area was still largely isolated from the rest of Jutland, and the peasants spoke their own dialect. The townspeople of Århus looked on them as rustics and told "*molbo* stories" which detailed their supposed stupidity. When the peasants decided to save their church bell from invaders, one story goes, they rowed out to sea and sank it. Then came the realisation that unless they marked the spot they would never find the bell again. Solemnly, they cut a notch in the side of the boat at the place where the bell lay and, congratulating themselves on their cleverness, rowed home once more.

closed Mon; entrance fee; tel: 86 48 30 01) west of **Auning**. The old house has 18th-century furniture, and an excellent agricultural museum traces the history of farming life from 1788 to the present day. An exhibition of country kitchens from 1788, 1888, and 1988 helps to give a good impression of life both outside and inside the farmhouse.

Beaches on the north side of the peninsula at **Fjellerup Strand** and **Skovgårde** have some of the best bathing waters in the country, and the nearby town of **Bønnerup Strand** is a local favourite for its fish market on the pier.

Tustrup, in the Hevring river valley 4 km (2 miles) southwest of Fjellerup Strand, contains an impressive prehistoric burial site, and 5 km (3 miles) to the southwest, the expansive forest surrounding the **Løvenholm manor house** is home to abundant wildlife. A few small roads transverse the forest; the one leading to the village of Marie Magdalene near Ryomgård passes several half-timbered, thatch-roofed houses, tucked into the trees.

On the east side of Løvenholm forest is **Djurs Sommerland ⑩** (open May: 10am–6pm; June–Aug: 10am–8pm; entrance fee; tel: 86 39 84 00), an amusement park built at the beginning of the 1980s. Its main attraction is Waterland for water fun of all sorts, as well as Cowboy Land, pony-riding, and a science centre – some 50 activities in all for families and children.

The port of **Grenå** is as far east as you can go on Djursland. Some three hours away by ferry from Grenå, is the small, desert-like island of **Anholt**.

Haunted dare

The southern peninsulas of Djursland jut down into the Bay of Århus, and the hills of Mols Bjerge can be seen easily from Århus itself. The ruins of the

Map on page 238

The ruined 15th-century monastery at Mariager.

BELOW: Gammel Estrup manor house, Djursland.

Legoland

More than a million people a year visit Legoland in the small town of Billund in the centre of Jutland. They come to marvel at the wonderful miniature world created from more than 35 million of the studded Lego plastic bricks, which have taken the world by as much storm as the Vikings did long ago.

The word Lego is a contraction of two Danish words, Leg Godt, which mean "Play well" and also, by coincidence, "I put together" in Latin. The name was coined by Ole Kirk Christiansen, a Danish carpenter who began making wooden toys when he was unemployed during the 1930s Depression.

By 1947, the company installed plastic injection moulding machinery and, by 1949, the plastic bricks were part of the Lego product range. During the 1950s they were developed to become the basic components of the then-revolutionary "Lego System of Play". Much of the toy's success has

stemmed from its versatility to click together in almost any way imagineable; six standard eight-stud bricks can be combined in as many as 102,981,500 different ways.

The son of the founder, Godtfred Kirk Christiansen, further developed the concept. He had the idea of creating a permanent exhibition of Lego buildings and models. This led to the opening of Legoland in 1968. Since then the park has found immense success with Danes and foreigners alike. Additional Legoland parks have opened in the USA and Great Britain, with another one planned for Germany in coming years.

The business remains under family control and the founder's grandson, Kjeld Kirk Kristiansen – the disparity in spelling of the surname was apparently an error by the registrar – has been managing director of Lego A/S since 1979.

The park's "Miniland" is a model-builder's dream world, with replicas of scenes from around the globe, including the Statue of Liberty, Rhineland castles and a Norwegian village. Danish scenes include the Amalienborg Palace and Nyhavn port in Copenhagen, and much more. With few exceptions, the buildings are made only from Lego bricks that can be bought anywhere.

A Lego train tours the park, and a safari ride is flanked by exotic Lego animals. Children can earn a Legoland Driver's Licence in the traffic school, based on the real Highway Code. In recent years other attractions have been added, including Castleland with its roller coaster, a Timber water ride, Pirateland and the Western Legoredo Town.

While the amusement park provides plenty for a day's activities, one of the most popular attractions is the indoor Lego Mindstorms Centre, which brings together modern computer technology and programmable Lego bricks. Children learn to build robots and bring them to life, testing them on a series of activities. In addition, giant bins of Lego bricks are found in an activity room, where children and adults can join daily building contests.

Legoland is open mid-June–Aug: 10am–9pm; Sept–mid-June: 10am–8pm; entrance fee (tel: 75 33 13 33). ❑

LEFT: Legoland in eastern Jutland, a colourful landscape created from millions of Lego bricks.

Kalø Slot , built in 1313, are situated on a small island on the edge of **Kalø Vig** cove on the north side of the bay. To reach the ruins, visitors walk along a cobbled road causeway and over grassy hillsides. Young Danes from the area test their bravery by attempting to camp overnight at the ruins, which are rumoured to be haunted.

Just below the Mols Bjerge on the Ebeltoft cove is the small, immaculate town of **Ebeltoft** ⓬, with the bright flowers of Rådhusgården echoing the tiles of the Gamle Rådhus, the old town hall built in 1789 and the smallest, unaltered town hall in Denmark. There are half-timbered houses, cobbled streets and even a night watch, to see that all is well. An additional interest is the **Frigatten Jylland** (Frigate *Jutland*), the last in a line of famous wooden battleships (tours: 10am–5pm; entrance fee; tel: 86 34 10 99). The Glasmuseet Ebeltoft (Ebeltoft Glass Museum) displays works from more than 500 artists from 40 countries (open 10am–5pm; entrance fee; tel: 86 34 17 99).

A house at Nordby on the island of Samsø, one of the prettiest villages in Denmark.

Island applause

The island of **Samsø** can be seen from Ebeltoft and Mols, but it must be reached by ferry from Hov, 25 km (15 miles) south of Århus. A haven for artists, farmers and nature-lovers alike, Samsø is renowned for its new potatoes and cheese. The north side of the island is blessed with a rolling green landscape formed during the Ice Age. On **Ballebjerg** hill, couples and families congregate to watch the sunset, applauding when the sun's daily performance is finished.

Nordby, on the northern tip, contains a wealth of colourful, cross-beam houses, as well as a proliferation of small art galleries. In the south, Brundby Rock Hotel, owned by a group of Danish rock musicians, is a great place to have dinner and hear live music.

BELOW: the town criers of Ebeltoft.

Fantasy land

Back on the mainland, 23 km (14 miles) west of Hov and 38 km (24 miles) south of Århus is **Horsens** ⓭, a modern, industrial city but one with a long history. Part of Horsens' **Klosterkirken (Abbey Church)** dates from 1200. Each year at the end of summer, the town hosts a **Middle Ages Festival**, with horseback duels between armoured knights, scores of activity booths for children, music and dance. The town goes out of its way to create the right atmosphere, covering streets with sand and wood chips and disguising rubbish bins under tree bark. Even the town's citizens dress up for the weekend – it's not uncommon to see robed peasants and wizards carrying groceries home in plastic shopping bags.

An imperative for children and youthfully-minded adults is a day at **Legoland** ⓮ (*see left*), Denmark's best known attraction, at **Billund** in the extreme southwest of East Jutland 50 km (31 miles) southwest of Horsens.

Lions at large

North of Billund, 8 km (5 miles) southeast of Give on highway 442 at **Givskud** ⓯, is **Løvepark** (Lion Safari Park; open May–Oct: 10am–2 hours before sunset; entrance fee; tel: 75 73 02 22). Lions, zebras,

Map on page 238

Dressed for Horsens' annual Middle Ages Festival.

BELOW: the valiant soldier at Fredericia.
RIGHT: field of wild flowers at Tvede.

elephants, giraffes, monkeys, and many more animals walk freely in the park, which tries to reproduce their natural environment as far as the unhelpful climate of a northern European country permits. Visitors view the wildlife from the safety of their cars.

Heading south, just 10 km (6 miles) towards Vejle in **Jelling** ⑯ is a memorial sometimes referred to as Denmark's birth certificate: the **Jellingstenene** (**Jelling Stones**), found beside the town church between two huge burial mounds. King Harald Blåtand (Harald Bluetooth) made the relief carving on the stones 1,000 years ago to proclaim his conversion to Christianity and in memory of his parents, King Gorm the Old and Queen Thyra Danebod, who were buried in the mounds. Jelling church has the oldest frescoes in Denmark, to make the town one of the most historic sites in an area which holds a great deal of Denmark's early history.

Vejle ⑰ has a commanding position at the head of the Vejle Fjord, and behind it lies the picturesque valley of Grejsdalen, 8 km (5 miles) long. The town has many relics illustrating its long history. An old monastery clock continues to chime, though it has long lost its monastery, which once stood where you find the 19th-century Rådhus (Town Hall). Another old building, the 1799 Smidske Gård, is now the tourist office and has an exhibition based on Vejle's history.

Rolled cigars

Fredericia ⑱, 20 km (12 miles) southeast of Vejle on a promontory that forms the bridgehead to the island of Funen, was yet another of the towns planned by Denmark's brilliant king, Christian IV, though it was built in 1650 by his son Frederik III, whose name it bears. Frederik III also conferred a special constitution, which granted right of asylum for religious refugees, debtors and even "foreign murderers and malefactors".

The privilege remained until 1820, when freedom of worship made it no longer necessary, and although many had moved there "in case", only around one person per year ever claimed asylum. Until religious freedom was established in Denmark in 1849, Fredericia was the only place where many religious sects were able to practise their religion. Not only was there a Jewish synagogue, but refugees from other countries arrived, including Huguenots – sorely persecuted in France – who brought a knowledge of cultivating potatoes and tobacco, and who also established a cigar-making industry. Until 1982, Fredericia had one remaining cigar manufacturer and, even today, you may find cigar-makers who roll cigars by hand, and the telephone book still contains French-sounding names.

Despite much strife, first with Sweden when Fredericia was barely completed, and between 1848 and 1864 in the wars between Germany and Denmark, the town inside its ramparts remains all that a planned town should be. But it has not forgotten its robust past. Every year, Fredericia celebrates the evening of 5 July, with a memorial service on the following morning, to commemorate a victory in 1849 when the Danes poured out to rout their German besiegers. ❏

ÅRHUS

Music, theatre and art lovers are captivated by historic Århus, "the world's smallest big city", situated on the picturesque east coast of Jutland

A rhus is Denmark's spunkiest "college town," a cultural magnet known for its music, theatre, art and cafés, its annual Festival Week in the autumn and its nearby forests, beaches and castles. Denmark's second largest city – with a population of about 280,000, only one-tenth the size of Copenhagen – Århus is the commercial centre of Jutland and likes to be known as "the world's smallest big city".

At its heart, however, Århus is provincial town through and through. Århus (pronounced as in *Oh, who's* there?) started life around AD 948 as a Viking settlement on the mouth of the river which now bears its name. From that time to the present, the port has had a significant role in the city's history and prosperity, and today Århus is one of the busiest ports in Scandinavia. The sound of cranes lifting cargo to and from ships can be heard throughout the town, along with the lonely call of a fog horn during the winter months.

Students and faculties at the University of Århus and several institutes of higher education give a spark to the city – from the Danish School of Journalism to a conservatory and schools for business, teachers, occupational and physical therapists, and many others. A project management school called The Kaos Pilots has also gained notoriety worldwide as a progressive business, first of its kind.

Immigrants are attracted to Århus, and foreigners from all over the world – particularly Africa, the Middle East, Europe and the Americas – have invigorated the city with restaurants, boutiques and new traditions. Turkish immigrants, for instance, have created a whole new shopping tradition with their colourful street markets. Kalamata olives, feta cheese, hummus and chilli peppers, bought from the markets' delis, are now as common as pizza – which itself was exotic in Denmark as recently as the 1970s.

Copenhageners poke fun at this "backwards town", joking about the way one must enter a bus at the rear and exit the front. As a provincial town, Århus is on the whole more subdued than its metropolitan rival – and much of its beauty is found in the details. Århusianers know, for instance, that one does not simply stroll through the town without looking up. Many buildings have been decorated with bizarre dragons, masks and gargoyles.

Seaman's saint

Begin with a visit to the **Domkirke Ⓐ**, the Cathedral of St Clement (open summer: 9.30am–4pm; rest of year: 10am–3pm; free). The nave of the church is a full 93 metres (316 ft), longer than any other in Denmark – and quite a stroll for the 50 or so brides who march down its candle-lit aisle every year. The pointed spire, 93 metres (316 ft) high, can be spotted

LEFT: fishing at Den Gamle By, Århus.
BELOW: interior of Århus cathedral.

miles away. The tower's bell room has one of the best views in the city. To get there means climbing an ancient, steep winding brick stairway – quite a thrill, but well worth the small entrance fee.

The first stage in the construction of the cathedral, which was consecrated to the patron saint of seafarers, was begun at the end of the 12th century and continued well into the next century. The cathedral was substantially rebuilt during the 15th century, and underwent restoration in 1877, 1907 and 1998. During the most recent work, restorers uncovered several frescoes under layers of whitewash on the high ceilings, including a Gothic-period work of Christ on the cross from 1470.

The cathedral's altar screen dates from 1479 and reveals a different scene for every major event of the Danish Lutheran calendar. Denmark's Queen, Margrethe II, has designed a complete set of chasubles, which also correspond to the church calendar and are worn by the priests at Domkirken. The Queen attends services here whenever she is staying at Marselisborg, her palace on the southern edge of Århus by the sea.

The area around the cathedral was a cemetery until 1813, and 1,000 bodies are buried under Domkirken's floor alone. In 1963, the city excavated the land to the southwest of the cathedral and unearthed remains of medieval houses and refuse heaps. A small **Vikingemuseet (Viking Museum)**, in the cellar of Unibank on Clemens Torv, houses some of the finds (open 9.30am–4pm, Thur 9.30am–6pm; free; tel: 86 27 24 33). From here, it's worth a walk around **Bispetorvet** square to the **Museum's Kopi Smykker** shop, which sells handcrafted copies of Scandinavian jewellery from the early Bronze age (1500 BC) to the Viking age (AD 1000).

Møllestien, near Vor Frue Kirke (church), is only a block long, but the craft shops and homes within the colourful cross-beam buildings give a glimpse of town houses of the past.

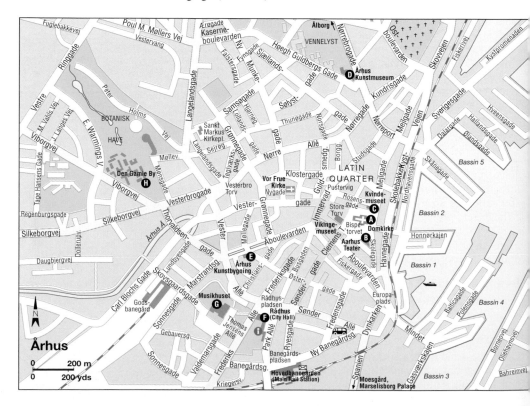

The town is a stage

The ornate facade of **Aarhus Teater** , at the head of Bispetorvet, is often called a stage backdrop to the city itself. Århus is said to have more working actors and playwrights per capita than Copenhagen. Theatres abound around town – from children's to experimental to classic to modern. Most performances are given in Danish, but some musicals and plays are in English.

On the other side of the cathedral on Domkirkepladsen is **Kvindemuseet** (The Women's Museum), which features women's culture and history in recent times (open 10am–5pm; Sept–May: closed Mon; entrance fee; tel: 86 13 61 44). One of the city's hippest bars, Under Masken, is located nearby on the corner of Rosengade and Bispegade.

At the end of Rosengade lies Pustervig square and the winding, cobblestone streets of the **Latin Quarter**, with quirky boutiques and trendy cafés and restaurants. Cafés Englen, Kindrød and Drudenfus are all within a stone's throw of each other in Studsgade.

The street of Graven – once a moat hundreds of years ago – has wonderful gourmet bakeries, starting with **Emmery's** at the corner of Guldsmedegade, and **Latin Brasserie Créperie** restaurant. At the outer edge of the quarter, on Nørregade, is one of the country's most unusual cafés, **Coffee & Silver**, a regular hang-out for local artists and creative thinkers. Here, almost everything in the place is for sale, from the mishmash of antique chairs and tables to the art on the walls and curios behind the bar.

North along Nørregade, at the base of the university's **Vennelyst** park, stands **Århus Kunstmuseum** (Art Museum), which has one of the oldest collections of Danish art outside the capital (open 10am–5pm, Wed 10am–8pm, closed

Map on page 248

In Denmark, it is said, chefs who cook and succeed at Latin Brasserie Créperie can work at any other restaurant they please in the country.

BELOW: browsing in the second-hand shops in Århus.

Changing the guard at Marselisborg Slot, Århus, the summer residence of the Danish royal family.

BELOW:
keep smiling.

Mon; entrance fee; tel: 86 13 52 55). This museum is a good place to get an overview of Danish art from 18th, 19th and 20th-century painters, with works ranging from C.W. Eckersberg, the "father of Danish painters", to Per Kirkeby, the contemporary Danish artist who has made the greatest impression abroad with his expressionist works.

Sun worship

From the square, Store Torv, in front of Domkirken, a series of streets form a long pedestrian mall all the way to the railway station. Some of the best local renditions of Danish waffle ice cream cones can be bought on the narrow Skt Clemens street (try the "Århus Vaffel" cone).

The river that runs through town, Århus Å, had been buried since 1935 under concrete and asphalt in the city centre, but since 1996 the city has been uncovering it, diverting traffic and renovating the area around it block by block. When the section within the pedestrian area was complete, it quickly become one of the best spots to relax in town. Numerous cafés and pubs line a riverside promenade on **Åboulevarden**, starting with the artsy Café Cross on the corner. Locals tend to drift to the banks of the river here any time the sun shines, no matter what the temperature – a natural response to the long, dark winters.

Further west along the boulevard at J.M. Mørks Gade, the **Århus Kunstbygning ❺** (Arts Centre) has some interesting exhibitions, as well as an exhibit dedicated to a history of Danish posters (open 10am–5pm, closed Mon; entrance fee; tel: 86 12 22 18).

At the southern end of the pedestrian mall towards the railway station stands the **Rådhus (City Hall) ❻**. It was built in 1941 and designed by Arne Jacobsen,

BIKE TOURS

The **Forhistorisk Museum** (Museum of Prehistory) housed in the manor house of Moesgård (*see page 252*) is a first-class destination to try out one of the many excellent bike paths through Århus. The 16-km (10-mile) tour starts by heading south of the city through the grounds of the majestic **Marselisborg Slot**, the summer residence of the royal family. When the Queen is at home, the Changing of the Guards takes place daily at noon. The castle grounds and the Queen's rose garden are open to the public when the royal family is not in residence.

The cycle route continues through the woods overlooking the sea (look out for sculptures formed from living wood), eventually coming to the **Dyrepark** (Animal Park), an open playground for humans, deer, and even wild boar (which are safely enclosed). As the sign says, remember to close the gate. Cyclists can then continue to Moesgård and even further southwards, joining the network of bike paths that cross the country.

Other fine bike tours are around **Brabrand Lake** to the west, or **Risskov forest** to the north. Cycle rentals are available from many bike shops in town, and the tourist information centre in the Rådhus, near the railway station, can supply maps (tel: 89 40 67 00).

one of Denmark's most notable architects and designers. Take the antique elevator to the top of the 60-metre (200-ft) high tower for a superb view of the city and the Bay of Århus. The local tourist information bureau is at the foot of the tower. Around the grounds of the building are several exquisite sculptures, including the funny fountain of a sow and her tinkling piglets.

Musical highlights

Nearby is **Musikhuset (Concert Hall)** , home of the Århus Symphony Orchestra, the Danish National Opera and DIEM, the Danish Institute for Electroacoustic Music. Live music performances of most genre are frequently staged at Musikhuset and a multitude of other venues around town.

The nearby Vox Hall on Vester Allé is one of the best places to hear rock and world music, while Fatter Eskild on Skolegade has terrific blues. Glazzhuset, under Clemens Bridge on Åboulevarden, and Bent J, on Nørre Allé, are the headquarters for the annual **Århus Jazz Festival**, which attracts international talent every summer. On Friday afternoon at the smoky Bent J, a gathering of talented musicians mingles with a regular crowd for the weekly jazz jam session. This is the perfect place to try the local Ceres brew – ask for a *"Top"*.

The annual **Århus Festival Week**, held every year in early September, fills nearly every performance spot in the city. With a theme on a certain foreign culture each year – such as Latin American, Eastern European or the Far Eastern – performers, artists and chefs from the featured area join their Danish counterparts to put on concerts, dance productions, plays and almost any type of performance you can imagine. (One year the John Cleese Society of Århus og Omegn held a "silly walk tournament".) An ultra-modern, white

Map on page 248

Map on page 248

TIP

The cobbled Studsgade, in Århus's Latin Quarter, has art galleries, shops selling trendy Danish Design knick-knacks, and some of the best cafés in town.

BELOW: cafés in Århus are busy all day long.

Map on page 248

Exhibit, Forhistorisk Museum, Moesgård.

BELOW: mural, Århus Town Hall.
RIGHT: cake shop in Den Gamle By.

tent called **Univers** jabs into the sky adjacent to the cathedral, filled with concerts, food booths and a bar.

The Old Town

Just to the northwest of the city centre is one of Århus's proudest attractions, **Den Gamle By (Old Town)** ⓗ, the national museum of urban culture and history (open June–Aug: 9am–6pm; Sept–May: hours vary; entrance fee; tel: 86 12 31 88 for details of tours in English).

In this open-air museum, 75 Danish urban buildings have been reconstructed. Most of them are from Jutland, and some from Zealand (the old theatre from Helsingør, for example) and Funen. From the front entrance onwards, the museum is a sensory overload in an environment that, at least, feels genuinely historic – with merchant and artisan houses and workshops, gardens, shops and stalls, streets and alleys.

The museum is under continual development. The most recent addition is the **Mintmaster Mansion** from Copenhagen from the 1680s, the largest half-timbered house in Denmark.

The Bog Man of Århus

One of the best single museum exhibits in Denmark is a 2,000-year-old man at the **Forhistorisk Museum (Museum of Prehistory)** at Moesgård, located about 8 km (5 miles) south of the city centre (open Apr–Sept: 10am–5pm; Oct–Mar: 10am–4pm; closed Mon; entrance fee; tel: 89 42 11 00). The Grauballe Man is named after the village where he was found in a peat bog near Århus in 1952, perfectly preserved. (Another Iron Age "bog man", the Tollund Man, was found

in the same area and is on display at the Silkeborg Museum; *see page 239.*) To stand face to face with the grimacing Mr Grauballe and count the whiskers on his chin and the whorl patterns on his fingers is quite a chilling experience.

The Moesgård Museum of Prehistory has an interesting collection of prehistoric finds from all over Denmark, as well as changing exhibitions from around the world.

Take in the indoor exhibits before setting out to walk the grounds along the "**Prehistoric Trackway**". The path begins in sheep pastures, leading through reconstructed Iron Age houses, graves and cult sites from the Stone and Bronze ages. Then the path enters a beech and oak tree forest and passes by **Skovmøllen** (the mill in the woods). The 200-year-old mill still functions, and the restaurant next door is famous for its hot chocolate and buns.

The well-marked path continues to the beach of Århus Bay at the mouth of Giber brook, the location for the annual **Viking Moot** during the last week in July, a fun re-enactment of duelling characters in full Viking garb.

A **Viking Settlement**, with a stave church and other reconstructed period buildings, is the final stop on this walking tour into the past.

Guidebooks are available in a variety of languages at the entrance to the museum. ❑

NORTH JUTLAND

Painters came first, lured by the "Nordic Light" of North Jutland,
followed by holidaymakers to the west coast sands, sailors
to the east, and walkers to the forests and heaths

Map
on page
258

I t only takes a few minutes in the small town of **Skagen** ❶ to understand
why this most northerly point of Denmark was an irresistible lure to the
Skagen painters, who made it their home in the second half of the 19th
century. The narrow strip of land where Denmark ends in a pointing finger is
so close to the sea and the vivid changing light of a wide, endless sky that it
seems to be part of both.

The "Nordic Light" (the name the painters gave themselves) is characteristic
of many parts of Scandinavia, but its quintessence surrounds Skagen. This is
what in the 1880s brought together artists such as Anna and Michael Ancher,
Christian Krogh, P.S. Krøyer, and the marine artist and poet Holger Drachmann
to flout the mainstream European Impressionist tradition and form their own
school of "Reality Painting". They took their inspiration from wide stretches of
silver-white sands spiked with marram grass, in raging seas and threatening
clouds that stormed across a metallic sky. Sea and sky seemed to meet. Locals
used cumulus clouds to predict the weather.

If the clarity of the air and changing sea makes it easy to understand why the
Nordic Light painters were conspicuous for the shimmering light of their
pictures, it is no surprise whatsoever to see that their influence continues. You
see it in **Skagens Museum**, Brøndumsvej 4, which
also has works from later periods (open Apr, May,
Sept: 11am–4pm, closed Mon; Jun–Aug: 10am–6pm
daily; Nov–Mar: 1–4pm, Sat 11am–6pm, Sun
11am–3pm, closed Mon; entrance fee; tel: 98 44 64
44), in **Anchers Hus**, Markvej 2–4, bought by the
Anchers in 1884 (open Apr: 11am–3pm; May–Sept:
10am–5pm; Nov–Mar: Sat–Sun only 11am–3pm;
entrance fee; tel: 98 44 30 09), and in **Drachmanns
Hus**, Hans Baghs Vej 21, a 19th-century villa which
became Drachmann's home at the beginning of the
20th century (open mid-Jun–mid-Aug: 10am–5pm;
mid-Aug–mid-Jun: 11am–3pm; entrance fee; tel: 98
44 28 22).

About 45 km (28 miles) south at Hjørring, the
Hjorring Kunstmuseum (Museum of Art) focuses
on the modern, and shows work by Poul Anker Bech,
Svend Engelund, and Johannes Hofmeister (open
mid-Jun–mid-Sep 10am–5pm; mid-Sep–mid-Jun:
Tue–Sun 11am–4pm; entrance fee; tel: 98 92 41 33).

For an idea of how the "Nordic Light" continues,
visit the exhibition held in August each year in **Vrå
Folk High School**, 12 km (7 miles) south. This
started in 1942 to show the works of Svend
Engelund, a native of Vrå, but now includes many
younger artists.

Today, Skagen is a fishing port with some 12,000
inhabitants, which still has the characteristic yellow

PRECEDING PAGES:
swans and their
young, Jutland.
LEFT: Anchers Hus,
the Painters' House,
Skagen.
BELOW: café
life in Skagen.

In Skagen, children should enjoy a visit to Bamse Hus, a teddy bear museum with hundreds of fuzzy friends. Some of them are historic, and some are downright hilarious.

fishermen's houses that also inspired the Skagen painters. Less than 5 km (3 miles) north, the road runs out at **Grenen**, where the trick is to stand with one foot in the Skagerrak and the other in the Kattegat, a temptation few can resist.

Skagen Fortidsminder is another of the open-air museums, much beloved of Scandinavia, which shows life and work from the past (open May–Sept 10am–5pm; Oct–Apr: 10am–4pm; closed Dec; entrance fee; tel: 98 44 47 60).

Just west of Skagen, peeping out of the dunes, is **Den Tilsandede Kirke** (the sand-covered church) with only the steeple visible (open Jun–Aug: 11am–5pm; entrance fee). In the 17th century, the church was the largest in Vendsyssel but the drifting dunes reached the church 100 years later. Though generations of parishioners fought to save it, they could not beat the endless drifts. In 1795, King Christian VII gave them permission to abandon their church. Who knows how long it will be before the top vanishes under the remorseless sand?

To understand how a church could disappear in the sand, you need go no further than **Råbjerg Mile ❷**, 10 km (6 miles) to the south, the largest example

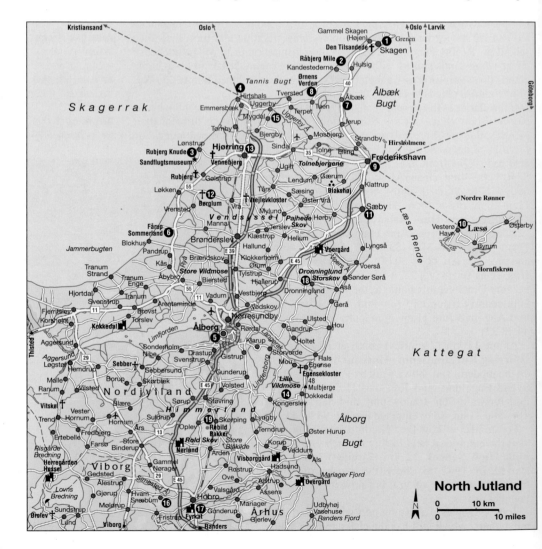

North Jutland

of migrating dunes in Denmark. Pushed by the wind and sea, the dunes travel a little further east every year, as tireless as the sands that overwhelmed the church. This Danish desert is beautiful. It can only be entered on foot and is protected by law. The usual entrance is from **Kandestederne**. The low-ceilinged church which has survived here contains fine baroque wood carvings.

Sand drifts are a feature of this part of Jutland; those at **Rubjerg Knude ❸**, 17 km (11 miles) south of Hirtshals, rise 74 metres (240 ft) from the sea. The lighthouse is now a Sand Drift Museum, **Sandflugbsmuseum**, and, when the wind blows, the sand is whipped up like a whirlwind (open May–Jun: 11am–4pm; Jul–Aug: 10am–5pm; Sept–Apr 1–4pm; entrance fee; tel: 98 92 06 77).

Many a ship has has been wrecked on this exposed coast and the disused Mårup church at **Lønstrup**, 4 km (2 miles) north, has an anchor from the British frigate *Crescent*, which ran aground here in 1808 with the loss of 226 lives.

In 1804 the citizens of **Hirtshals ❹**, on the most northwesterly point, wanted to build a harbour but were rebuffed by the government. They stubbornly pursued their aims and in 1917, 113 years after the first application, the harbour received approval. Even so, it was not finished until 1930. It is now an important fishing centre with ferry connections to Norway.

Holidaymakers' haven

The radiant light, the sea and shore still draw painters to Skagen and North Jutland, but the area has also become one of Denmark's most popular family holiday spots. The beaches are among the best in Northern Europe and a hot sunny day means that the cities of the north are deserted as everyone heads for the sea. Not just Danes are attracted. North Jutland is a magnet for holiday-

Map on page 258

Lifeboat building at Fortidsminder, the open air museum on the dunes at Skagen (tel: 98 44 47 60).

BELOW: the shifting sands of the north.

makers from all over Scandinavia, as well as Germany, Holland and other parts of Western Europe. Holiday cottages have mushroomed in the sheltered areas behind the dunes and defensive tree plantings of the west coast.

This is especially true of the northernmost area of **Vendsyssel**, which few realise is actually an island, cut off from the rest of Denmark by the Limfjord, just north of the city of **Ålborg** ❺ (*see page 267*).

Blokhus, 35 km (22 miles) northwest of Ålborg, is a lively holiday centre with a superb broad, sandy beach stretching 16 km (10 miles) north to the next holiday resort of Løkken. Near Saltum, 7 km (4 miles) east from Blokhus, **Fårup Sommerland** ❻ offers a huge range of children's activities (open mid-May–Aug: 10am–6pm; Jul: until 8pm; entrance fee; tel: 98 88 16 00).

Its very popularity can make the Danish high season, from late-June to mid-August, a time to avoid unless you enjoy being part of a crowd. But the beaches are so endless along these northern coasts that even at high season it is relatively easy to find somewhere not crowded, particularly on the less populated eastern side facing the Kattegat. Small coastal towns and villages such as Ålbæk, Sæby, Aså and Hals, an old fishing village that guards the eastern gateway of the Limfjord, are certainly calmer and quieter. The east also has more holiday marinas than the less sheltered northwest.

Ålbæk ❼, on the east coast, 5 km (3 miles) south of Råbjerg Mile, is an old fishing port, surrounded by the typical moor and open countryside of North Jutland. It is popular with those who want to avoid the summer crowds. About 8 km (5 miles) west of Ålbæk is one of Denmark's greatest natural attractions, **Ørnens Verden (Eagle World)** ❽, at Tuen. Here, some of the world's shyest eagles fly free and the Wenzel family, which owns the sanctuary, has succeeded

Nordsømuseet, the North Sea Museum in Hirtshals, has been named Denmark's best aquarium. All kinds of North Sea marine life is on view (open Jun–Aug 9am–6pm; Sept–Apr: Mon–Fri 9am–4pm, Sat–Sun 10am–5pm; entrance fee; tel: 98 94 48 44).

BELOW: Jutland's northeast shore is often quieter than the busy western coastline.

in getting large eagles and falcons to breed (open Apr–Aug one hour before each demonstration; tel: 98 93 20 31 for times; entrance fee).

Frederikshavn ❾, 15 km (9 miles) south of Ålbæk, is one of the busiest ferry ports in the world. It grew from a fishing village to a fortified town, and traces of that period lie around the harbour. **Krudttårnet**, the Gun Tower Museum, dates from 1686 and has collections of weapons and uniforms (open Jun–mid-Sept: 10.30am–5pm; entrance fee; tel: 98 43 19 19).

Today, Frederikshavn's main function is as a busy port with connections to Sweden and Norway and, most important for visitors, to the island of **Læsø**.

Island beaches

Læsø´s population of less than 3,000 inflates like a balloon at holiday times. It is less than two hours away by ferry from Frederikshavn. Two-thirds of the island is uncultivated land with pools, heaths and scrub, and the northern coast has fine beaches. Many of the island houses are thatched with seaweed, some are now restaurants and small hotels; there are also lots of holiday cottages, camping sites, and beaches with the European Union blue flag that indicates clean sea water and unpolluted sand. A bicycle is an ideal way to get around and it is easy to hire one. An organised island tour combines nature and cycling in a five-day holiday for both children and adults, and is led by an experienced natural historian who can explain the mysteries of plant, bird and animal life.

In the past, while the men of Læsø fished and sailed, the women worked the land. The **Søfarts-og-Fiskerimuseet (Museum of Fishing and Shipping)** in **Vesterø ❿**, where the ferry arrives, recalls their roles (open May–Oct: 1–3pm; entrance fee; tel: 98 49 80 45). There are two other communities, **Østerby** on

Map on page 258

Råbjerg Mile is a gigantic sand dune that was formed on Jutland's northwest coast about 500 years ago. Winds are gradually pushing it east at a rate of 15 metres (50 ft) a year.

BELOW: east coast fisherman at Aså.

the northeast coast and **Byrum** in the south, which has a viewing tower overlooking the island and sea.

Ancient heritage

Sæby ⑪, 15 km (9 miles) south of Frederikshavn, is a town for strolling. It is said to have inspired the dramatist Henrik Ibsen, but judging by the small, spiteful societies he usually portrayed, this is not necessarily a compliment. This is an old town, founded in the early 16th century around **Vor Frue Kirke** which dates from 1460, with an altarpiece, choir stalls and frescoes added over the next 100 years. One of Denmark's loveliest manor houses is the 16th-century **Sæbygård Herregårdsmuseum**, Sæbygaardsvej 49. It lies north of town in a small forest (open 10am–5pm, closed Mon; entrance fee; tel: 98 46 10 77).

Voergård Slot (Castle), 15 km (9 miles) southwest along the river Voerså at Flauenskjold, is a beautiful Renaissance building with a large collection of antiques and paintings, including works by Goya, Raphael and Rubens (open Apr–mid-Jun, mid-Aug–Sept: Sat 2pm–5pm; Easter and mid-Jun–mid-Aug: 10am–5pm; entrance fee; tel: guided tours 98 46 90 72, information 98 86 71 08). **Voer Kirke** stands nearby with an imposing monument to Ingeborg Skee, who founded the Voer estate in 1586.

Small churches and religious houses are scattered widely in northeast Jutland. **Børglum Kloster** ⑫, 8 km (5 miles) east of Løkken, was built by monks in the 11th-century as a monastery, and later became the Bishop's House. Along with other religious buildings in the area, Børglum became a manor house after the Reformation (open May–Aug: 10am–6pm; entrance fee; tel: 98 99 40 11). The largest cluster of old churches can be found in **Hjørring** ⑬. The town itself is

Protected by a wide moat, Voergård Slot, near Saeby, houses a fine collection of art, porcelain, silverware and furniture.

BELOW: the pick of the catch, fresh from the boat.

Map on page 258

13th century, but Skt Olai Kirke predates it by 100 years. Skt Kathrine Kirke is 13th century Romanesque with three aisles and transepts. Skt Hans Kirke, erected around 1350, has some fine murals, rivalled by those in Bindslev Kirke, to the northeast of the town. It has one of Denmark's finest pieces of medieval art, a Madonna painted in the early 13th century, and murals with a strong Byzantine influence.

Vrejlevkloster, 10 km (6 miles) south of Hjørring, was once a convent and has a church built around 1200. **Vennebjerg Kirke**, 7 km (4 miles) west of Hjørring, has the tallest steeple in Vendsyssel and is used as a navigation mark that can be clearly seen from far out at sea.

Golden riches

The varied Jutland landscape is not just used for pleasure and leisure. It is also working land. The richer soil of the south produces crops of wheat and barley, as well as cows and pigs, while further north, farmers grow potatoes, rye and oats. Even the bog areas can be of use. On the east coast, south of Limfjord, **Lille Vildmose ⓮** is the largest raised bog in Denmark. Alongside a sphagnum moss industry, it has acres of unspoiled landscape, with herds of wild boar and deer. Although the public is not admitted, it is possible to get a view of the bog from the nearby Mullbjerge (hills).

On the sea shore you can sometimes find nuggets of amber, a golden petrified tree resin that washes ashore. Amber has been traded in North Jutland since the Stone Age, and the area still has stone-cutters and jewellers who specialise in it. At Gerå, on the east coast, Osvald Højer works with the stones, and at **Mygdal ⓯**, 12 km (7 miles) north of Hjørring, his son, Benni Højer, has

TIP

Along the west and north Jutland coasts, look for amber, the "gold of the north". These valuable nuggets of solidified resin are usually found on the beach after a westerly storm.

BELOW: today Dronninglund Slot houses a fine hotel.

WILD EATING – AND DRINKING

The Danes refer to their gently rolling landscape as "gold and green forests", the gold being the intensely yellow rapeseed that blooms when spring turns into summer. One forest delight that all Scandinavians enjoy is berry picking.

The woods yield wild raspberries, blackberries, lingon, multer, and strawberries. The heath areas are rich in cranberries and blueberries. Both habitats hold many more with Danish names that are guaranteed to produce confusion in translation. Late summer is the time for mushrooms and, though local mushroomers may be reluctant to disclose their secret locations, sharp eyes will certainly spot boletus and ink caps. The best informed visitor will keep a lookout for *pors* (bog myrtle or sweet gale) and juniper berries.

It's well known that Ålborg produces excellent *akvavit*, but Vendsyssel claims to have given the world an even better drink, *bjesk* (pronounced "*byesk*"). To make *Juniper Bjesk*, put 12 dried black juniper berries in a half bottle of akvavit and leave them to soak for a week. Strain and save the *akvavit*, then discard the berries. For *Pors Bjesk*, put a twig of *pors* into a half bottle of *akvavit* and leave to soak for a week until the twig is golden. Then pour. *Skål!*

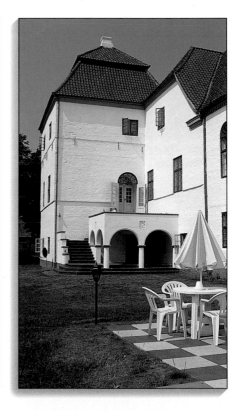

Map
on page
258

*Reconstructed
dwelling at Fyrkat,
the Viking village.*

BELOW: on the
beach near Aså.
RIGHT: forest
stream in full flow.

Jutland's largest amber workshop, Højers Rav Sliberi, Højtvedvej 7 (open Mon–Fri 10am–5pm; free; tel: 98 97 52 23).

Relics of early times are everywhere, for this northern island was, not surprisingly, Viking territory. Even before the days of these great seafarers, the lives of prehistoric people can be traced through the relics they left. The long barrow at **Blakshøj**, just inland from Gærum on the east coast, is one of the country's longest passage graves. Also among the best preserved passage graves are the 5,000-year-old specimens at **Snæbum** ⑯, 12 km (7 miles) west of Hobro in the south of Himmerland. For closer inspection, visitors can clamber through one of the passage graves here, **Snibhøj**.

A thousand years ago, also near Hobro, the Vikings built **Fyrkat** ⑰. Four earth fortifications enclosed 16 large houses, and one of these longhouses has been rebuilt (open Apr–Oct: 10am–5pm; entrance fee; tel: 98 51 19 27). **Hobro Museum** houses some of the finds from Fyrkat (open Apr–Oct: 11am–5pm, closed Mon; entrance fee; tel: 98 51 50 55).

A walk in the forest

North Jutland may be best known for swimming, sunning and sea sports, but the countryside is also remarkable inland, with many special conservation areas and bird territories. It goes without saying that the long coastline, and the rivers and lakes, make for good fishing. A inexpensive licence is required for public waters but private property often costs more. Ask at tourist offices for details.

Cycling or walking is a good way of getting close to nature and many districts hire out horses for the day. One of the best cycle tours consists of seven gentle days around the Mariager Fjord, starting and finishing at Hobro, and taking in historic ruins and stately homes, as well as beautiful countryside and the idyllic town of roses, **Mariager**.

One of the most popular areas for cycling and walking is the Jutland Ridge. The 30 km (21 miles) between Dronninglund Storskov (forest) and Pajhede Skov (wood) at Øster Vrå further northwest has a special cycling and walking track, which wends its way through beech woods, fir trees, heath and bogland.

In **Dronninglund** ⑱ itself is **Dronninglund Slot**, a former convent later used by Charlotte Amalie, the wife of King Christian V. Today it is a conference centre, but the chapel with its frescoes is open to the public (open late-Jun–early-Aug: guided tours 11am; entrance fee; tel: 98 84 30 00). Further north, the Tolne Hills, 12 km (8 miles) west of Frederikshavn, are clad in beech and fir. A good starting point for a walk is the old pavilion near Tolne station.

In Himmerland you find Denmark's biggest forest, Rold Skov, around the town of **Skørping**. The area includes the **Rebild Bakker (Hills of Rebild)** ⑲, a national park, and the car park makes a good point for starting a walk in the heather hills, beech woods and conifer forests. Good targets are the springs of **Lille Blåkilde** and **Store Blåkilde**, where 30,000 cubic metres (1 million cu ft) of water come gushing out each day. Each 4th of July, Rebild National Park celebrates American Independence Day, the biggest such celebration outside the United States. ❑

ÅLBORG

Map on page 268

Ålborg, the "city that never sleeps", owes its origins to the Vikings. Today, its combination of history and modern culture make this an inviting base for exploring North Jutland

When the bustling, successful commercial town of **Ålborg** was at its most prosperous in the Middle Ages, its rich merchants enjoyed the ostentatious display of their considerable wealth. None enjoyed it more than Jens Bang, whose opulent six-storey **Stenhus (Stone House)** , on Østerågade, was built in 1624 to show off his wealth. It is still the largest preserved citizen's house from the period.

Today, Ålborg is Denmark's fourth-largest city with a population of 155,000. It is still a busy commercial centre, owing much of its success to its position at the narrowest point on the south bank of the Limfjorden. This advantageous site was the reason the Vikings settled here, and it soon became one of Denmark's busiest trading centres and a focal point for communication. Jens Bang, as well as being rich, was an argumentative and obstinate man who made enemies, and was not averse to taking revenge on them. This, they say, is why he caricatured them in the grotesque carvings on the front of his house. He was also annoyed that he had never become a town councillor and, again, his house shows his anger at that omission. On the south facade of the Stenhus is the clear carving of the merchant himself, sticking his tongue out at the town hall across the street. Inside this historic house is a basement wine bar, open to the public.

LEFT: 16th-century Ålborghus Slot.
BELOW: Budolfi Domkirke, Ålborg's cathedral.

Another well-preserved merchant's mansion on Østerågade is **Jørgen Olufsens Gård** , a three-storey, half-timbered building from 1616, complete with its hoists and doors where the storekeepers once hauled the merchant's newly-bought grain up to the loft (not open to the public).

Budolfi Domkirke , the 15th-century cathedral on Gammel Torv, is dedicated to the English saint, Botolph, the seamen's patron. It has a richly furnished and colourful interior, a large altarpiece from 1689 and a carved pulpit dating from 1692. The baroque baptismal font was completed in 1728, and the impressive spire (1779) has a carillon of 48 bells.

Just as interesting is **Helligåndsklosteret**  (the Monastery of the Holy Ghost), on C.W. Obels Plads, with its 15th-century cloisters. It is Denmark's oldest welfare institution and is still in use as a home for the elderly (for tours contact Ålborg Tourist Information, tel: 98 12 60 22). Nearby is the **Vor Frue Kirke**  (Church of Our Lady) and the little traders' houses of Hjelmerstald and Peder Barkesgade, much as they have always been.

Ålborghus Slot  (Castle) is 16th-century, but only the eastern of the three original wings remains, along with the fortress wall (gardens open all year: 8am–9pm; dungeons May–Sept: 8am–3pm; subterranean hallways 8am–9pm; free). A new northern wing was built in 1633 and is now the residence of the

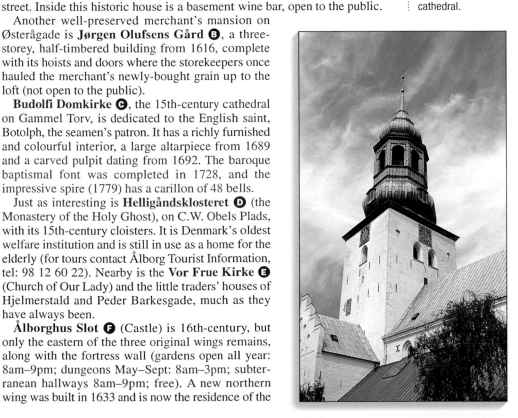

*Portico of Ålborg's
18th-century Town
Hall, Gammel Torv.*

Lord Lieutenant. This old townscape lends itself to exploration by foot and the tourist office has a useful booklet, *Good Old Ålborg*, to guide visitors around all the key attractions. It has long had Scandinavia's largest cattle market, at **Nyhavnsgade ⓖ**, on Tuesday and Friday.

Aqvavit capital

Commerce has always been the bedrock of the city's existence and today three industries dominate: cement, tobacco, and *aqvavit*, which the Danes call "*snaps*". The latter is probably Ålborg's best known product – many claim the best *aqvavit* of all – and has been distilled here since 1846.

Two statues are closely associated both with the city and with two of these major industries. **The Goose Girl** by Gerhard Henning was presented in 1937 by C. W. Obel's Tobacco Company. **The Cimbrian Bull** by A. J. Bundgaard, which has a poem by Nobel prize-winner Johannes V. Jensen on its base, was presented in the same year by Danish Distilleries.

A little art, a lot of industry and some history are not the sum total of Ålborg. More recently there has been a greater emphasis on culture in its broadest sense. The **Ålborghallen (Ålborg Halls) ⓗ**, Europa Plads, were built between 1949 and 1953 with the aim of providing a suitable venue for the well-patronised concerts, theatrical productions, sporting events, congresses and art exhibitions.

BELOW: Jørgen
Olufsens Gård, a
merchant's house.

The opening of the **Nordjyllands Kunstmuseum (North Jutlands Art Museum) ⓘ**, at Kong Chr. Allé 50, in 1972 provided an outstanding centre for international art (open July–Aug: daily 10am–5pm; Sept–June: closed Mon; entrance fee; tel: 98 13 80 88). Designed by a Finnish architectural couple, Elissa and Alvar Aalto, and a Dane, Jean-Jacques Baru'l, it houses a permanent

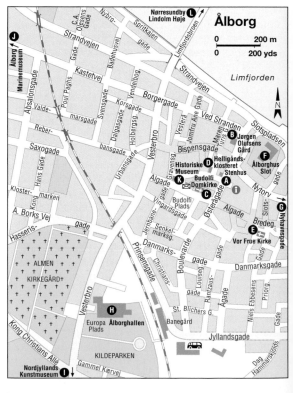

Ålborg

0   200 m
0   200 yds

collection of Danish art from 1890 to the present day and distinguished works by foreign artists such as Picasso, Chagall, Le Corbusier, and many others. These are supplemented by visiting exhibitions. The city also holds concerts in the museum and popular summer outdoor entertainment in the amphitheatre.

The **Ålborg Marinemuseum (Shipping and Naval Museum)** ◑, at Vestre Fjordvej 81, opened in 1991 near the western end of the harbour area (open May–Aug: 10am–6pm; Sept–Apr: 10am–4pm; entrance fee; tel: 98 11 78 03). Its star attraction is *Springeren*, the last submarine built in Denmark. It is installed on dry land with access in the bow and stern to allow visitors to walk through.

The **Historiske Museum** ◉ (Museum of History), Algade 48, covers the past in all its aspects (open Tue–Sun 10am–5pm; entrance fee; tel: 98 12 45 22). It includes finds from Scandinavia's largest burial ground from the Germanic Iron Age and the Viking period at **Lindholm Høje**. This lies across the Limfjord to the northwest of Nørresundby and, with more than 600 graves, is well worth a visit (open Easter–May and Sept–Feb daily: 10am–5pm; June–Aug: 10am–7pm; Oct–Easter: Tue–Sun 10am–4pm; entrance fee; tel: 98 17 55 22). About 150 graves are in the shape of stone ships.

Nørresundby ◑ has grown from an old village to become one of the largest towns in the north with 37,000 inhabitants. The church is the original 13th-century village church and the **Nørresundby Local Collection** has a large garden area of aromatic and medicinal herbs (open May–Aug: 9am–9pm; Sept–Oct 9am–7pm; free).

Today, this north side of the fjord is linked to the city by road and rail bridges, and a six-lane underwater tunnel for the E45 motorway. The entire area of Jutland north of the Limfjord is, in fact, an island. ❑

Map on page 268

TIP

Every Sunday from late June to early September, a steam train chugs out of Ålborg Station for a two-hour return trip along the Limfjord line to Greenland Harbour. All aboard!

BELOW: transport on two wheels – the Danish way.

THE BEATING HEART OF ÅLBORG

The city of Ålborg, with its university and international commerce, has a booming downtown area. Jomfru Ane Gade is the main entertainment artery where about 30 of Ålborg's 300 restaurants and nightspots are shuffled shoulder-to-shoulder, with competing prices for food and drink. It pulsates into the wee small hours, and the crowd is both Danish and international. Jomfru Ane Gade lies in the middle of the old downtown district, the heart of shopping and dining. A number of good restaurants are situated in centuries-old, half-timbered courtyards; the cuisine ranges from traditional Danish to Mediterranean nouvelle. If you're dining Danish, especially on open-face sandwiches with fish or potent cheese at lunchtime, accompany your meal with an icy jigger of a famous Ålborg product, *akvavit*. It's a kind of lightly spiced vodka, served cold, extremely so.

You can spend a day here browsing in Ålborg's many stores and art galleries, sampling a restaurant or two, then topping it off with a promenade down Jomfru Ane Gade. There is even a casino at the harbour's edge.

During the summer, you can tour the Limfjorden and Ålborg's bustling harbour aboard the *Hornfisken*. Don't miss the Ålborg Karneval in late May.

WEST JUTLAND

Silvery sands, migrating dunes and tranquil lakes attract holidaymakers and watersports enthusiasts from far and wide to Denmark's westerly shores

Map on page 274

Copenhagen

Distances rarely seem long in Denmark. Thanks to the Store Bælt bridge, it takes just three hours to cross the country from east to west, and you could tour round the island of Funen in a day. West Jutland is a bit different, with a sense of space and long coastlines which have beautiful, almost unbroken beaches stretching ahead.

Much of this western coastline is still in a state of movement. Sand dunes and narrow land strips change at the whim of the North Sea tides, to form and reform and to build up into great hills more than 60 metres (200 ft) high. These silver-white beaches are frequently backed by sand hills with marram grass. Inland, the scenery is a mixture of fertile farmland and heath, moor and planted forests which the Danes call *plantage*. There are slow-moving rivers and streams, and placid lakes. The **Limfjorden**, like an inland sea in the northwest, is a sailing paradise.

Although parts of West Jutland cannot be called anything but flat, stretches of gently undulating hills help to avoid monotony. In winter, the weather can be rugged, with storms blowing in off a turbulent North Sea and the prevailing westerlies bending the trees towards the east. In summer, the combination of wind and sun can easily burn a sensitive skin, which needs protection. This part of Jutland is popular with holidaymakers, as one can see from the countless summer cottages, each with its flagpole, camping sites, and holiday centres.

Fishing first

The loss of South Jutland to Germany in the war of 1864 led to the development of **Esbjerg ❶** on the west coast. From a village with few inhabitants, it has become a major port, the country's biggest fishing harbour and its fifth largest city (population 81,000). It is the main gateway for ferries from Britain.

The importance of the fishing industry is reflected in the **Fiskeri og Søfartsmuseet (Fisheries and Maritime Museum)** with its collection of fishing gear and models of boats (open July–Aug: 10am–6pm; Sept–Jun 10am–5pm; entrance fee; tel: 76 12 20 00). Its saltwater aquarium has 200 species of fish found in Danish waters and there is a seal aquarium where you can watch the seals under, as well as in the water.

The development of the town from 1900 to 1950 is shown in the **Esbjerg Museum**, where a complete urban environment has been created, with shops, houses, workshops and other town features (open 10am–4pm; Sept–May closed Mon; entrance fee; tel: 75 12 78 11).

The town history archives have a large collection of documents, maps and old photographs, while the **Bogtrykmuseet (Printing Press Museum)** illustrates

PRECEDING PAGES: leisurely dinner at Sønderho Inn
LEFT: windy walk on the west coast.
BELOW: fishing boats on the sand at Nørre Vorupør.

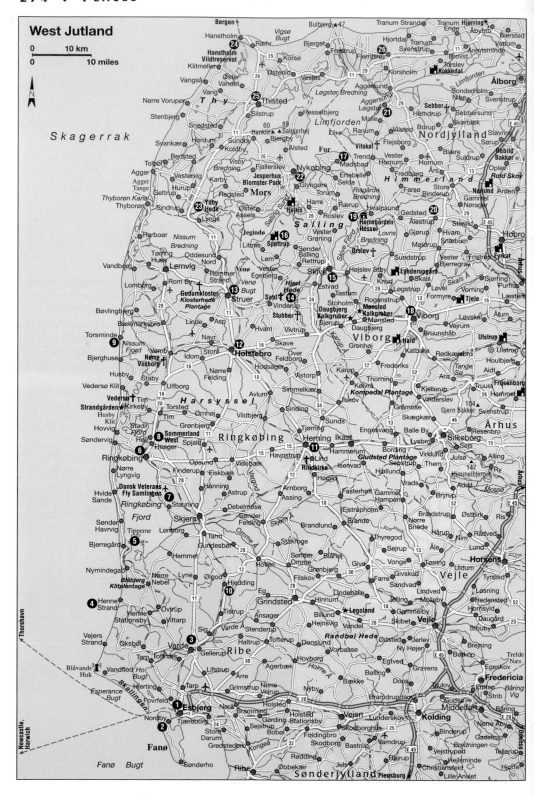

West Jutland

Map on page 274

the craft of printing over 500 years (open Jun–mid-Sept: Mon only 12 noon–4pm; entrance fee; tel: 75 13 04 05). **Esbjerg Kunstmuseum** (Modern Art Museum) features the work of contemporary Danish artists (open 10am–4pm; entrance fee; tel: 75 13 02 11).

A monument in the fishermen's **Memorial Grove** is dedicated to the many local fishermen who have died at sea. There are also monuments to allied airmen, German refugees, and military personnel killed in World War II.

Seafaring Fanø

Guarding the entrance to Esbjerg harbour and a 20-minute ferry ride away is the 11-mile (18-km) long island of **Fanø**. This must be the first example of a successful "buy-out". Until 1741, the island belonged to the King of Denmark; then, when he was short of cash, he offered it for sale by public auction. Fanø's inhabitants bought the island and also obtained the right to build ships. In one move, they had kept their island and created a major industry, which constructed 1,000 sailing ships between 1741 and 1900.

Today, Fanø has long forgotten its busy industrial past and relaxed into a role as a holiday island. The only town is **Nordby** ❷, which has narrow streets and typical thatched Fanø houses. The Seamen's Church (1786) includes ship models, and there are more to be seen in the Fanø Søfarts og Dragtudstilling (Fanø Shipping and Costume Museum; open May–Sept: 11am–4pm; Sep–Apr: 11am–1pm, closed Sun; entrance fee; tel: 75 16 22 72).

Sønderho in the south of the island is the jewel in Fanø's crown, with its old cottages, inn, and Seamen's Church (1782). The local museum, Hannes Hus, also reflects the great days of sailing. For today's holidaymakers, the west coast is a superb stretch of white sandy beach backed by sand hills, and the rest of the island is characteristic West Jutland scenery: dunes, heath and forest.

Dunes on the move

About 17 km (11 miles) north of Esbjerg, **Varde** ❸ has some preserved houses but a visitor gets a better idea of how the town looked in 1800 from the 1:10 miniature town model which has some 150 buildings.

On the coast, 30 km (19 miles) west, is **Blåvands Huk Lighthouse**, Denmark's westernmost point. There are many summer cottages here, seemingly oblivious to the Danish Army's noisy training area nearby. Good beaches line the coast; two fine ones are at Vejers Strand and **Henne Strand** ❹.

North of Henne Strand on the way to Nymindegab is the **Blåbjerg Klitplantage**, a 68-metre (210-ft) high sand ridge that changes its shape as the wind blows and the tides wander, to form what is called a "migrating dune".

From Nymindegab to Søndervig, the sea is also still forming the coastline. A narrow strip of land runs north, separating the sea from **Ringkøbing Fjord**, a broad, shallow expanse, the direct opposite of the conventional idea of a fjord. Once, this salt-water "lake" was part of the sea with an entrance at its northern end. Today, the shifting sands have left only a narrow channel half way along at the fishing village

The wide, sandy beaches of West Jutland are a magnet for bathers and windsurfers. In summer the most common language is German. But no matter how crowded, there's always plenty of space.

BELOW: drying fish is a common sight on the west coast.

*Beacon of light:
Bovbjerg lighthouse
at Torsminde.*

BELOW: Torsminde's
Shipwreck Museum
with relics from
the British flagship
"St George".

of **Hvide Sand** (appropriately translated as "white sand"), big enough to allow a small boat through.

From the road that runs along the sand hills, the view of the fjord is fascinating, with reeds and water plants pushing up above the surface. But from this road, the sea view is rather disappointing, scarcely visible through the dunes with their many cottages and camping sites. At **Tipperne** ❺, at the southern end of Ringkøbing Fjord, there is a bird sanctuary.

Ringkøbing ❻, once one of the west coast's busiest ports, is now on the inner coastline of the fjord, 10 km (6 miles) from the sea. This ancient port was founded in 1250 and has retained much of its old atmosphere, with typical West Jutland houses along the little streets.

About 17 km (11 miles) south of Rindkøbing, at Stauning airport is the **Dansk Veterans Fly Samlingen (Veteran Aircraft Museum)** ❼ (open May–Oct: 11am–5pm; entrance fee; tel: 97 36 93 33), and 8 km (5 miles) to the north of Rindkøbing at Hee is **Sommerland West** ❽. This children's activity park has more than 40 attractions and is crowded all summer (open late May–Jun: 10am–5pm; July: 10am–6pm; Aug: 10am–5pm; entrance fee; tel: 97 33 54 11).

Heading north from Rindkøbing on route 181 past beaches and sand dunes, stop at **Husby Klit** for **Strandgården**, a museum which includes all the first editions of the poet-vicar Kaj Munk, who was also a staunch member of the Resistance movement in World War II. He is buried 4 km (2 miles) south at **Vedersø Kirke** (museum open Apr–Jun and Sept–Oct: 11am–6pm, closed Mon; July–Aug: daily 11am–6pm; entrance fee; tel: 97 33 10 22).

All the way north the natural coastal phenomenon of sand hills and dunes repeats itself again and again, and has left stretches of salt water cut off from the sea. The strip that divides the Nissum Fjord from the North Sea is at one point wide enough to allow for the attractive small village of **Torsminde** ❾ and gives better sea views than the Ringkøbing "strip".

North again, you come to **Nissum Bredning.** To the east, Nissum Bredning becomes the westernmost part of the marvellous Limfjorden, which winds and wriggles right through to the east of Denmark and eventually empties into the Kattegat, east of Ålborg. This effectively turns North Jutland into an island.

Nissum Bredning opens into the sea at what is called the **Thyborøn Kanal** – even if it looks more like a narrow, natural opening.

A good catch

For excellent fishing, turn inland from Ringkøbing, where there are some splendid angling rivers. The **Skjern**, for example, has more than 100 km (60 miles) of river banks which give good sport.

Late in the 19th century, Danish farmers were pioneers in forming agricultural co-operatives. At **Hjedding** ❿, near Ølgod, 37 km (23 miles) north of Esbjerg, is Denmark's first co-operative dairy with its original 1882 machinery, now the Mejerimuseum (open Jun and Aug–mid-Sept: Sun 2–5pm; Jul Sat–Sun 2–5pm; tel: 75 24 50 11).

Herning ⓫, 45 km (28 miles) northeast, is an ancient settlement which in the past 100 years has

Map on page 274

expanded from a few houses to become the centre of the Danish textile industry. It is also an exhibition and congress town, which means that at times it is full to overflowing.

Herning Museum, Museumsgade 32, includes a delightful series of 57 detailed little dioramas depicting *A Year at Jens Nielsen's Farm* created by the artist Inge Fauertof (open Tue–Fri 10am–5pm, Sat–Sun 11am–5pm, closed Mon; entrance fee; tel 97 12 32 66). Another collection of 46 dioramas, *A September Day at Jens Nielsen's Farm*, are at the **Blichermuseet på Herningsholm**, Viborgvej 72, an old mid-Jutland manor house (1579) which is now a museum (open May–Oct 11am–6pm, closed Mon; tel: 97 22 22 99). It has a period interior and is dedicated to the moorland poet, Steen Steensen Blicher.

The **Herning Kunstmuseum (Art Museum)**, at Birkecenterpark 3, has an important contemporary collection (open 12 noon–5pm, Sat–Sun 10am–5pm, closed Mon; entrance fee; tel: 97 12 10 33). Also, there is a large sculpture park and photographic museum, the Foto Galleriet, Museumsgade 32, featuring exhibitions by Danish and international photographers (open 1–5pm; closed Mon; Jul: daily 1–5pm). Herning may have risen from the Jutland moorland, but it is not being left behind in the race for culture.

Forming the apex of a triangle made up of Ringkøbing and Herning is **Holstebro** ⑫, a busy commercial town 32 km (20 miles) north. Lacking historical associations, it has also decided to make a cultural name for itself as an art centre. There is an impressive range of sculptures and fountains throughout the town, the latest being the high-tech laser sculpture of Frithoff Johansen.

Holstebro has a whole raft of museums covering art and graphics, including the **Kleinkunstmuseet (Museum of Miniature Art)**, Sønderlandsgade 46,

At Christmas 1811 the English flagship "St George" and the warship "Defence" went down on the west coast with the loss of 1400 men. The Shipwreck Museum, Torsminde, bears witness to this and other North Sea dramas.

BELOW: Esbjerg, one of Denmark's busiest ports

BELOW: snail house at Thyboron covered with shells.

containing 400 international works each no larger than 10 by 15 cm (4 by 6 in) (open Sun–Fri 1pm–5pm, Sat 11am–1pm closed Mon; entrance fee; tel: 97 40 43 99). Collections of pipes and dolls, the history of a Dragoon regiment and the World War II Resistance are other subjects.

About 20 km (12 miles) west of Holstebro, at **Ulfborg**, the village church has an unusual preaching chair which runs from wall to wall. The countryside around these three towns seldom rises over 90 metres (300 ft) above sea level and, apart from a scattering of villages and hamlets, there is little to take the eye.

Watery landscape

The coastline north, with almost continuous beaches, eventually thins to a finger at the fishing village of **Thyborøn**, where there is a ferry (12-minute crossing) over the Thyborøn Kanal to another spit of land, Agger Tange. In the south, the Nissum Bredning narrows sufficiently at **Oddesund** for there to be road and rail bridges, and the waters then continue northeast to become Limfjorden. This is a region of islands separated by narrow sounds and peninsulas which project into the fjord itself. A spit of land may have the fjord on both sides, an island may be linked by a bridge. If sailing is not possible, this is an area for slow, leisurely driving on roads that link the fjord towns and villages and wind across farmland and heath. You are always at water's edge. On these twisting roads, directions can be difficult and a map is essential.

Struer ⓭, 12 km (7 miles) north of Holstebro, is another of Denmark's "young towns" and has major industries. Not least is Bang & Olufsen, the maker of state-of-the-art stereos, televisions and electronics. The **Struer Museum**, Søndergade 23, is in an old farmhouse and vicarage next to the home of the poet

SUN, SAND AND SURF

The west coast of Jutland is an unspoilt stretch of grassy dunes, glowing sunsets and the incessant crash of waves on broad, sandy beaches. Brisk North Sea breezes make it a windsurfer's El Dorado. This is where the Danes come for a carefree holiday and the entire area is dotted with summer cottages.

One should be careful with the term "summer cottage", however, because these holiday houses range from the modest to the outright luxurious. They can be rented not just in summer, but all year round, even at Christmas. The cottages offer privacy and a degree of solitude, but not isolation. In summer and other holiday periods, visitors often form a lively community.

Just up the road, the local town will probably have a weekly market day where you can buy anything from farm-fresh eggs and produce, to knick-knacks, even a horse. Stay until evening and chances are that the local jazzmen or provincial musicians will strike up the band. When the locals begin to dance, just join in.

The North Sea and Danish fjords offer their own bounty. Meet the fishermen down at the harbour and you can buy fresh herring, cod, salmon, plaice, eel or sea trout directly from the boats.

Johannes Buchholtz (1882-1940) (open Jul–Aug: 10am–4pm, Sat–Sun 1am–4pm; Sept–May: 1pm–4pm, closed Mon; entrance fee; tel: 97 85 13 11).

Near the Oddesund bridges are two major wind farms for the generation of electric power. Without the benefit of oil or hydro-electric power, Denmark has experimented hard with many forms of alternative energy and wind now produces 10 percent of the country's power.

The island of **Venø**, with 150 inhabitants, lies to the northeast of Struer, connected by ferry. It features the smallest village church in Denmark, from the 16th century. To the west of Struer, the **Klosterhede Plantage** is the biggest planted forest in Denmark and covers an area of 65 sq km (25 sq miles).

Hjerl Hede ⓮, 20 km (12 miles) east of Struer, is one of the country's most impressive natural areas covering 810 hectares (2,000 acres) and all preserved since 1934. **Hjerl Hede Frilandsmuseum (Open Air Museum)** has a large collection of historic buildings which have been moved from other parts of Jutland, including a smithy, dairy and an inn, as well as a rope walk (open Apr–Oct: 9am–5pm; Dec: various weekends 10am–5pm; entrance fee; tel: 97 44 80 60). Nearby Sahl Kirke has a so-called golden altar made of delicately beaten copper plates on oak.

Skive ⓯, 35 km (22 miles) northeast of Struer, on the River Karup, is an old, well established town which today is a busy road and rail junction, and a good base for exploration. It lies at the foot of the **Salling peninsula**, a pleasant rural area of farmland and rolling hills which reaches out into the Limfjord. Historically the most interesting building is **Spøttrup Slot ⓰**, 16 km (10 miles) west of Skive. This is one of Denmark's finest medieval fortresses, surrounded by a double moat, and has a well-preserved interior. Adjoining it is a medieval

Map on page 274

BELOW: medieval Spøttrup Slot.

herb garden and rose park (open Dec–Apr: Sun, Tue, Wed and Easter 11am–5pm; May–Aug: 10am–6pm; Sept: 10am–5pm; Oct: 10am–4pm; Nov: 11am–3pm; entrance fee; tel: 97 56 16 06).

To the west, the Salling peninsula is linked to the island of Mors by an impressive bridge spanning Salling Sund. At the northern tip of Salling is the island of **Fur**, a five-minute ferry crossing. Erosion by the sea has created steep molar cliffs, and Fur Museum at **Madsbad** ⑰ has a rare collection of fossils (open: Apr–Jun and Sept–Oct: 1–4pm; Jul–Aug: 10am–5pm; tel: 97 59 34 11).

Vantage point

Facing the Søndersø and Nordsø lakes is the hilltop town of **Viborg** ⑱ with its magnificent **Domkirke (Cathedral)**. At this junction of six main roads, east and west meet (Viborg is a town that either East or West Jutland can claim).

Although the cathedral was founded in 1130, the present building was completed in 1876. It contains some beautiful frescoes by Joakim Skovgård. The Skovgård Museet, at Domkirkestræde 2–4, features paintings, sculptures and art works by five generations of the Skovgård family (open: May–Sept: 10am–12.30pm, 1.30pm–5pm; Oct–Apr: 1.30–5pm; tel: 86 62 39 75).

Viborg Stiftsmuseum, Hjultorvet 4, traces the history of the town and its people and contains workshops and products of the local craftsmen (open Jun–Aug: 11am–5pm, closed Mon; Sept–May and Tue–Fri 2–5pm, Sat–Sun 11am–5pm; entrance fee; tel: 87 25 26 10). The pews at Søndersogn Kirke (Church) are covered by some 200 paintings.

At **Thorning**, 15 km (9 miles) south of the town, the **Blicheregnens Museum** covers 19th-century peasant culture and the life of the writer, Blicher, a vicar of

BELOW: Feggerklit, cliff-face of Mors.

Thorning (open: May, Sept: 1–5pm; Jun–Aug Mon–Fri 10am–5pm, Sat–Sun 1–5pm; Oct–Apr: 1–5pm; tel: 86 88 08 77).

Map on page 274

West of Viborg is an area of disused limestone mines. The **Mønsted Kalkgruber** (**Mønsted Mines**) are open to the public, with galleries 35 metres (114 ft) below ground (open mid-May–Sept: 11am–5pm; entrance fee; tel: 86 64 60 11). Some galleries are used to mature cheese because of their even temperature. At the **Daugbjerg Kalkgruber** (**Daugberg Mines**), 4 km (2 miles) west, the galleries are up to 70 metres (230 ft) deep, and there is a bat museum (open Apr: Sat–Sun noon–4pm; May and Sept–Oct: noon–4pm; June: 10am–4pm; July–Aug. 10am–6pm; entrance fee; tel: 97 54 83 33). The mine owner is an enthusiastic violinist who holds concerts underground. Limestone was first extracted as long ago as the 10th century and was used in the building of Ribe Cathedral in South Jutland.

Heather turns the Jutland moors purple in autumn. A refreshing stroll will show you that the heather varies in colour from almost burgundy to white.

Yacht haven

To the east of the Salling peninsula is **Himmerland**, a region of gently rolling farmland with some wide swathes of moorland and heath. On two sides, the waters of the Limfjord vary from narrow sounds and sheltered coves to broad stretches of open water with islands and peninsulas. They are a pure delight for the sailing enthusiast.

Herregården Hessel ⑲, on Skive Fjord near Hvalpsund, is the last completely thatched manor house in Denmark, now an agricultural museum with a period interior and a collection of implements (open May–Sept: 10am–5.30pm; entrance fee; tel: 98 63 81 25). **Ålestrup ⑳**, 20 km (12 miles) east, has the Danmarks Cykle Museum (Denmark's Bicycle Museum), with more than 100 machines, as well as some early sewing machines and radios (open May–Sept: 10am–5pm; entrance fee; tel: 98 64 19 60).

BELOW: ladybirds on the dunes of Rudbjerg Knud.

Between Ranum and Trend, 25 km (15 miles) northwest of Ålestrup, are the remains of what was intended to be a great church and monastery, **Vitskel-Kloster**. It was given to the Cistercian monks in 1157 by King Valdemar. Only ruins now remain and the monastery, which became a manor house in 1668, is now a correction centre for young offenders.

A small town with a long history is **Løgstør ㉑**, on the east of the Limfjord 15 km (9 miles) north of Vitsel-Kloster, which was a Viking fortress in AD 1000. In the 16th century it was the centre of the herring fisheries, but the disappearance of the fish meant a change to commerce and shipping. This was at first thwarted by the shallow waters of the Aggersund but resolved in 1861 with the construction of the Frederik VII's canal, 5 km (3 miles) in length. It continued in use until a new channel was made through the shallows at the turn of the century.

Today, part of the canal is a yacht harbour, and the **Limfjordmuseet** is in the former canal warden's house (open Jun–Aug 10am–5pm; Sept–May: Sat 2–5pm, Sun 10am–5pm; tel: 98 67 18 05). Løgstør has reverted to being a quiet town, quite different from its past as a Viking fortress or commercial port. **Nibe**, 23 km (14 miles) east of Løgstør, was also founded

Map on page 274

because of the herring fisheries and, like Løgstør, today is a quiet little place and the best preserved community in the Limfjord area.

Mors in bloom

The island of **Mors**, the largest in the Limfjord, lies between the Salling peninsula and that part of West Jutland traditionally called Thy. Mors includes a microcosm of all West Jutland's landscape, from salt marshes to great molar cliffs. **Hanklit** is 60 metres (215 ft) high and embodies tertiary flora and fauna, and layers of black volcanic ash. Nearby is **Salgjerhøj**, 89 metres (293 ft) high, offering panoramic views over the waters of Limfjord.

The principal town, **Nykøbing** ㉒, grew up around the Abbey of St John (1370). The Morsland Historisk Museum is in the former Dueholm Kloster (open mid-Jun–mid-Aug: 10am–5pm; mid-Aug–mid-Jun 10am–4pm, Sat–Sun 12–4pm; entrance fee; tel: 97 72 34 21). To the south is **Jesperhus Blomster Park**, the largest flower gardens in Scandinavia with more than 500,000 species (open mid-May–mid-June and Sept: 10am–5pm, Sat–Sun 10am–6pm; mid-June–July 10am–8pm; Aug 10am–6pm; free; tel: 97 72 32 00).

Thy peninsula

The narrow peninsula of Thy is like a long pincer, with its jaw at the Thyborøn Kanal to the northwest of the Limfjord. At **Ydby Hede** ㉓, overlooking the Skibsted Fjord, there are 50 grave mounds from the Bronze Age. **Vestervig** has Scandinavia's biggest 12th-century village but the surrounding scenery is more likely to catch the visitor's attention. From the fishing village of **Agger**, in the south of Thy to **Hanstholm** ㉔ in the north, there is a splendid coastline with good beaches. Inland are extensive areas of heath, forest and lakes.

At the village of **Nørre Vorupør** the fishermen still haul their cutters up on the beach, but at **Klitmøller** fishing has given way to holiday cottages. Between Klitmøller and Hanstholm is a stretch of spectacular scenery: the Hanstholm Vildtreservat (Hanstholm Nature Reserve) is a treeless heathland which is rich in birds and wildlife (closed during springtime breeding).

In 1917 the Danish government decided to build a harbour at Hanstholm but work proceeded slowly. In World War II, the German occupation forces turned it into a heavily fortified zone. Work resumed in the 1960s, and the harbour was built out of sight at the base of steep cliffs, with the town spread out above.

Thy's principal town is **Thisted** ㉕, a commercial centre to the south of the peninsula. The Gothic church dates from about 1500 and Thisted Museum honours two townsmen, the poet J. P. Jacobsen and the educator Kristen Kold (open Jun–Aug: 10am–5pm; Sept–May: Mon–Fri 9am–3pm; Sun 2–5pm; tel: 97 97 42 77).

Beyond Hanstholm at the northern end of the Vigsø bay is **Bulbjerg**, a limestone cliff 40 metres (130 ft) high with good views of the area. It is known as the "shoulder of Denmark". Inland, 45 km (28 miles) east of Bulberg, **Fjerritslev**'s ㉖ claim to fame is its preserved brewery, now a museum. ❏

SOUTH JUTLAND

Map on page 288

*In the low-lying land of South Jutland, guarded by ancient castles,
the night watchman still walks the streets of medieval Ribe
and Viking life is re-enacted in Jels*

The half-timbered and gabled houses in the marshes of South Jutland richly illustrate the region's historic past. Here you find Scandinavia's oldest town, Ribe, which has played an important role. In 1864, the Danes lost southern Jutland to Prussia after a heroic battle at Dybbøl. It became part of Schleswig-Holstein, and Denmark only recovered it again in 1920. At that time, in a plebiscite, North Schleswig voted overwhelmingly to return to Denmark, and the border was redrawn to form the area that is now southern Jutland.

Though the landscape is basically flat and alternates between heath, marshland, dunes and forest, with a network of well-stocked rivers to keep the anglers happy, history gives this area an added interest.

Cathedral city

Ribe **❶**, built around its 12th-century cathedral, is the first town you encounter as you travel south along the west coast. It ranks high on the list of historic centres in Scandinavia with 560 buildings included in a municipal preservation project. The houses, courtyards and inns (*kro*) are much as they were hundreds of years ago. But Ribe is no mere museum; the houses are homes to local people, their windows colourful with potted plants and bright curtains.

Ribe began as a Viking settlement in the 9th century and was of great importance in the Middle Ages. Its days of glory ended in the 17th century when economic and political power moved to Copenhagen. Its industries foundered in the 19th century when South Jutland was lost to Germany.

Ribe Domkirke (Cathedral) dates from 1150 but stands on the site of one of Denmark's earliest wooden churches, built around AD 860. It has five aisles. The red brick tower is 14th-century and the 234 steps to the top are worth climbing for the splendid views over the surrounding countryside.

In days past, that high tower had a highly practical use. Before the construction of dykes and barriers, this low-lying area was periodically inundated by floods, and the church bell in its tower tolled out as a warning of danger. The "Cat Head Door" was said to be the entrance for the Devil.

Quedens Gård, Overdammen 10, a four-winged, half-timbered merchant's house, is now a museum of interiors with exhibits that reflect local crafts, trade and industry (open Mar–May: 11am–3pm, closed Mon; Jun–Aug: 10am–5pm daily; Sept–Oct: 11am–3pm, closed Mon; Nov–Jan: 11am–1pm, closed Mon; entrance fee; tel: 76 88 11 22).

The old grammar school was in use from the early 1500s to 1856, and the 15th-century town hall was the seat of local government from 1709 to 1966. **Ribe**

PRECEDING PAGES: thatching a roof, a skilled art.
LEFT: on the harbour at Ribe.
BELOW: view from Ribe Cathedral.

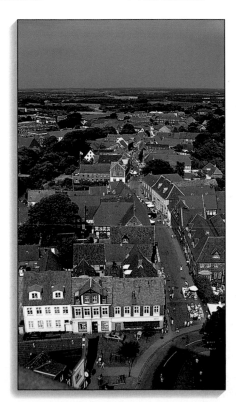

A night watchman walks through the old streets of Ribe on summer evenings, recounting the town's history in song.

Kunstmuseum (Art Museum), Skt Nicolajgade 10, features works by Danish artists from the "Golden Age" of the 19th century, including Michael Ancher's *A Christening in Skagen* (1888) (open mid-Jun–mid Sept: daily 11am–4pm; mid-Sept–mid-Jun: 1–4pm, closed Mon; entrance fee; tel: 75 42 03 62).

In Ribe marketplace is an ancient inn called **Weiss' Stue**, panelled with biblical pictures, where the courtyard makes a fine outdoor restaurant in summer. The town continues the Middle Ages tradition of **night watchmen**. Each evening at 10pm, the watchman walks around singing the traditional songs that once told the people that they could sleep soundly, all was well. In summer, he is most often accompanied by a crowd of visitors.

Ribe was once a seaport, and the old quay has a column whose highest watermark shows the height of the 1634 flood which reached as far as the cathedral. The silting up of the river means that now **Ribe Harbour** can be used only by small pleasure craft.

To the islands

Off the coast is the tiny, windswept island of **Mandø** which can be reached by a tractor bus at low tide. (Your own car is not recommended.) It is an isolated community of some 100 inhabitants.

To the south, the larger island of **Rømø** is accessible along a 5-mile (9-km) causeway and is a favourite of German visitors. It has wide, sandy beaches on the west coast, and **Havneby** has a ferry connection to the island of **Sylt**. The island was once the home of prosperous whaling fleet commanders and one of their houses (*circa* 1746) at **Toftum ❷** is now a museum, Nationalmuseets Kommandørgård (open May–Sept: 10am–6pm, closed Mon; Oct: 10am–3pm,

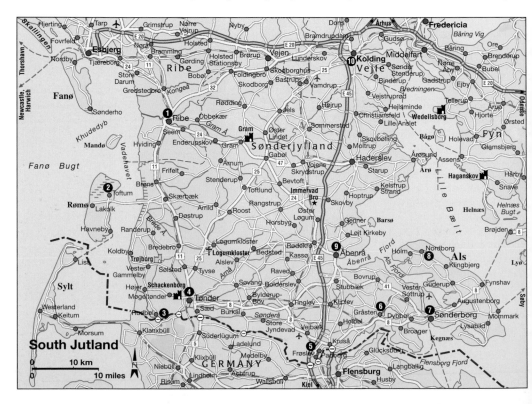

closed Mon; entrance fee; tel: 74 75 52 76). In summer, this house is the setting for folk dancing, lace-making and similar demonstrations of traditional skills.

Nearer the German frontier, 45 km (28 miles) south of Ribe, **Højer** is also one of the oldest villages in Denmark where 250 houses and farms are preserved, though still lived in. Højer's windmill is the tallest in northern Europe.

Map on page 288

Exploring inland

Inland areas of South Jutland, once little more than marsh and moor, have few major centres of population, but it is easy driving and, like so many parts of Denmark, it's good for cycling. One characteristic sight in this marshland area is the isolated farms built on high mounds to protect them from floods that came frequently and suddenly before the earthworks were built.

The little town of **Gram**, surrounded by moors, heath and pine forests 18 km (11 miles) east of Ribe, is typical of an old market town which grew up around its castle. The present castle dates from 1664 and the west wing houses a geological museum, **Midsønderjytllands Museum** (open May–mid-Sept: 10am–5pm, closed Mon; mid-Sept–Aug: 1pm–4pm, Sun 10am–4pm, closed Mon; entrance fee; tel: 74 82 01 11).

The village of **Rudbøl ❸** straddles the frontier. Here you see Danish locals wheeling their shopping trolleys past the border post after a visit to a German supermarket, where prices and taxes are lower. This area is famous for its local produce. A good place to try the local speciality of a marsh sausage is the Rudbøl Grænsekro, an inn that has been serving them since 1791.

Møgeltønder's village street, 6 km (4 miles) north of Rudbøl, is lined with lime trees and can with justification claim to be one of the most beautiful in this

Vikings come alive in Jels, east of Ribe, in early July. The annual outdoor pageant features blood oaths and battles, but also the everyday lives of the traders and farmers who earned their fame as warriors.

BELOW: Denmark's oldest hotel, the Dagmar at Ribe.

Christiansfeld, south of Kolding, is "world famous in Denmark" (as the Danes say jokingly) for its honey cake. This baking tradition is almost as old as the town itself, dating back to 1783.

part of Europe. The little houses are of typical Friesian design and at one end of the village, the church has Denmark's oldest working organ from 1679. At the other end is **Schackenborg Slot**, built as a church property and now the residence of Prince Joachim (second in succession) and Princess Alexandra.

Just 3 km (2 miles) to the east, **Tønder** ❹ is the "capital" of this southwestern region. This former port, which received its charter in 1243, is now a considerable distance from the sea. It became famous as a lace-making centre and in its heyday when 12,000 young women were employed in this work. The excellent **Tonder Museum**, Kongevej 51, covers the history of the area, particularly the lace-making industry, and shows a collection of silver and tiles (open 10am–5pm, closed Mon; entrance fee; tel:74 72 26 57).

Tønder has a well-preserved, attractive 17th- and 18th-century townscape, and many houses have distinctive painted doorways. In the 12th century, Cistercian monks established a church and monastery at **Løgumkloster**, 15 km (9 miles) to the north. The present church combines Romanesque and Gothic styles. The old buildings now house a retreat and a school for bell-ringers.

Reminders of war

Moving 40 km (25 miles) east from Tønder towards Kruså, **Frøslev** ❺ has a reminder of World War II, as parts of a German internment camp have been kept as a museum, **Frøslevlejren** (open Tue–Fri 9am–4pm; Sat–Sun 10am-5pm; entrance fee; tel: 74 67 65 57). Some 16,000 Danes were imprisoned here; for many it was only a temporary stay along the road to the concentration camps.

The key frontier town is **Padborg**. Neighbouring **Kruså** is the gateway to Sønderborg and the island of Als which stretches east at the mouth of the Lille

BELOW: Dybbøl windmill, near the 1864 battlefield.

SOUTHERN APPEAL

The fairy-tale villages and gentle farmlands of South Jutland appear to have been created by Hans Christian Andersen himself. In fact, the author was quite enchanted by the serene beauty of the region. **Schackenborg Slot** in Møgeltønder is the residence of a real prince, Joachim, and his princess. Denmark's royal grandmother, Queen Mother Ingrid, spends her holidays at **Gråsten Slot** on Flensborg Fjord, a short distance to the east.

South Jutland features more than 100 museums with art, historical and specialised exhibitions. One of the best ways to learn about the ancient town of Ribe is to wander along the cobbled streets with the night watchman as he sings his traditional song and tells about its long history.

A major event in the south is the annual **Tønder Festival** in late August with folk musicians from around Europe and further afield. On the first weekend in July, Åbenrå hosts the **Regional Tilting Tournament** when horses' hooves thunder under more than 500 riders.

Along both east and west coasts of South Jutland are miles of clean beaches for swimming, diving, windsurfing or simply lolling in the sand. Active visitors will find excellent places to golf, fish, bicycle, watch birds or hike across the gentle countryside.

Bælt, looking across to Funen. Heading east, the most scenic route is the secondary coast road alongside Kobbermølle Bugt.

On the outskirts of **Gråsten** ❻, 15 km (9 miles) northeast of Kruså, is the magnificent white **Gråsten Slot**. Apart from the chapel with its impressive floor-to-ceiling altarpiece, the original 17th-century buildings burned down in 1759. The palace was rebuilt and in 1935, was presented to the Danish crown prince and princess at the time. It is now a summer residence of the Danish royal family but, when Queen Margethe II and their highnesses are away, the chapel and parkland are open to the public (8am–7pm).

Almost on the outskirts of Sønderborg is another dramatic area, **Dybbøl**, which played a major role in the war of 1864. The area is a national park and includes the ramparts and old cannon from the battle which resulted in South Jutland disappearing from the Danish map for 50 years, to become part of Germany. All over the area museums have reminders of this era. The **Dybbøl Vindmølle** (windmill), restored and painted white, and its museum are open to the public (Apr–Oct: 10am-5pm; free; tel: 74 48 69 91).

Sønderborg ❼ (population 30,000) calls itself the largest town in South Jutland – although the majority of the town lies across the sound on the island of Als. The town has grown up around mighty **Sønderborg Slot**. It was begun by King Valdemar the Great about 1100 as a defensive fortress. Today the castle houses a museum of Danish history, Museet på Sønderborg Slot (open May–Sept: 10am–5pm, Oct–Apr:10am–4pm, Nov–Mar:1–4pm; tel: 74 42 25 39).

Als is a pleasant island designed for pottering around, with some good sandy beaches in the north and south. At Mommark, 13 km (8 miles) east of Sønderborg, there is a ferry to **Søby** on the island of Ærø, on the opposite side of the

Map on page 288

Memorial to the night watchmen of old at Åbenrå.

BELOW: walking along Hærvejen, the ancient drove road.

Lille Bælt. At Fynshav, 7 km (4 miles) north, another service runs to Bøjden on Funen. The only other town of any size on Als is **Nordborg ❽** which features a castle and one of Denmark's major industrial concerns, Danfoss, which manufactures and exports refrigeration, heating and water controls all over the world. **Egen Kirke** has a wooden bell tower – unusual in Denmark. A graceful, twin-spired church at **Broager** has frescoes from 1250.

Seafaring centre

Going north on the eastern side of the peninsula, the first town of importance is **Åbenrå ❾** (population 20,000). The town, set on the Åbenrå Fjord, should in theory have a beautiful location but, alas, the view is spoiled by oil storage tanks and a massive power station. Granted a charter in 1333 by Duke Valdemar, Åbenrå became a major port in the 17th and 18th centuries. Its maritime heritage is reflected in the shipbuilding artefacts in **Åbenrå Museum** (open Jun–Aug: 10am–4pm, closed Mon; Sept– May: 1–4pm, closed Mon; entrance fee; tel: 74 62 26 45). Impressive houses in the town and on the **Løjt Kirkeby peninsula** are reminders of the good shore life enjoyed by sea captains in bygone days.

The church at **Løjt Kirkeby** has South Jutland's longest late-Gothic triptych (1520). The oldest Åbenrå church is the 13th-century **Skt Nikolaj**, which features a baroque altarpiece, pulpit and baptismal font.

ABOVE AND BELOW: ancient and modern are combined at Koldinghus Slot. **RIGHT:** musician wearing traditional Tønder dress.

When farming was at its height, from the 16th century to the middle of the 19th century, South Jutland's best-known drove road was called **Hærvejen** (the Army Road) and ran south to north through the area from Bov to Jels-Rødding, and then up through Jutland to Viborg. Along this road, the farmers herded their cattle on the hoof to market. A section of the old road is still preserved 14 km (9 miles) north of Åbenrå, near **Immervad Bro**, an old granite boulder bridge, and the local authorities are making strenuous efforts to have the whole of Hærvejen reinstated as a walking and cycling route.

Kolding ❿, 33 km (20 miles) to the north, next to the Lille Bælt Bridge to Funen, has been involved in many wars over the centuries and not much is left of the original castle, **Koldinghus Slot**, built in 1208 (open 10am–5pm; entrance fee; tel: 75 50 15 00).

The castle's last burning in 1808 was caused not by direct attack, but from shivering Spanish troops which Napoleon stationed there during Denmark's confused alliance with the French emperor. Faced with the chill of a Scandinavian winter, the Spaniards stoked up their fires so well that the old royal castle went up in flames. Nevertheless, the Spaniards were popular in Kolding and are credited with, or blamed for, teaching the Danes to smoke cigarettes. Today, Koldinghus is restored and furnished with collections of wartime memorabilia, as well as arts and crafts .

The town of Kolding is a junction on the east–west route across Denmark. The main railway line runs through the centre and the motorway lies to the north.

Southern Jutland was once torn by war but today this gentle area is better summed up in **Kolding's Geographical Garden** where more than 2,000 varieties of trees and shrubs from all over the world have brought about a more peaceful invasion. ❑

GREENLAND

The Land of the Midnight Sun offers some awesome adventure travel and spectacular scenery. For the less intrepid, there are boat cruises, nature walks and helicopter rides

Map
on page
298

The world's largest island is a place of stunning natural beauty, dramatic weather and fascinating culture. Greenland, like the Faroe Islands, is a former Danish colony that has become a member of the kingdom, but with its own home-rule government.

A visit to Greenland is like no other place. Its vast Arctic solitude is profound and its silence almost consumes you. Try touring the coastal settlements, ice plains and glaciers by dog sled for a lifetime experience. Here, where the North Atlantic meets the Arctic Ocean, is the cleanest environment in the world, and measurably the oldest. Greenlandic rocks have been dated back 3.7 billion years. Where else can you sip a drink cooled by a 1,000-year-old ice cube?

Greenland is called Kalaallit Nunaat (Land of Man) by its own people. They number only about 45,000 (plus an additional 10,000 Danes) in an area of 2,175,600 sq km (840,000 sq miles). The distance north to south is 2,670 km (1,655 miles), and the widest part east to west is 1,000 km (620 miles). Its closest neighbour is Canada. The capital is **Nuuk** ❶ (Godthåb) on the west coast.

Over four-fifths of Greenland lies under 3 km (2 miles) of pack ice but the southern coastal regions, mainly to the west, are green and mild during late spring and summer. The southernmost point of Greenland, Nunap Isua (Kap Farvel), is on the same latitude as Oslo, Norway's capital.

PRECEDING PAGES: canoeing in Greenland waters. **LEFT:** Qasigiannguit on the west coast. **BELOW:** dressed in traditional costume.

Icy conditions

There are three main types of ice in Greenland: compact ice, field ice and icebergs. Compact ice is frozen salt water that covers the fjords in winter.

Field ice, however, is formed in the Arctic Ocean north of Greenland and is carried by currents down the east coast, around Kap Farvel, and up the west coast. Field ice can create havoc for shipping, making many towns inaccessible except by air or dog sled.

Icebergs break off glaciers at the edge of the inland ice, which is frozen fresh water. This ice can range in age from hundreds to millions of years old.

The ice-free strips along Greenland's coast are only a few miles wide before the land climbs steeply to the inland ice. These are green in spring and summer, and offer a surprising array of plants, flowers and wildlife. As for trees, there are none.

The ice cap and the deep-cut fjords make sea or air the only links between the isolated settlements. Road travel exists only in towns and their immediate surroundings, but not between them.

Greenlanders are Inuit, traditionally referred to as Eskimos, and live in small towns around the coast, especially the west. Most of these people still earn their livelihoods by fishing and hunting. But thanks to its long association with Denmark, Greenland has a

TIP

Greenland welcomes
tourists but asks that
you treat the natural
environment with the
same respect that
they do. Leave behind
only your footprints,
take with you only
memories and
photographs.

modern infrastructure and burgeoning tourist industry. In north and east Greenland, some of the people still follow the ancient ways of seal hunting by kayak. The sealing families partly subsist on a barter economy. They eat or use every part of the seal, but they also earn money by selling seal skins.

The majority of export income today, however, stems from shrimp, salmon and cod fishing – often with the use of large, highly sophisticated trawlers – and several townships have modern fish-processing plants. Greenland's future wealth might come from underground, however. Coal, lead, graphite and zinc have all been extracted in the past, but geologists have identified at least 200 more metals and minerals. Exploration projects are now under way for oil, gas, zinc and gold with an eye to future commercial exploitation.

Despite all the ice, Greenland has a surprisingly mild spring and summer along much of its coast. The average temperature in mid-Greenland, for instance, can soar to a balmy 70°F (26°C), but in winter, it can plunge to a bone-cracking –25°F (–32°C). The spring and summer climate makes for excellent hiking and camping, not to mention some of the best fishing anywhere. Skiing, of course, is an option year-round, both alpine and cross-country.

Adventure tours

An ancient but still thrilling way of touring Greenland is by dog sled. You can hire a team and driver for a short sightseeing tour or for a long journey over days. Outfitters can provide you with the food and equipment you need. The season is usually from late February to May, but summer trips are also possible. In western Greenland in season, it's possible to arrange trips from **Sisimiut ❷**, **Qeqertarsuaq (Disko Island) ❸** and points further north of the Arctic Circle.

BELOW: a
fresh catch is
brought ashore.

Map on page 298

On the barely-populated east coast, you can dog sled from **Tasiilaq** ❹ and **Ittoqqortoormiit** ❺, and some smaller villages.

A classic though physically demanding dog sled tour is the eight-day trip between Sisimiut and **Kangerlussuaq** ❻ at Søndre Strømfjord on the west coast, which is possible in March and April. You enter vast and beautiful landscapes of mid-Greenland, across frozen lakes and over hilly terrain. You travel five to seven hours a day, and sleep in hunting huts or solid tents.

Boat tours also offer breathtaking scenery and wildlife. Summer cruises to towns along the east and west coasts take you through sparkling seas alive with seals and other marine life, even whales. You can disembark at these harbours and settlements for hiking trips, or dog sled tours in season. Between ports, you sail past icebergs and glaciers. On land you might see reindeer and musk oxen, and polar bears have been spotted. Bird life is not abundant in Greenland but you can encounter arctic terns, ravens, peregrine falcons and eagles.

Helicopter is an important, often essential means of transportation here. Chopper tours are a breathtakingly beautiful way to travel around Greenland and understandably, more expensive. Greenlandair operates domestic helicopter passenger services, but private companies also offer sightseeing flights.

Hiking and trekking tours in Greenland are possible at all levels of ability. You can join guided expeditions for days or weeks into the wilds, or modest day trips. A novel way of exploring Greenland's nature is aboard a sturdy Icelandic pony. From Kangerlussuaq, you can join riding tours over gentle or demanding terrain, if you like, past lush flora and fauna, and inspiring scenery.

This vast, half-frozen island draws an increasing number of anglers each year. They come after the trout and Arctic char in lowland lakes, rivers and

Greenland Outfitters are self-employed people who are trained and certified in one or more of some 10 adventure fields, including hunting, fishing, kayaking, dog sledding and more.

BELOW: a fishing boat in Greenland's icy waters.

Nuuk, the capital of Greenland and seat of government.

BELOW: bronze figures by the artist Sven Havsteen, at Kagssiarssuq.

streams. Off the coast and sometime through ice, they reel in Greenland halibut, Norway haddock, catfish and cod. Fishing licenses are required for all adults, but they are inexpensive.

Wild weather and northern lights

The most essential – perhaps the only – word you need to know in Greenlandic is *imaga*. It means maybe, some time, or perhaps. In a climate which changes from hot sun and clear bright air to a deluge of rain in a moment, the weather decides whether it's possible to keep to a plan made the day before.

Many a visitor has "overnighted" at **Narsarsuaq ❼** in the south because aircraft couldn't land, and all Greenland airports have transit hotels. The record is held, so the story goes, by a plane load that waited three weeks at the "all-weather" **airport** at Søndre Strømfjord – but that was during the worst of the winter weather, they add reassuringly.

Among exquisite natural phenomena in Greenland are the northern lights and the midnight sun. The *aurora borealis*, or northern light, occurs all year long but is only visible in a clear, night sky in autumn and winter. These splendid lights can appear as colourful curtains, veins of silk ribbon or as ghostly souls flying to heaven. The summer midnight sun keeps the night sky blue but whether it's a bright glow or direct sunshine depends on where you view it. At Disko Bay, for instance, you see midnight sun from late May to late July.

Getting there

The only way to travel to Greenland is by air, either via Copenhagen; Keflavik, Iceland; or Ottawa, Canada. Greenland has four international airports: Narsarsuaq in the south, Kulusuk near Tasiilaq in the east, and Nuuk and Kangerlussuaq on the central west coast. **Thule,** home of the US air base in the extreme northwest, is served via Kangerlussuaq by helicopter to **Qaanaaq ❽**. All domestic air services are handled by Greenlandair, either with fixed-wing aircraft or helicopters.

Once in Greenland, sailing is an option year-round, but schedules are highly dependent on the changing weather. The same applies to air services.

Food and accommodation

Most towns in Greenland, the largest of which is Nuuk with 12,000 inhabitants, have modern hotels in various categories of comfort. These and the local tourist offices are the best places to book excursions. The more footloose visitor may prefer a hostel, seaman's home, or a cabin.

Virtually all forms of accommodation are available. More and more camping sites are appearing in Greenland these days, meaning sites with toilets and hot bathing facilities. Tent roughing is permitted virtually everywhere, so long as campers observe the rules of nature and common politeness. The only area that is off limits is in southern Greenland, on land used for grass harvesting.

Heart disease is a rarity for Greenlanders, thanks to a diet that is based heavily on the sea. Greenlandic

specialities also include fowl, game and berries. The national dish is *suasaat*, seal meat cooked with rice and onions. A particular delicacy is *mattak*, pieces of whale skin with a thin layer of blubber. Slow chewing brings out its nutty flavour. If your taste buds are more "Western", try musk ox steak or Greenlandic lamb cutlets, considered to be some of the best in the world. The reindeer venison and honey-roasted eider duck breast aren't bad, either.

Then, of course, there is any kind of fresh Greenlandic seafood. This includes trout, salmon, Atlantic halibut, redfish, whale, bay scallops and the world-renowned large Greenlandic prawns. Smoked fish is a traditional lunch, and its aroma is delicious.

In the summer, families take to the highlands to cook in traditional Greenlandic style. They build a raised, flat stone base, gather heather and branches for a fire and place a pot or a piece of meat directly on the stone. Soon comes the delicious aroma of heather smoke and cooking fish or seal meat.

Handicrafts are the most popular souvenirs of Greenland. These include figures of people and animals carved in walrus ivory, reindeer antler and soapstone. Then there are *tupilak*, grotesque little figures that Greenlanders once used to put a spell on their enemies. Today they are high ethnic art.

If you travel to Greenland in summer, it's wise to bring shorts, gloves and everything in between, plus waterproof clothing. The most appropriate footwear is light, waterproof hiking shoes or boots.

The changeable weather makes it a good idea to check travel connections and excursions ahead of time. Greenlandair's outstanding safety record is based on high technical skills and prudent weather precautions. No matter when you travel to Greenland, you should be prepared for adventure and fantastic nature. ❑

Map on page 298

Greenlandic is an Inuit language similar to those spoken by Inuit people in Canada, USA and Russia. Although there is no common, written Inuit language, Greenlandic has a literary heritage.

BELOW: Narsarsuaq, on Greenland's south coast.

GREENLAND'S PLACE IN HISTORY

Greenlanders share their heritage with the Asian tribes who crossed the Bering Strait and migrated into what is now Alaska and northern Canada. The Danes came to Greenland as Vikings in about AD 985. They established settlements in the south, from where they sailed further to North America. In 1721, a priest, Hans Egede, founded a Danish mission and trading station in western Greenland. New stations proliferated over the next 150–200 years. Greenlanders sold skins, blubber and walrus tusks through a Danish-controlled trading company.

As a Danish colony, the island was all but isolated from the rest of the world until the start of World War II when links with Denmark were severed as German forces occupied the Danish mainland. The United States sent its military forces to Greenland, and set up radar stations and airfields. Suddenly Greenlanders were exposed to the good and bad influences of modern Western civilisation.

After the war, the country began a gradual improvement in education, health care and fishing industries. In 1953, a constitutional amendment made Greenland an integral part of the Kingdom of Denmark, and in 1979 the island gained Home Rule. Greenland received its own flag in 1985.

THE FAROE ISLANDS

Map on page 306

Fishing and fish-processing are the keys to prosperity on the far-flung Faroes. Visitors are attracted by the natural beauty of the rocky islands and the remarkable bird life

The sea is serious business in the Faroe Islands and nothing shows that more clearly than the harbour **Tórshavn ❶**. It is stuffed with boats of all kinds – visiting ships, inter-island ferries, sailing boats and other pleasure craft and, most numerous of all, the fishing boats which disgorge their cargoes at one of the big fish processors scattered around the islands' coasts. The fishing fleet is one of the most modern in Europe. Fish products make up more than 95 percent of the country's export earnings and the not-to-be missed tang of fish permeating the harbour is also the smell of money.

The sea is not only serious business, it is basically the only export business the islands have. Consider this; the number two export product from the Faroes is postage stamps. And for the philatelist, they are really something special.

The islands lie far to the north of mainland Europe, halfway between Iceland and the Shetland Islands, some 450 km (320 miles) south of the former, and 225 miles (300 km) north of Scotland's northernmost outpost. The sailing distance between the Faroes and Copenhagen is around 1,500 km (900 miles).

But though the Faroe islanders are prosperous with a high standard of living – they claim to have more cars and more video recorders per head than anyone else in Europe – everything is relative. Only 43,700 live on the 18 inhabited islands – a dozen more are home only to the huge colonies of birds – and most are clustered in coastal communities. The islands are great slabs of rock that were pressed upwards from the earth's crust. Much of the surface area is virtually bare rock, and only a few areas are inhabitable.

As though to contrast with the muted blues, greens and greys of rocks, sea and hills, modern Faroese favour brightly painted houses of the most unlikely hues. The old tradition was black paint, which helped to preserve the timber, with roofs of living green turf, and this is becoming popular once more.

PRECEDING PAGES: a remote Faroe Islands settlement. **LEFT:** turf-roofed buildings, Mykines. **BELOW:** cathedral in Tórshavn.

Warm and wet

Far north as the islands are and feel, the Gulf Stream, keeps the climate maritime and mild. The seas do not freeze and in the coldest month the average temperature is around 3°C (36°F). In the warmest, it reaches 11°C (52°F). Yet the climate is changeable; one minute the sun is hot against the back, followed by driving rain as the mist comes down.

No self-respecting tree could grow to reasonable height against that constant wind – though, as a joke, the Faroese call the small copse in the shelter of the park in the capital, Tórshavn, the islands' "forest". The Faroe's other name is the Sheep Islands – even today, there are thousands more sheep than people, and lamb is a basic food. The islands are scattered

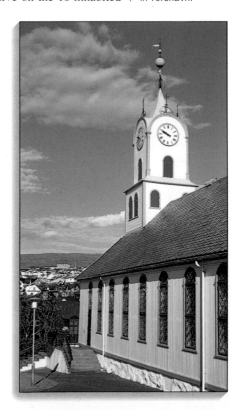

with a type of Arctic willow, and some heather and bilberry. The amount of arable land is extremely limited. Small kitchen gardens will have robust plants, leeks, cabbages, carrots, and any small patch where there is soil will be utilised. Outside the houses people will hang fish and lamb/mutton to dry. The constant winds make short work of this job. Dried fish and meats were once a means of survival, and the Faroese still relish these treats.

On the trail

The inland trails are a wonderland of stunning terrain that the visitor shares with roaming sheep and the near-constant wind. Footpaths criss-cross all the islands and were originally the main routes between settlements. Most of the paths are marked by cairns, but some of them are not regularly maintained, and it's imperative to carry a map and compass. Campers may pitch tents virtually anywhere, but many a tent has been swept into the North Atlantic by powerful gusts, so remember to find a spot in the lee of a cliff and weigh the tent down.

It is important to carry the right equipment. Outerwear that repels wind and rain is a must as are tents without pegs. Since the weather can change quickly, hikers should also carry a whistle, the obligatory compass, maps and some sweets. It is advisable to tell the hotel or local host what route you will be taking and when you expect to return.

Birds everywhere

BELOW:
face of the Faroes.

Though Faroe has few mammals, the rich bird-life is outstanding, especially on the cliffs. The towering faces of the stacs and cliffs are home to thousands of sea birds and in the sheltered pools live phalaropes and red-throated divers. The stiff-

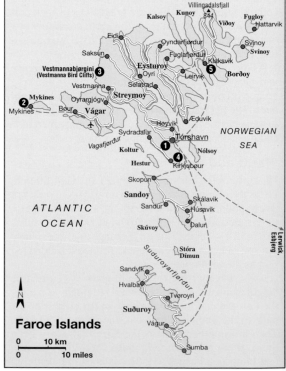

winged flight of the fulmars follows the boats without ever tiring and clown-faced puffins gaze solemnly from cliff burrows. The Faroes' national bird, the black and white oyster catcher, calls worriedly from every small hillock.

The luckless puffin is a delicacy, caught during the open season in July with a curious instrument of pole and net, and served stuffed and cooked. It has a tangy sea-poultry flavour. The island of **Mykines ❷** is its stronghold and attracts birders from many lands. Visitors wishing to stay there should book a room at the B&B Kristianshús (tel: 31 09 85) well in advance, especially in summer.

For the seafaring adventurer, two boat operators sail from Vestmanna on an excursion of the islands to view the bird cliffs of **Vestmannabjørgini ❸**, or Enniberg, a sheer cliff that rises 640 metres (2,100 ft) from the sea. The restored sloop, *Norolysio*, takes visitors on an enchanting tour of the islands, sailing into fjords and grottoes when the seas permit. On most tours, the crew will provide a freshly-caught seafood dinner or lunch.

Anglers may find great challenges in the brooks and lochs which hold trout and salmon. The season extends from 1 May to 31 August and regulations are printed on fishing permits. Your own equipment must first be disinfected before use. Contact the tourist office in Tórshavn for details (tel: 31 60 55).

Early settlers

The islands' first substantial settlers came from Norway in the 9th century. Even before that time, an early township, **Kirkjubøur ❹**, had been the centre of life for a group of Irish friars who colonised the islands around the 8th century. In 1380, as Norway came under Danish Rule, the islands, too, became part of Denmark and, when the union dissolved in 1814, the Faroes continued as a

Map on page 306

The varied bird life of the Faroe Islands is a major attraction for ornithologists.

BELOW: Tórshavn, capital of the Faroe Islands.

Danish county, under the Danish crown. Gradually a strong movement for independence arose, with demands for more self-government.

This was intensified during World War II when Britain occupied the islands and the Faroes had little or no contact with a Denmark occupied by the Germans. The modern airport on **Vágar** was originally built as a landing strip for the RAF. After the war, a strong faction favoured separation from Denmark and, though the demand for independence has rumbled on, negotiations between the two governments resulted in the present system of Home Rule from 1948.

Self-government is by a democratically elected Assembly (*Lágting*) made up of 32 members and with legislative powers in all local affairs. Executive power is entrusted to a local government (*Landsstyret*). The Faroe islands also send two representatives to the Danish Parliament.

The population of the Faroes tripled during the 19th century, and then again in the 20th century as the people found they could make a better living from the sea than from the land.

Seafaring history

The dominant industry is fisheries, accounting for more than 95 percent of the islands' exports. Fishing is traditionally concentrated on cod, which is processed into split, dried or salted cod, but the modern boats also catch large quantities of blue whiting, coalfish and shrimp. Drastic changes in fishing have taken place, first from fishing in local waters to deep-sea fishing, with ocean-going trawlers that travel throughout the North Atlantic, and then back to local fishing with the use of sophisticated equipment.

This long seafaring history is traced in the **Fornminnisavn (National Museum)** at Hoyvik, 2km (1 mile) north of Tórshavn (open mid-May–mid-Sept: Mon–Fri 10am–5pm, Sat–Sun 2–6pm; mid-Sept–mid-May: Sun only, 2–5pm; entrance fee), and also in the **Nordoya Fornminnasavn** (North Islands

BELOW: preserving cod before export on the southerly island of Sud006.

Museum; open summer: 2–4pm; other times by appointment) at **Klaksvík ⑤**, the second largest town, on Bordoy island.

Most towns have museums featuring folklore, history or art, which are open in the summer months or by appointment. Also, in Tórshavn there is the **Norourlandahúsid (Nordic Centre)**, which aims to bring together the best of Nordic culture in art exhibitions and concerts, and other performances.

Island lifestyle

The Faroes, together with Denmark, belonged to the European Free Trade Association (EFTA) from 1967, but the islands declined to follow Denmark into the European Community in 1973 largely at the insistence of the fishing industry. Thanks to the fishing income, the Faroese live well. Around 85 percent of families own their own houses, with well-stocked modern facilities. The Faroes have had a radio station since 1957 and their own television since 1984.

Life is very much home and family-centred. A wandering child is everyone's concern, neighbours work together, and Faroese often set off over long distances to visit friends at a time when most people might be thinking of going to bed. Precise time-keeping is not something that worries the Faroese unduly, and this draws its logic from the past. Then and (still to a large extent) now, the priority is to do what must be done when the weather is right.

Besides the fishing industry, there are shipyards and other trades aimed almost exclusively at the fishing industry. Faroese manufacturing has specialised in production machinery and equipment for fishing, fish-farming and fish-processing. Computer systems developed for the monitoring of fish-processing are exported to several countries. To counterbalance their dependence on fish-

Map on page 306

Vesturkirkjan, in the capital, Tórshavn. Almost every settlement on the Faroes has a church.

BELOW: aboard the Sildberin ferry in traditional attire.

MAKING CONNECTIONS

The Faroe Islands have put immense sums of money into transportation so the inhabitants can get around. In the old days, people either rowed, walked or travelled by horseback to get to work, buy provisions or visit family and friends. Narrow paths, which still exist, wound through the rocky terrain between settlements. Water transport was operated by private companies which used discarded fishing vessels. In the second half of the 20th century, vessels were improved and car ferries introduced. Today the ferries are an integral part of the road network.

The first road, between Sandur and Skopun on Sandoy, was completed in 1916. In the following two decades around 200 km (120 miles) of unpaved roads were built to link the main points on the larger islands. The first cars arrived on the Faroes in the 1920s.

In the 1980s and 1990s, the islands undertook an expansive road-building and tunnel-boring project to connect as many settlements as possible to one another by road. To the outsider it would seem frivolous to spend millions on a road that linked but a few score inhabitants, but to the natives it was a prestigious building of infrastructure even though the hefty investment put Faroe finances into a slump that can still be felt.

Map on page 306

The Faroes national football team's win over Austria in a European Cup match in 1990 prompted the building of a national football stadium on Eysturoy. Here players have to pit their skills not just against the opposition, but also the elements.

BELOW: well clad for a Faroese hike.
RIGHT: voyage to the islands.

ing, the Faroese have sought to diversify and have started a popular Philatelic Bureau which provides some monetary jam on the daily bread and butter. Due to the modest size of the Faroes, there is a limit to the scope of industrial development and the islands are among the most heavily indebted country in Europe.

The economic situation could change drastically as the Faroes plan to tap into the seabed for oil. Faroe territory extends westward to British territory, and investigations indicate that there are vast oil reserves under the seabed.

Faroese traditions

The Faroese are proud of the rich culture and traditions of their islands, where the language, costumes and customs are kept very much alive. On festive occasions, all still join in the special Faroese chain dance, which can last all night. Participants hold hands and do a slow, hypnotic dance while chanting. At first it may seem monotonous to the newcomer, but little by little the cadence will seduce the listener. The chants narrate a story: one popular one is about a maiden and a seamen, although it is not as ribald as it may sound.

An older tradition that is still practised is the "door snaps". Visitors are greeted at the door with a horn full of snaps (*akvavit*) and everybody takes a sip before entering. When visiting the "**smoke room**" in Kirkjubøur, the first order of the day is a nip from the horn. The building is allegedly the oldest wooden structure in the world, built from logs that were towed from Norway. The room has an open fireplace in the middle, and VIPs gathered around the flames to discuss business and politics (open daily June–Sept, or by appointment).

For the thirsty, the Faroes is not an easy place to find a drink. Alcoholic beverages are sold only at state-run monopoly stores. Hotels generally have fully stocked bars, as do restaurants. The Faroes are semi-dry due to strict interpretations of Christianity that came from Denmark. While Denmark has eased its regulations, the other Nordic countries still have relatively strict rulings about drink.

Music festivals

Theatre and music abound and, based on the size of the population, the Faroese must be the world's most eager buyers and readers of books and newspapers. But what else are they to do in the long, dark winter, unless it be the chain dance?

In truth, there are other things to do. The **Faroese Cultural Evening** is a series of events held in the summer months on the island of Eysturoy and at Tórshavn. It includes music, theatre, literature, traditional food and of course, chain dancing. In late June and July the **Summartonar Music Festival** is staged at venues around the islands. These concerts feature classical and contemporary music.

The **Torshavnar Jazz, Folk and Blues Festival** is a four-day event held in August and spotlighting local, Scandinavian and international musicians. The **Folk Music Festival** takes place in July in Tórshavn.

What is important to understand is that while the Faroe Islands may be singular in tradition and geography, they still want to be an integral part of a global community, but without losing their identity. ❏

INSIGHT GUIDES
Travel Tips

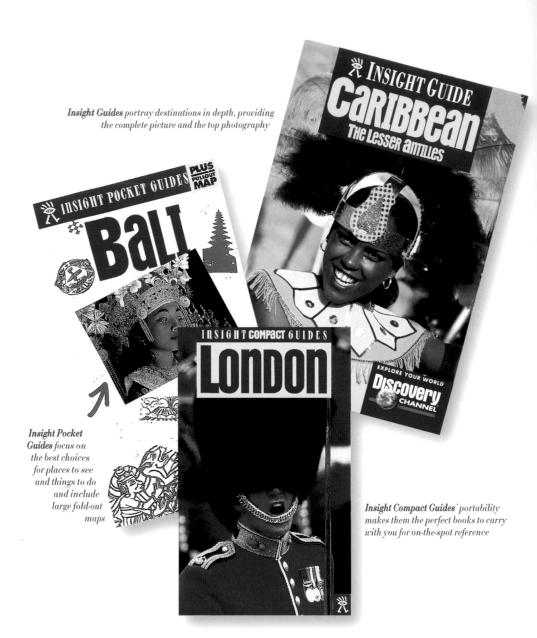

Insight Guides portray destinations in depth, providing the complete picture and the top photography

Insight Pocket Guides focus on the best choices for places to see and things to do and include large fold-out maps

Insight Compact Guides' portability makes them the perfect books to carry with you for on-the-spot reference

Three types of guide for all types of travel

INSIGHT GUIDES Different people need different kinds of information. Some want *background information* to help them prepare for the trip. Others seek *personal recommendations* from someone who knows the destination well. And others look for *compactly presented data* for on-the-spot reference. With three carefully designed series, Insight Guides offer readers the perfect choice. Insight Guides will turn your visit into an experience.

The world's largest collection of visual travel guides

CONTENTS

Getting Acquainted

The Place

Situation: Located between the North Sea and the Baltic.
Area: 430,094 sq km (166,059 sq miles) consisting of one peninsula and 405 islands of which 7,314 km (4,542 miles) is coastline.
Capital: Copenhagen.
Highest Point: Yiding Skovhøj, 173 meters (568 ft) in eastern Jutland.
Largest Lake: Arresø, in Northern Zealand, covering 41 sq km (16 sq miles).
Population: 5,294,860 of whom 1,379, 413 live in the Copenhagen area, 215,587 in Århus and 145,296 in Odense.
Life Expectancy: 73.58 years for men and 78.64 for women.
Language: Danish.

New Link to Sweden

The Øresund railway, road, tunnel and bridge, due to open on 1 July 2000, is a remarkable feat of engineering connecting Denmark and Sweden. The 3,510-metre (11,516-ft) immersed tunnel contains four traffic lanes and two railway tracks. Starting off from the coast of the Copenhagen Kastrup Airport, the tunnel extends 4 km (2 miles), and emerges on a 4,000-metre (13,000-ft) long artificial island connected to Sweden by Denmark's longest free-span bridge. The bridge has a 490-metre (1,608-ft) free span. In all, 16 km (10 miles) of tunnel, island and bridge, making it only a 20- to 30-minute drive from Copenhagen Airport to the Swedish city of Malmö.

Religion: 89 percent of Danes are registered as belonging to the Evangelical Lutheran church, although only a small segment of the population attends services.
Time Zone: Central European time zone. One hour ahead of Greenwich Mean Time (GMT), six hours ahead of Eastern Standard Time (EST). Clocks are put forward by one hour between the end of March and the end of October.
Currency: Danish *krone* (crown); plural *kroner*, marked kr in shops or DKK internationally; and split into 100 *øre*.
Weights and Measures: Metric.
Electricity: 220 volts AC, two-pin round plugs.
International dialling code: + 45. There are no separate city codes, The first two digits of any Danish phone number identifies its location.

Geography

The Kingdom of Denmark – the word originally meant "border district of the Danes" – is the smallest Scandinavian country apart from Iceland. It sits between the North Sea on the west and the Baltic Sea on the southeast. Germany borders to the south for 69 km (43 miles), and Sweden is just a 25-minute ferry ride away to the east. Jutland, which makes up about 70 percent of the country, is a peninsula jutting into the North and Baltic Seas. The rest of the land consists of nearby islands – 405 in all, of which the major islands are Bornholm, Zealand (where Copenhagen is situated), Falster, Fyn and Lolland. There are many small islands, yet only one-fifth of them are inhabited. Because of Jutland's deeply indented coastline and the many islands, Denmark has more than 7,300 km (4,500 miles) of coast, and no-one lives farther than 53 km (33 miles) from the ocean.

More than three-quarters of the land lies below 100 metres (330 ft) and is flat or gently undulating. Denmark was totally or partially covered by ice sheets at least four

times over the past 2 million years, and the limit of the most recent ice advance can be seen in Jutland where a range of low hills extends north-south through the peninsula.

The natural vegetation is a mixed forest covering one-eighth of the country, with beech the most common tree. Around seven-tenths of the land is used for farming. Most farms are family-run and the average size is just over 20 hectares (50 acres). Barley, used for cattle feed, is the main crop.

There are few valuable minerals, but limestone and gravel are widely mined. Oil and gas have been found in the Danish sector of the North Sea.

High Season

The high season for tourism in Denmark is May through September, while the Danes usually take their holidays in July or early August.

Climate

Denmark's temperate marine climate keeps the weather mild, with the North Atlantic Drift, part of the Gulf Stream, providing a warming influence. The mean temperature for February, the coldest month, is –0.6°C (31°F), and for July, the warmest month, 17°C (63°F). Average rainfall is 660 mm (26 in) a year. The Danish climate is extremely variable and temperatures can change drastically from one day to another.

Falling night-time temperatures account (at least in part) for the low averages. The swimming season starts (except for true masochists) in the middle of May and ends in September. The best part of the summer usually falls between May 10 and June 20 with short, light nights. Sometime around the summer equinox (June 23) it often starts to rain, and sometimes carries on until August, when school begins and most Danes have already spent their summer holidays on a Mediterranean

Mean Temperatures

January	−4°C	(25°F)
February	−1°C	(30°F)
March	−1°C	(30°F)
April	6°C	(43°F)
May	10°C	(50°F)
June	14°C	(57°F)
July	16°C	(61°F)
August	15°C	(59°F)
September	12°C	(54°F)
October	9°C	(48°F)
November	5°C	(41°F)
December	2°C	(36°F)

island. But other summers bring beautiful sunshine and warm nights.

It seldom rains all day long; one will often have a couple of hours to dry off between showers. Remember to dress for cold and wet weather in the winter and spring.

The People

Most Danes are Nordic Scandinavians, although a German minority can be found in south Jutland. Around 85 percent of the population lives in towns or cities. There is a growing resident foreign population; the greatest influx of refugees and immigrants originate from Turkey (47,000), the former Yugoslavia (38,000) and Germany (25,000). In all, 6.8 percent of the population derive from different cultural backgrounds.

The Economy

Denmark, a member of the European Union, is one of the world's great trading nations. Grain was the major export until the 19th century; dairy products then became dominant. Although they remain the best-known exports, dairy products account for only 30 percent of export turnover, with light industrial goods accounting for the rest. Denmark has a growing industry based on environmental development, inventing and producing a wide variety of products that span from energy-saving light bulbs to high-tech windmills, which are sold on the local and international markets. Heavy industry never really developed because of the lack of raw materials. Germany and the UK are Denmark's major customers for dairy products, and Sweden for industrial goods.

As elsewhere in western Europe, service industries have been providing an increasing proportion of employment, and only one-fifth of workers are now engaged in manufacturing.

Economic conditions have been favorable throughout the second half of the 1990s. An economic growth factor of around 3 percent or more per year has led to a collective "spending spree" that the government at present is doing its best to curb. A major task for any Danish government is to change the habits of what have been called "Europe's most optimistic consumers". The fact that the public administration has one-third of all Danish workers on its payroll adds to the problem.

The goal for Danish politicians has for many years been to create a society where "few have too much and fewer have too little" and, even if the political debate has sharpened in recent years, the average income and the benefits of the social welfare system are still among the highest in the world – but so are personal income taxes. The latter means that a growing number of people feel that they have too little left for themselves when the rent and union dues have been paid. The average family spends about 30 percent of its net income on rent, 20 percent on food and 15 percent on transport.

Government

Denmark has been a kingdom for over a thousand years and is therefore the oldest monarchy in the world. The reigning monarch, Queen Margrethe, has no real political power or influence, yet no laws or governments are recognized without her signature.

Members of the Danish Parliament decide on the laws and policies of the country. To be able to stand for parliamentary election a party must collect at least 10,000 signatures, and to get into parliament a party needs at least 2 percent of the votes. At local elections it is common for people to stand for so-called independent lists. These may be, for instance, environment or immigrant lists. The great majority of governments since World War II have been coalitions, yet the Social Democrats have remained the most influential political party throughout the greater part of the 20th century.

The Danish parliament has 179 members, including two from Greenland and two from the Faroe Islands (Færøerne). Both are former colonies of Denmark and have their own languages. The Faroes have been self governing since 1948, and Greenland since 1979.

Public Holidays

● January 1	New Year's Day
● April	Maundy Thursday, Good Friday, Easter Day and Easter Monday
● May 1	Workers' Day
● May/June	Whit Monday
● Jun 1	Ascension Day
● Jun 5	Constitution Day
● Dec 24–26	Christmas

A floating holiday is **Prayer Day** (*Store Bededag*), which falls on a different day each year. All shops close on holidays.

Planning the Trip

Visas and Passports

A valid passport entitles you to a stay of up to three months. Visas are not required for EU citizens, and those from Canada and the US. Other nationalities may need to obtain a visa before arriving. If in doubt, ask at the nearest Danish Embassy or Consulate. If you arrive from another Scandinavian country, you will often find that passports aren't checked at all. If you intend to stay longer than three months you will have to obtain a resident's permit.

Customs

Danish customs formalities are usually painless and baggage is rarely opened, but it´s sensible to observe the duty free limits and other rules.

Cigarettes, spirits, perfume, cameras and other luxury items are relatively expensive in Denmark. The rules about how much one can bring into Denmark depend on whether or not you are coming from an EU country. To be safe, bring only one litre of spirits or two litres of wine; 200 cigarettes or 50 cigars or 250 g of tobacco; 500 g of coffee; 100 g of tea; 50 g of perfume; 250 ml of eau de toilette; and goods/gifts not exceeding 1.350DKK in value. It is wise to check with your local Danish consul if in doubt.

Money and cheques may be brought in freely.

Duty Free

Visitors from countries outside Scandinavia and the EU are entitled to claim back the taxes paid on purchases when leaving Denmark. All purchases are subject to value added tax (VAT – in Danish, *moms*) Many shops can mail goods home to you, avoiding VAT payment. For visitors wishing to take goods with them straight away, shops displaying Global Refund Denmark or Tax Free International emblems offer tourists personal export service with VAT refunds on purchases of over 300DKK. You must declare your purchase and get a stamp from customs authorities upon departure from the last EU country.

Health & Insurance

Standards of hygiene in Scandinavia are among the highest in the world. Visitors often comment upon how clean Denmark is. There are no major health hazards. No inoculations are needed and the tap water is safe to drink.

The Danish medical system will immediately assist anyone in an emergency situation; however, you should take out travel insurance before you leave. Travellers with chronic diseases should be aware of international rules and the policies of their insurance company before arriving in Denmark.

You can bring medicines into the country, but take the prescription with you if they contain drugs.

● **Global Refund Denmark** offers cash payment at almost every international airport in Europe and on different ferry lines, including Scandinavian Seaways (to Norway), the Polish line and Color line. Refunds by cheque, bank account and credit card are also available without extra charge.
● **Tax Free International** offers cash payment at Copenhagen airport and by credit card. Refunds by cheque and bank account will be charged an extra fee.

If leaving Denmark for a non-EU country, all you have to do is show your boarding card in the airport shops and you will be able to buy any item there tax free. If your final destination is an EU country it is quite a different story. The rules have not been finalised and it would be best to check with the tax free office at Copenhagen Airport, tel: 32 47 09 00, concerning the items you wish to purchase.

Money Matters

Currency
Coins are 25 øre and 50 øre (copper in color), 1 krone, 2 krone, 5 krone (silver colored with a hole through the center), 10 and 20 krone (solid, gold colored coins that are similar except that the 20 krone piece is a little bigger than the 10 krone piece). Notes come in 50, 100, 200, 500 and 1000 denominations. A series of new coins and bills has been introduced since 1996. The bills are now smaller and feature the portraits of famous Danish authors, scientists and celebrities.

Changing Money
There are exchanges open outside normal business hours at the **Copenhagen Central Railway Station**, and in the centre of the city. **Den Danske Bank** (tel: 33 12 04 01) is open Monday–Sunday 8am–8pm; and **Forex**, Monday–Sunday 8am–9pm. There are three open-air exchange machines with 24-hour service near Copenhagen City Hall.

How to Pay
Visa and MasterCard are widely accepted in the shops. Diner's Club cards are accepted in many, but not all restaurants, while American Express cards can be used in major hotels and shops, but are not very popular in general. All banks and a few shops take travellers' cheques.

Most travellers find it convenient to use Visa, MasterCard or travellers' cheques. The exchange rates are more favorable for Visa and MasterCard than for travellers' cheques. See page 318 for banking hours.

What to Wear

The average mean temperature in July, the hottest month of the year, is 16°C (61°F), so even if you are lucky enough to travel in a year with a *real* summer, expect to find cold and rainy days as well. Yet it can also be very hot – well above 20°C (70°F). The only time of year with consistently good weather is from mid-May to mid-June. In any case, it is wise to bring a sweater and a rain jacket. Shoes that can stand a little water are also a good idea.

Many Danes find it practical to dress in several layers: a shirt over a T-shirt and a cardigan casually swept around the shoulders will be appropriate for cool summer or early autumn evenings. Temperatures of 0°F (–17°C) are not uncommon during the winter. A flexible wardrobe is usually necessary.

Danes dress casually when they go out for the evening and at work. Young people are generally fashion conscious, spending great sums on designer sweatshirts and tennis shoes or carefully assembling their own look from second-hand shops. When going out for the evening it isn't necessary for men to put on a suit and tie (apart from at a handful of smart night spots).

Getting There

BY AIR

The two main airports in Denmark are Copenhagen Kastrup Airport and Bilund Airport in Jutland. Denmark's national carrier is SAS or Scandinavian Airlines System, which is primarily for international traffic. Maersk Air and Cimber Air serve most of the domestic routes. British Airways operates direct flights five times daily from London Heathrow to Copenhagen Kastrup Airport.

There are many charter flights that leave daily from Copenhagen airport. The Danes often fly south to the Canary islands, Northern Africa, and different parts of Southern Europe to escape from the long cold winter. Almost all

Danish Tourist Offices Abroad

● **UK:** The Danish Tourist Board, 55 Sloane Street, London SW1X 9SY. Tel: 020 7259 5959. Fax: 020 7259 5955. Website: www.dtb.dt.dk E-mail: dtb.london@dt.dk
● **Germany:** Dänisches Frendemverkehrsamt, Glockengiesserwall 2, Postfach 10 13 29, 200095 Hamburg. Tel: 40-32 02 1122. Fax: 40 32 02 1111. Website: www.daenemark.dt.dk E-mail: daninfo@dt.dk
● **US:** The Danish Tourist Board, 655 Third Street, 18th Floor, New York, NY 10017. Tel: (212) 885-9727. Fax: (212) 885-9726. Website: wwwvisitdenmark.com E-mail ac@dt-nyc.com

travel agencies are located in close proximity to Copenhagen Central Railway Station.
SAS Tel: 32 32 00 00 Website: www.sas.dk
Maersk Air Tel: 32 31 45 45 Fax: 32 31 45 90
Cimber Air Tel: 74 42 22 77
British Airways Tel: 80 20 80 22 Website: www.british-airways.com

BY SEA

Reaching Denmark by sea can be a beautiful experience, and there are many routes to choose from.

From Germany and Poland

From Germany, ferries connect Puttgarden and Rødby (Lolland). Ferries also run between Warnemünde and Gedser, and in the summer, Sassnitz and Rønne (Bornholm). Swinoujscie in Poland sends a daily ferry to Copenhagen.

From Sweden

Sweden operates several lines from Helsingborg to Helsingør (North Zealand) and from Helsingborg to Grenå (East Jutland); other ferries go from Varberg to Grenå and from Göteborg to Frederikshavn (North Jutland); ferries bound for Copenhagen go from Landskrona to

Tuborg Havn, from Malmö to Nyhavn (Copenhagen), and from Limhamn to Dragør; from Rønne (Bornholm) there is a ferry to Ystad.

From Norway

Lines go from Oslo to Copenhagen or to Hirtshals and Frederikshavn in North Jutland; from Hirtshals there are ferries to Bergen, Egernsund, Kristianssand and Stavanger. Ferries from Larvik and Moss (Norway) go to Frederikshavn.

From Britain

Departure harbours in Britain are Harwich, which has ferries to Esbjerg and, in the summer, Newcastle has another line to Esbjerg.

BY RAIL

Trains arrive daily from Germany, Britain and Sweden. There are direct trains to Germany five times daily and connecting trains to Sweden three to six times a day.
● For information on trains travelling outside Denmark. Tel: 70 13 14 16. E-mail tlfsalg@dsb.int.dk
● For inland trains, tel: 70 13 14 15 Website: www.dsb.dk

Scandinavian Tourist Board, 150 North Michigan Avenue, Suite 2110, Chicago, Il 60601. Tel: (312) 726-1120.
Scandinavian Tourist Board, 8929 Wilshire Blvd, Beverly Hills, CA 90211; tel: (213) 854-1549.
● **Canada:** The Danish Tourist Board, P.O. Box 115, Station N, Toronto, Ontario M8V 3S4. Tel: 416/823-9620.
The Danish Tourist Board also has offices in Paris, Madrid, Milan, Leiden, Hamburg, Tokyo, Stockholm, Oslo and Helsinki. There are no offices in Australia or New Zealand but the Danish Consulate/Embassy supplies information and literature.

BY BUS

Call HT bus transport in Copenhagen for information about bus schedules. Tel: 36 13 14 15. Website: www.ht.dk

There are many bus lines that travel throughout Europe and Denmark, among others:
- **Daniaturist**, tel: 45 28 02 81.
- **Combus**, tel: 32 52 66 31.
- **Viking Bus**, tel: 32 66 00 00.

Tour Operators

It is best to contact the tourist information office in the area of Denmark you want to know about.

Copenhagen Guides
For an authorised guide to the city, apply to: **Wonderful Copenhagen**, 1 Gammel Kongevej, 1610 Cph.V; tel: 33 25 38 22.

In the weekly *Copenhagen This Week* (website: www.ctw.dk available free of charge at almost all hotels and tourist agencies), you will find a comprehensive list of new and standard tours for the city. It also covers tours of Zealand.

Rest of Denmark
The following two operators run many tours on Zealand and throughout Denmark:
Copenhagen Excursions
Tel: 32 54 06 06; fax: 32 57 49 05; website: www.copenhagen-excursions.dk
Auto Paaske
Tel: 32 66 00 00. Fax: 32 66 00 25

Border Traffic

Traffic across the German border can be heavy at times, and some waiting time should also be anticipated at the car ferries. Friday and Sunday evenings are the worst. It pays to make reservations for a vehicle for both domestic and international ferry routes as early as possible.

When coming to Denmark from the south, be sure to fill the tank before crossing the border as petrol is expensive.

Practical Tips

Business Hours

Most **offices** are open from 8am or 9am until 4pm or 5pm. Rush hours can be tiresome, but the traffic is usually moving. The heaviest hours are 7.30–9am and 3.30–5.30pm.

Most **shops** close at 5.30pm Monday–Thursday and at 7pm (8pm in Copenhagen) on Friday. Supermarkets remain open until 7 or 8pm, at least in Copenhagen. Opening hours on Saturday are 9am–2pm, or 5pm in Copenhagen, but 9am–noon in most other places. On the first Saturday in each month, most shops remain open until 4pm or 5pm. All shops are closed on Sunday. Exceptions are the bakeries and kiosks, some of which are open around the clock.

In addition, the supermarket at the Central Railway Station and Steno Apotek (the pharmacy across Vesterbrogade from the train station) are open all day, every day. Keep the closing hours in mind when planning any day trip. There has been a rash of 7-Elevens recently opened in every major city.

Banks are open 9.30am–4pm Monday–Friday, but sometimes stay open till 6pm on Thursday. They are closed on Saturday and Sunday.

Media

NEWSPAPERS AND MAGAZINES

English-language newspapers are widely available at all central train stations in major cities throughout Denmark, as well as at the larger neighbourhood kiosks. You can also read them for free at the **Central Library** on Krystalgade 15 or **Café Europa** on Amagertorv 1 in the

middle of Copenhagen.

An English language weekly newspaper, *The Copenhagen Post* (tel: 33 36 33 00; e-mail: info@cphpost.dk; website: www.cphpost.dk), contains lots of local news, practical information for foreign residents and visitors, entertainment and restaurant guides. Available at tourist information offices, it costs 15DKK

Look out also for a magazine called *Playtime* (website: www.useit.dk), a guide for those on a limited budget, published by Youth Information Copenhagen and available free of charge.

Copenhagen Living is a Scandinavian lifestyle magazine about the city, its people, architecture, design, food, fashion, shopping and the environment; it is available at book shops and museums.

BOOKS

Many of the public libraries have a good selection of books in English, and Copenhagen has book shops which specialise in foreign literature. See *Shopping* for more details.

TELEVISION

There are many satellite/cable channels featuring CNN, BBC and MTV, broadcast in English. In addition, there are often English-language movies to be found on the national channels DR1, DR2 and TV 2.

RADIO

A high percentage of music on Danish radio is in English. For news in English, tune to Radio Denmark, programme 3 at 93.8 MHZ, Monday–Friday at 8.31–8.36am. **Radio Denmark** tel: 35 20 30 40; e-mail: dr@dr.dk; website: www.dr.dk

Postal Services

Post offices are generally open 9am–5pm on weekdays, and

9am–noon on Saturday.

For more urgent matters, the Customer Service at the **Main Post Office**, Titgensgade 37, 1500 Copenhagen V. Tel: 33 33 89 00. The website: www.postdanmark.dk can direct you to the nearest office.

In an emergency go to the **Central Railway Station post office**, open Monday–Friday 8am–10pm, Saturday 9am–4pm and Sunday 10am–5pm.

Poste Restante letters should be collected at the main post office in the region you are in, unless they are specifically addressed to a local post office.

Money orders can be collected or dispatched at all post offices during normal business hours, and **telegrams** can be sent by phone – dial 122 (168 for information) – or from any post office. To send a telex or fax ask for assistance at a post office or at your hotel.

Telecommunications

Phone calls to foreign countries can be placed from **Statens Teletjeneste** offices, above the post office in the Central Railway Station, and next door to the post office in Købmagergade in Copenhagen.

Calls cannot normally be charged to credit cards. However, if you're an American "Calling card" customer you may have your calls charged in the US by dialling 800 100 10 (free of charge) and you will be put through to an American operator. The same number should be used for collect calls to America. For information on other telephone services dial 141.

Tipping

Tips are included in all bills, but there are certain situations where a sign of appreciation will be welcomed. When arriving at your hotel, give the porter 5 to 20 DKK for carrying luggage to your room.

In restaurants, it is a friendly gesture to pick up the notes but leave the coins for the waitress.

Copenhagen Card

We recommend that you buy a Copenhagen Card at your hotel, the Central Station, or at the tourist bureau. The card gives you free entry to Tivoli and nearly 60 other attractions, and it can be used as a bus/train ticket as well. There is a 108-page booklet giving information about the museums and sights included which is exclusively for Copenhagen card holders.

It's a good idea to invest in a telephone card because many pay phones no longer take change. Cards cost between 30 and 100DKK and you can buy them at kiosks throughout the country.

Telephone numbers in Denmark carry no separate city codes – the first two digits of any Danish number identifies its location.

Useful Numbers

● Danish directory enquiries **112**
● International directory enquiries **118**

Tourist Offices

There is a tourist office in almost every city, with knowledgeable and friendly staff waiting to help and answer questions. They can assist in planning a trip and making the necessary reservations, or just by providing directions and reference materials. Tell them what your interests are – from fishing or bird watching, history or 18th-century art, to organ or rock music, nouvelle cuisine or old locomotives

Excellent service should be rewarded a little more generously. It is unusual to tip a waitress in a bar or café, and never tip the hairdresser. Cab drivers will appreciate it if the fare is rounded up to the nearest 5 or 10DKK.

When in doubt, ask directly whether a tip is appropriate.

– and there is a good chance they can find something of interest in the area you are visiting.

For access to websites and information about all tourist offices in Denmark, visit the central website: www.visitdenmark.com.

Some of the tourist bureaus are:

Copenhagen
Turist information
Bernstorffsgade 1, 1577 Copenhagen V (at the main entrance of Tivoli)
Tel: 33 11 13 25. Fax: 33 93 49 69
Website: www.woco.dk

North Zealand
Helsingør Turistforening
Havnepladsen 3, 3000 Helsingør
Tel: 49 21 13 33. Fax: 49 21 15 77
Website: www.helsingerturist.dk

Southwest Zealand
Roskilde Turistforening
Fondens, Bro 3, Postboks 278, 4000 Roskilde
Tel: 46 35 27 00. Fax: 46 35 14 74

Bornholm
Bornholms Turistbureau
Munch Petersensvej 4, 3700 Rønne
Tel: 56 95 95 00. Fax: 56 95 95 68
Website: wwwbornholminfo.dk

Funen
Svendborg Turistforening,
Møllergade 201, 5700 Svendborg
Tel: 62 21 09 80. Fax: 62 22 05 53
Website: www.turistbureausydfyn.dk
Odense Turistforening
Rådhuset, 5000 Odense C
Tel: 66 12 75 20. Fax: 66 12 75 86
Website: www.odenseturist.dk

Funen Archipelago
Ærøskøbing Turistforening
Torvet, 5970 Ærøskøbing
Tel: 62 52 13 00. Fax: 62 52 14 36

East Jutland
Århus Turistforening
Rådhuset, 8000 Århus C
Tel: 89 40 67 00. Fax: 86 12 95 90
Website: www.aarhus-tourist.dk
Silkeborg Turistforening
Torvet 9, Postboks 950, 8600 Silkeborg
Tel: 86 82 19 11. Fax: 86 81 09 83

Useful Websites

● **Danish Tourist Board**
www.denmark.dt.dk
● **Denmark Hotel list**
www.dkhotellist.dk
● **Wonderful Copenhagen**
(Guide to the City)
www.woco.dk
● **Copenhagen Airport**
www.cph.dk

● **The Danish Ministry of Culture**
www.kulturnet.dk
● **Currency Converter**
www.oanda.com/converter/classic
● **Danish Meteorological Institute**
www.dmi.dk/eng/index.html
● **Use It Youth Information**
www.useit.dk

Turistforeningen for Ebeltoft og Mols
Torvet 9–11, 8400 Ebeltoft
Tel: 86 34 14 00. Fax: 86 34 05 28

North Jutland
Skagen Turistforening
Skt Laurentiivej 22, 9990 Skagen
Tel: 98 44 13 77. Fax 98 45 02 94
Ålborg Tourist Bureau
Østerå 8, 9000 Ålborg
Tel: 98 12 60 22. Fax: 98 16 69 22
Website: www.tourist-aal.dk

West Jutland
Holstebro Turistbureau
Brostræde 2, 7500 Holstebro
Tel: 97 42 57 00. Fax: 97 42 57 47
Viborg Turistkontor
Nytorv 5, 8800 Viborg
Tel: 86 61 16 66. Fax: 86 60 02 38

South Jutland
Haderslev Turistforening
Søndergade 3, 6100 Haderslev
Tel: 74 52 55 50. Fax: 74 53 46 67
Ribe Turistforening
Torvet 3–5, 6760 Ribe
Tel: 75 42 15 00. Fax: 75 42 40 78

Travelling with Children

Denmark is ideal for travelling with children. It's a peaceful, safe country with many suitable attractions, such as amusement parks, playgrounds, parks and children's theaters. Many museums have recently opened children's sections, and music festivals are often arranged so that children can take part in them.

The family is very much in focus at present. The birth rate has fallen and the government is in the middle of a campaign encouraging Danes to have more children; for example, new parents are entitled to between six months and a year's paid leave to be with their children. Some companies have invested in playgrounds and day care nurseries for the offspring of their employees.

Babysitters
● **Studenternes Babysitters**
Lykkesholmsallé 33 C,
1902 Frederiksberg C
Tel/fax: 70 20 44 16.
Monday–Friday 10am–3pm,
Thursday until 6pm. Closed at the weekend.
● **H-H Babysitting**
Open daily from 6.30am–10pm
Tel: 38 74 81 51. Fax: 38 76 17 17
E-mail hh.baby@hh-baby.dk.

Gay Travellers

There is a liberal attitude towards gays in Denmark. The age of consent is 18, and there is a lively scene in Copenhagen, with many bars and clubs for gay people.

Gay Organisations
Forbundet af 1948 (gay association headquarters with club and disco):
Knabrostræde 3,
1023 Copenhagen K
Tel: 33 13 19 48.
Pan-Information
PO Box 1023, Copenhagen K
Tel: 33 13 01 12.

Business Travellers

The Danes are not excessively formal when it comes to business attire. Punctuality is appreciated and it's probably best to make business appointments for morning or early afternoon. Offices are often deserted on Friday afternoons and the country seems to close down from July to August.

BUSINESS SERVICES

Bella Centre
(trade shows and conventions),
Center Blvd Copenhagen S
Tel: 32 52 88 11. Fax: 32 51 96 36
Dansk Industriråd
(Federation of Danish Industries), H. C. Andersens Blvd 18,
1553 Copenhagen V
Tel: 33 77 33 77. Fax: 33 77 33 00
Regus Business Centre
Regus House, Lars Bjørnsstræde 3,
1454 Copenhagen K
Tel: 33 32 25 25. Fax: 33 32 43 70
Udenrigsministeriet
(Ministry of Foreign Affairs) Asiatisk Plads 2, 1402 Copenhagen K
Tel: 33 92 00 00. Fax: 32 54 05 33

Travellers with Disabillities

The Danish tourist board publishes *Access in Denmark – A Travel Guide for the Disabled.*

For a list of hotels with facilities for disabled guests, consult the *Danish Accommodation Guide.* Tourist information offices have a list of restaurants and businesses with special facilities for disabled guests. In Denmark as a whole, a lot of thought and consideration is given to the comfort and unhindered access to all parts of society for citizens and visitors with disabilities.

Medical Services

Health care is generally free in Denmark. Acute illnesses or accidents will be treated at the casualty department of the nearest hospital. It may be possible to have costs reimbursed on return. If you are too ill to visit the doctor, you may be asked to pay for the consultation on the spot. Outside normal business hours you can contact a doctor on 38 88 60 41 or 32 84 00 41.

PHARMACIES

Pharmacies are open during normal business hours, but there is a 24-hour pharmacy in every region. The names and addresses are posted on the door of every pharmacy (or look in the yellow pages under *Apotek*).

In Copenhagen, use **Steno Apotek** on Vesterbrogade, across the street from the Central Railway Station. Prescriptions are required for most drugs other than aspirins and pain relievers of equivalent strength.

In an Emergency

For police, ambulance or the fire service **call 112** for assistance.

DENTAL SERVICES

Dental care is available by appointment only. Check the listings under *Tandlæger* in the business directory to find the closest to you. Dentists' fees are paid in cash, and the same guidelines for reimbursement apply as for other health care. Outside normal business hours you can call Tandlægevagten, tel: 35 38 02 51 (no appointment necessary). In Copenhagen the address is Oslo Plads 14 near Østerport Station.

Religious Services

Services are normally conducted on Sunday at 10am, and they are often repeated at 2pm. There are several foreign congregations in Copenhagen.
English Church
At Esplanaden near Amaliegade.
Sankt Petri Church
On the corner of Nørregade and Skt. Pedersstræde. Ceremonies in German.
Church of the Reformation
At Gothersgade across the street from Rosenborg Castle. Shared by a German and French congregation.
Jewish Synagogue
Krystalgade,
1172 Copenhagen
Tel: 33 12 88 68.

Lost Credit Cards

● If you lose your **MasterCard** or **Visa** card, call the 24-hour service on 44 89 25 00.
● For missing **American Express** cards, call 80 01 0021, and if you have lost your Diners Club card, call 36 73 73 73.

Nusrat Jahan Mosque
Eriksminde Alle 2
Tel: 36 75 35 02 (reached by bus numbers 10, 21 and 22 02).
Roman Catholic Church
Skt. Ansgars, Bredgade 64
Tel: 33 13 37 62.

Security and Crime

Denmark is generally a very safe country, but you should not take any risks. To recover lost or stolen property, contact the nearest police station for assistance, or try the lost and found offices at the train station.

Police stations in Copenhagen can be found on Central Station, tel: 33 15 38 01, and at Polititorvet, tel: 33 14 14 48.

Consulates

The following embassies and consulates are all located in Copenhagen:
● **Australia**
Strandboulevarden 122
Tel: 39 29 20 77.
● **Canada**
Kristen Bernikowsgade 1
Tel: 33 13 22 99/33 12 22 99.
● **Ireland**, Østbanegade 21
Tel: 35 42 32 33.
● **New Zealand** There is no consulate or embassy in Denmark. The nearest is in The Hague, Netherlands, tel: 31 703 469 324
● **United Kingdom**, Kastelsvej 40
Tel: 35 44 52 00
Fax: 35 44 52 93.
● **United States**
Daghammarskjolds Allé 24
Tel: 35 55 31 44
Fax: 35 43 02 23.

Getting Around

On Arrival

Almost all international flights arrive and depart from Copenhagen Airport. There is a train running three times an hour directly from terminal 3, the international terminal, at Copenhagen Airport, to the Central Station. It takes 12 minutes and leaves at 15, 35 and 55 minutes past the hour, running from 4.55am to 12.15am. A ticket from the airport to Central Station costs 16.50DKK.

An **intercity express** train runs from the airport daily to Frederikshavn, Struer, Herning and Esbjerg.

There are white **SAS buses** that run between the airport and Central Station every 15 minutes. They cost 35DKK and stop at the Radisson SAS Scandinavian hotel. There are also bus connections between the airport and all major Swedish cities with **Combus Denmark**, tel: 32 52 66 31.

A **taxi** from the airport to the centre of town will cost around 140DKK or more. There is a taxi stand right next to terminal 3

By Air

Flight times within Denmark are short – in less than an hour you can be on the other side of the country.

Maersk Air and **Cimber Airways** have daily flights from Copenhagen to Bornholm, Odense, Århus (Tirstrup) and several other destinations in Jutland. A one-way ticket from Copenhagen to Århus will cost around 750DKK and from Copenhagen to Bornholm around 720DKK.

Help for the Disabled

If you are disabled, call the minibus number below for help in getting around.
● **Minibus and Handicap bus**
Tel: 35 39 35 35.

By Bus

There is an extensive network of buses throughout Denmark. You can get virtually anywhere within the country by bus. **HT Customer Service** (tel: 36 13 14 15; website: www.ht.dk; open daily from 7am–9.30pm) will give you all the information necessary for planning any bus trip in Denmark.

By Train

There is a very efficient train service, linking all major cities and some of the smaller towns. Danish trains are usually a relaxed and comfortable way to travel, allowing you the pleasure of getting off the main tourist circuit and enjoying a pleasant view of the countryside.

There is an **Inter-Rail Centre** at the Central Station, where young travellers can meet like-minded souls, get a shower and stock up on information. Only available for those with Inter-Rail cards, Eurail Youthpass, BIGE tickets and *ungdoms kort Norden*; open daily from 6.30am–10pm, or midnight from late May until September,

Useful Numbers
General information
Call DSB information
Tel: 33 14 17 01
Website: www.dsb.dk
Long-distance trains
(travelling out of the country)
Tel: 70 13 14 16.
Inland trains
Tel: 70 13 14 15.

By Car

Travel time in Denmark is not great however you travel, but a car gives you the freedom to go anywhere quickly.

It is neither easy nor cheap to get a driving license in Denmark, and most drivers have had at least 20 hours of classroom and behind-the-wheel training. They know the rules of the road, and expect that everyone else does also.

Danish Highway Code
Remember to drive on the right, and drive politely. Always give way at pedestrian crossings and look out for bicycles when turning right. Look over your left shoulder every time you open the doors on the driver's side – bicycles are everywhere. Drivers and passengers must wear seat belts at all times, and dipped headlights are required.

Speed limits are enforced – for cars and motorcycles they are 50kph (30mph) in built-up areas; 80kph (50mph) on main roads and 110kph (70mph) on motorways. If you have a car with a trailer, the limits are 50kph (30mph), 70kph (40mph) and 90 kph (55mph) respectively. Look out for the road signs which on occasions indicate alternative speed limits. Overtake on the left only.

When parking the car in a controlled parking area, you should buy a parking ticket from a nearby vending machine, and display the ticket behind the windscreen.

Roadside Assistance
If you break down, use the

On Your Bike!

The best way to enjoy the Danish landscape is on a bicycle. You'd do best to bring your own bike if you want to tour the country, but for getting around the city, a rented one will do. The local tourist information office can tell you where to pick one up.

● For information on routes and practical advice, contact:
Dansk Cyklistforbund (Danish Association of Cyclists)
Rømersgade 7,
1362 Copenhagen K
Tel: 33 32 31 21

emergency telephones set up by the roadside to call FALCK, the Danish motorists' aid organization, tel: 70 10 20 30. If FALK can't repair your car on the spot it will be towed to a garage, for a fee. FALCK is open 24 hours a day.

CAR RENTAL

It pays to shop around when renting a car. Ask your travel agency if they have a special offer, or try the yellow pages. **Avis** (tel: 33 15 22 99) and **Hertz** (tel: 33 17 90 27) have offices all around the country, but it is often possible to make a better deal with smaller companies like **Europcar** (tel: 33 55 99 00) and **Lej et lig** (tel: 39 29 85 05). You need a valid international driving license and must be 20–25 years old to rent a car.

Taxis

Taxis are available at airports, central train and bus stations and in the centre of all major Danish cities. Prices are standard, starting with a fare of 22DKK for a standard taxi ride, and adding 7.70DKK per km between 7am and 4pm, 9.60DKK per km between 4pm and 7am, and 11.60DKK per km on Friday and Saturday night from 11pm–7am.

Companies to try include:

Fax: 33 32 76 83.
Open: summer, Monday–Friday 9.30am–5pm; winter, Monday–Friday 9.30am– 3pm. Late night: Thursday to 7pm in summer or 6pm in winter.

● There are also **free bikes** you can borrow in the centre of Copenhagen! You pay 20DKK, which is then refunded when you deliver the bike back to the stand.
City Bikes
Tel: 36 30 02 86
Website: wwwbycyklen.dk

Drinking and Driving

Alcohol is involved in one-third of all traffic accidents resulting in fatal injuries in Denmark. The best advice is not to drink alcohol at all when driving. The blood alcohol level maximum is 0.5% (the equivalent of two units of alcohol). Danish police frequently set up road blocks (unannounced and at different locations) to test all who drive past for alcohol and to conduct a cursory inspection of their vehicles. Remember that public transportation is reliable, cheap and easily available – use it as an alternative to the car if you've been partying.

● **Copenhagen taxi**
Tel: 35 35 35 35
● **Øbrotaxi**
Tel: 32 51 51 51
● **HS taxi**
Tel: 38 77 77 77

Where to Stay

Choosing a Hotel

Danish hotels are good in a clean, well-run Scandinavian way. They are not cheap, but have first-class facilities and are very much business-oriented. They are now classified by one to five stars by HORESTA (Danish Hotel, Restaurant and Tourist Employers' Association). As more and more hotels go in for extensive refurbishment, it is harder to find the small, traditional hotel with character.

Nevertheless, as in other Scandinavian countries, almost all hotels slash their rates in the summer months when business visitors are scarce, and offer fine value if you visit from June to late August, when the Danes take to their summer cottages. Watch the dates though – a difference of a week can almost double the price. Always ask when you book. Scandinavian hotels, including Danish, more often have showers than baths in the rooms. If you want a bath, ask before you book.

Greenland

In Greenland, which until recently had only a few hotels, the move into modern hotels aimed at the conference market has been rapid and the list of hotels is now longer than you might expect in such a remote, snow-covered area. In general, these hotels come into the expensive category and there is not a wide selection of alternatives. Make sure of your accommodation before you go, and do not expect to rent rooms in private houses.

Faroe Islands

Hotels here were until recently largely designed for visiting sailors.

Apart from a few in Torshavn (of which at least two have good facilities), modern hotels are not plentiful. Private houses and youth hostels provide an alternative.

Information and Reservations

The **Denmark Accommodation Guide** is available free from the Danish Tourist Board, tel: 33 11 14 15; fax: 33 93 14 16; e-mail: dt@dt.dk; website: www.dt.dk. This lists hundreds of hotels, holiday centres and inns in Denmark.

You can book a hotel at the tourist information office right across from Central Station, or book directly through **Hotel Booking Copenhagen**, tel: 33 25 74 00; fax: 33 25 74 10 (open daily from 9am–4pm); or **Easy book**, tel: 35 38 00 37; fax 35 38 06 37.

For further information try the Danish Tourist Board in your home country or contact **Tourist Information in Copenhagen**, Bernstorffsgade 1, 1577 Copenhagen V, tel: 33 11 13 25.

Hotel Listings

Hotels are listed by area, starting with Copenhagen. Within each city or region, they are listed by price category, with the most expensive first.

COPENHAGEN

Hotel d'Angleterre
Kongens Nytorv 34
DK-1050 Copenhagen K
Tel: 33 12 00 95
Fax: 33 12 11 18
E-mail: anglehot@remmen.dk
Website: www.remmen.dk
This is Copenhagen's "Royal" hotel, which has many times entertained European royalty and famous people. Its pavement café is popular with the less exalted. 243 beds. Suites. **$$$**
71 Nyhavn
Nyhavn 71
DK-1051 Copenhagen
Tel: 33 11 85 85
Fax: 33 93 15 85
An unusual atmospheric hotel built

into a converted warehouse along the waterside at Nyhavn near the quay. Most rooms have splendid harbor views. 110 beds. **$$$**

Savoy Hotel
Vesterbrogade 34
DK-1620 Copenhagen V
Tel: 33 26 75 00
Fax: 33 26 75 01
133 beds in a 1906 building in a garden courtyard off Vesterbrogade. Carefully restored in the mid-1980s with advice from the National Museum. **$$–$$$**

Copenhagen Admiral Hotel
Toldbodgade 24–28
Tel: 33 11 82 82
Fax: 33 32 55 42
E-mail: admiral@admiral-hotel.dk
Website: www.admiral-hotel.dk
Another delightful conversion of an old building – this time a 1787 granary with excellent facilities. 815 beds. **$$**

Hotel Excelsior
Colbjørnsensgade 4
DK-1652 Copenhagen V
Tel: 33 25 22 33
Fax: 33 25 69 99
100 beds in an old building well modernised. It has a plant-filled atrium were you can sit for drinks. No restaurant but choice of many nearby. Rooms well furnished in cool Scandinavian style. **$$**

Sophie Amalie Hotel
Sankt Annæ Plads 21
DK-1250 Copenhagen K
Tel: 33 13 34 00
Fax: 33 11 77 07
E-mail: anglehot@remmen.dk
Website: www.remmed.dk
This well renovated old building is not far from the quayside near Nyhavn. Some rooms with a harbour view. Quiet. **$$**

Hotel Amager
Amagerbrogade 29
DK-2300 Copenhagen S
Tel: 32 54 40 08
Fax: 32 54 90 05
On the way to the airport but only five minutes' bus ride to the centre. A traditional "pension" hotel, with rooms without private facilities. **$**

Top Hebron
Helgolandsgade 4
DK-1653 Copenhagen V
Tel: 33 31 69 06

Fax: 33 31 90 67
E-mail: tophotel@hebron.dk
Website: www.hebron.dk
A quiet, well located hotel near the Central Railway Station and Tivoli. Only a few minutes' walk from City Hall. 3 stars. **$**

Hotel 9 Små Hjem
Classensgade 38–42
DK-2100 Copenhagen Ø
Tel: 35 26 16 47
Fax: 35 43 17 84
Website: www.9smaahjem.dk
Situated in the quiet embassy area of Copenhagen just 10 minutes from the centre of town. 2 stars. **$**

Price Guide

Copenhagen hotel price categories are as follows:
  $$$ = 955–2,995DKK
  $$ = 725–1,050DKK
  $ = under 450–835DKK.

Prices given are the average cost of a double room for two, and *usually* include breakfast.

Hotel Rossini
Gammel Jernbane 27-35
2500 Valby
Tel: 36 45 45 72
Fax: 43 69 14 79
Ten minutes by train or bus to the Central Station. Located in the old part of Valby near the zoo, with many historic sites within walking distance. A family hotel right next to the Big Bowl bowling and entertainment complex. **$**

Hotel Fy and Bi
Valby Langgade 62, 2500 Valby
Tel: 36 45 44 00
Fax: 36 45 44 09
A charming 100-year-old hotel and restaurant painted in the traditional yellow Danish color and situated in the centre of the old part of Valby. Only 10 minutes by bus or train to the centre of the city. Quiet and exceedingly quaint. 3 stars. **$**

NORTH ZEALAND

Hotel Hamlet
Bramstræde 5, 3000 Helsingør

Tel: 49 21 05 91
Fax: 49 26 01 30
E-mail: hotelhamlet@internet.dk
Website: www.hotelhamlet.dk
$$

Hotel Frederiksværk
Torvet 6, 3300 Frederiksværk
Tel: 47 72 22 88
Fax: 47 72 01 13
$

Strandhotel "Højbohus"
Hovedgaden 75
3220 Tisvildeleje
Tel: 48 70 71 19
Fax: 48 70 71 77
$$

Hotel Store Kro
Slotsgade 6, 3480 Fredensborg
Tel: 48 48 00 47
Fax: 48 48 45 61
$$

Hotel Marina
Vedbæk Strandvej 391
2950 Vedbæk
Tel: 45 89 17 11
Fax: 45 89 17 22
E-mail: marina@hotelmarina.dk
Website: www.hotelmarina.dk
$$

Bregnerød Kro
Bregnerød Byvej 2, 3520 Farum
Tel: 42 95 00 57
Fax: 42 95 06 55
$$

FUNEN

Odense
Hotel H.C. Andersen
Claus Bergs Gade 7
DK-5000 Odense
Tel: 66 14 78 00
Fax: 66 14 78 90
Good, modern hotel in the old part of Odense, next to museum. 250 beds all with private facilities. Also conference facilities. **$$$**

Odense Congress Hotel
Ørbækvej 350
DK-5220 Odense SØ
Tel: 66 15 55 35
Fax: 66 15 50 70
E-mail: konf@occ.dk
Website: www.occ.dk
In the southeastern part of Odense city, this is both a congress centre and hotel. 4 stars with 218 beds. A good hotel for business visitors. **$$**

Motel Brasilia/Blommenslyst Kro
Middelfartvej 420
DK-5491 Blommenslyst
Tel: 65 96 70 12
Fax: 65 96 79 37
Beautiful motel added to old *kro* (inn) in lovely garden. Excellent traditional food at the inn. Five miles (8 km) west of Odense. **$$**

Missionhotellet Ansgar
Østre Stationsvej 32
DK-5100 Odense C
Tel: 66 11 96 93
Fax: 66 11 96 75
The old mission hotels nowadays have all the facilities and are usually very good value. 70 rooms. **$**

City Hotel Odense
Hans Mulesgade 5
DK-500 Odense C
Tel: 66 12 12 58
Fax: 66 12 93 94
A moderately priced 3-star hotel with all the modern comforts. Situated in the historical precinct of the city only a few minutes' walk from the centre. **$$**

Det Lille hotel
Dronningensgade 5
DK-5000 Odense
Tel: 66 12 28 2
Fax: 66 12 28 21
A charming little family hotel on a quiet street near the centre of Odense. Comfortable and inexpensive. **$**

Pjentehus Bed and Breakfast
Pjentedansgade 14
DK-5000 Odense C
Tel: 40 31 76 12
E-mail: pjentehus@teliamail.dk
A beautiful villa in the city with a relaxed atmosphere and pleasant rooms. **$**

Ydes Hotel
Hans Tausensgade 11
DK-5000 Odense C
Tel: 66 12 11 31
Website: www.ydes.dk
A small hotel that serves an English breakfast. **$**

NORTH JUTLAND

Danhostel Skagen
Rolighedsvej 2
DK-9990 Skagen
Tel: 98 44 22 00

Kroer/Inns

For character, turn to the *kro* (inn), once 17th- and 18th-century coaching inns, which are scattered throughout Denmark. Most preserve the past by leaving the original inn intact and building on extra accommodation motel-style. They are usually outside the main towns.

Nearly 70 *kroer* combine to provide Inn Cheques (*Dansk Kroferie*), which can be bought in advance and are valid for an overnight stay at very reasonable prices.

● Details from:
Dansk Kroferie,
Horsens Tourist Bureau,
Søndergade 31, 8700 Horsens
Tel: 75 64 87 00
Fax: 75 64 87 20.

Fax: 98 44 22 55
E-mail: danhostel.skagen@adr.dk
Website:
www.danhostelnord.dk/skagen
$

Kokkedal Slot
Kokkedalsvej 17
DK-9460 Brovst
Tel: 98 23 36 22
Fax: 96 44 10 29
E-mail: royal-classic@internet.dk
Website:
www.royal-classic.dk/kokkedal
$$

Hotel Skagen Strand
Tranevej Hulsig
DK-9990 Skagen
Tel: 98 48 72 22
Fax: 98 48 71 15
Website:
www.hotel-skagen-strand.dk
$$

Park Hotel
J.F. Kennedys Plads 41
DK-9000 Aalborg
Tel: 98 12 31 33
Fax: 98 13 31 66
$$

Hotel Frederikshavn
Tordenskjoldsgade 14
DK-9900 Frederikshavn
Tel: 98 43 32 33
Fax: 98 43 33 11

E-mail: hotel.frh@post3.tele.dk
Website: www.hotel-frederikshavn
$$

Hotel Strandlyst
Tornby Strand
DK-9850 Hirtshals
Tel: 98 97 70 76
Fax: 98 97 70 76
$

SOUTH JUTLAND

Munkebjerg Hotel
Munkebjergvej 125
DK-7100 Vejle
Tel: 79 42 79 10
Fax: 79 42 79 01
Website: www.munkebjerg.dk
$$–$$$

Hos Gert Sørensen
Lindegade 25
DK-6070 Christiansfeld
Tel: 74 56 17 10
Fax: 74 56 36 40
Website: www.sima.dk/hos-gert-s
$

Sønderho Kro
Kropladsen 11
6720 Fanø
Tel: 75 16 40 09
Fax: 75 16 43 85
E-mail: sonderho@relaischateaux.fr
$$

EAST JUTLAND

Århus
SAS Radisson
Margrethepladsen 1
DK-8000 Århus
Tel: 86 12 86 65
Fax: 86 12 86 75
The most modern and luxurious hotel in Århus, just recently finished with a top-class restaurant, meeting facilities and every convenience that is to be found in a first-class hotel. A large building of steel and glass, fast becoming one of the major conference centres in Jutland. Situated in a beautiful green area beside the Music and Culture House and within walking distance of the city centre. **$$$**

Hotel Marselis
Strandvejen 25
DK-8000 Århus C

Tel: 86 14 44 11
Fax: 86 11 70 46
Situated between a bathing beach and Marselisborg Forest, across from the royal summer residence of the Danish Queen. With a café and restaurant which both have a beautiful view of the seaside. Conference facilities and live music. **$$$**

Price Guide

Hotel price categories outside Copenhagen are as follows:
$$$ = 640–1,710DKK
$$ = 525–675DKK
$ = under 330–550DKK.

Prices given are the average cost of a double room for two, and *usually* include breakfast.

Hotel Royal
Store Torv
Box 43, Århus
Tel: 86 12 00 11
Fax: 86 76 04 04
Beautiful building, more than 150 years old. Modernised in character, with a fine conservatory restaurant in the Queen's Garden. 186 beds with private facilities. **$$$**
Hotel La Tour
Randersvej 139
DK-8200 Århus N
Tel: 86 16 78 88
Fax: 86 16 79 95
Two hundred beds, all with private facilities. **$$**
Hotel Ritz
Banegårdsplads 12
Postboks 37, Århus
Tel: 86 13 44 44
Fax: 86 13 45 87
Very central and close to station with interesting decor. 110 comfortable beds. All private facilities. **$$**
Plaza Hotel
Banegårdspladsen 14
DK-8100 Århus C
Tel: 87 32 01 00
Fax: 87 32 01 99
E-mail: post@plaza-hotel-aarhus.dk
Website: www.plaza-hotel-aarhus.dk
Totally renovated in 1997, the Plaza is centrally located, with a bar,

fitness centre, jacuzzi and indoor parking. **$$**

GREENLAND

Nuuk
Hotel Hans Egede
Aqqusinersuaq 1–5,
Box 289 DK-3920 Nuuk
Tel: 0299-32 42 22 and 32 59 30
Fax: 0299-32 44 87
E-mail: hhe@greennet.gl
Website: www.greenland-guide.dk
Big, modern conference hotel in Greenland's capital. Has 250 beds with private facilities. **$$$**

Aasiaat
Hotel Nanoq
Frederiklyngesvej 12
Box 29 3950 Aasiaat
Tel: 0299 89 21 21
Fax: 0299 89 25 06
Just north of Nuuk with large exclusive rooms and a beautiful unique view out over the fjords of Greenland. **$$**

Kangerlussnag
Hotel Kangerlussnag
Box 1006-3910 Kangerlussnaq
Tel: 0299 84 11 80
Fax: 0299 84 12 84
This hotel is situated on the inland tip of one of Greenland's longest fjords. With 269 rooms, a conference capacity of 300, swimming pool, bowling alley, restaurant and bar. **$$**

Narsarsuaq
Hotel Narsarsuaq
The Airport
DK-3921 Narsarsuaq
Tel: 0299-35253
Fax: 0299-35370
The airport hotel, 10 miles (16 km) or so from the start of the Inland Ice, with a good view of the icebergs in the fjord. 192 rooms, all with private facilities. **$$$**
Hotel Perlen
Box 8 DK-3291 Narsarsuaq
Tel: 0299-57 20 17 and 66 17 13
Fax: 0299-66 13 33
Comfortable, family-run hotel with good food and beautiful view of the Narsarsuaq sound and its icebergs.

Bed and Breakfast

Danes are relative newcomers to the idea of entertaining bed and breakfast guests, and you should check that breakfast is included in the price. Even when it is not, it can usually be arranged. In Danish, "bed and breakfast" is *Logi/Morgenmad*. For detailed information contact:

Dansk Bed and Breakfast,
tel: 39 61 04 05;
fax: 39 61 05 25;
website: www.bbdk.dk;
E-mail bed@bbdk.dk

60 rooms, some with private facilities. Ideal for fjord and iceberg tours, and tours of the mountains behind. **$$**

Illulisaat (Jakobshavn)
Hotel Arctic Illulissat
Box 501
DK-3852 Illulissat
Tel: 0299-44153
Fax: 0299-43924
Good quality modern hotel at the top of the hill, with a superb view overlooking the bay and Disko island. Best reached by helicopter from Søndrestrømfjord Airport, the all-weather airport that is part of the US Air Force base. **$$$**
Disco Bay House
Tel: 0299 91 10 81
Fax: 0299 91 15 24
Qaanaaq (Thule)
Hotel Qaanaaq
Box 88
DK-3971 Qaanaaq
Tel: 0299-50120
Fax: 0299-50064
A small, simple hotel on the remote northwest coast of Greenland, which can be reached through Thule air base. Ten rooms without private facilities. **$**

THE FAROE ISLANDS

Torshavn
Hotel Borg
Oggjarvegur,
PO Box 105

FR-110 Torshavn
Tel: 0298-17500
Fax: 0298-16919
A big, modern hotel but built in traditional style, with dark timber walls and turf roof, in a beautiful position above the hill behind Torshavn, looking across the harbor to the island of Nolsoy. All private facilities. **$$$**
Hotel Hafnia
Aarvegur 6 1B
FR-110 Torshavn
Tel: 29 81 12 70
Fax: 29 81 52 50
Some 100–200 meters from the harbor. 76 beds all with private facilities. Sauna. **$$**
Torshavn Sjomansheim
Torsgata 4
PO Box 97
FR-110 Torshavn
Tel: 0298-13515
Fax: 0298-13286
Comfortable hotel with 72 rooms, some with private facilities. Restaurant with good, simple fare. **$**
Hotel Vagar
Sørvagar
FR-380
Tel: 29 83 29 55
Fax: 29 83 23 10
Rooms with bathroom, radio and TV. Restaurants; conference facilities, audio visual equipment and an international kitchen with Faroe specialities. They also book and arrange sightseeing tours. **$$**

Mykines
Kristianshus
Tel: 18 433
Fax: 10 985
Situated on the beautiful outlying island of Mykines. Open May through September. **$**

Eystoroy, Eidi
Hotel Eidi
Tel: 23 456
Fax: 23 200
In the north of this northern island on the Sundini Channel. 31 beds without private facilities but with mini-bars, an asset in a country without licensed restaurants and bars. **$**

Eystoroy also has two youth hostels, as do many other islands.

Bordoy, Klaksvik
Klaksvikar Sjomansheim
Vikavegur
FR-700 Klaksvik
Tel: 0298-55333
Fax: 0298-57 233
The main accommodation in the Faroe Islands' second largest community, handy for the ferry to Leirvik. 61 rooms, some with private facilities. Restaurant. **$$**

Self-catering/Camping

These options are always popular in Denmark, particularly for people who bring their own cars north from Germany or across the North Sea from Britain; they are an ideal way of seeing the country in summer. Summer houses are reasonable to rent but normally require a guest to stay at least a week. Whether it is rented out centrally or not, the house may well belong to a Danish family. Danes, known homemakers, often spend even more money and thought on their holiday home than they do on their permanent house, and the standard will be high.

You can hire stationary caravans or huts on many campsites, or take your own tent. There are 525 well-equipped star-rated camping sites. Ask the Danish tourist board (*see page 317*) or the local tourist information office for a list of camping sites. There is also a camping voucher, similar to the Inn

Castles and Manor Houses

Several Danish castles and manor houses have been converted into hotels or guest houses, giving you a chance to go back in time and live in the midst of ancient gardens and hallways. Many of the castles have excellent restaurants and wine cellars.

● For further information contact:
Danish Castles and Manor Houses, 8000 Viborg
Tel: 86 60 38 44
Fax: 86 60 38 31.

Cheque mentioned under *Kroer*/Inns (*see page 325*). For further details, contact: **Camping Club Denmark**, Horsens Tourist Bureau, address and phone under *Kroer*/Inns.

Farm Holidays

Danish farmers have long been happy with the idea of inviting guests to stay as one of the family on their comfortable farms, with their well-kept courtyard gardens. You get an excellent insight into Danish life, and can volunteer to help when needed. This type of accommodation is popular with children, and the farmer at harvest-time. The main centre is Jutland.
● Contact:
Horsens Tourist Board
Søndergade 31, 8700 Horsens, Denmark
Tel: 75 60 21 20
Fax: 75 60 21 90.

Youth Hostels

As in most countries, youth hostels cater to people of all ages, and Denmark has around 100 of them, with a standard of facilities higher than in most European hostels. You need a valid membership of the Youth Hostel Association in your home country. Details from:
Denmarks Vandrerhjem,
Vesterbrogade 39, DK-1620 Copenhagen V, price 20DKK, plus postage, tel: 31 31 36 12. The Danish Tourist Office also has a free list of sites.

The **YMCA** and **YWCA** run one Inter-Rail point in Copenhagen. Open: June to mid-August. They offer accommodation for around 65DKK. and breakfast for 29DKK; at
Inter-Rail Point
Valdemarsgade 15,
DK-1663 Copenhagen V
Tel: 31 31 15 74.

For information on youth hostels and inexpensive accommodation, also contact the **Youth Information Centre – USE IT**, Rådhusstræde 13, DK-1466 Copenhagen, tel: 33 73 06 20; website: www.useit.dk. Outside hours, consult the outdoor notice board for information.

Where to Eat

What To Eat

Within the past couple of decades the Danish kitchen has gone through a quiet revolution. Not only have the traditional hearty meals of pork and beef seen new low-calorie, high-fibre varieties, but words like pizza, pasta, quiche and kebab have also gone into the everyday vocabulary. These days one can eat in a variety of languages and still not be exotic. (*See also chapter on Danish food, page 123.*)

Traditional Danish food

However, the food that is usually associated with Denmark has not suffered from this clash of cultures: open sandwiches (*smørrebrød*) are still most common for lunch. If you don't count calories, try a lunch buffet of cold dishes (*smörgåsbord* is originally a Swedish word, but the tradition is Danish, too), where you can pick and choose from a range of Danish specialities. A beer and an *aqvavit* are also traditional and go well with lunch.

Fish, fowl and game

When in Denmark take advantage of the varieties of fish available from the Baltic and North Seas. Freshwater fish, whether from the rivers of northern Scandinavia or the fish farms of Jutland, is excellent. Relatively inexpensive meals can be prepared easily, and are common in restaurants. Fowl and game are common, especially in autumn, and should by all means be sampled.

Eating on a Budget

You can often eat well but cheaply at cafés, most of which serve chili con carne, quiche, a salad and soup, and several kinds of sandwiches. Among the money savers are also many oriental restaurants, especially those with Chinese menus; 85–100DKK or less will usually cover a main course and a beer.

Many restaurants offer "a two-course meal of good, Danish food" for 85–125DKK. This is where one finds pork roast, minced beef, meat or fish balls, and other traditional dishes with ice cream for dessert. Drinks are not included.

Restaurant Listings

Restaurants in the capital are featured first, divided into different categories of food. The various regions of the country follow. Within the regional sections that follow, restaurants are listed in alphabetical order.

COPENHAGEN

Danish
Bjælkehuset
Valbylanggade 2
Tel: 36 30 35 96
(Not open in the winter.) A beautiful place for a traditional Danish lunch in the middle of the oldest park in Copenhagen. **$$**
Brasilko
Østergade 36
Tel: 33 12 08 86
Traditional Danish grilled meat. **$$**
Dockside Steak and Lobster
Langelinekaj 5
Tel: 35 55 75 80
Excellent seafood with one of the most beautiful views in the city. Not far from the Little Mermaid. **$$–$$$**
Krogs Fiskerestaurant
Gammel Strand 38, 1202 K
Tel: 33 15 89 15
Fax: 33 15 83 15
Possibly the best (and most expensive) fish restaurant in town. **$$$**
Nikolaj Church
Nikolaj Plads
Tel: 33 93 16 26
Lovely outside in the summer.
Peder Oxe
Grobrødretorv 11

Tel: 31 11 99 11
A good choice for lunch, with an excellent salad bar and Danish *smørrebrød* on the menu. **$$$**
St. Gertrude's Kloster
Hauserplads 32d
Tel: 33 14 66 30
Built in 1397 as a monastery, with candlelit narrow passageways. Specialising in medieval Danish dishes. **$$$**
Torvaldsen
Gammel Strand 34
Tel: 33 32 04 00
Fish and seafood specialities. **$$$**

International
Barpck NR. 1
Nyhavn
Tel 33 33 01 51
Danish/French food by the waterside. **$$**
L'Education Nationale
Karsbjårnstøde 12
Tel: 33 91 53 60
El Gusto
Havnegade 47
Tel: 33 11 32 16
Copenhagen's oldest and largest Mexican restaurant.
Indian Taj
Jernbanegade 3–5
Tel: 33 13 10 10
Traditional Indian cuisine. Good value for money. **$$**
Mitsu
Jagtvej 101
Tel: 35 85 79 97
Excellent Japanese food. **$$**
Pasta Basta
Valkendorfsgade 22 (between Stråget and Gråbrødretorv)
1151 K
Tel: 33 11 21 31
Try their first-rate buffet of hot and cold pasta dishes at reasonable prices. **$**
San Giorgio
Rosenborggade 7
Tel: 33 12 61 20
One of the best Italian (Sardinian) restaurants in Copenhagen: it goes by the motto of "tradition and quality". **$$$**
White Clouds
Strandvejen 26
Tel: 39 29 07 33
Chinese specialities; well worth a try. **$$**

Cafés

Café Chips
Øster Farimagsgade 53
Tel: 35 38 47 91
A cosy little place, often with live
music on Sunday afternoon. **$**

Café Dan Turell
Store Regnegade 3, 1110K
Tel: 33 14 10 47
Fax: 33 14 60 47
Artists often frequent this café.**$**

Krasnapolsky
Vestergade 10, 1456 K
Tel: 33 32 88 00
Fax: 33 32 22 50
This café is popular with the
younger, fashion-conscious crowd.**$**

Café Norden
Østergade 61, 1100 K
Tel: 33 13 59 59
Beautiful upstairs, hung with old
paintings.**$**

Park Café
Østerbrogade 79, 2100 Ø
Tel: 35 42 6248
Often live music. **$**

For Vegetarians

Atlas Bar, Larsbjørnstræde 18
Tel: 33 15 03 52
A popular vegetarian restaurant
with international cuisine. **$**

Den Grønne Kælder
Pilestræde 48
Tel: 33 93 01 40
An excellent place for a
vegetarian lunch. **$$–$**

Els, Store Strandstræde 3
Tel: 33 14 13 41
International cuisine.

Riz Raz, Kompagnistræde 20
Tel: 33 15 05 75
One of the top vegetarian
restaurants in Copenhagen, with
a great variety of dishes to
choose between. **$$–$**

ZEALAND

Anno 1880
Kongensgade 6, 3000 Helsingør
Tel: 49 21 54 80
Fax: 49 20 18 18

Restaurant Brede Spisehus
I.C. Modewegsvej
2800 Kongens Lyngby
Tel: 45 85 54 57

Fax: 45 85 57 67

The Cottage
Skansensvej 19, 4880 Nysted
Tel: 54 87 16 00
Fax: 54 87 16 44
Danish/French cuisine.

Dronning Louises Kro
Gl. Strandvej 1, 2990 Nivå
Tel: 49 18 04 18

Hos Karen og Marie
Ndr. Havnevej 3, 3250 Gilleleje
Tel/Fax: 48 30 21 30

Middelaldercentret
Ved Hamborgskoven 2,
4800 Nykøbing Falster
Tel: 54 86 19 34
Fax: 54 8618 34
An inn that serves traditional
dishes.

Sletten Kro
Gl. Humlebækvej, 3050 Humlebæk
Tel: 49 19 13 01
Fax: 49 19 13 91

Slotskroen
Slotsgade 67, 3400 Hillerød
Tel: 48 26 01 82
Fax: 48 24 08 82
Website: www.slotskroen.dk
Fax: 49 14 31 62
E-mail: dronning-louise@post.tele.dk

BORNHOLM

Fredensborg
Strandvejen 116, Rønne
Tel: 56 95 44 44
Fax: 56 95 03 14
High gastronomic standard with a
view of the forest and the sea.

ODENSE

AirPub
Kongensgade 41
Tel: 66 14 66 08
Typical Danish food and beer. **$$**

Amfita Café – Brandts Klædefabrik
Brandts Passage 37–43
Tel: 66 13 78 97
Fax: 66 13 73 10
An immense art gallery and lovely
café. **$$**

Den Gamle Kro (The Old Inn)
Overgade 23
Tel: 66 12 14 33
Fax: 66 17 88 58
International cuisine in an historicl

Price Guide

The following prices are for an
average two-course meal
(excluding drinks) per head:
  $$$ = 120DKK or more
  $$ = 70–120DKK
  $ = less than 70DKK.

building built in 1683. **$$$**

**Den Grimme Ælling (The Ugly
Duckling)**
Hans Jensens Str. 1
Tel: 65 91 70 30
A great place for a Danish lunch in
the old quarter of town. **$$**

Kreta
Vestergade 98
Tel. 66 19 44 40
A three-course menu of excellent
Greek food at inexpensive prices. **$**

Restaurant Le Provence
Pogestræde 31
Tel: 66 12 1296
Fax: 65 90 69 63
Popular, relaxed restaurant in the
centre of Odense serving, as the
name suggests, French cuisine.
$$

Olivia
Vintapperstræde 37
Tel: 66 17 87 44
A cosy little café with delicious
home-baked pies. A good place for
a light lunch. **$**

Restauranten Søhesten
Pantheonsgade 5 B
Tel: 66 91 46 96
Specializes in fish and seafood.
$$–$$$

NORTH JUTLAND

Brøndums Hotel
Anchersvej 3, 9990 Skagen
Tel: 98 44 15 55
$$

Det Gule Pakhus
Tordenskjoldsgade 14
9900 Frederikshavn
Tel: 98 42 98 10
$$

Restaurant Jeckels
Jekelsvej 5, 9990 Skagen
Tel: 98 44 63 00
Website: www.jeckels.dk
$$

Restaurant "Mortens Kro"
Algade 37
9000 Aalborg
Tel/fax: 98 12 48 60
Website:
www.spiseguiden.dk/mortenskro
$–$$
Rold Gammel Kro
Hobrovej 11
9510 Arden
Tel: 98 56 17 00
Fax: 98 56 25 11
$$
Sallingsund Færgekro
Sallingsundvej 104
7900 Nykøbing Mors
Tel: 97 72 00 88
Fax: 97 72 25 40
Website: www.sima.dk/sallingsund-
faergekro
$–$$

Price Guide

The following prices are for an
average two-course meal
(excluding drinks) per head:
   $$$ = 120DKK or more
   $$ = 70–120DKK
   $ = less than 70DKK.

EAST JUTLAND

Norsminde Gl. Kro
Gl. Krovej 2, 8340 Malling
Tel: 86 93 24 44
Fax: 86 83 14 24
Website: www.norsminde-kro.dk
Slotskroen
Slotsgade , 8900 Randers
Tel: 86 43 56 64
Fax: 86 42 69 41
Website:
www.spiseguiden.dk/slotskroen

Århus
Restaurant De 4 Årstider
Åboulevarden 47
8000 Århus C
Tel: 86 19 96 96
Fax: 86 18 07 78
$$$
Chez Tony
Tordenskjoldsgade 25
Tel: 86 16 88 30
A popular neighbourhood Greek
restaurant. Casual. Exceptionally
tasty food at moderate prices. **$$**

Emmery's
Guldsmedegade 24
Tel: 86 13 04 00
Gourmet bakery and tapas. **$$**
Latin Brasserie & Crêperie
Klostergade 2
Tel: 86 13 78 12
Elegant, French, romantic. Chefs of
the highest calibre in an arty,
bohemian-type setting. **$$$**
Le Canard
Frederiksgade 74
Tel: 86 12 58 38
Classical, top-class French cuisine.
$$$
Makies Pizzeria
Sct. Clemens Torv 9
Tel: 86 12 36 61
Excellent hamburgers and pizza in a
fun atmosphere, at the foot of the
pedestrianised mall near the
cathedral. **$**
Pind's Café
Skolegade 29
Tel: 86 12 20 60
An Århus institution. To see what all
the fuss over a Danish lunch is
about, order anything here with a
shot of aquavit and a beer. Feels
like a hunter's lodge. **$$**
Prins Ferdinand
Den Gamle By
Tel: 86 12 52 05
Contemporary Danish gastronomy.
$$$
Café Smageløs
Klostertorv 7
Tel: 86 13 51 33
Their brunch is famous in Århus. A
modern, arty spin on the traditional
open sandwiches, in a trendy spot.
Amazing bread. **$$**

SOUTH JUTLAND

Den Gamle Gæstgivergård
Lindegade 25, 6070 Christiansfeld
Tel: 74 56 17 10
Fax: 74 56 36 40
An historic site and top-class
restaurant that specialises in
classic Danish cuisine. **$$$**
Krusmølle
Krusmøllevej 10
Feldstedskov, Aabenraa
Tel: 74 68 61 72
Fax: 74 68 62 10
Danish and international cuisine. **$$**

Nightlife

Information

The best entertainment is found in
Copenhagen, Århus and Odense.
Check the local newspapers or, as
always, call the tourist information
offices for information about what's
currently on (*see page 319*).

The pedestrian street in the
centre of any town is a good place
to look for a café or a bar. Most
Danes welcome a chance to
practise their English, and will be
proud to unload an insider's view
on the best places to go in their
own city.

BILLETnet is an entertainment
information network. You can
reserve tickets through BILLETnet
and also receive information on
everything from concerts to sports
events.

BILLETnet has a telephone line
open everyday from 10am–9pm,
tel: 70 15 65 65; website
www.billetnet.dk.

You will also find BILLETnet at
many post offices throughout
Denmark.

For further information about the
music scene in Denmark, contact:
Danish Music Information Center
Tel: 33 11 20 66
Fax: 33 32 20 16
Website www.mic.dk

Listings
COPENHAGEN

Theatre
Most theatre is in Danish even
though the piece may have been
originally written in another
language.

The London Toast Theatre,
Kochsvej 18

Tel: 33 22 86 86.
The only English language theatre in Copenhagen, showing plays of a high standard.
Det Konglig Teater
(The Royal Theatre)
Kongens Nytorv
Tel: 33 69 69 33
Website: www.kgl-teater.dk
Major operas and symphonies are performed here.

Live Music
The Australian Bar
Vestergade 10
Tel: 33 15 04 80
DJ, film and disco.
Café Baptof
Nodre Fasanvej 46
Tel: 38 86 90 67
Folk, Irish, American.
Café Barcelona
Fælledvej 21
Tel: 31 35 76 11
Hip hop, disco, R&B.
Blågårds Apotek
Blågårdsgade 20
Tel: 35 37 34 42
Blues, country.
Café Chips
Øster Farimagsgade 53
Tel: 35 38 47 91
Jazz and folk.
Copenhagen Jazz House
Niels Hemmingsensgade 10
Tel: 33 15 26 00
This is *The* place for those interested in jazz.
Mojo
Løngangsstræde 21 C
Tel: 33 11 64 53
Live blues every night.
Pumpehuset
Stidiestræde 52
Tel: 33 93 14 32
Big names in modern music.
Café Svejk
Smallegade 31
Tel: 38 86 25 60
Blues, rock and folk.
Vega
Enghavevej 40
Tel: 33 25 70 11
African, latin, pop and world music.
Woodstock
Vestergade 12
Tel: 33 11 20 71
Lots of 60s oldies and basic rock.

ODENSE

Badstuen
Østre Stationsvej 26
Tel: 66 13 48 66
Rock, blues, latin and pop.
Brandts Klædefabrik
Brandts Passage 37-43
Music, dance and theatre.
Grønttorvet
Sortebrødre Torv 9
Tel: 66 14 34 37
Jazz.
Odense Koncerthus
Claus Bergs Gade 9
Tel: 66 12 44 80
Classical music.
Café Oscar
Vestergade 75
Tel: 66 14 25 35
Rock.
Rytmeposten
Østre Stationsvej 35
Tel: 66 13 60 20
Rock, blues, pop.

ÅRHUS

The night life in Århus is centred around **Skolegade**. One can zig-zag down the street from bar to bar. (The same is true of Ålborg in Jomfru Ane Gade.) Århus has fostered a great number of cafés in recent years. Many cafés and bars are near the cathedral and in the old streets leading up to Guldsmedegade. You should also take a stroll through Vestergade and Jægersgårdgade.

Bent J
Nørre Allé 66
Tel: 86 12 04 92
Famous jazz bar.
Glazzhuset
Åboulevarden 35
Tel: 86 12 13 12
Live jazz.
Fatter Eskild
Skolegade 25
Tel: 86 19 44 11
Blues music.
Musikcaféen
Mejlgade 53
Tel: 86 76 03 44
Rock, blues, folk all kinds.
Musikhuset Århus
Thomas Jensens allé

Tel: 89 31 82 10
All kinds of music, dance and theatre. Classical orchestras and major artists.
Naxos Vinkælder
Mindebrogade 2
Tel: 86 19 01 01
Live music; small, cosy place.
Train
Toldbodegade 6
Tel: 86 13 47 22
Live music.
Vox Hall
Vesterallé 15
Tel: 86 12 26 77
Rock and world music.

Cinema

All foreign films are shown with their original sound track. Local newspapers have all the details as to which movies are playing when and where. There are several film guides available in Copenhagen at the tourist information office, cafés and movie houses. You will find most of the cinemas in the city centre, often within walking distance of the Central Station.

Music Festivals

These are just a few of the 180 music festivals taking place in Denmark every year.

Copenhagen Jazz Festival
For several weeks in July the streets of Copenhagen are filled with the sound of jazz. One of the world's best jazz festivals.
Midfyns Festival
In July on the Island of Fyn. Rock, pop, blues and heavy music in a beautiful country setting.
Roskilde Festival
Always in July near Roskilde on Zealand. The largest music festival in Denmark, featuring major acts from around the world.
Skagen Festival
In June at the northern most tip of Denmark – beautiful windswept Skagen. One of Denmark's largest folk music festivals.

Children

Amusements

Denmark is a great place for children; here we list a few of the highlights.

COPENHAGEN

Experimentarium
A hands-on science museum where you can try more than 300 experiments with sound, light, water, currents and more. With short demonstrations and special exhibits. Open daily. Tel: 39 27 33 33.

National Zoo
There is a special children's zoo here, where children are allowed to pat the animals, watch chickens peck their way out of eggs and ride on ponies. Open every day of the year from 9am–4pm or 6pm. It is near the centre of Copenhagen on Roskildevej 32, tel: 36 30 20 01.

Puppet Theatre
From the beginning of summer until the end of August there are free puppet shows in **Kongens Have** (the Royal Gardens) near Rosenborg Palace. At 2pm and 3pm, Tuesday to Sunday.

Tivoli
The world famous amusement park, Tivoli, just across from Central Station, is a delight both for children and adults. For more than 156 years it has fulfilled every child's dream of a fantasy world. There is a 125-year-old pantomine theatre that still presents Italian-style Commedia dell´Arte twice daily, and an endless variety of rides and amusements that will

satisfy even the most energetic child. Open from April 23 to September 26. Sunday–Thursday from 11am–12pm, Friday and Saturday from 11am to 1am.

OUTSIDE COPENHAGEN

Bakken
Bakken is a traditional amusement park located in the beautiful Dyrehaven area near Klampenborg in north Zealand, with more than a 100 rides to choose from. Situated in the former royal hunting forest, it is a perfect place for a beautiful walk through traditional Danish countryside, with free ranging deer in sight, or for a ride in a horse-drawn carriage. Open every day from March 25–August 30, noon–midnight, free of charge.

Benneweis Circus
The largest circus in Northern Europe and the most famous one in Denmark. It is situated in Dronningmølle. 3120-DK; website: www.cirkus-benneweis.dk

Legoland
A world famous amusement park near Bilund airport in Jutland, built out of 33 million Lego brick blocks. Open daily May until mid-September. Be sure to make reservations ahead of time. Tel: 75 33 13 33 and 32 54 06 06.

Lejre Research Centre
An historical-archaeological research centre with a reconstructed Iron age village, ancient agriculture and houses from 1850, this is definitely one of the most marvellous places in Denmark for a family outing. Children can learn to grind their own flour, cut wood, and make Viking bread on an open fire under adult supervision. They can make clay figures, and colour wool, in just a few of the many workshops where teachers and families live during the summer period. Situated in beautiful countryside on Zealand, Lejre brings the past into the present. Tel: 46 48 08 78.

Sport

Spectator Sports

The Danes are very proud of their soccer teams. When Denmark wins a big soccer match you can hear loud, happy exclamations throughout the city streets. When it doesn't go so well, the silence is deafening.

Long-distance cycling has also become a major sport and many watch the *Tour de France* with bated breath.

Participant Sports

ANGLING

Anglers must have fishing permits in Denmark. These can be obtained at any post office or tourist office. Fishing rights in lakes and streams are usually privately owned but can often be hired from the local tourist office.

CYCLING

Denmark was made for the bicycle, with its gentle terrain and general lack of mountainous countryside. The bicycle itself has become an integral part of Danish culture and a major form of transportation. Danes cycle to work, to visit friends, to pick up their children and to go shopping. It is sheer pleasure to bicycle through the winding streets of Copenhagen on a summer day, or out through the lovely countryside taking all the small seldom frequented side roads.

Rental
There are a number of places where you can rent a bike at a reasonable rate. Try:

Dan Wheel
Colbjørnsgade 3
Tel: 33 21 22 27; or
Cyklebørs
157 Gothersgade
Tel: 33 14 07 17.

You can also borrow a bike for free at **City Bikes** 1 Store Kirkestræde Tel: 36 30 02 86
Website: www.bycyklen.dk

GOLF

There are more than 120 golf courses to choose from in Denmark. Green fees are about 180DKK during the week and 200DKK during the weekend. Try **Copenhagen Pay and Play** Smørem Golf centre
Skebjerg 46
Tel: 44 97 01 11; and
Furesø
Tel: 42 81 74 44.

HIKING

There are many beautiful places for hiking in Denmark. Local tourist offices have maps of tested walks and will help you plan routes of special interests. Try walking along the lovely chalk white cliffs of **Stevens** or through the peaceful forest of **Bøgeskov**, just an hour south of Copenhagen.

SAILING

Sailboats and yachts are available for hire on a weekly basis. Visitors should ask to see a certificate from the Shipping Inspection office before hiring a boat. Two major boat charter companies are:
Nordia Boat Charter
Tel: 97 20 99 22
Fax: 97 11 88 70; and
Maritim Camping
Tel: 46 73 28 28
Fax: 46 73 28 11.

Shopping

What to Buy

Danish design is famous all over the world, especially in the area of **kitchenware, furniture** and **stereo equipment**. Beautiful **amber necklaces** are to be found in all jewellery stores, along with exquisite replicas of ancient Viking jewellery in silver and gold. **Ceramics and glassware** are a tradition in Denmark and, in addition to Royal Copenhagen Porcelain, there are many small ceramic studios throughout the country. Danish **furs** are very popular among tourists and countless shops specialise in **traditional and modern knitwear.** **Lego** bricks are known throughout the world, but most children's toys are made of strong, durable wood with designs and functions that are based on educational principles. **Feather bedding** is common in Denmark and many stores sell feather comforters and pillows. **Pipe makers** carve with excellent craftsmanship wood and meerschaum pipes.

Denmark is full of small interesting stores. There are not that many large shopping malls in Denmark as yet, and part of the cities' charm is that they have retained their small speciality shops, some of them for over a hundred years.

Tax-free shopping

Part of the reason for the high prices is a value-added tax (called MOMS) of 25 percent, added to all sales and services. Visitors can avoid making this contribution to the Danish state by having their purchases shipped home or by shopping in stores that offer a tax-free service.

Shops that cater to tourists will provide information about the procedures. If you buy something and want to take it with you immediately, look for a sign saying "Danish Tax-Free Shopping." About 1,500 shops are members of this association, and the MOMS spent in them will be refunded on departure from Denmark. Show the tax-free invoice to the customs officer *before* checking in. He will return customs stamps which can be presented for cash at the Office for Repayment of VAT in the transit hall (minus a small service charge). If leaving by land, ask for the stamps and send the invoice back to "Danish Tax-Free Shopping" for a refund. A minimum purchase is required – check for the latest information before arriving.

Complaints

If you want to complain about poor service or merchandise, and the matter cannot be sorted out on the spot, try using **Forbrugerrådet** (The Consumer Council), Købmagergade 7, 1150 Copenhagen K, tel: 33 13 63 11 (10am–1pm weekdays).

Copenhagen Shopping

Copenhagen never fails to appear on lists of the most expensive cities in the world, usually rated among the top 10, accompanied by the other Scandinavian capitals. The main shopping areas are of course the pedestrianised streets, and first among them Strøget. When there, take a look inside **Illums Bolighus** (at Amagertorv). They sell everything from furniture to kitchenware, all of it high quality. Jørn Utzon, the designer of the Sydney Opera House, was invited to design the **Paustian** furniture store in Nordre Frihavn and it is also an interesting place to visit.

Visit **Krea** in Vestergade and **BR** across the street from **Magasin** ("the largest department store in Scandinavia") for toys and gifts for kids. Around the corner in Lars Bjørnstræde are street fashion and secondhand shops. Pistolstræde is more pricey, and here you will find the name of **Birger Christensen,** the owner of Café Bee Cee, Birger Christensen Furs and several other food and fashion shops in the neighbourhood. **Georg Jensen's** silver shop is at Strøget and Pilestræde, near Illums.

The department store **Magasin** is always crowded, no matter which city you browse in. Fashion bargains can be made in **Hennes & Mauritz,** originally a Swedish company, but now an enormous success with younger Danes.

Copenhagen is packed with antique shops, many to be found in Strædet (Kompagnistræde and Læderstræde) Ravnsborggade. Some are very exclusive and expensive while others do business on the pavement. They're fun to explore and spend money in – don't be afraid to negotiate a price, or to walk away from the shop if it seems too expensive. You will find many amber shops around the city, and jewellery stores specialising in replicas of Viking jewellery.

There is an information center for Danish handicrafts on Amagertorv 1,1160 Kbh. K, tel: 33 12 61 62; website: www: craftsdk.com

BOOKS

The following shops are worth trying for foreign-language literature:
● **Arnold Busck,** Købmagergade 49 Tel: 33 73 35 00. Fax: 33 73 35 35
● **Atheneum,** Nørregade 6 Tel: 33 12 69 70. Fax: 33 14 69 33
● **English Books and Records** Fredriksalle 53 Tel: 86 19 54 55.
● **GAD** At the Central Station and Fiolstræde 31-33; Tel: 33 12 91 48 Website: www. gad.dk Books in English, German and French.
● **Buchandlung** Vester Voldgade 83 Tel: 33 13 60 16.
● **The French Book Shop** Badstuestræde 6 Tel: 33 14 20 71.

Language

Pronunciation

The old joke says that Danish is not so much a language as a disease of the throat, and so it sometimes seems. To make the language even more difficult, Danish has three extra letters – æ, ø, and å – plus unpronounceable sub-glottal stops, and myriad local dialects and accents. It almost seems like a conspiracy. No sooner have you got used to one set of sounds than the next town or village produces a new cacophony. Although the Danes are always helpful, a knowledge of a few basic pronunciation rules will also help to fathom out a notice, road sign or headline.

Despite their clear differences of grammar, usage and vocabulary, Danes, Norwegians and Swedes are still able to understand one another. In a tripartite conversation, each will speak his or her own national language, and on an SAS (Scandinavian Air Services) flight the captain and head steward will make the flight announcements in their native tongue. The advent of cross-border television has helped inter-Scandinavian knowledge of all three forms, but claims to perfect understanding of each other's language are better taken with a pinch of salt.

Modern Danish is no more rational than English and has far fewer words. In addition to the many dialects and various pronunciations in the different areas, another difficulty for foreigners is that many existing letters are pronounced in a different way from other European languages.

There are a few simple rules of thumb for vowels which may help:

Although none of this will mean you can speak Danish within a few days, it should help in getting place names right. It will also kindle a polite mirth in your hosts because all Danes love to hear a foreigner attempting to wrap a reluctant tongue round words such as *sikkerhedsforanstaltninger* (security precautions) or *anti-ubådskrigsførelse* (anti-submarine warfare) and not forgetting *rødgrød med fløde på* (a fruit dessert with cream).

A quick look into any telephone book will reveal another quirk of the Danish language: the predominance of certain names. Around 7.7 percent of the population is called Jensen, 7.3 percent Nielsen and 6.2 percent answers to the name of Hansen. These are closely followed by umpteen Christensens, Andersens, Pedersens and Petersens. In all, two-thirds of the entire Danish population is a *-sen* of one sort or another.

The reason is historical, dating back to the days when sons and daughters took their surnames from their fathers. Thus, Anders Nielsen's son was called Jonas Andersen and his daughter Gudrun Andersdatter. Then, as the population grew, a new fad for fashionable names brought the whole system into chaos. In 1828, the government passed the Name Law, which stipulated that all families should choose and retain a surname for the future. Iceland is now the only country in the western hemisphere to use the old system, reintroduced in a spate of historical patriotism in the 1970s.

None of this makes Danish any easier to understand, let alone speak. But at least your efforts will amuse the Danes.

Visitors who plan to stay for a longer period will find several language schools for non-native speakers (the **Berlitz School** and **K.I.S.S.** in Copenhagen offer intensive training; **Studieskolen** is a more humane alternative, and private tutors can be found), but the following words and phrases might ease your trip a little:

Useful Words & Phrases

General
yes/no *ja/nej*
big/little *stor(t)/lille*
good/bad *god(t)/dårlig(t)*
possible/impossible *muligt/umuligt*
hot/cold *varm/kold*
much/little *meget/lidt*
many/few *mange/få*
and/or *og/eller*
please/thank you *vær så venlig/tak*
I *jeg*
you (**formal**) *du (de)*
he/she *han/hun*
it *den/det*
we *vi*
you (**formal**) *I (de)*
they *de*
foreigner *udlænding*
foreign *fremmed*

Food and Drink
breakfast *morgenmad*
lunch (**break**) *frokost (pause)*
dinner *middag*
tea *te*
coffee *kaffe*
beer *fadøl*

Getting Around
left *venstre*
right *højre*
street *(en) gade/vej*
bicycle (**path**) *(en) cykel (sti)*
car *(en) bil*
bus/coach *(en) bus*
train *(et) tog*
ferry *(en) færge*
bridge *(en) bro*
traffic light *(et) trafiklys*
square *(et) torv*
north *nord*
south *syd*
east *øst*
west *vest*

Money
how much is it? *Hvad koster det?*
can I pay with... *Må jeg betale med...*
travellers' cheques *rejsechecks*
money *penge*
notes/coins *sedler/mønter*
Please may I have the bill? *Må jeg få regningen?*
May I have a *Må jeg få en*

receipt? *kvittering?*
bank *(en) bank*
exchange *veksle*
exchange rate *kurs*
business hours *åbningstider*
open *åben*
closed *lukket*

Medical
pharmacy *(et) apotek*
hospital *(et) hospital*
casualty *(en) skadestue*
doctor *(en) læge*

Time
what time is it? *hvad erklokken?*
good morning *godmorgen*
good day/evening *goddag*
goodnight *godaften/godnat*
today *i dag*
tomorrow *i morgen*
yesterday *i går*
morning (**9–12**) *formiddag*
noon *middag*
afternoon *eftermiddag*
evening *aften*
night *nat*
what time is it? *hvad er klokken?*
It's five *Den er fem*

Places
Copenhagen *København*
Elsinore *Helsingør*
Zealand *Sjælland*
Funen *Fyn*
Jutland *Jylland*

Vowels
a – a, as in *bar*
å – aw, as in *paw*
æ – e, as in *pear*
e – as in *bed*
i – ee, as in *sleep*
ø – u, as in *fur*

Abbreviations
A/S Ltd/Inc.
Dkr. Danish Kroner
DSB Danish State Railways
e.Kr. AD
f.Kr. BC
HT Copenhagen Transit Authority
Kbh. Copenhagen
KFUK YWCA
KFUM YMCA
km/t. kilometres per hour
MOMS value-added tax

Calendar
Weekday names are from Nordic mythology (reflected in the English):
Monday *mandag* (moon day)
Tuesday *tirsdag* (from the Latin *dies Martis*)
Wednesday *onsdag* (Odin's day)
Thursday *torsdag* (Thor's day)
Friday *fredag* (Freja's day)
Saturday *lørdag* (from the Old Norse *laurgardagr/*"washing day")
Sunday *søndag* (from the Latin, *dies soils*, the day of the sun).

Numbers

1	*en/et*	18	*atten*
2	*to*	19	*nitten*
3	*tre*	20	*tyve*
4	*fire*	21	*enogtyve*
5	*fem*	30	*tredive*
6	*seks*	32	*toogtredive*
7	*syv*	40	*fyrre*
8	*otte*	43	*treogfyrre*
9	*ni*	50	*halvtreds*
10	*ti*	54	*fireoghalvtreds*
11	*elleve*	60	*tres*
12	*tolv*	65	*femogtres*
13	*tretten*	70	*halvfjerds*
14	*fjorten*	76	*seksoghalvfjerds*
15	*femten*	80	*firs*
16	*seksten*	90	*halvfems*
17	*sytten*	100	*hundrede*

Further Reading

General

A History of Denmark, by Palle Lauring. (Høst, Copenhagen, 1986.) An authoritative account of Danish history that brings historical personalities alive and makes fascinating reading.
Our Nordic Heritage (KOM 1997). 256 pages with colour illustrations about world heritage sites in the Nordic countries.
Children's Culture in Denmark (Danmarks Lære Højskole 1997). On children's cultural development and creativity in Denmark.
An Account of Denmark as it was in the Year 1692: Robert Molesworth. (Wormanium Publishers, Aarhus, Denmark.)
An Outline History of Denmark, Helge Seidelin Jacobsen. (Høst, Copenhagen, 1986.)
Copenhagen This Week, Folia Publishers, Copenhagen (monthly).
Country Report: Denmark Reuters News Agency, London (current electronic database).
Danmark Fra Luften (Denmark from the Air), Torkild Balslev. (Bogan's Forlag A/S; Viborg, 1984.) In Danish – English edition available.
Danmarks Arkitektur: Kirkens huse (Danish Architecture: Churches), Hugo Johannsen and Claus M. Smidt, Ed. by Hakon Lund. (Gyldendalske Boghandel, Nordiske Forlag A/S; Copenhagen, 1981.) Text in Danish, captions in Danish and English.
Denmark: An Official Handbook, Press and Information Department, Danish Ministry of Foreign Affairs. (Kraks Publishers, Copenhagen, 1970.)
Denmark – Praise and Protest, Alan Moray Williams. (Høst, Copenhagen, 1969.)
Denmark Today – The World of the Danes, Danish Ministry of Foreign Affairs. (Copenhagen, 1979.)

Environment DENMARK: Denmark's national report to the United Nations on the human environment, Danish Ministries of Foreign Affairs, Housing, Cultural Affairs and Environmental Protection. (F.E. Bording, Ltd, Copenhagen, 1972.)
Facts About Denmark, Danish Ministry of Foreign Affairs (Press and Cultural Department); Danish Foreign Ministry/Forlaget Aktuelle Bøger. (Copenhagen, 12th edition 1995.)
Historisk Atlas Danmark, Ed. by Jette Kjærulff Hellesen and Ole Tuxen; G.E.C. Gads Forlag; København, 1988 (in Danish and English).
Kraks kort over København og omegn (Krak's Map of Copenhagen and Environs), 63rd Edition, 1987. (Kraks Forlag; Copenhagen, 1986.) In Danish, with museums and sights also listed in English.
Prehistoric Denmark National Museum of Denmark. (Copenhagen, 1978.)
The Art of Scandinavia, Volumes 1 & 2, Peter Anker and Aron Andersson (translated by Vivienne Menkes from the French original).

Other Insight Guides

Companion volumes to this book include *Insight Guide: Finland*, *Insight Guide: Norway*, *Insight Guide: Sweden* and *Insight Guide: Iceland*. Each contains a wide range of topical essays and a comprehensive Places section.
   In addition, **Insight Pocket Guide: Oslo and Bergen** provides carefully structured itineraries suitable for those on a tight schedule and contains a full-size pull-out map.
   Compact Guide: Denmark is an encyclopaedic yet highly portable guide with detailed text, pictures and maps all carefully cross-referenced for easy on-the-spot use.

Insight Guide: Norway ranges from Oslo to Telemark, from Stavanger to beyond the Arctic Circle. Its features cover the Sami, the cost of living, boat building, skiing, fishing, alcoholism, and much more.

Insight Guide: Finland reveals all that is most interesting about Europe's fifth largest country, ranging from Helsinki to Lapland, with Apa's customary eye-catching photography.

Insight Guide: Sweden ranges from Stockholm to Gothenburg, from Alfred Nobel to Ingmar Bergman. As well as a comprehensive Places section, it offers a penetrating analysis of this fascinating society.

ART & PHOTO CREDITS

Picture Spreads

INSIGHT GUIDE
DENMARK

Cartographic Editor **Zoë Goodwin**
Production **Stuart A Everitt**
Design Consultants
Carlotta Junger, Graham Mitchener
Picture Research **Hilary Genin, Britta Jaschinski**

The World of Insight Guides

400 books in three complementary series cover every major destination in every continent.

Insight Guides

Alaska
Alsace
Amazon Wildlife
American Southwest
Amsterdam
Argentina
Atlanta
Athens
Australia
Austria
Bahamas
Bali
Baltic States
Bangkok
Barbados
Barcelona
Bay of Naples
Beijing
Belgium
Belize
Berlin
Bermuda
Boston
Brazil
Brittany
Brussels
Budapest
Buenos Aires
Burgundy
Burma (Myanmar)
Cairo
Calcutta
California
Canada
Caribbean
Catalonia
Channel Islands
Chicago
Chile
China
Cologne
Continental Europe
Corsica
Costa Rica
Crete
Crossing America
Cuba
Cyprus
Czech & Slovak Republics
Delhi, Jaipur, Agra
Denmark
Dresden
Dublin
Düsseldorf
East African Wildlife
East Asia
Eastern Europe
Ecuador
Edinburgh
Egypt
Finland
Florence
Florida
France
Frankfurt
French Riviera
Gambia & Senegal
Germany
Glasgow

Gran Canaria
Great Barrier Reef
Great Britain
Greece
Greek Islands
Hamburg
Hawaii
Hong Kong
Hungary
Iceland
India
India's Western Himalaya
Indian Wildlife
Indonesia
Ireland
Israel
Istanbul
Italy
Jamaica
Japan
Java
Jerusalem
Jordan
Kathmandu
Kenya
Korea
Lisbon
Loire Valley
London
Los Angeles
Madeira
Madrid
Malaysia
Mallorca & Ibiza
Malta
Marine Life in the South China Sea
Melbourne
Mexico
Mexico City
Miami
Montreal
Morocco
Moscow
Namibia
Native America
Nepal
Netherlands
New England
Northern California
Northern Spain
Norway
Oman & the UAE
Oxford
Old South
Pacific Northwest
Pakistan
Paris
Peru
Philadelphia
Philippines
Poland
Portugal
Prague

Provence
Puerto Rico
Rajasthan
Rhine
Rio de Janeiro
Rockies
Rome
Russia
St Petersburg
San Francisco
Sardinia
Scotland
Seattle
Sicily
Singapore
South Africa
South America
South Asia
South India
South Tyrol
Southeast Asia
Southeast Asia Wildlife
Southern California
Southern Spain
Spain
Sri Lanka
Sweden
Switzerland
Sydney
Taiwan
Tenerife
Texas
Thailand
Tokyo
Trinidad & Tobago
Tunisia
Turkey
Turkish Coast
Tuscany
Umbria
US National Parks East
US National Parks West
Vancouver
Venezuela
Venice
Vienna
Vietnam
Wales
Washington DC
Waterways of Europe
Wild West
Yemen

Insight Pocket Guides

Aegean Islands★
Algarve★
Alsace
Amsterdam★
Athens★
Atlanta★
Bahamas★
Baja Peninsula★
Bali★
Bali *Bird Walks*
Bangkok★
Barbados★
Barcelona★
Bavaria★
Beijing★
Berlin★

Bermuda★
Bhutan★
Boston★
British Columbia★
Brittany★
Brussels★
Budapest & Surroundings★
Canton★
Chiang Mai★
Chicago★
Corsica★
Costa Blanca★
Costa Brava★
Costa del Sol/Marbella★
Costa Rica★
Crete★
Denmark★
Fiji★
Florence★
Florida★
Florida Keys★
French Riviera★
Gran Canaria★
Hawaii★
Hong Kong★
Hungary
Ibiza★
Ireland★
Ireland's Southwest★
Israel★
Istanbul★
Jakarta★
Jamaica★
Kathmandu *Bikes & Hikes*★
Kenya★
Kuala Lumpur★
Lisbon★
Loire Valley★
London★
Macau
Madrid★
Malacca
Maldives
Mallorca★
Malta★
Mexico City★
Miami★
Milan★
Montreal★
Morocco★
Moscow
Munich★
Nepal★
New Delhi
New Orleans★
New York City★
New Zealand★
Northern California★
Oslo/Bergen★
Paris★
Penang★
Phuket★
Prague★
Provence★
Puerto Rico★
Quebec★
Rhodes★
Rome★
Sabah★

St Petersburg★
San Francisco★
Sardinia
Scotland★
Seville★
Seychelles★
Sicily★
Sikkim
Singapore★
Southeast England
Southern California★
Southern Spain★
Sri Lanka★
Sydney★
Tenerife★
Thailand★
Tibet★
Toronto★
Tunisia★
Turkish Coast★
Tuscany★
Venice★
Vienna★
Vietnam★
Yogyakarta
Yucatan Peninsula★

★ = Insight Pocket Guides
with Pull out Maps

Insight Compact Guides

Algarve
Amsterdam
Bahamas
Bali
Bangkok
Barbados
Barcelona
Beijing
Belgium
Berlin
Brittany
Brussels
Budapest
Burgundy
Copenhagen
Costa Brava
Costa Rica
Crete
Cyprus
Czech Republic
Denmark
Dominican Republic
Dublin
Egypt
Finland
Florence
Gran Canaria
Greece
Holland
Hong Kong
Ireland
Israel
Italian Lakes
Italian Riviera
Jamaica
Jerusalem
Lisbon
Madeira
Mallorca
Malta

Milan
Moscow
Munich
Normandy
Norway
Paris
Poland
Portugal
Prague
Provence
Rhodes
Rome
St Petersburg
Salzburg
Singapore
Switzerland
Sydney
Tenerife
Thailand
Turkey
Turkish Coast
Tuscany
UK regional titles:
 Bath & Surroundings
 Cambridge & East Anglia
 Cornwall
 Cotswolds
 Devon & Exmoor
 Edinburgh
 Lake District
 London
 New Forest
 North York Moors
 Northumbria
 Oxford
 Peak District
 Scotland
 Scottish Highlands
 Shakespeare Country
 Snowdonia
 South Downs
 York
 Yorkshire Dales
USA regional titles:
 Boston
 Cape Cod
 Chicago
 Florida
 Florida Keys
 Hawaii: Maui
 Hawaii: Oahu
 Las Vegas
 Los Angeles
 Martha's Vineyard & Nantucket
 New York
 San Francisco
 Washington D.C.
 Venice
 Vienna
 West of Ireland

Copenhagen S-tog (S-train) System

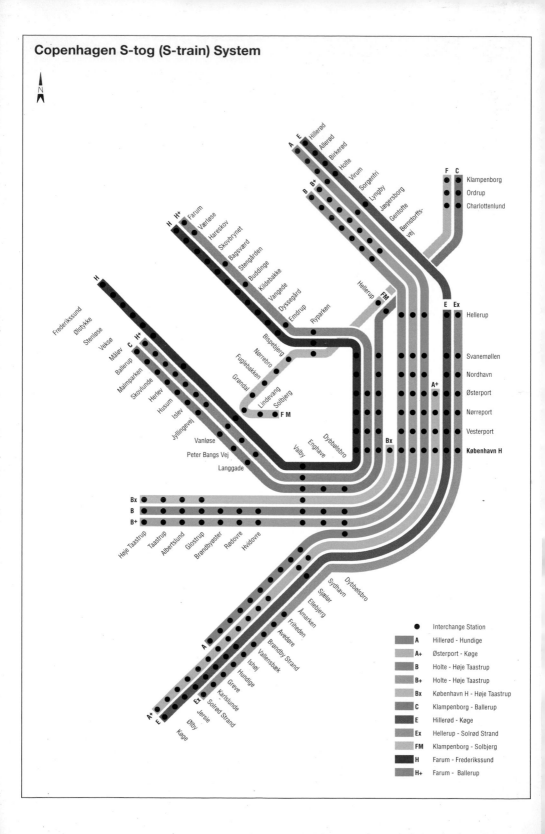